PCs made easy

STAGE

5

A PRACTICAL COURSE

PCs made easy

STAGE

5

A PRACTICAL COURSE

PUBLISHED BY THE READER'S DIGEST ASSOCIATION LIMITED
LONDON NEW YORK SYDNEY MONTREAL

PCS MADE EASY
A PRACTICAL COURSE – STAGE 5

Published by the Reader's Digest Association Limited, 2001

The Reader's Digest Association Limited
11 Westferry Circus, Canary Wharf, London E14 4HE
www.readersdigest.co.uk

We are committed to both the quality of our products and the service we provide to our customers, so please feel free to contact us on 08705 113366, or by email at cust_service@readersdigest.co.uk
If you have any comments about the content of our books, you can contact us at gbeditorial@readersdigest.co.uk

For Reader's Digest
Series Editor: Christine Noble
Assistant Editor: Caroline Boucher
Art Editor: Julie Bennett

Reader's Digest General Books
Editorial Director: Cortina Butler
Art Director: Nick Clark

PCs made easy was created and produced for The Reader's Digest Association Limited by De Agostini UK Ltd, from material originally published as the Partwork *Computer Success Plus.*

Printing and binding: Printer Industria Gráfica S.A., Barcelona

ISBN 0 276 42637 1

CONTENTS

6

Windows

Extra Windows utilities

Windows has its own built-in facilities to keep your PC system in tune, but there are also many other maintenance programs available. Pick the right ones and keep your computer trouble-free and running smoothly.

In Stage 3, pages 8-11, we looked at how the system tools that are built into Windows can keep your PC working efficiently. Programs such as Disk Defragmenter, ScanDisk and Backup come as part of Windows and can be used for a variety of useful housekeeping and maintenance tasks.

However, these tools have their limitations. As a result, many independent companies have developed their own system tools, either to perform tasks that are not carried out by the tools already supplied with Windows or to perform similar tasks in a more effective way.

Many of these utilities do such an important and useful job that it is well worth purchasing them. In addition, there are many shareware programs that do less important jobs, but which can add extra functions and options to your system.

Some of the important functions utility software can do for you include:

▶ Crash protection: this kind of software automatically monitors your PC to prevent crashes or to allow you to save your work if one should occur.

▶ File recovery: unerase (or undelete) programs allow you to recover files you have deleted, even if you have already emptied the Recycle bin. Deleted files sit on your hard drive until the space they take up is needed, so for a while at least, the files are not lost.

▶ Software removal: uninstall programs offer an efficient method of removing software you no longer require from your system.

▶ Virus protection: this kind of software monitors incoming files for the presence of viruses, and can also remove a virus should it detect one on your PC. It is essential to have active virus protection software if you use the Internet.

● All-in-one utilities

The most popular additional system tool is Norton Utilities (see pages 10-13), which has been around in various forms since the dawn of the PC age. It is a collection of utility programs that perform a number of useful tasks, from monitoring your PC or protecting against crashes to recovering files that you might have accidentally deleted. In addition, the package contains a number of other programs to help optimize the performance of your system. Other popular all-in-one utility programs include Clinic and CheckIt Suite.

● Anti-virus software

Anti-virus software (see pages 18-19) is one of the most important

WINDOWS ME

Windows Me closely follows the format of Windows 98, at least for the purposes of the average user. Therefore, unless indicated otherwise, all the exercises in *PCs made easy* work on both operating systems, with only minor differences in screen layout.

system tools, not necessarily because viruses are particularly common or difficult to remove, but because it gives you peace of mind knowing that your PC isn't suddenly going to be invaded by a malicious program.

Anti-virus software varies quite widely in price, with the top-of-the-range version of Dr Solomon's Active Virus Defence costing upwards of £300. This price reflects the fact that the software not only contains an enormous database of viruses and their antidotes, but also ensures that the database is updated regularly via the Internet. Other leading anti-virus software includes McAfee VirusScan and Norton AntiVirus.

● Software removal

Although Windows has its own Uninstall program, many people still find it useful to purchase separate versions of the same type of utility. Programs such as CleanSweep are more versatile and will work even with software that the usual Windows Uninstall process can't remove.

CleanSweep, and other uninstallers such as UnInstaller, are more thorough and reliable than the built-in Windows uninstaller. These programs retail at around £30.

● Shareware

In addition to commercially retailed programs you can also download a number of very useful utilities from the Internet. These are usually shareware programs; you may use them for nothing at first, but you are expected to pay for them after the evaluation period. These shareware utilities are often just as useful as the commercial titles – and they have the added bonus that you can try before you buy. Paint Shop Pro, for example, features many of the tools and commands of Corel PHOTO-PAINT and is invaluable when converting between file formats and making quick changes to your stored pictures.

● Compression software

Compression software can create and extract compressed files, which is indispensable when sending files over the Internet or when trying to squeeze a large number of files onto a floppy disk. WinZip is one of the most popular shareware utilities. Without it you'd be unable to use most of the files you can download, and would find moving a large number of files via floppy disk very difficult; we look at WinZip on pages 14-17.

● Handy notes

There are many other, smaller, shareware utilities that may be less essential, but which are still fun and useful. NiftyNotes, for example, is an electronic version of those little squares of (usually) yellow paper with an adhesive strip at the top. Now you can actually stick notes on to your PC's Desktop! There is a commercial notes program from 3M called Post-it® Software Notes (below). Both NiftyNotes and Post-it® Software Notes are great ways to give yourself reminders.

Post-it® Software Notes are the PC equivalent of the paper Post-it® notes from 3M and as such they are a very useful way of putting reminders on your screen so you won't forget what you have to do.

CONTACT POINTS

The following are some of the most popular programs in each of the main categories. You may well find them on sale for less than this – typically, the mail-order price will be around 20 per cent lower. This guide gives you a rough idea of how they compare with each other.

Norton Utilities
Price: £30*
Norton AntiVirus
Price: £25*
Norton CleanSweep
Price: £25*
Symantec
Tel: 020 7616 5600
www.symantec.co.uk

McAfee Office
Price: £60*
McAfee Utilities
Price: £25*
McAfee VirusScan
Price: £25*
Uninstaller
Price: £25*
Network Associates
Tel: 0800 092 7160
www.mcafee-at-home.com

*UK prices

Housekeeping with Norton Utilities

Windows has its own housekeeping tools, but you can buy specialist software dedicated to making it even easier for Windows to run smoothly. Here we look at Symantec's Norton Utilities.

Windows isn't perfect. However, this is just as well for all the software companies that make a very healthy living from creating Windows utilities (see pages 8-9). Some are quite specific in their remit, such as Norton CleanSweep, which simply clears out all the old, unnecessary files left behind by programs you no longer use.

Other specific utilities include virus checkers and unerase programs. If you think of each specific type of program as the computer equivalent of a spanner or hammer, the complete toolbox is represented by a suite of software utilities. Of these, the most popular and most widely used is Norton Utilities.

Symantec's Norton Utilities has been around for many years. The core of the suite has remained largely unchanged, simply being upgraded to take into account the changes in versions of MS-DOS and Windows. With each successive version, extra tools have been built into the suite while others have been dropped.

The latest incarnation – Version 2001 – offers diagnostics, which automatically track down and repair any errors; optimization tools, which ensure your computer is running at peak efficiency; and the creation of emergency rescue floppies.

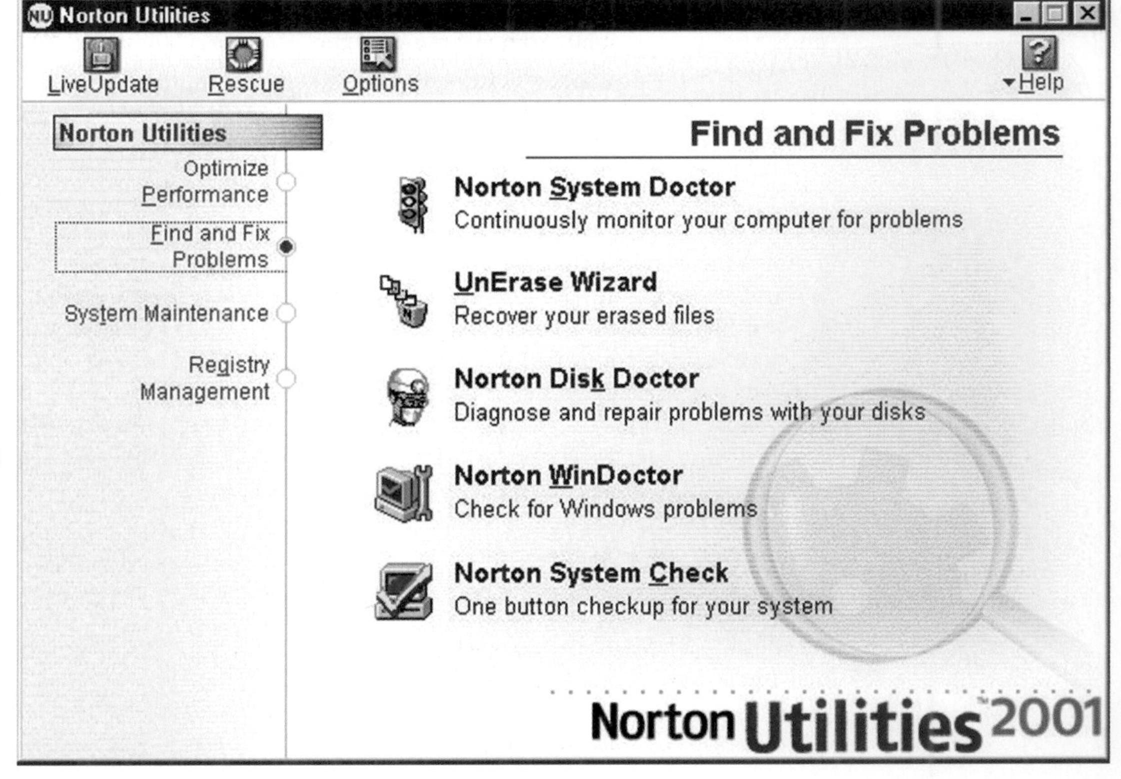

Even though you can do some powerful and quite technical things with Norton Utilities, it has a friendly face and is very easy to use.

A good deal of what Norton Utilities does takes place in the background. It periodically checks that everything is running smoothly and warns you if it thinks there is a problem.

● Nasty surprises

When you first install Norton Utilities this warning capability can be quite a daunting business, as it seems to find quite a few problems very quickly. It might then badger you constantly to fix these problems you never knew you had. Don't worry about this: it's just the utilities bedding down and ensuring that the system is set up to run as it thinks fit. A dialog box will pop up telling you what to do: follow the on-screen instructions and the program will sort it all out.

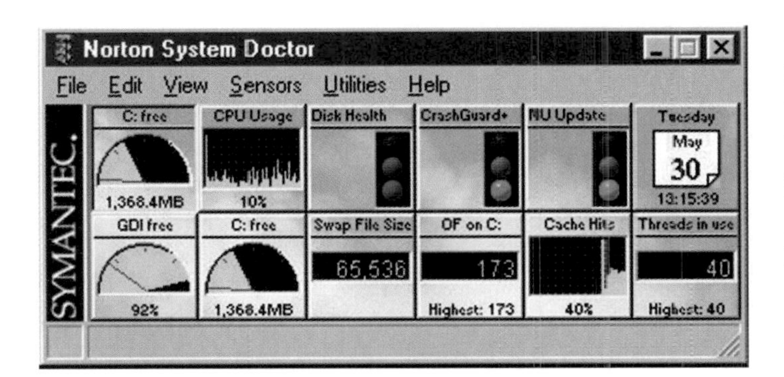

With Norton System Doctor it's very easy to get a clear and concise picture of how your computer is performing.

● The Doctor will see you now

WinDoctor is the tool that checks Windows' internal workings, alerting you to problems it finds with your system. Some of these might be trivial, some of them might be important – and some might be critical. After all, the aim of Windows, and modern software generally, is to hide the real 'behind the scenes' action. Without tools that can 'look inside' Windows, where do you look if things go wrong? The WinDoctor knows what to do, and cheerfully offers up a list of the problems, asking you whether it should fix them or not. Similarly, Norton DiskDoctor will check your hard disk and the way files are stored for errors and offer to fix things accordingly. You can run WinDoctor and DiskDoctor when you see fit, and/or run them in the background as part of Norton System Doctor.

Norton Utilities also allows you to retrieve deleted files – even after you have emptied the Recycle Bin. This is possible because when you delete a file, the information it contains isn't wiped from the hard disk immediately. Instead, the part of Windows that deals with the hard disk simply notes that the area on the disk that stored the file is available for re-use. Eventually these areas will be overwritten by new files, but until that happens, the file is recoverable. Norton Utilities keeps track of the areas taken up by deleted files: if they haven't been overwritten, it can then retrieve them.

There is also a utility to speed up your disk. This is essentially a disk defragmenter (much quicker than the Windows one!), which repositions important files for easy access. If you want virus protection as well, you can opt for Norton SystemWorks. This combines Norton Utilities with Norton AntiVirus.

PC TIPS

Trust the Doctor

Often, the WinDoctor tool will identify problems that seem to involve obscure parts of Windows and lots of jargon. You might be told, for example, that there are 15 problems with Invalid ActiveX/COM entries. Generally, it's best to accept WinDoctor's suggestions for solving the problems rather than worrying about such obscure technical terms.

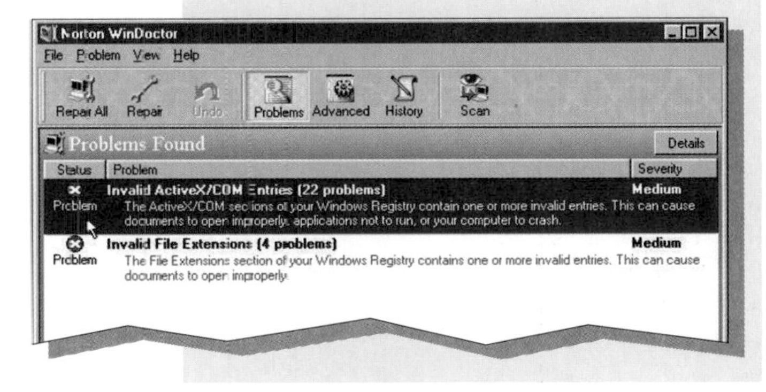

EMERGENCY

The 2001 version of the Norton Utilities CD-ROM is bootable. This means that if your PC refuses to start Windows from the hard disk, you may be able to fix the problems by inserting the Norton Utilities CD into your CD-ROM drive and restarting the PC. Your PC manual will tell you how to boot from the CD-ROM drive.

Checking your hardware

The Norton Diagnostics program carries out a thorough check of all your PC's hardware to help with troubleshooting.

While Disk Doctor looks after your hard disk and WinDoctor checks that the thousands of Windows files are operating properly, you need a completely different type of utility to check the PC's hardware.

There are 13 separate tests that run on everything from the processor within the PC to the printer on your desktop. For example, the graphics card check displays test patterns and colour palettes on your computer monitor, and also runs through lightning fast tests of how quickly the card can handle data. At the end of the test a screen appears which lists the results.

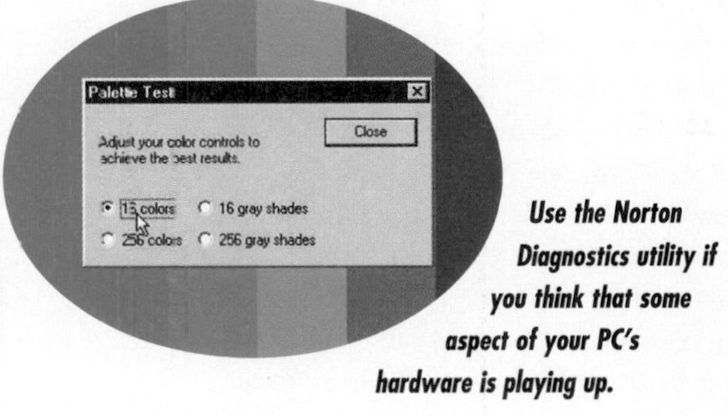

Use the Norton Diagnostics utility if you think that some aspect of your PC's hardware is playing up.

The Optimization Wizard

Norton Utilities is easy to use. It's simply a case of starting up whichever wizard-style utility you wish to run and following the instructions.

AT FIRST THERE appears to be a bewildering number of programs in Norton Utilities. However, this is a little misleading, as the same functions are available from several different sources: the Start menu, the System Doctor and Norton Utilities Integrator, which is placed on your Desktop automatically. You will come across Norton's diagnostic, fix-it programs, WinDoctor and DiskDoctor, soon after installation. Here, we run the Optimization Wizard.

1 The best way to see the breadth of the Norton Utilities suite is to use the Norton Utilities Integrator. Double-click on its Desktop icon.

2 The main window is divided in two. The left panel shows the four different Norton Utilities areas. Click on Optimize Performance.

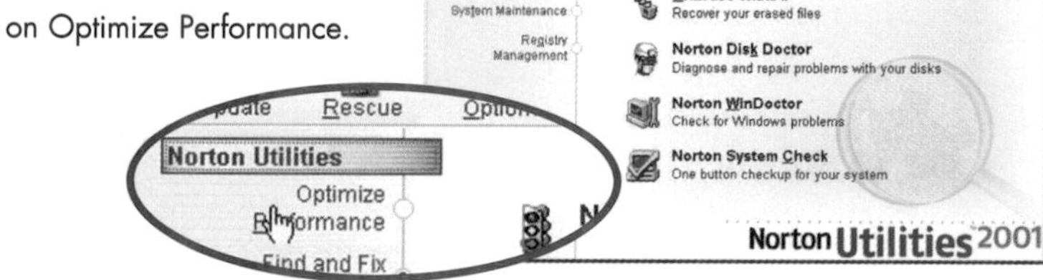

WHAT IT MEANS

SWAP FILE

This is a special area of the hard disk that is used as a temporary store for information that cannot be stored in the computer's memory due to lack of space.

3 The panel on the right changes to show new options. Click on the Norton Optimization Wizard.

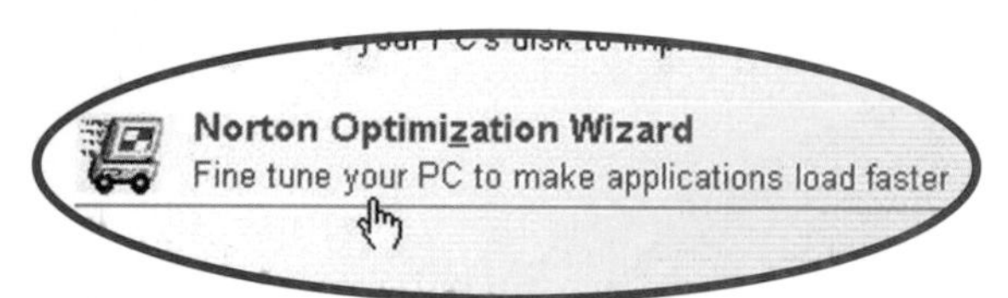

4 The first screen of the Wizard explains what the Wizard does. Click the Next button.

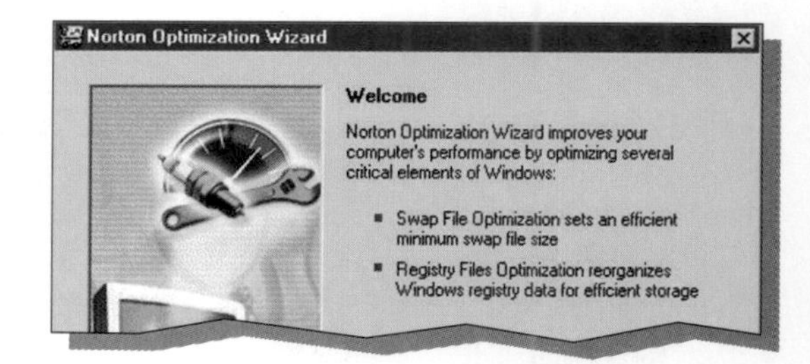

5 The next screen explains what optimizing your **swap file** means. The Wizard can set an optimum size for this file: first it will check to see if your swap file has been optimized. If it hasn't, tick the box before pressing the Next button.

6 The next screen tells you how the Wizard can optimize the Registry – primarily by storing Registry information more efficiently and allowing faster access and better all-round performance. Tick the Optimize my Registry box and click the Next button.

7 The Finish screen confirms your choices and asks you to restart your computer. As requested, shut down all other programs first and then click the Reboot button.

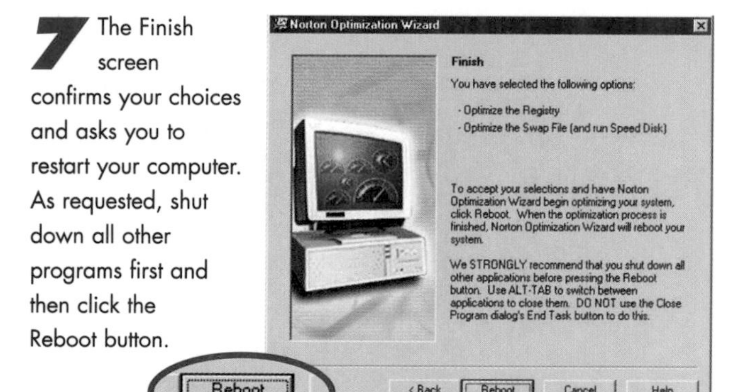

8 Depending on the level of defragmentation and the size of your disk, this might take a while – so you can leave the computer during the process.

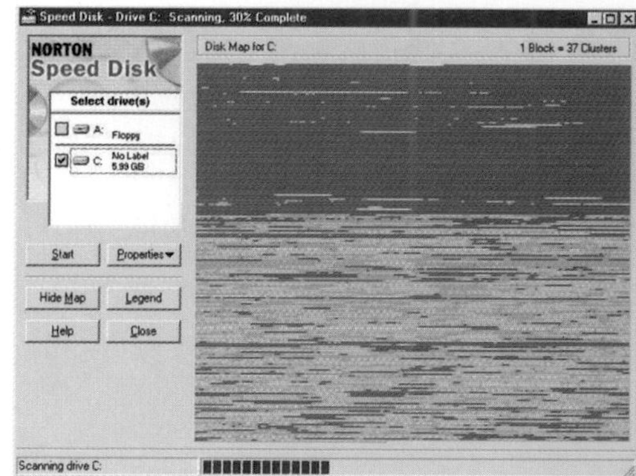

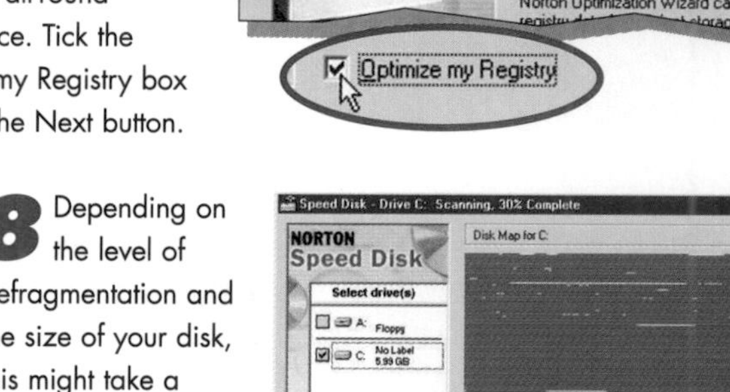

Using the LiveUpdate program

Once you buy Norton Utilities you can make sure it stays up to date by logging onto the Symantec Web site with its LiveUpdate function.

NORTON UTILITIES includes a handy service that allows you to hook up to Symantec's special Norton Utilities site on the Internet. You can check that you have the latest Norton software and that your files are up to date with the LiveUpdate program. If there are more recent versions of the utility files on the Symantec Web site, you can download them to your PC, ready to install where Norton needs them.

PC TIPS

Smart updating

You don't have to install all of the updates listed in the LiveUpdate dialog box (see Step 3). Depending on the time of day when you log on to LiveUpdate, it may be better to defer the downloading process. For example, if you find there are a lot of files to update – perhaps 2MB or more – it's best to do the update early in the morning while the USA is still asleep and the Symantec site is less busy.

1 Start up the Norton Utilities Integrator and click the LiveUpdate button.

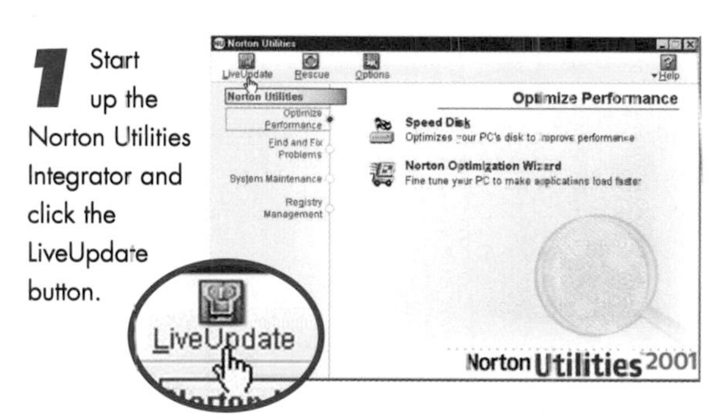

2 In the dialog box that appears, click the Next button and then connect to the Internet when prompted.

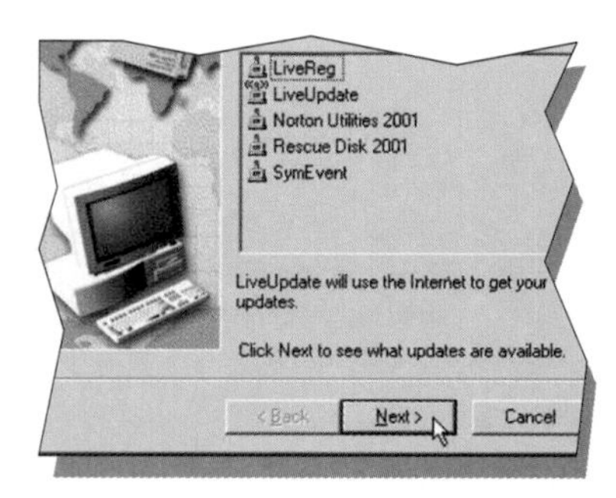

3 LiveUpdate now connects to the Internet and then communicates with a special part of Symantec's Web site. It downloads a list of updates that have been released since your version of Norton Utilities was distributed on CD-ROM. The software you see will vary depending on when you bought your Utilities and when you last updated. Tick the upgrades you want and then click the Next button.

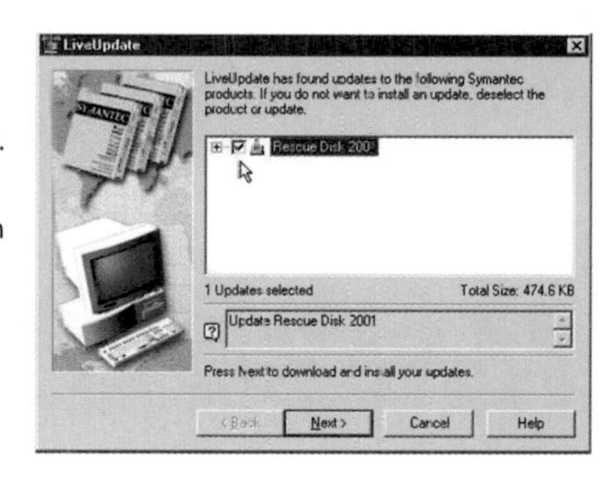

REGULAR UPDATES

It pays to use the LiveUpdate command regularly so that all aspects of your Norton Utilities software are up to date, and any useful advances that Symantec release are available for use as soon as possible. Even if you opted to do a LiveUpdate check immediately after installing the program, make a point of checking the site every month or two.

4 LiveUpdate stays connected to the Internet so you can download the necessary material directly. Wait while the new software is downloaded to your computer.

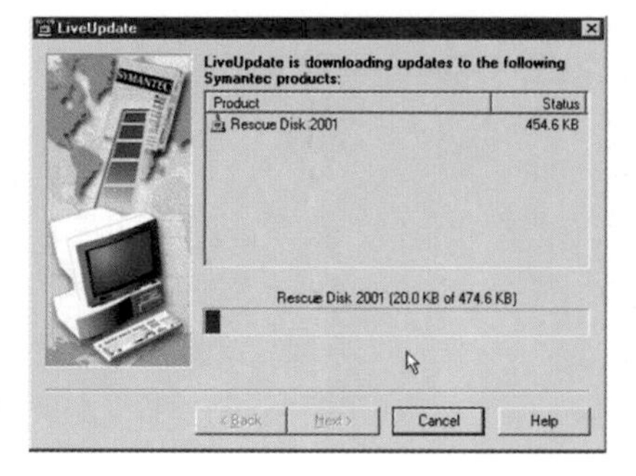

5 When the download is complete a Please Read! dialog box appears. Click OK.

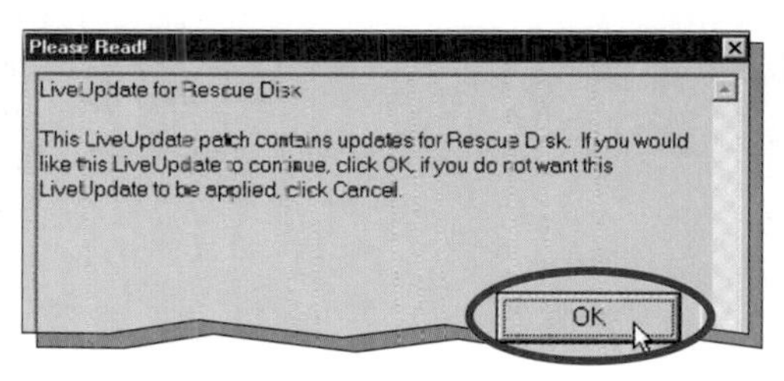

6 The downloaded software automatically installs itself on your computer. The process only takes a few minutes.

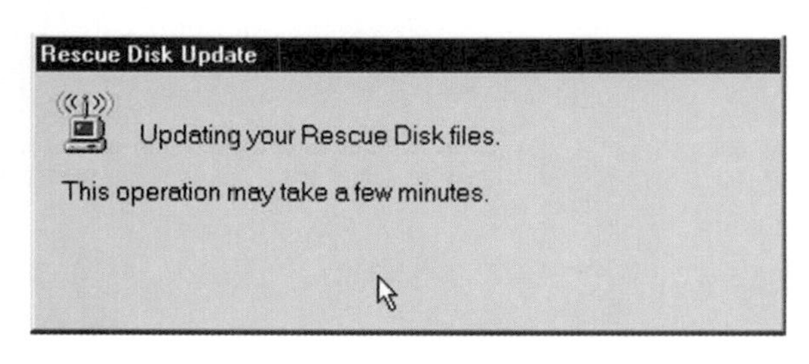

7 The final screen confirms the details of the update. The green ticks indicate all the components of Norton Utilities which are up to date. Press the Finish button to restart your computer for the changes to take effect.

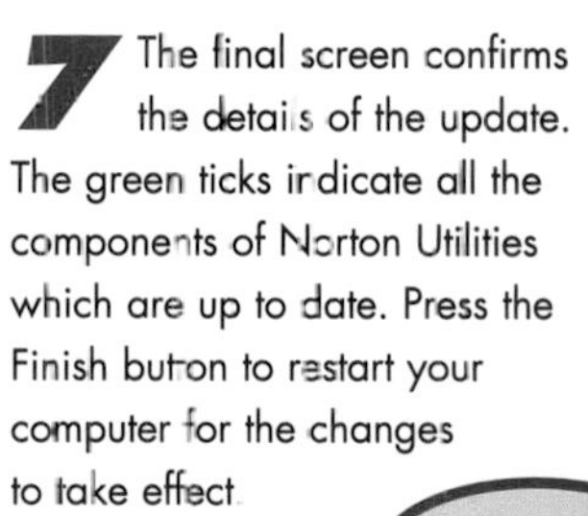

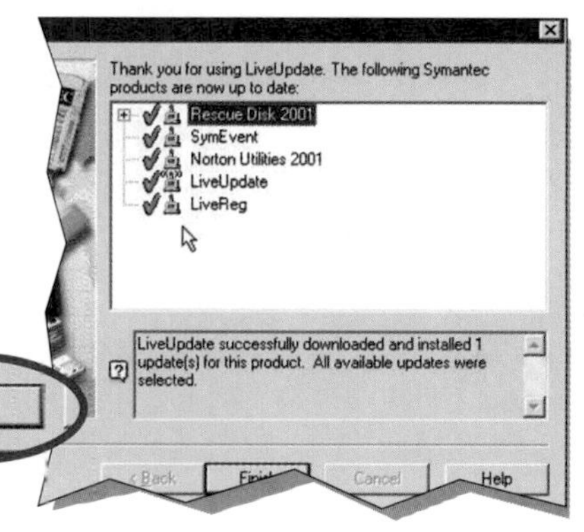

Making files smaller

Storing important files can take up valuable space on your hard drive, or fill up hundreds of floppy disks. However, by using WinZip to compress files you can make the most of your available storage space.

Using WinZip allows you to squeeze more information into the same space and then restore it to its original state whenever necessary.

Storage devices have a limited amount of space available in which to hold data. However, WinZip can help to overcome this problem by compressing files so that they take up less space. When a file is stored using WinZip, it is put through a complex mathematical process that results in any unused space being freed up. The zipped file still contains all the original information, but it is smaller and takes up less storage space. This smaller file can be unzipped when you are ready to retrieve the information.

The exact reduction in file size depends on the type of file you compress. For example, it's possible to squeeze Microsoft Word's .DOC documents down to around 25 per cent of their original size. At the other extreme, some types of graphics files might compress to only 90 per cent of their original size.

The process can be used either on a single file or on several files at once. Without a program such as WinZip, it would be impossible for you to zip up a file, and you'd also be unable to unzip files that have already been compressed. This includes Internet files you have downloaded – the majority of which are generally supplied in zipped form.

● By popular demand

WinZip's popularity is also helped by its easy-to-use design. This has been improved with successive versions of the software to the point where it now offers a choice of interface: WinZip Wizard or WinZip Classic.

The Wizard is a simplified interface for first-time users, which looks similar to the Wizard dialog boxes in Word. As we show opposite, it takes you through the process one step at a time and immediately knows where all the zipped files are on your PC and which folders you usually prefer to unzip them to. The Classic version is for confident WinZip users, although it is still relatively easy to use.

WHAT IT MEANS

ZIPPED

When files are used in conjunction with WinZip they are said to be zipped or unzipped. Zipped files are files that have been compressed by WinZip and they cannot be used until they are unzipped. Although an unzipped file is technically any one that isn't zipped up, it usually refers to files that have previously been compressed.

Getting and using WinZip

Here we look at how easy it is to download and use WinZip.

THE FASTEST WAY to acquire the shareware version of WinZip Wizard is to download it from the Internet. We've already seen how to download files (see Stage 2, pages 146-149), where the example given was an anti-virus program, and you follow pretty much the same procedure to download WinZip.

Go to www.winzip.com and follow the download links. For this exercise, we suggest you download WinZip from one of Download.com's international sites. The download will take approximately ten minutes.

At the same time, download a normal zip file to use at the end of this exercise. You can choose any zip file you like. In our example we've chosen a waterfalls screen saver (saved as wtrFall3.zip) from Download.com's list of popular downloads.

1 Once the program has downloaded, double-click on the WinZip program icon to begin the installation process. Click Setup in the first window that appears.

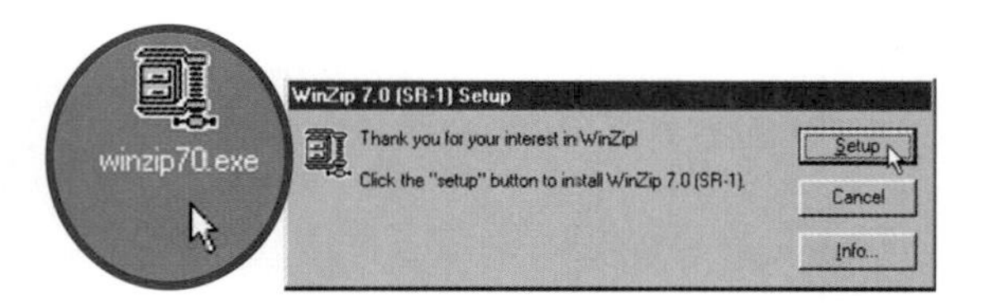

2 A second window will pop up, asking you where you want to install WinZip. The default option is to install it into the Program Files Folder. Press OK. On the next screen, click the Next button, then press the Yes button after reading the License Agreement.

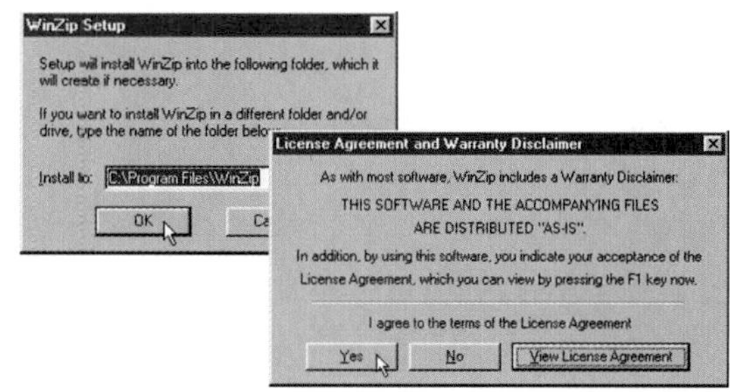

3 Once you've accepted the licence agreement, you will be able to choose between the Classic or Wizard interface. Click on the WinZip Wizard option, then click Next to proceed.

4 WinZip will now search through the folders on your PC adding those that contain zip files to a Favorite Zip Folders list. When this is done, installation will be complete. Accept the Search Entire Hard Disk option and click Next to start the WinZip Wizard.

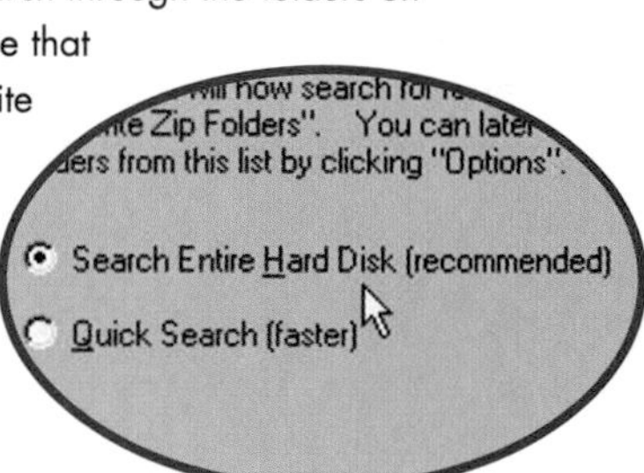

PAYING FOR IT

WinZip is not a full-priced program, but it's not free either. It is shareware, which means that you can try it out for free for a specified period, but if you continue to use it, you have to pay for the right to do so.

In the case of WinZip, the price is currently $29 (around £20), which is not much for a program that you will probably use frequently. The WinZip Web site contains all the information you need, as well as a facility to pay by credit card.

5 The first screen of the WinZip Wizard gives you the option to change your favourite folders and alter other options. Click the Next button and a scrollable window will appear, listing all the .zip files on your computer. Choose the screen saver zip file you downloaded earlier (or any other .zip file) and click the Next button.

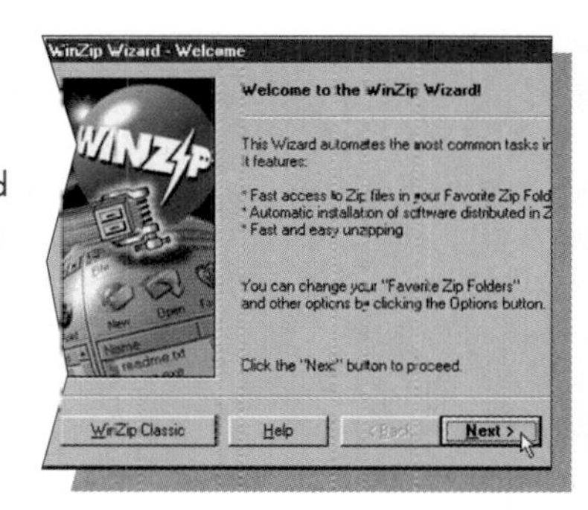

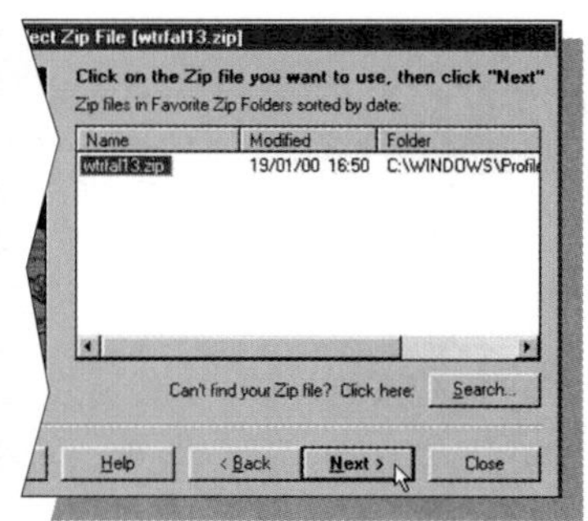

6 Click the Next button on the next screen, then click the Install Now button to get WinZip to install the screen saver.

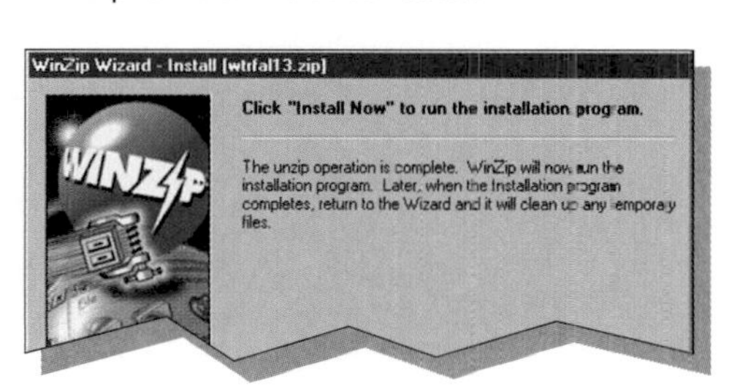

7 The waterfalls setup program starts. Follow the on-screen instructions to install it. When the process is complete, the WinZip program cleans up the setup files. Click the Close button to quit WinZip.

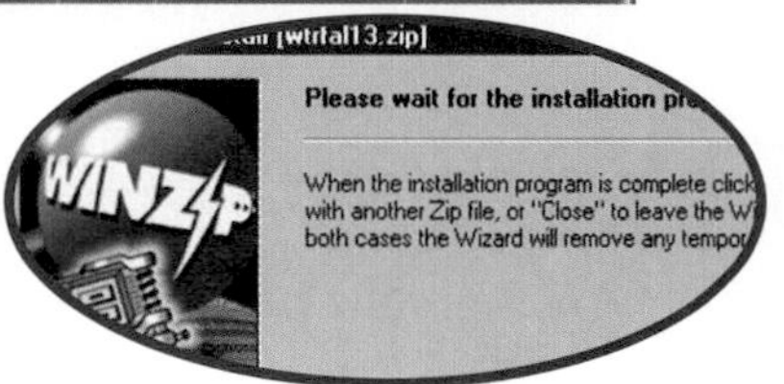

Getting the most out of WinZip

For a program that costs around £20, WinZip is an extremely useful addition to your PC. And you can get even more out of it if you learn a few of its time-saving and space-saving tricks.

On pages 14-15 we introduced the shareware program WinZip, an incredibly useful piece of software which is almost essential to anyone using a modern computer. Those who want to download files from the Internet or to send files via email or on floppy disks would be lost without WinZip – and it is also useful for compressing large files so that they take up less space on your hard disk or Web site.

WinZip has a further use if you want to send data to someone else as it can turn a collection of files into a single zip file, which is much smaller than the sum of the individual elements you put in – and much easier to copy onto a floppy. WinZip can then be used at any time to decompress the zipped files and recover the original data.

● A choice of interface

Our introduction to WinZip used its simple Wizard interface to carry out the necessary steps for compressing and extracting files. But although the Wizard works well and is ideally suited to a WinZip beginner, it allows you to use only the program's basic extraction and compression options. Once familiar with WinZip, most users prefer its Classic interface, which is almost as easy to understand but adds a great many other options.

● Using WinZip Classic

Opposite we show you how to get started with WinZip's Classic interface. The most useful functions are still New and Extract – used to zip and unzip files – but even these basic options have additional features that give you more control over the size and type of zip files you create. The Classic interface also opens up a number of other functions, of which perhaps the most useful is the ability to save zipped data as an executable WinZip file.

An executable file can be run on any PC and will unzip itself without the need for an additional program. This means that you can send a zipped file to someone who does not have a copy of WinZip and they will still be able to use it. The only disadvantage is that an executable file is slightly larger than an ordinary WinZip file.

WHAT IT MEANS

EXECUTABLE

An executable file has the extension .EXE. This indicates that a computer file is a program instead of a document. A normal zip file is a document much like a Word letter or an Excel worksheet, but an executable zip file contains both the compressed files and a miniature program that can unzip them.

Using WinZip Classic

If you are familiar with what the WinZip Wizard can do, click on the WinZip Classic button and discover even more powerful features.

1 WinZip Wizard is the default option when you first install WinZip. To change to the Classic interface, click on the WinZip Classic button on the bottom left of the Wizard window.

2 You'll see a new window with a blank workspace and a large toolbar (below). To create a new zip file, click the New button. The New Archive dialog box (right) asks you to choose a name and location for your zipped file. We've called ours Important.zip. Click OK when you are finished.

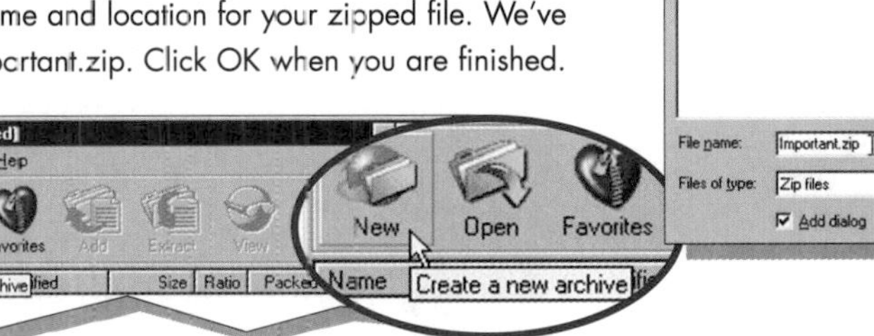

3 You will now see the Add dialog box. This works rather like a Save or Open dialog box, except you can add several files at once. Find the folder containing the files you want zipped and select a file. To select multiple files, as seen here, just hold down the [Ctrl] key as you click on each one. Now press the Add button.

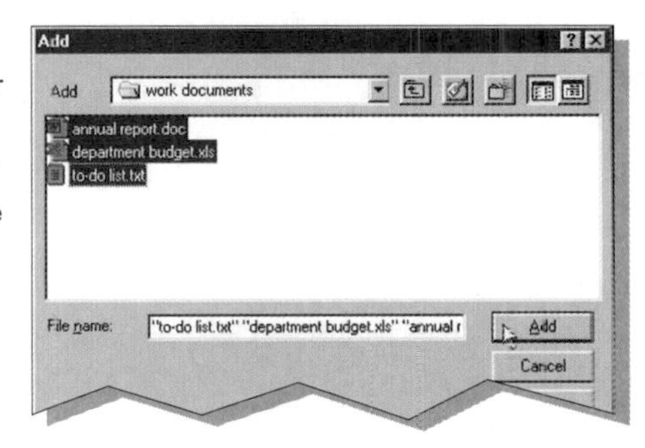

4 Close WinZip and you will see that the file has now been zipped. Decompressing a zipped file with the Classic interface is simple: just double-click on the file and WinZip will load up with the file selected. Press the Extract button (inset) to open the Extract dialog box.

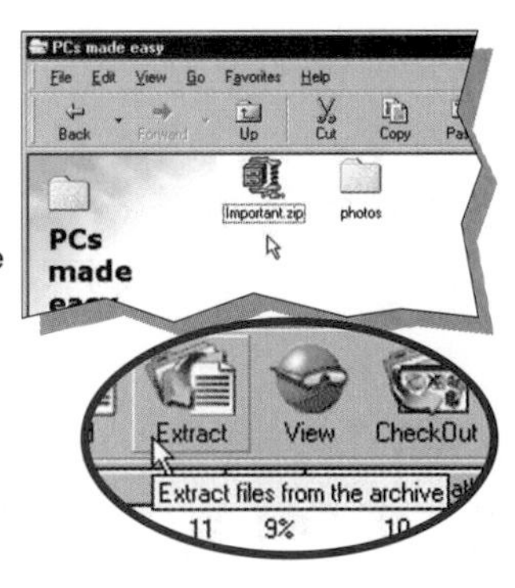

5 Use the Folders/drives panel of the Extract dialog box to choose where you want the decompressed files to go. When you're ready, click the Extract button. Now if you look in the folder you chose, you'll find the files that were contained in the zip file.

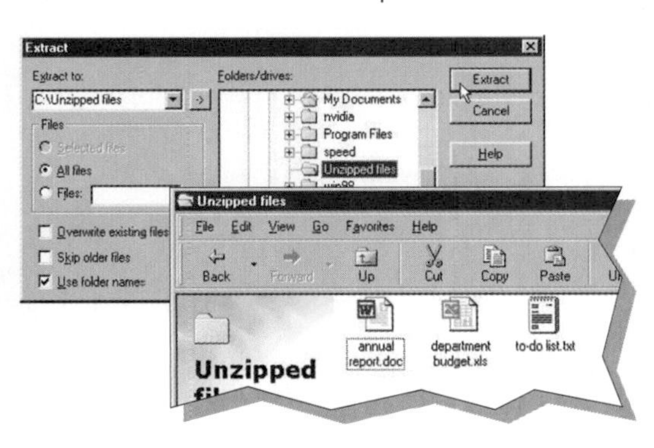

6 To make the zipped file executable, find the Important.zip file you created and double-click on it. This time choose Make .Exe File from WinZip's Actions menu (right). A new dialog box appears; leave the settings as they are and press the Make .Exe button to create a self-extracting zip file.

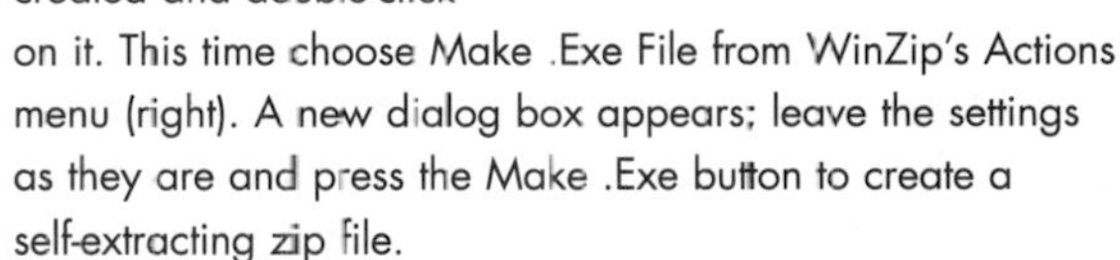

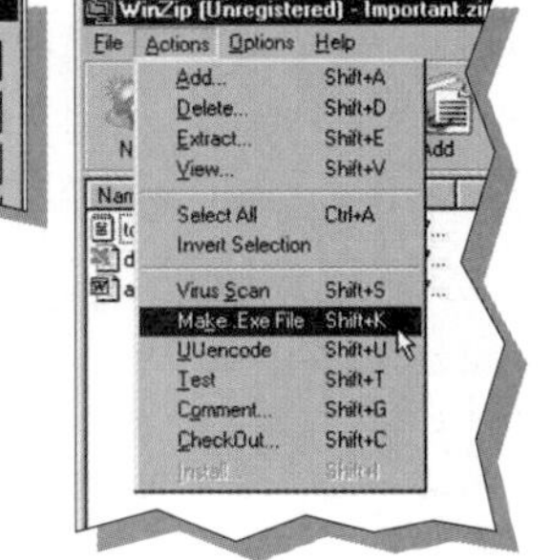

7 A dialog box will appear, suggesting that you test the self-extracting zip file. Click the Yes button.

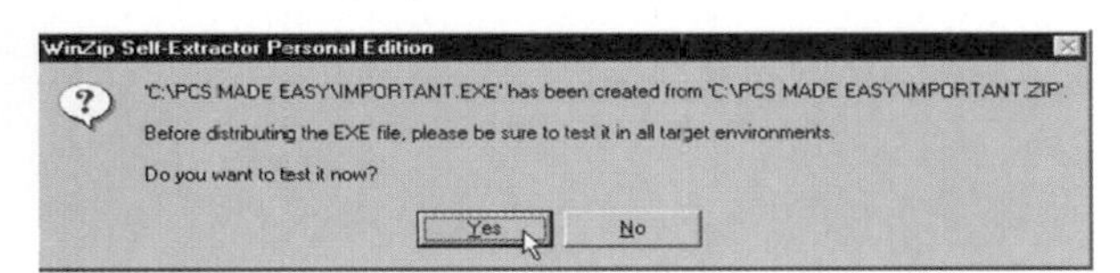

8 The WinZip Self-Extractor lets you specify which folder to put the unzipped files in by typing a path in the Unzip to folder box. We've used a temporary folder. Click the Unzip button and the files will be decompressed without needing WinZip itself.

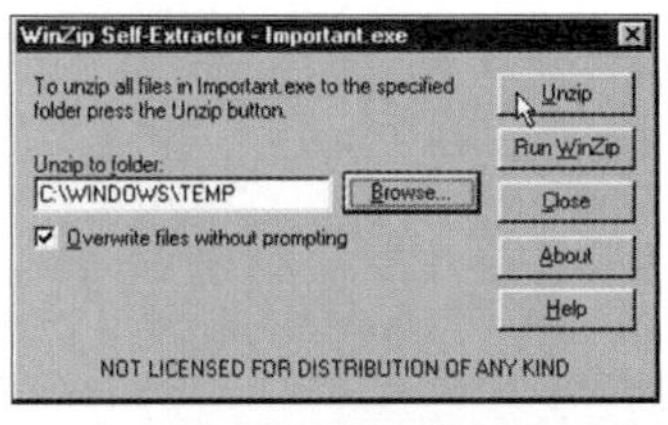

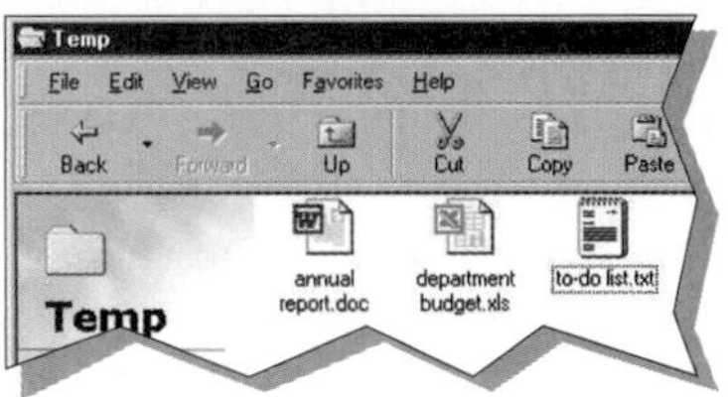

Virus checking

Like a good insurance policy, anti-virus software gives you peace of mind, letting you go about your business in the knowledge that almost any virus trying to infect your computer will be eradicated.

We have seen how third-party utility software can help you to manage your system better, (see pages 8-9). One of the most vital utilities you can buy is a virus checker – used to protect your computer against these malicious and damaging little programs. Anti-virus software will search for, and erase, any viruses it finds. You can set it to run in the background and automatically check all, or only some, of the files coming onto your computer from outside sources.

● Almost foolproof

While anti-virus software is usually 100 per cent effective in removing infection, this is usually at the cost of some of your data. Often it will not be possible to both remove a virus from a file that has been badly infected and to recover all the original data. In extreme cases the entire file might be lost.

Prevention is always better than cure and this is provided by the automatic virus guards that are supplied as part of most programs. These anti-virus utilities have to be ever-alert to keep one step ahead of the virus makers themselves, and they must be able to recognize thousands of different viruses. Anti-virus companies estimate that there are more than 50,000 viruses, with over 200 new viruses and subtle mutations being discovered every month.

With this volume of new viruses, you obviously need to keep up to date. For example, an anti-virus utility bought two years ago will not afford complete protection now. For this reason, when you buy an anti-virus utility you can receive free updates for a certain period – usually a year. These updates are usually available as small, downloadable files from the software publisher's Web site.

There are several good virus checkers available but we've chosen McAfee's VirusScan program for the following exercise as it is one of the most popular programs available.

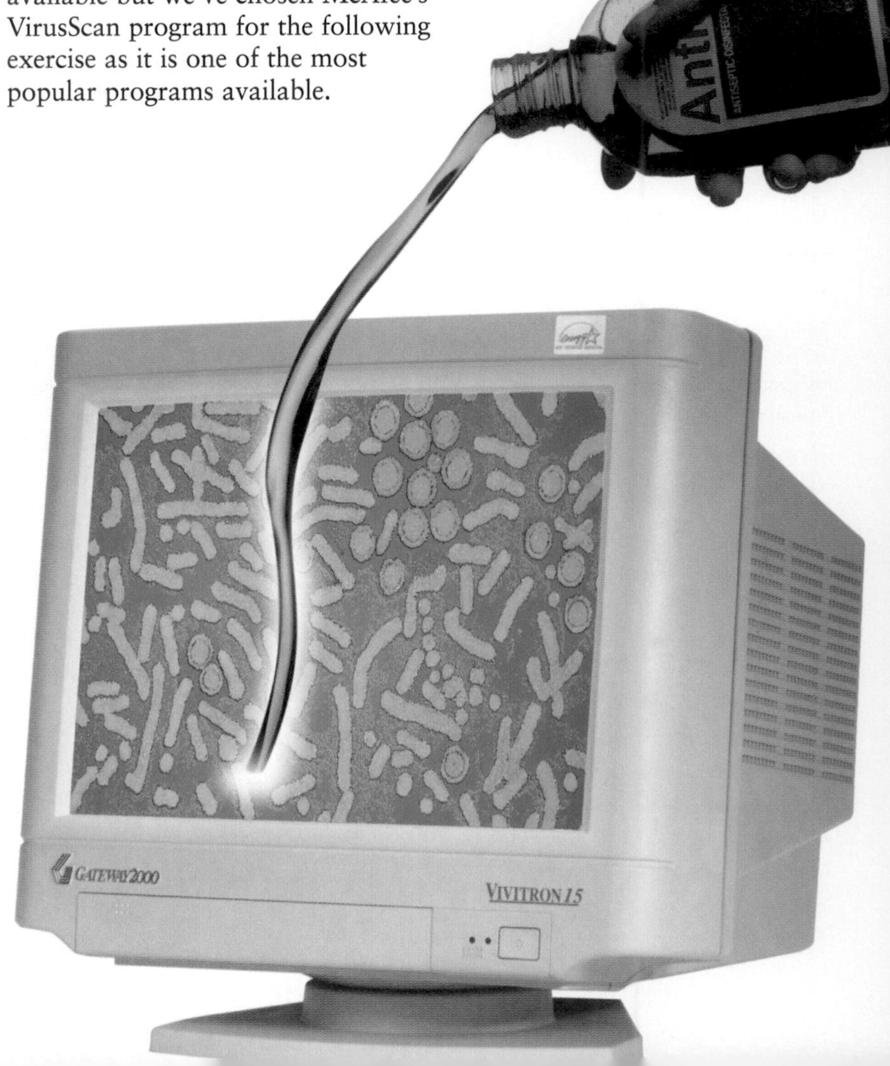

If a virus is detected by your anti-virus program, you simply press a button to 'disinfect' your computer so that all traces of the virus are eradicated.

THE EVILS OF THE COMPUTER VIRUS

Computer viruses are mini-programs that have the ability to pass from one computer to another, usually without the user being aware of their presence until it is too late.

They are all man-made: some might be written as a prank, others with malicious intent. Viruses range from the merely annoying, but relatively harmless, to the seriously damaging, which can destroy valuable data or cause your PC to crash.

Viruses usually spread from machine to machine when files are transferred – either over the Internet or via a floppy disk or other storage media. Often a virus won't show up until some time after the computer has been infected. This means that people might unwittingly pass on a virus without even knowing that they are doing so. This is why it is essential to check all disks, even from reliable sources.

Virus Checking with VirusScan

McAfee's VirusScan is one of the most popular anti-virus programs. Here's how to give your PC a thorough health check.

1 Most virus checkers are installed and work in the same way. Insert the CD-ROM and follow the on-screen instructions, choosing the Typical option.

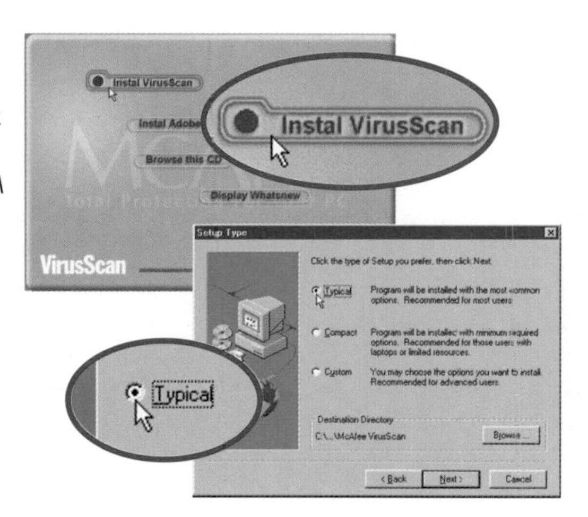

2 After copying the files to your hard disk, the setup program carries out an immediate check on your PC. At the end of this check, you will have to restart your PC to complete the installation.

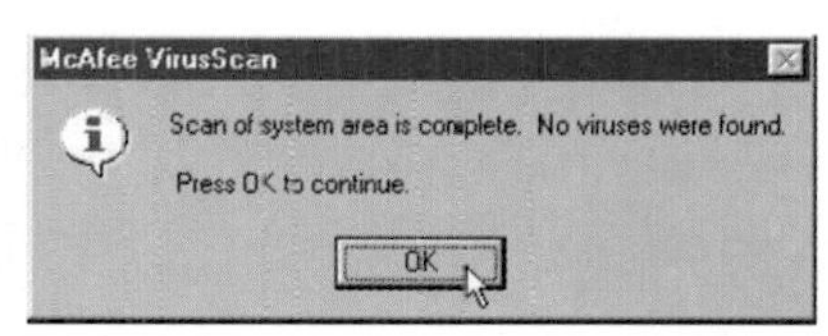

3 When Windows restarts, there are some new icons in the Taskbar's system tray and a new Desktop icon. Double-click on the VirusScan Desktop icon.

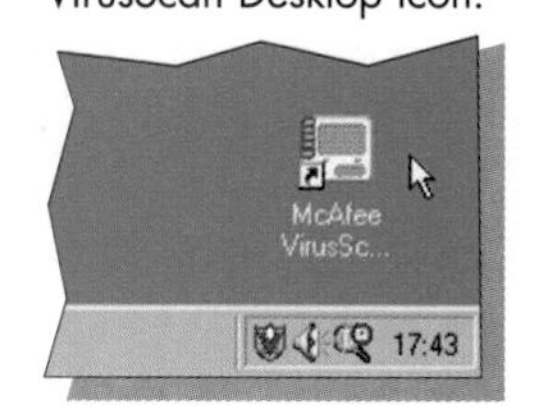

4 VirusScan alerts you to the fact that your computer hasn't recently been checked. To carry out an immediate scan, click on the Scan button.

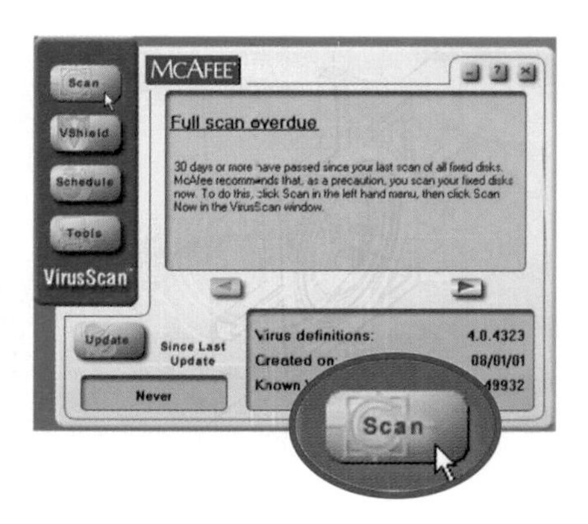

5 Ensure that the All fixed disks option is selected in the Scan in box and click the Scan Now button. VirusScan takes several minutes to check every program on your hard disk; if everything is clear, it tells you so at the bottom of the dialog box.

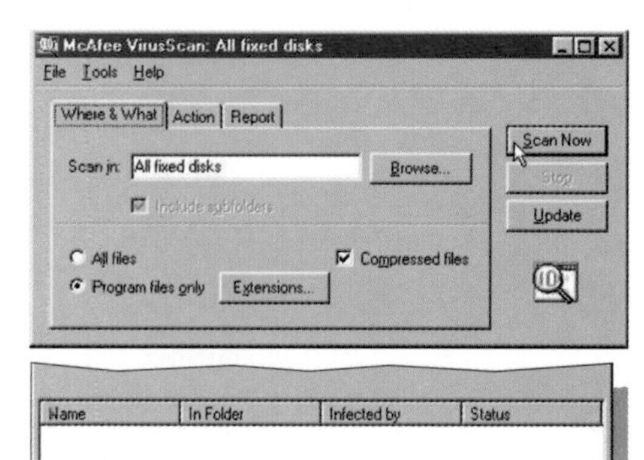

6 If a virus is found, the program alerts you and offers several options. If possible, try the Clean option and VirusScan will try to restore the file to its original form. If VirusScan says that cleaning the file isn't possible, click the Delete button. If necessary, re-install the affected program from its original CD-ROM or reinstate the file from your back-up version if you have one.

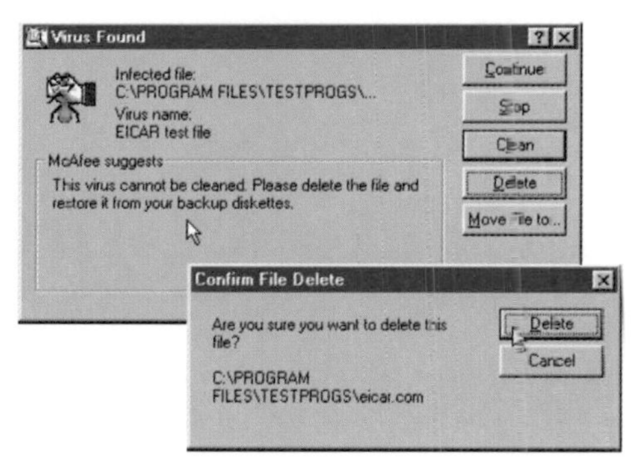

7 VirusScan records the actions it takes for all infected files and shows them as a list at the bottom of the VirusScan dialog box.

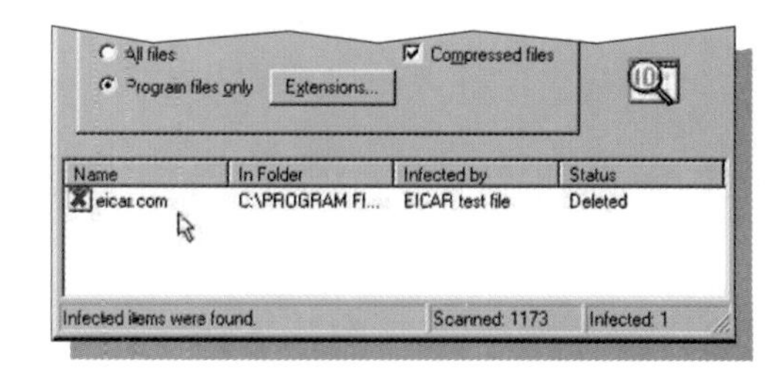

8 As part of the program, McAfee VShield is loaded into the system tray, and starts up with your computer. All new files copied to your hard disk – from floppy disk, Internet or email, for example – will be checked. You'll get an immediate warning of any infected files before they can do any damage. (Note: you must still update your virus data files to keep up with new viruses.)

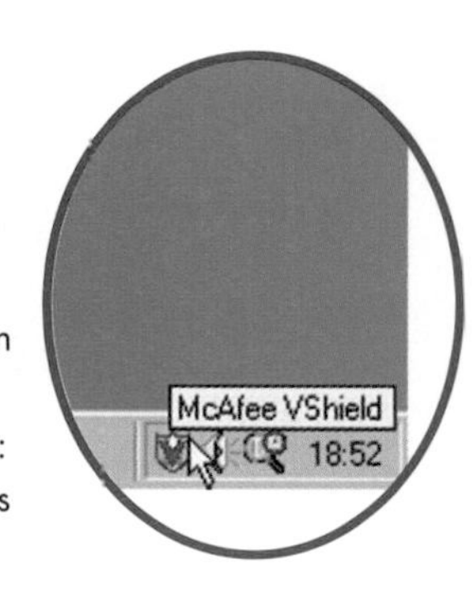

CONTACT POINTS

Anti-virus programs aren't cheap, but if you've ever suffered from a virus, you'll know that, despite the cost, they're well worth it.

Norton AntiVirus
Symantec
Tel: 020 7616 5600
Price: £25*

McAfee's VirusScan
Network Associates
Tel: 0800 092 7160
Price: £25*

*UK prices

Recording and playing sounds

Multimedia computer users will already have noticed that Windows makes certain sounds to indicate when common system events occur – but it is also easy to record and play your own sounds on the PC.

With a Multimedia computer you have your own private sound studio which can play and record sounds of a quality that's every bit as good as sound from a compact disc. Some musicians even use computers exclusively to create their music. If you don't want to go that far, however, you can use some of Windows' simple sound tools to customize your computer in order to make it friendlier and more fun to use.

You'll have noticed that when starting up, Windows welcomes you by playing a short musical sound. Depending on how your computer is set up, other sounds might accompany certain events. For example, some common error messages are accompanied by a bell, which rings to draw your attention to a problem. But if you're not happy with these sounds, Windows will let you change them. You can either replace them with a pre-recorded sound file – changing a bell to a beep, for example – or record and use new sounds of your own.

It's easy to use your Windows Multimedia PC to record sounds and play them back. You can, for instance, customize the alert sounds your computer makes, or get it to play a special noise when it starts up.

PC TIPS

If you want to play around with pre-recorded sound files, you can use Windows' Find command (see Stage 2, pages 8-9) to locate all the sounds stored on your computer as wave files. In Windows Me, the Find command has been renamed Search. The Find and Search commands are available from the Start menu. Just type *.wav in the Named field and Find will locate all the .wav files on your computer.

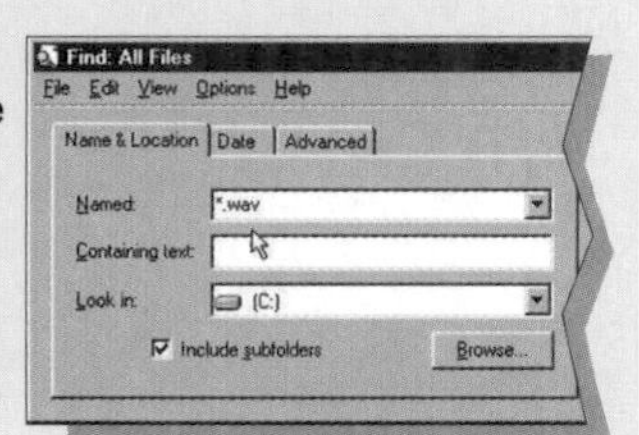

● What is a sound file?

Your computer uses many different types of sound files, but the simplest and most common is called a wave file. This is like a computerized tape recording – but the sound wave is converted into digital computer data so that it can be stored on disk. Such files normally have a .wav extension. For example, the Windows welcome sound is called 'The Microsoft Sound.wav' and the bell

HOW YOUR COMPUTER RECORDS AND REPLAYS SOUND

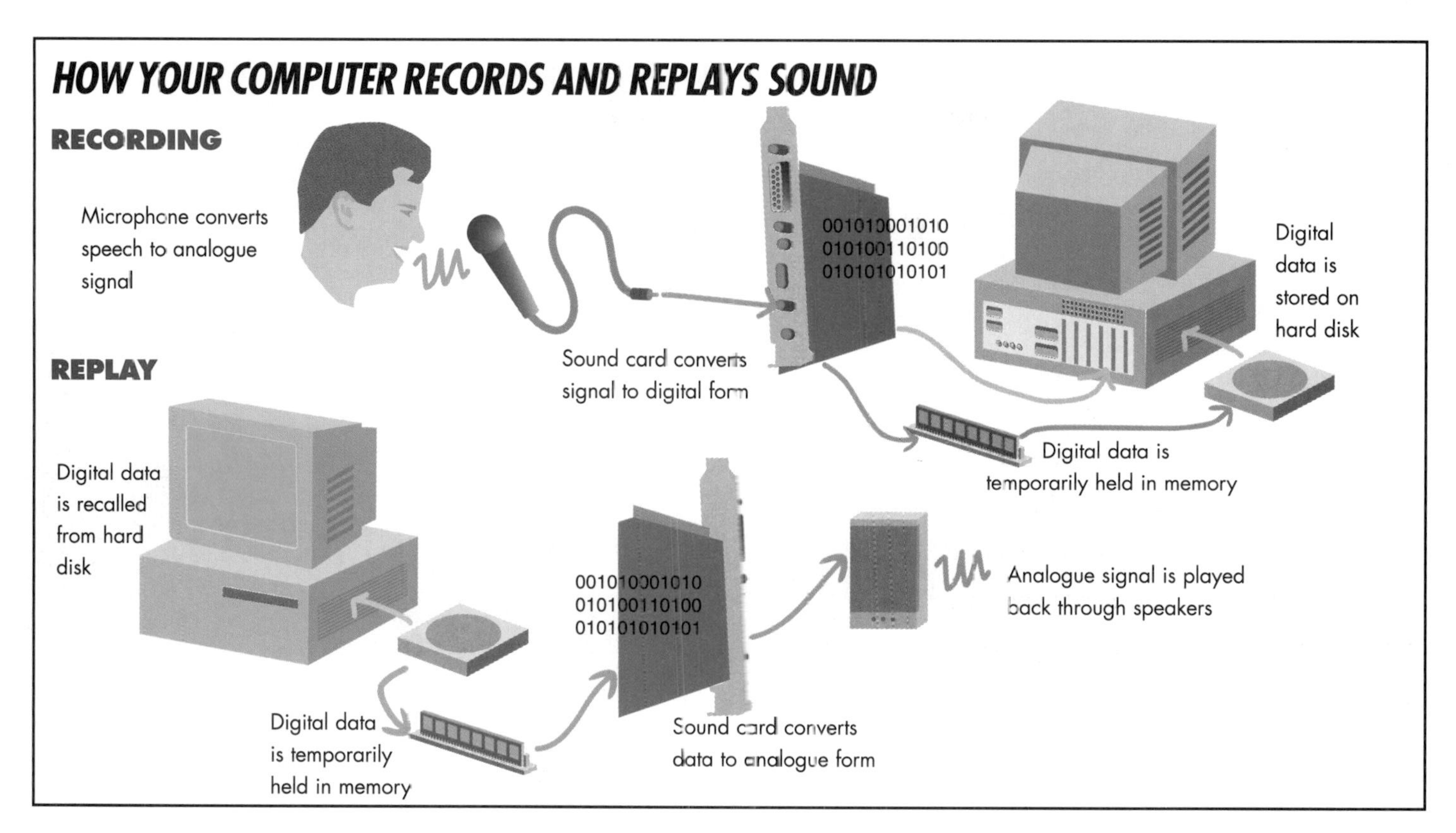

sound is called 'ding.wav'. Windows installs a number of wave files on your computer; the PC Tips box on the opposite page shows how to find them.

● Getting sound files

Recording your own sounds to play in Windows is a great way of making your computer sound unique. It's an easy process, too (see page 22). However, if you want to change lots of sounds, it can be very time-consuming and you should consider obtaining pre-recorded sounds instead. Several software companies sell disks packed with a wide range of sound files. These often have a theme, such as birdsong or a particular TV show. Titles such as *The Simpsons* and *Star Wars* are among the most popular.

These collections usually come on CD-ROMs and cost around £10-20. However, you may find that many high-street shops do not stock these sound file CD-ROMs, so you will need to check mail-order dealers. Mail-order companies sell from warehouses which enable them to carry a much wider range of software. Browse through one of the computer magazines to find adverts from mail-order dealers.

Alternatively, if you have Internet access, you'll be able to look for other collections of sounds which are available there, often free of charge. Try using a search engine to look for 'Windows sound files'.

● Recording sounds

If you prefer to make your own, original sounds, Windows includes a simple program called Sound Recorder, which makes recording sound files easy. It can record CD-quality sounds and the only hardware you need – a sound card and a microphone – are built into your Multimedia computer (see Checkpoint, left). If you want to record from music or sound effects CDs, you don't even need the microphone, as you can record directly from your CD-ROM drive.

CHECKPOINT

Before you can record sounds onto your PC, you need the following pieces of hardware and software:

SOUND CARD You must have a sound card to record and play back any sounds through your PC. All new Multimedia computers come with a sound card installed, but if you don't have one already, make sure you buy a Sound Blaster-compatible device.

MICROPHONE You need a microphone to record sounds. Many sound cards come supplied with a microphone for this purpose. If you don't have one, you can use any of the standard microphones widely available in high street electrical stores (although you might need an adaptor plug to fit the socket in the sound card).

SPEAKERS You won't hear the sounds you have recorded unless you have these; refer to Stage 2, pages 92-93 for information on the types of speakers you can buy.

SOFTWARE The final necessity is a program to convert the sounds to a digital format. Windows is supplied with a standard program called Sound Recorder, which we show you how to use on page 22. If you want to do anything more complex with sounds, then programs such as Creative's WaveStudio will give you more options to work with.

Recording your own sound files

If you're bored with Windows' sounds, why not record your own? With a microphone or a CD in the CD-ROM drive, you can record any sound you want.

1 Insert the jack plug of the microphone into the microphone socket of your sound card (see Stage 2, page 93). The microphone has no external power source, so this is the only hardware connection you need to make.

2 The Sound Recorder program is buried quite deep within your computer. From the Start menu, choose the Programs folder, then Accessories, followed by Entertainment. Select Sound Recorder from this final folder.

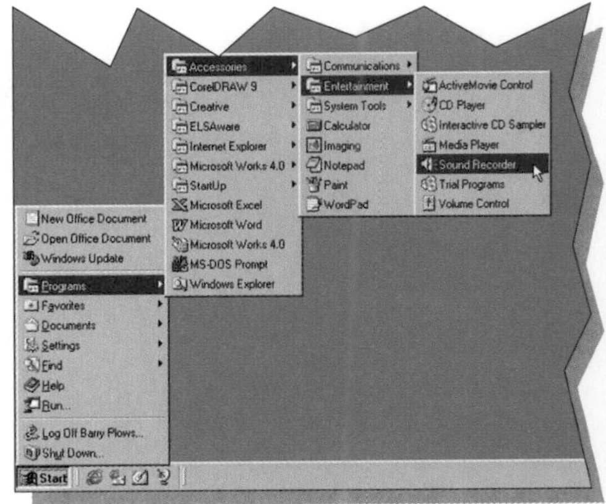

3 A small program window appears. Sound Recorder uses buttons that look very much like those on the cassette tape recorder on your hi-fi. When you are ready to record, press the big red record button and speak into the microphone.

4 As sound is picked up, you will see the green wave in the centre of the Sound Recorder window change. Press the square black stop button when you are finished.

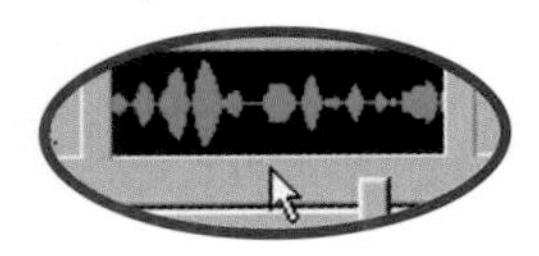

5 Check the sound you have recorded by pressing the button with the single black arrow. If your recording isn't quite right, you can discard the sound: select New from the File menu and press the No button when Windows asks if you want to keep the old sound.

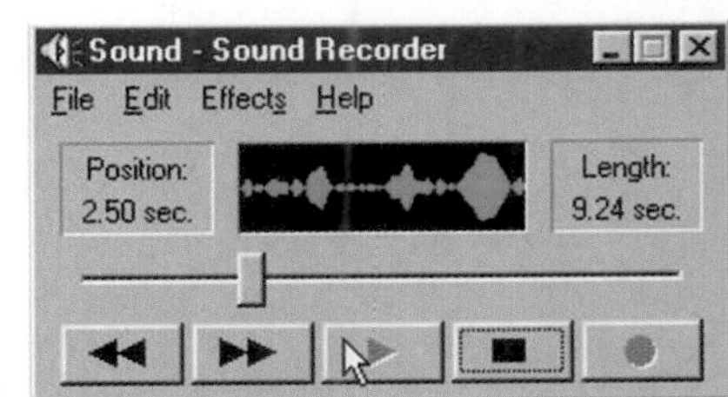

6 To save the sound file, go to the File menu and choose the Save As option.

7 The standard Save As dialog box appears: use the Save in drop-down list to find the PCs made easy folder. When you are in the right folder, type in a name for the file and click the Save button.

Note: if you don't have a PCs made easy folder, create it now. Select the C: drive from the Save in drop-down list, press the New Folder button and type in 'PCs made easy' to name the new folder that appears in the directory list. Name and save your sound file.

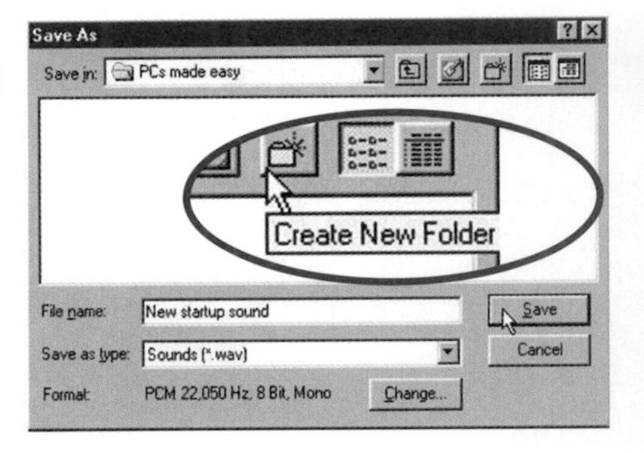

PC TIPS

Recording sound files is great fun, but try not to get too carried away as you need to be careful of the space they take up.

If you speak for more than a few seconds, the recorded sound can take up a huge amount of space. Even a collection of just 10 six-second sounds can take up over 10MB of disk space. Once you are happy with the sounds you've created, delete the unwanted ones to make sure you're not wasting space.

COPYRIGHT WARNING

When recording music CDs, you must be careful that you do not contravene copyright laws. For personal use, recording music and sound effects from a music CD is fine. However, it is illegal to copy and distribute any files you record from music CDs to other people.

8 You can also record music straight from a music CD. Put your chosen CD into the computer's CD-ROM drive, and after a few moments you will see the Windows CD Player start automatically (see Stage 2, pages 26-27).

Use the CD Player's fast forward and rewind buttons to locate the piece of music you want to record. Press the Sound Recorder's Record button just before your chosen piece of music starts to play. Press the Stop button to finish recording, then save the file as described in Steps 6 & 7.

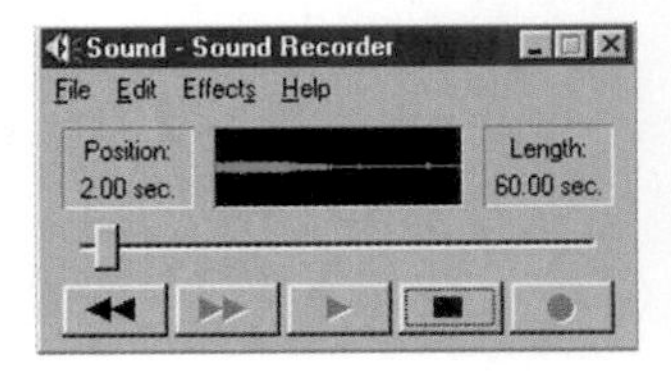

Assigning sounds to events

Once recorded sounds have been stored on your computer, it's easy to choose which ones are played back when Windows starts up or particular events occur.

IT'S EASY TO play a sound file: you don't even have to start the Sound Recorder program. If you find a sound file you need, simply double-click on its icon. Windows will automatically start up the Sound Recorder program, play the sound and then close the program again.

If you want to replace the standard Windows sounds with new sound files, this is also easy to do. All you have to do is use the Sounds program, which is contained in the Windows Control Panel. Here we show how to assign a sound file to a Windows event. This process can be used for any Windows event.

PC TIPS

Size matters

Be careful about assigning long sounds to lots of events; handling numerous large sound files at the same time can slow down your computer. If you stick to sounds of between one and two seconds, you should have no such problem.

You might also find that lots of long sounds can become annoying after the initial novelty wears off. Keep long sounds for infrequent events – such as the Windows startup sound – and stick to short, simple sounds for more frequent Windows events, such as opening a program.

1 Click on the Start button. From the menu, choose the Settings folder, followed by Control Panel.

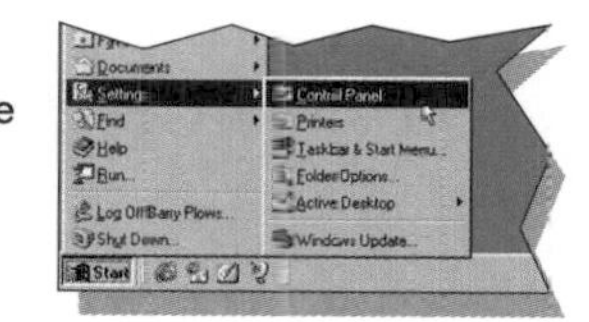

2 Locate the Sounds icon in the Control Panel window and double-click on it.

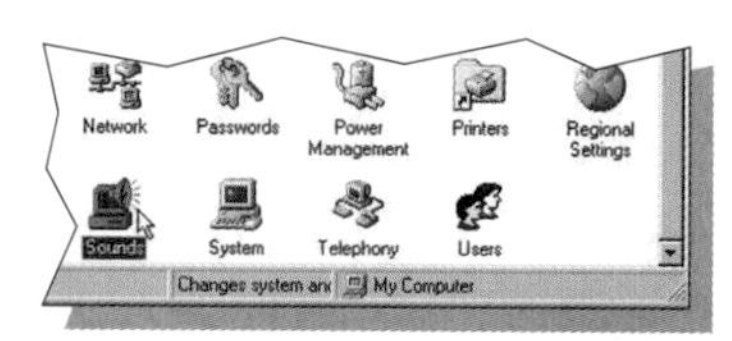

3 A large window appears. The top section lists all the possible Windows events that can have a sound associated with them. Any event that has a speaker icon to its left already has a sound assigned to it.

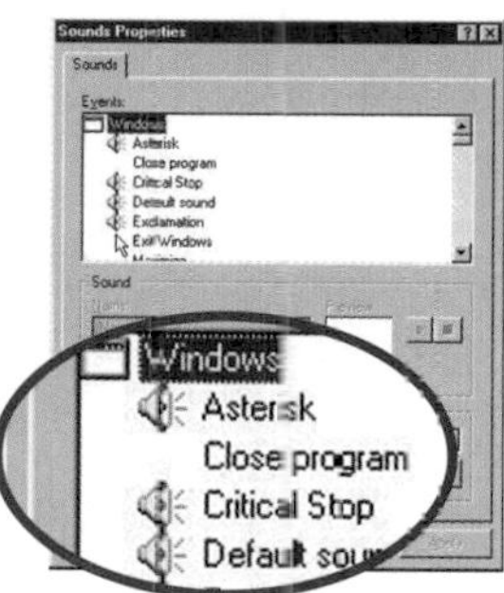

4 To play any of the event sounds, click on the name of the event to highlight it. You will see an icon appear in the Preview window. Press the small play button just to the right of the Preview window to hear the sound.

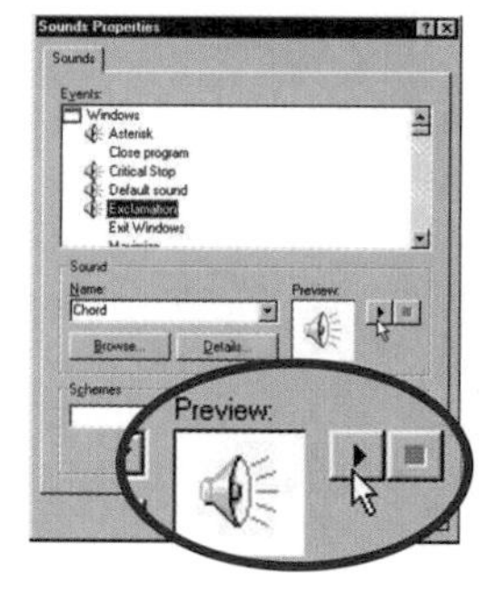

5 We'll now assign our new sound file to one of the common Windows events that does not already have a sound. Scroll down the list of events until you find Minimize. Click on it once, then click on the Browse button.

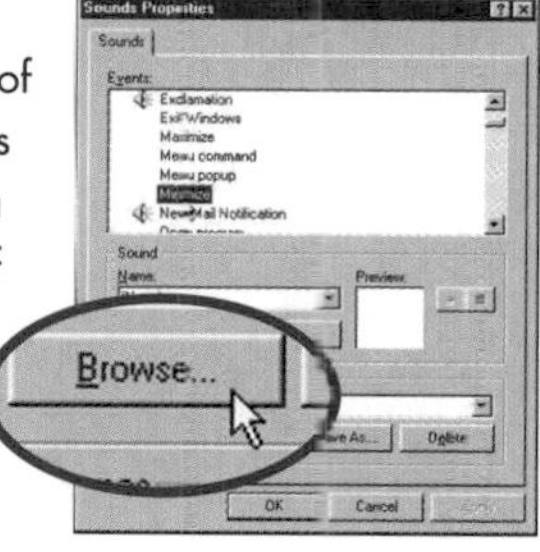

6 Use the Browse window to locate the sounds that you have recorded. If you want to check the sound first, select it and press the play button at the bottom of the window. Press the OK button when you have done so.

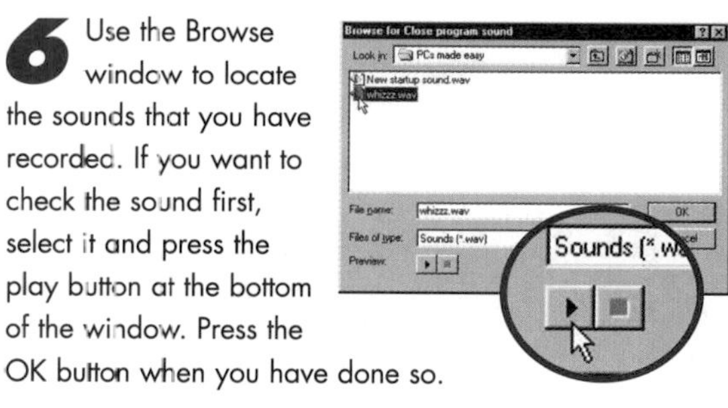

7 You will see that the Minimize event now has a speaker icon to its left. This confirms that a sound has been assigned to it. Press the OK button.

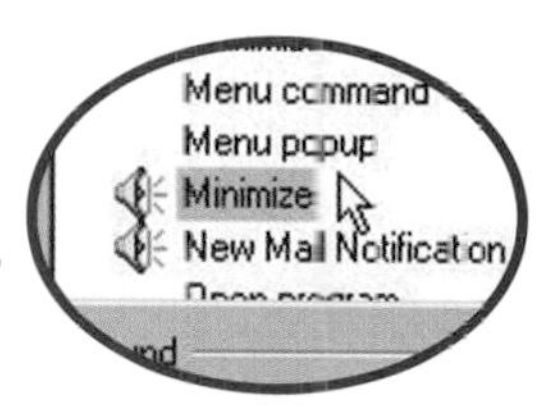

8 Now, whenever you minimize a window, you will hear the sound you previously recorded. Repeat Steps 5 to 7 for each Windows event to which you want to assign a new sound.

USING WINDOWS' DESKTOP SCHEMES

Once you have assigned sounds to several Windows events, you can save the combination as a Scheme: click on the Save As button in the Schemes section of the dialog box and give the scheme a name. Each new one will appear in the Schemes drop-down list. If you share your computer, saving each combination with a different name, means it's a quick job to change from one to another.

Windows Default
No Sounds
Windows Default
Dad's sounds
Dinosaur sounds

Windows Phone Dialer

You can use a modem for more than just connecting to the Internet. Windows includes a simple and effective program that can store and dial any telephone number for you.

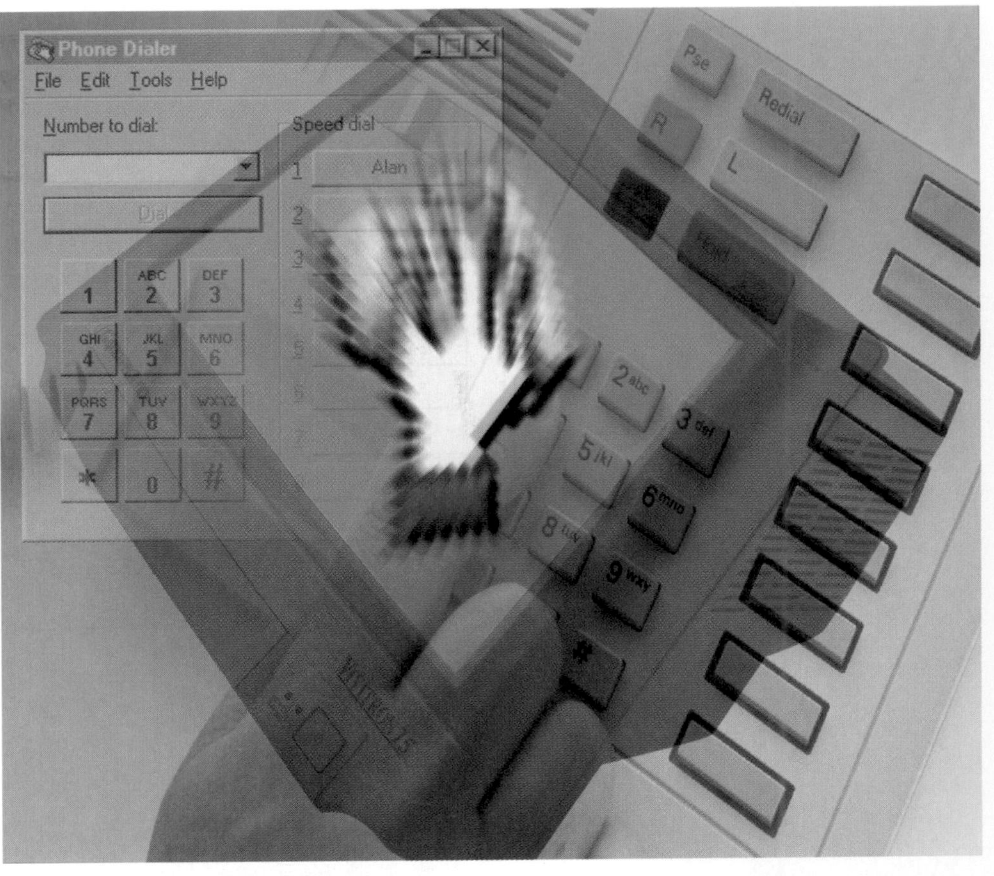

If you have a telephone near your computer, you can easily use the power of your PC to operate it more efficiently.

If you have a modem attached to your computer, Windows comes with several small but useful programs to help you exploit it to the maximum. Among the easiest to set up and use are the Phone Dialer and Microsoft Fax. We'll look at faxing with Word on pages 42-45, but here we'll examine the handy, but often overlooked, Phone Dialer.

This simple program gives you the ability to dial phone numbers from your computer, rather than using the buttons on the telephone. Phone Dialer uses the circuitry inside your modem to dial numbers by using tones just like those you hear when you press a button on your telephone. You simply tell it which phone number to dial and it plays the tones, then you pick up your ordinary telephone handset to speak when the person at the other end answers.

● Better than a telephone

Like most modern telephones, the Phone Dialer can store your selected numbers but on top of that it also lets you add text names to the buttons – Mum & Dad, Work, Doctor and so on. That way, you don't get confused about which speed-dial button belongs to which number.

Telephones have a very small amount of memory to store information, but the Phone Dialer takes advantage of your computer's huge storage. It keeps a full log of the calls you make from the Phone Dialer, as well as listing the number, date, time and duration of the call. You can check and clear the log at any time.

● Installing the Phone Dialer

If the Phone Dialer program is already installed on your computer, you'll find it in the Communications folder in the Start menu's Accessories folder. If it's not there, you can add it from your Windows CD-ROM. Insert the CD-ROM and double-click the Add/Remove Programs icon in the Control Panel window. In the Add/Remove Programs window, click the Windows Setup tab, then select the Communications category and click the Details button. In the new list of items you'll see the Phone Dialer. Click on it and then press OK. Windows will add the program to your PC.

PC TIPS

A phone that remembers

All modern telephones have a last number redial button, which can save you time and effort when you want to dial a number that was engaged a few minutes before. However, a telephone can remember only the last number. If you have called someone else since trying the engaged phone, you have to dial again. Not with the Phone Dialer, however: this is much more effective, as it keeps a record of all the numbers you have used. You just pick the one you want to dial from the list.

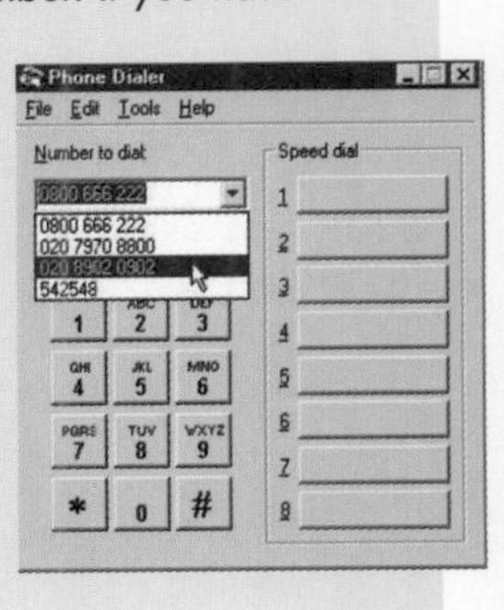

Dialling by computer

If you have a phone near your modem-equipped computer, you can use your computer's intelligence and memory to operate the telephone for you. Here's how to do it.

1 Start the Phone Dialer program and you'll see a window that looks a little like the front panel of a business telephone.

2 To dial a number, you press the buttons on the Phone Dialer's numerical keypad or type it on your computer's keypad. The number appears in the Number to dial box. When you have typed the complete number, press the large Dial button.

3 You'll hear the modem dial the number. Two small dialog boxes pop up. The first box confirms the number being dialled. Almost immediately, the Call Status dialog box appears with two buttons: Talk and Hang Up.

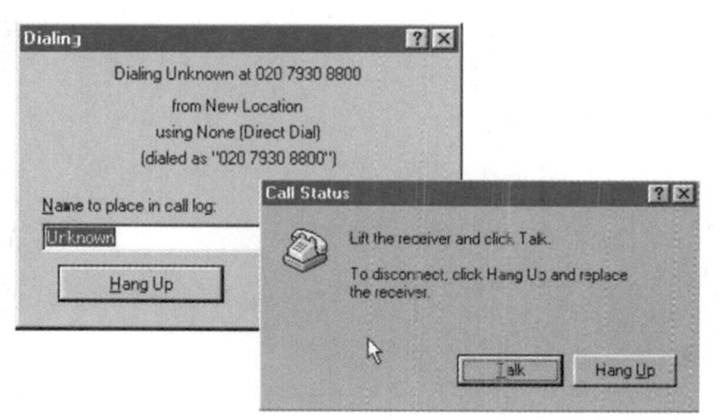

4 When you hear the person at the other end pick up the telephone, lift the handset of your phone and press the Talk button on your computer screen. The Call Status dialog box disappears and you can have a conversation as you usually would.

Once you have added Speed dial numbers to the buttons on the right of the Phone Dialer, you can use a keyboard command to dial them. For example, use [Alt]+[1] to dial the first button, [Alt]+[2] to dial the second, and so on.

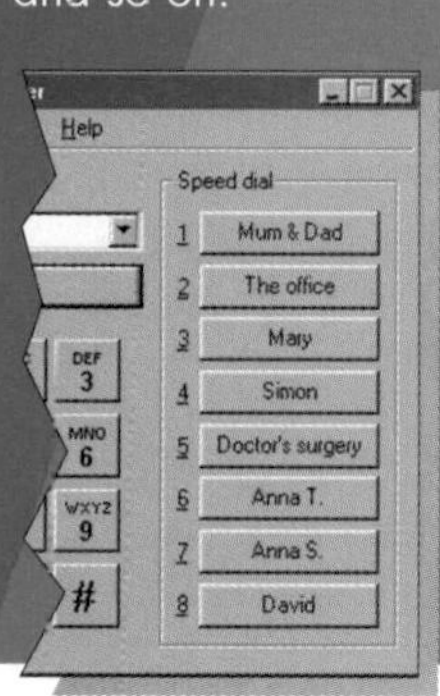

5 When you have finished the call, hang up the telephone handset. The Active call dialog box remains on screen so that you can add a name or description to the telephone number. Type a suitable name and then press the Hang Up button. This information is saved in a log.

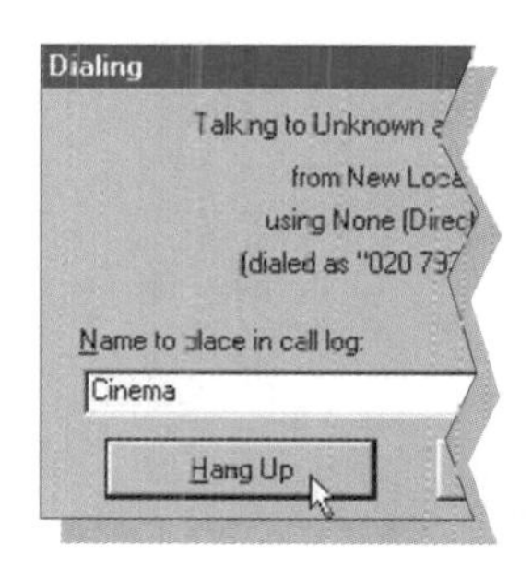

6 You can check the log details at any time by clicking on the Show Log entry in the Phone Dialer Tools menu.

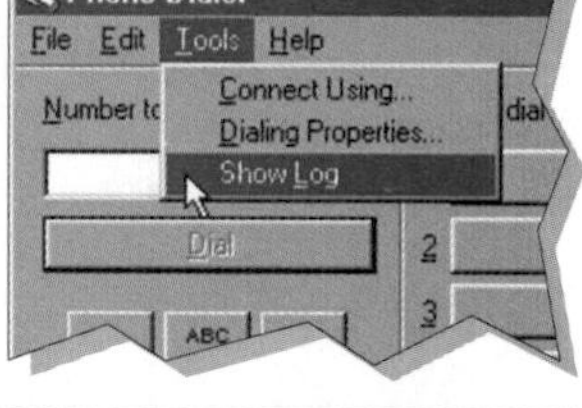

Call Log

To:	Gary	020 8902 0902	24-05-01	09:13AM	2 min
To:	Cinema	020 7930 8800	24-05-01	17:46PM	5 min
To:	Gary	020 8902 0902	25-05-01	10:20PM	10 min
To:	Car competition	0800 666 2222	26-05-01	22:01PM	7 min

7 You can add your most used numbers to the Speed dial buttons. These are on the right of the Phone Dialer window. Select the Speed Dial option from the Edit menu and the Edit Speed Dial dialog box appears.

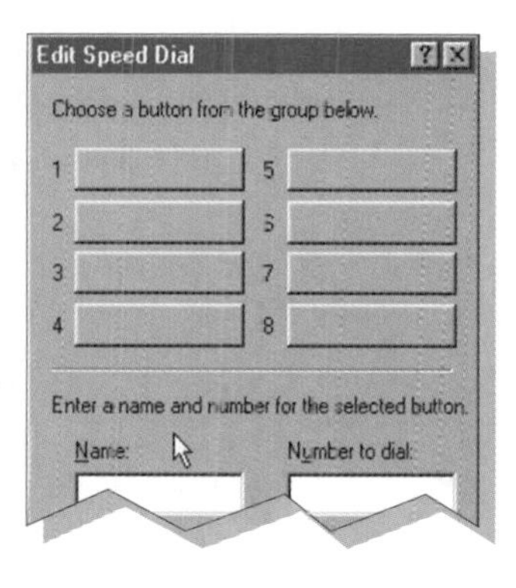

8 For each number you want to add, click a button and then type a name and phone number in the two spaces at the bottom of the dialog box. When you have finished, click Save.

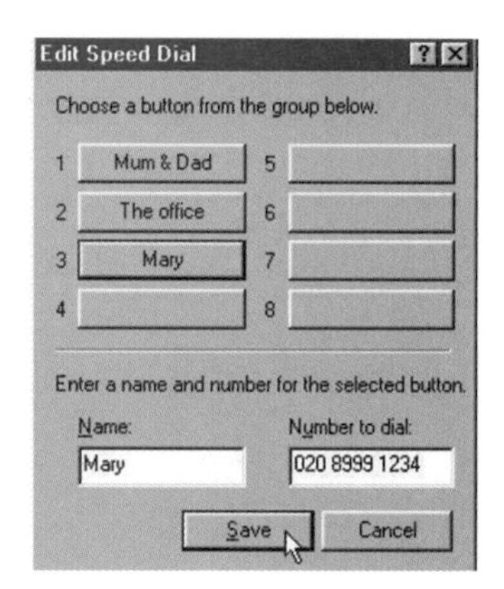

Faxing with Windows

You might think that your modem is only there to let you surf the Net and email. With fax software, however, your computer and modem turn into a fax machine, sending and receiving pages so that you don't have to handle any paper at all.

Although the main reason why most people buy a modem is to get on to the Internet, the electronics inside the modem can be turned to other uses. Most useful – and often overlooked by modem buyers – is faxing. A modem can fax a page to any fax machine in the world as easily as it sends and receives email.

● Fax software

In order to send and receive faxes, some special software has to be installed. Windows includes some basic fax software, but it's buried in an obscure part of the Windows CD-ROM. It's also very complicated to install, with the result that very few Windows users bother with it. Fortunately, most modems come with faxing software that's a lot easier to get working. Check your modem's manual and CD-ROM to see what's available. You might find that the fax software was already installed when you first added your modem (see PC Tips box, opposite).

Once your modem's fax software is installed, you're just seconds away from being able to send and receive faxes. Sending faxes is as easy as printing a document. Instead of printing out the page, the fax software creates an electronic version of the document in the computer's memory. It then uses the modem to dial the fax number you type in and sends this electronic document to the remote fax machine. This is a great way to save paper (see pages 42-45).

● Incoming

Your modem and PC can also receive faxes, and most fax programs have several different ways of working to suit the way you use your phone. If you have a second phone line dedicated to your modem, for example, you can set up the fax software so that it automatically answers incoming calls to receive faxes. When the modem detects the phone ringing it wakes up the fax software, which receives the document that you are being sent. You can then read the document on the computer screen. If necessary, you can print it out for permanent storage.

If you have only one phone line, you can set up the fax software so that you answer the phone for all calls. If you hear the high-pitched bleeps and whistles of a fax machine, you can tell the fax software to take the call. This method is a little less convenient, but fine if you get only a few faxes.

EXTRA FEATURES

If you check your modem's manual, you might find that the software it comes with can extend your PC's communications capabilities. Some software can turn your PC into an answering machine as well as a fax.

Installing your fax software

If there's no fax software installed on your computer, you can use the CD-ROM supplied with your modem to add it. Our fax software is called Xtreem Machine, but most will follow similar steps. First, investigate whether or not fax software is installed (see PC Tips box).

1 Insert the CD-ROM that came with your modem. When the intro screen appears, choose the option that lets you install the software. In this example, it's also necessary to choose the correct language before starting.

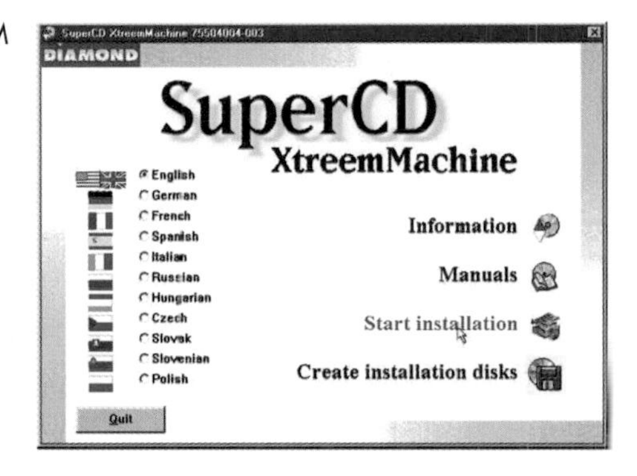

2 If your modem is already installed and working for Internet access, look for the option that lets you install the extra software and click it.

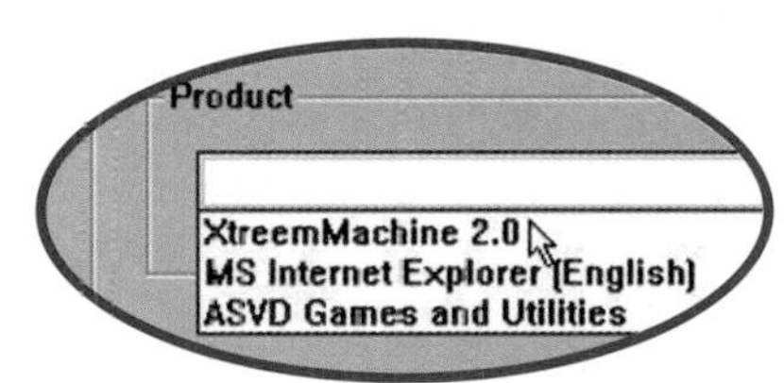

3 Follow the instructions on the fax software setup screens. The files that the software needs will be copied from the CD-ROM to your computer's hard disk.

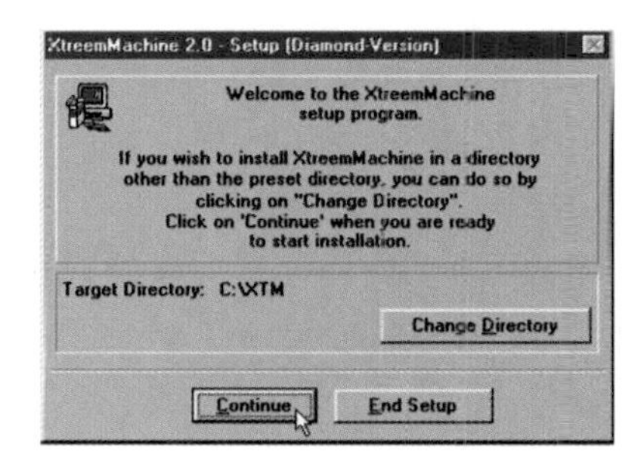

4 When the installation is complete, click the OK (or Yes) button to return to Windows.

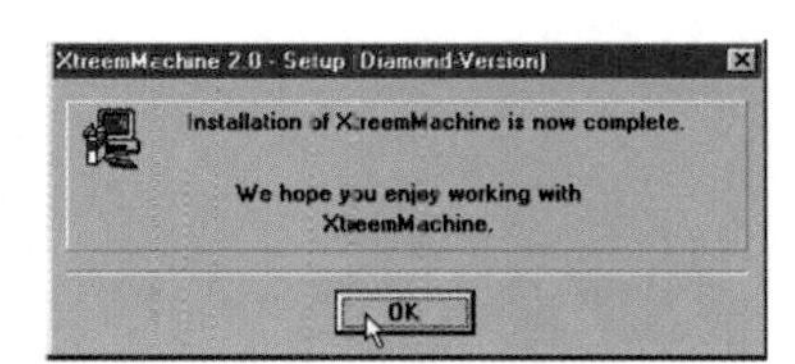

5 In most cases, you will find that the setup program has added an extra folder of programs to the Start menu's Programs folder.

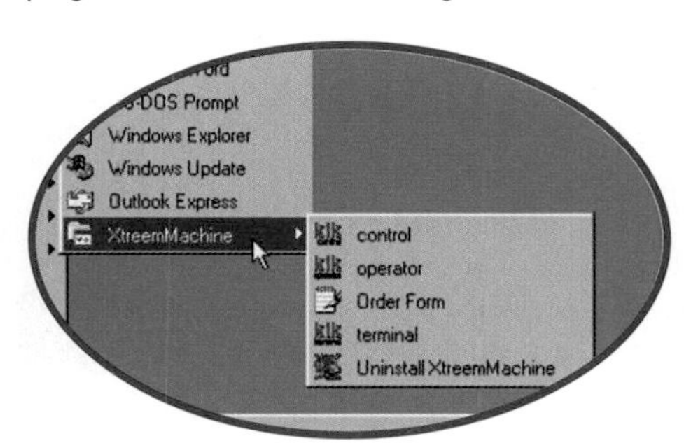

6 Many modem manufacturers don't include printed manuals for the fax software. It's easy to use the basic fax-sending features, but to use the more advanced fax features you might need to refer to the electronic manuals on the CD-ROM. Re-insert the CD and look for the manuals or user guide section.

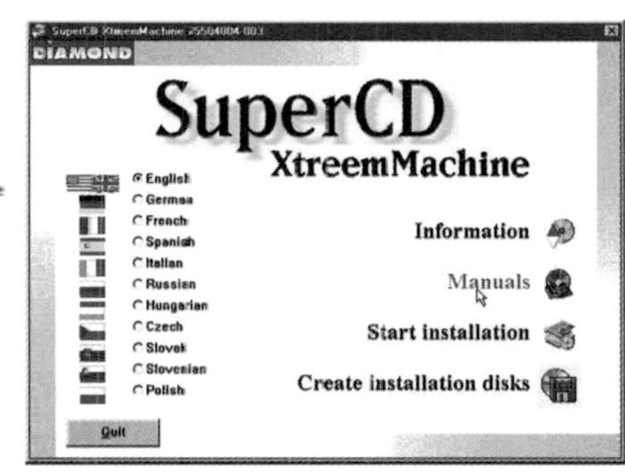

7 When the manual appears, you can use the Find or Search command to locate the section you need.

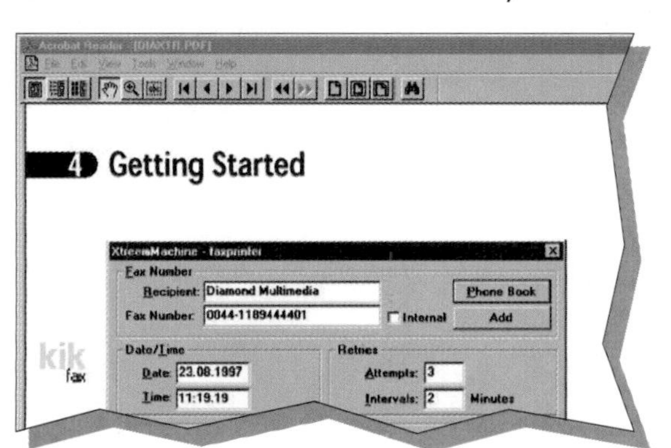

8 Your fax software is now ready for action. Contact a friend who has a fax machine and use Word to send a short and simple fax message to make sure everything's working smoothly (see pages 42-45).

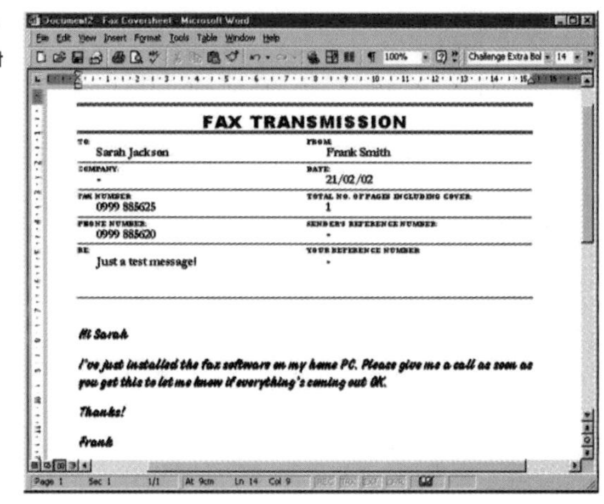

PC TIPS

Testing for installation

Although reinstalling fax software won't do any harm, you can save having to reinstall by doing a simple test to see if it's present. First, check the modem's manual to see what fax program is included. Then start a program such as Microsoft Word and select Print from the File menu. Click on the arrow beside the Name box to see what other devices are listed. If you see the fax program in addition to the printer, the software is already installed.

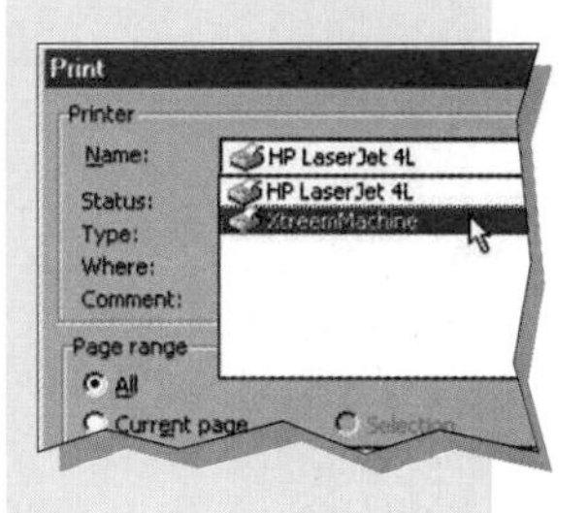

Software

Microsoft® Word

Microsoft® Excel

CorelDRAW™

Intuit™ Quicken®

Introduction to macros

If there are tasks you find yourself having to do over and over again when working on a document, why not get Word to record them? A simple key combination will make Word do the tasks for you.

Imagine being able to automate all the tasks involved in making a pot of tea. Instead of having to boil the kettle, get out a pot, put in the teabags and all the rest, you could have a custom machine that does it all for you – just the way you like it – at the press of a button. This is the sort of thing a macro does in Word, allowing you to carry out a sequence of related tasks at the press of a single key or the click of a button on the toolbar.

A macro is simply a name for a sequence of operations. It is a way of bolting together a lot of different tasks into a single command, which you can then activate with a single instruction. Macros take the hard work out of those boring tasks that you perform time and time again – sometimes so often that you don't even realize the number of tasks you have to perform to achieve something simple.

● Saving space

For example, a common formatting exercise, such as checking for and removing double spaces, can be automated. Many typists have been taught to put in two spaces after each full stop – an essential aid to legibility in typewritten text. However, text keyed into a word processor doesn't need extra space after the full stops and it makes text look 'gappy'.

Usually, the best way to remove unwanted spaces is with Word's Replace command. Call up the Replace dialog box, tell it to change double spaces to singles, and then run it. With a macro, you can do all this with a single command – as we show you opposite.

This is a very simple example, but macros can be a good deal more complex, as we will show you over the next few pages. You can create macros to carry out more involved formatting tasks, to set up tables, save pages with custom names in custom folders, or to carry out any task involving a regular sequence of commands.

● Setting up a macro

Macros are easy to create. By entering a series of keyboard commands and/or menu selections, dialog box choices and button presses, you can create a basic macro and achieve the result you want.

All you have to do is start Word's built-in macro recorder, perform the various commands that make up the task you wish to automate and then tell the macro recorder to stop recording. It's up to you then whether you want to assign a special keystroke to your new macro or put a button for it on a toolbar, which is every bit as easy as customizing the regular toolbars (see Stage 4, pages 32-33). The only thing to bear in mind is that you shouldn't give it a keystroke that's already been assigned to another task in Word as, when you hit that key, it will perform your macro and not the original command.

WORD 2000

Word 2000 has most of Word 97's commands, so whichever program you use, future Word exercises in *PCs made easy* will work in both programs. Where there are any differences, we'll highlight the Word 2000 method with this type of box.

Creating a simple Word macro

Here's how to create a basic macro that removes double spaces from a document by just pressing a simple key combination.

1 Open a document. Select Macro from the Tools menu and Record New Macro from the sub-menu.

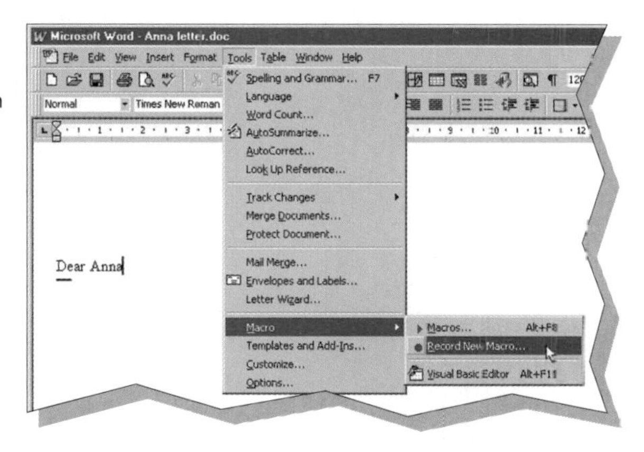

2 In the Record Macro dialog box, give the macro a name, such as 'Spaces'. The Store macro in box offers a list of options for storing the macro. Choose the current document (see PC Tips, below). Add a description of the macro in the box underneath. Click the keyboard button to show that you want to assign the macro to a keystroke.

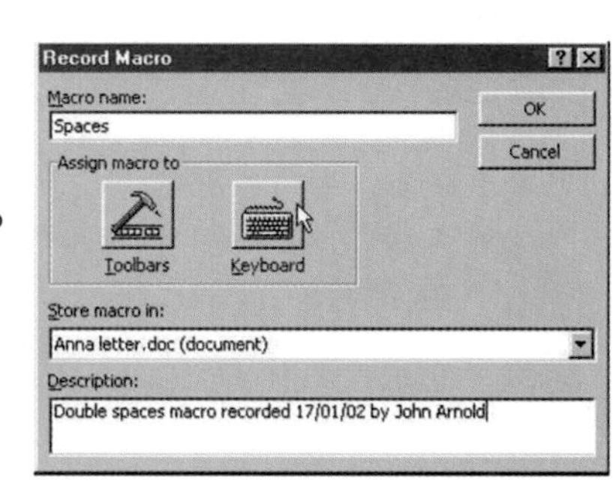

3 The Customize Keyboard dialog box lets you set up your keystroke. Press the [Ctrl] and [9] keys at the same time. This is an unassigned key combination that can be used to activate your macro. You'll see Ctrl+9 appear in the Press new shortcut key box. Press Assign to confirm.

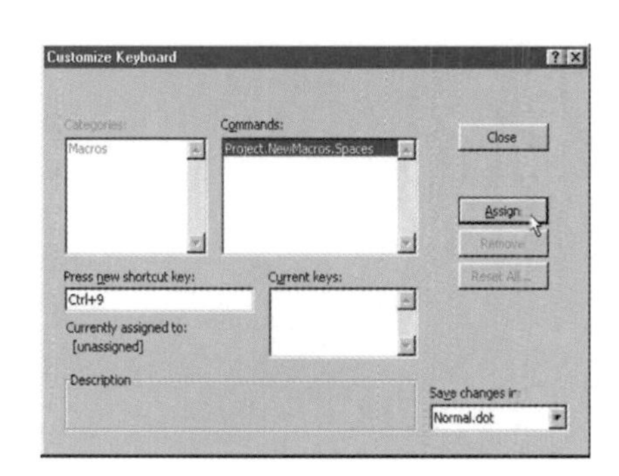

4 After you have closed the box you will see a small floating toolbar with Stop and Pause buttons similar to those on a tape recorder. The mouse pointer also has a tiny cassette icon to remind you that your actions are now being recorded.

5 To remove the double spaces, move the insertion point to the start of the document. Press [Ctrl]+[Home] to do this. Then select Replace from the Edit menu.

6 The Find and Replace dialog box appears. Type two spaces in the Find what box and a single space in the Replace with box. Click on Replace All.

7 Word now searches the current document and replaces any spaces. When it's finished, it will tell you that the search is complete. Click OK to close this box and then close the Find and Replace dialog box.

PC TIPS

In the above example, we stored the macro in the current document. If you start a new document and press [Ctrl]+[9] nothing will happen. To make a macro work in all documents, you must store it in the Normal.dot template. To do this, select All Documents (Normal.dot) instead of your current document in Step 2 above. This tells Word to store the macro in the template from which new documents are created.

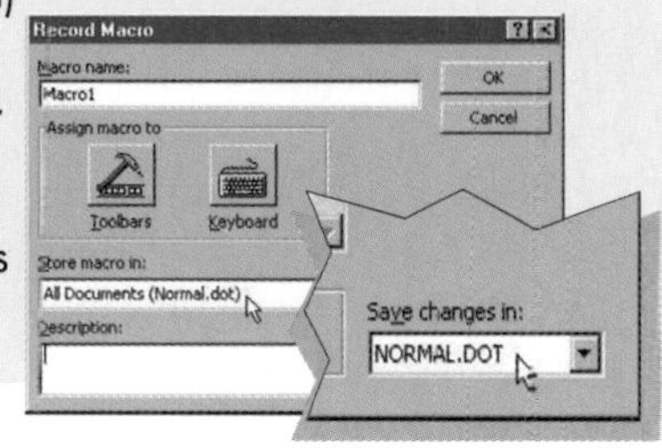

8 Now, all you need to do is just click the Stop icon on the macro toolbar. Whenever you press [Ctrl]+[9] while working on this document, Word will check for double spaces and replace them with single spaces. Try it and you'll see that it all happens automatically; there's no need to click any buttons and you don't even see any dialog boxes.

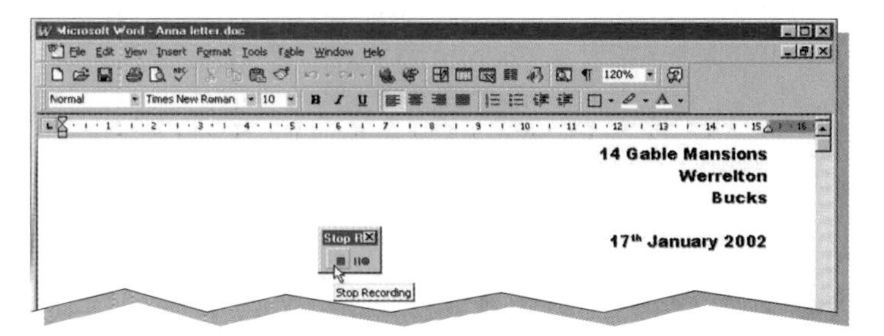

More advanced macros

Here we show you how to create a more complex sequence of macro commands and how to place a customized button on a toolbar.

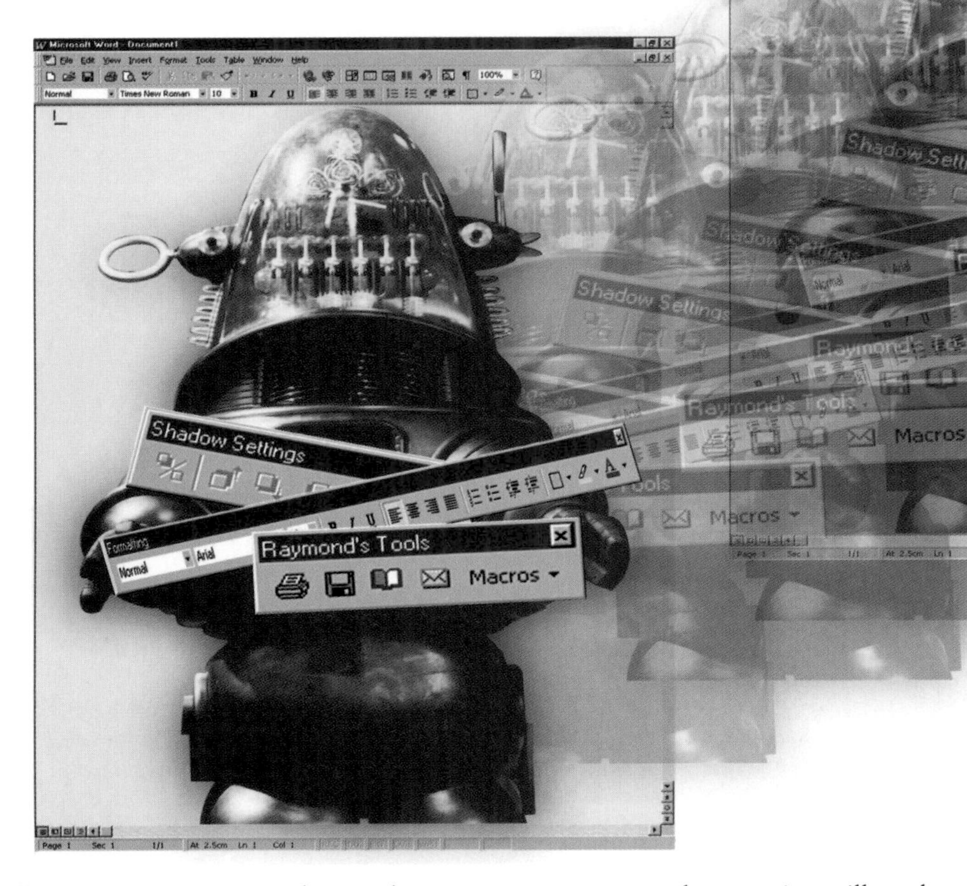

Now, with a single click, you will be able to operate your macros from your own customized toolbar, and take them with you from document to document.

We've covered a simple formatting macro (on pages 30-31), which automated the task of removing unwanted double spaces from a document. Now we're going to create a slightly longer macro to give you a better idea of how powerful macros can be – and how carefully you need to think through the actions to make the most of them.

Once you begin creating macros, it's important that you also start managing them properly. As soon as you commence recording a macro, it will be created and saved – regardless of whether you get it right or not. So if, as is quite possible, you have four or five goes at getting a macro right, you will create four or five different macros. This is not necessarily a problem, as the keyboard command you assign will apply only to the last macro created. However, if you plan to create several macros, it will help you to keep track of which one does what if you give each a meaningful name. You can also delete all of your unwanted macros by using the Macros and Organizer dialog boxes.

● The Macros dialog box

The Macros dialog box lets you list or alter any macro. It will show all the macros attached to your current document or, if you change the viewing option, all the macros stored in the Normal template, as well as all the macros used by Word itself. From the Macros dialog box, you can run or delete any macro, while a set of advanced controls allows you to edit an existing macro or create a new

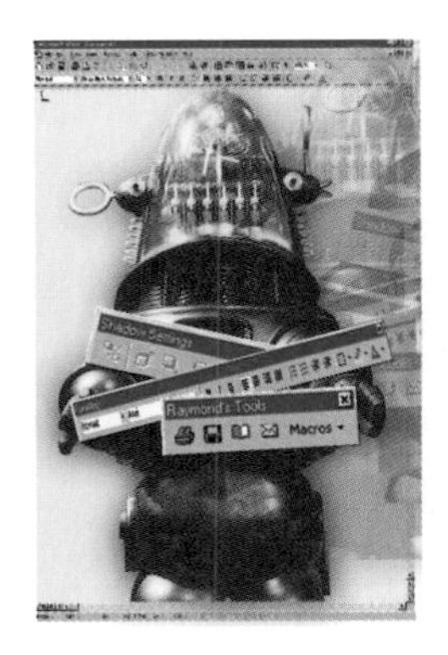

one. You can also call up the Organizer dialog box (see panel below).

You won't need many of the Macros options at this stage. Run is of limited use, as you will probably find it far easier to give your macros keyboard or toolbar shortcuts instead. It's best for macro novices to steer clear of the Step Into, Edit and Create options, because all these plunge you straight into Visual Basic, Word's built-in program language. When you record a macro, it is stored as a set of Visual Basic commands, but these are normally hidden from view. Step Into shows you the macro command-by-command, highlighting each step as it is executed, to help you find out where a troublesome macro is going wrong. Edit lets you alter the Visual Basic commands, while advanced users can choose Create and type in a macro directly in Visual Basic.

The Macros dialog box shows all the macros in the location you specify in the Macros in list box. You can run or modify any macro, or go to the Organizer dialog box.

● The basic difference

The Description panel in the Macros dialog box differentiates between recorded macros and created macros that were set up in Visual Basic. This is because macros that were created or edited in Visual Basic can be much more powerful than the basic recorded ones. On pages 36-37, we'll discuss in more detail the custom macros you can buy and install in Word to perform specific tasks.

● Let's get organized

The most useful option at this stage is the Organizer button. As explained in detail below, this allows you to delete macros or copy them between documents and templates. It also lets you move and copy customized styles, autotext entries and toolbars, which is extremely handy. You can also use it to assign macros for different tasks to different templates, depending on what you use the templates for.

On page 31, we took care to save our macro in the active document, rather than the Normal template. When you store a macro in the Normal template, it becomes available to every document you then create (unless you specify otherwise). But you must take care of what's put there; unless you're careful, you can end up with your Normal template becoming an untidy mess of half-finished and trial-and-error macros.

Earlier on, we showed you how to create a macro and assign it a keystroke (on page 31). Now we're going to look at setting up another one and adding a button to one of Word's toolbars. In this way, you will be able to activate your macro with a single click.

The Organizer

The Organizer is a powerful (and well hidden) tool, which allows you to move text styles, autotext entries, macros and toolbars between documents and templates. On pages 36-37 we will show you how to copy a custom macro step-by-step. The principle is fairly simple. If you want to copy a macro, you simply choose the Macro Project Items tab, open up a document which you know contains the macro and then copy it to where you want it.

Note that Word automatically puts all macros you create via the Record New Macro command into a single 'Project', which it calls NewMacros by default. This means that if you store several macros in one document, you cannot see them individually. You can see and move them only by the group or project name – which means you will also have to transfer or delete them as a whole. This probably won't be a problem, unless you are planning to create a lot of macros.

However, since you can change the group/project name by using Organizer's Rename button, it's a good idea to arrange your macros by group/project, and give them meaningful names (for example, Letter macros, or Newsletter macros) so that you can move them around together.

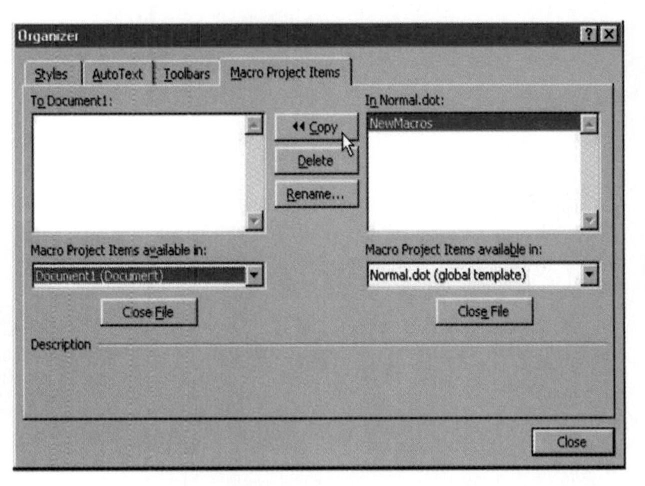

With Organizer (above), you can easily keep an eye on exactly what macros you have created and where they are.

Removing unwanted line breaks

Some tasks you need to perform on a regular basis are ideally suited to the use of a macro. Here we create a simple macro to reformat email documents in Word with a single click.

1 We've started with a simple message, which we've cut and pasted from the email program into Word. As you can see, the lines of text don't extend all the way across the page. This is because the email program has included line breaks at the end of each line.

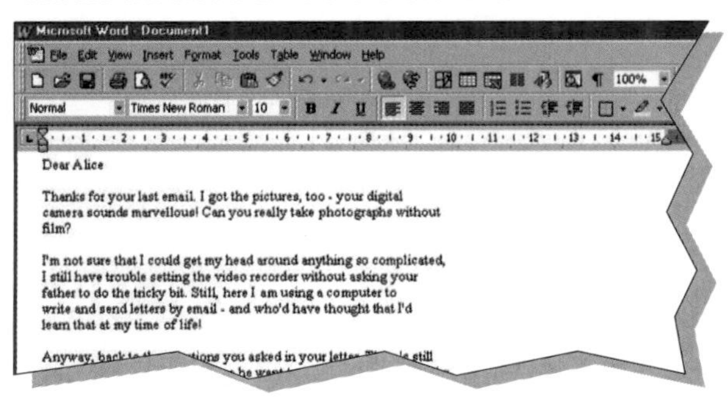

2 Click on the Tools menu, then the Macro option and finally the Record New Macro command.

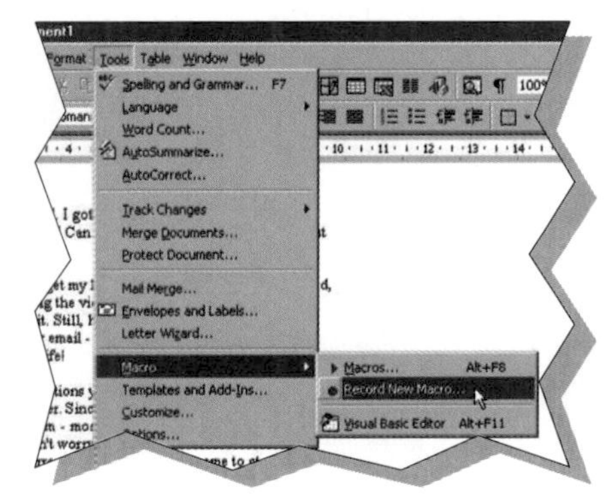

3 Type Linebreaks into the Macro name box and select the file, which is called Document1 (document), from the Store macro in drop-down list box. Click the Toolbars button.

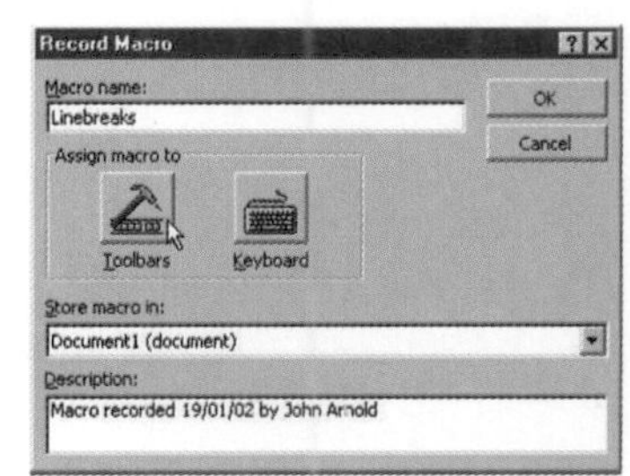

4 The Customize dialog box appears. Select the Document1 option from the Save in list box, and then drag your macro command onto the toolbar (inset). Click the Close button.

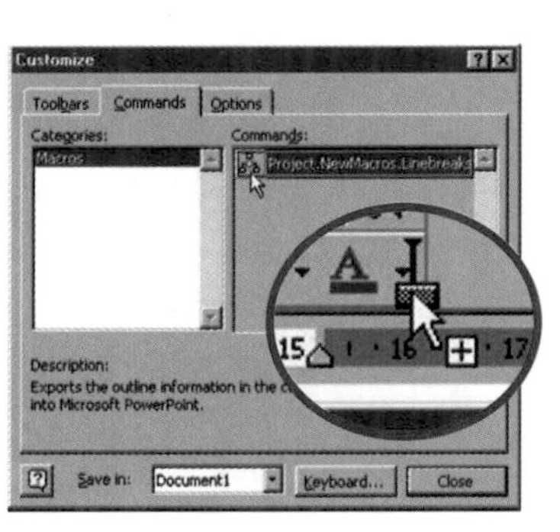

5 You'll see a button appear on the toolbar, and the mouse pointer changes to the cassette pointer to show that your actions are being recorded.

6 Press [Ctrl]+[H] to bring up the Find and Replace dialog box. We need to remove the line breaks at the end of each line, but not those between paragraphs. To preserve the latter, temporarily replace the double line breaks between paragraphs with four asterisks. Type ^p^p (see Special characters below) into the Find what box and **** into the Replace with box. Then click the Replace All button.

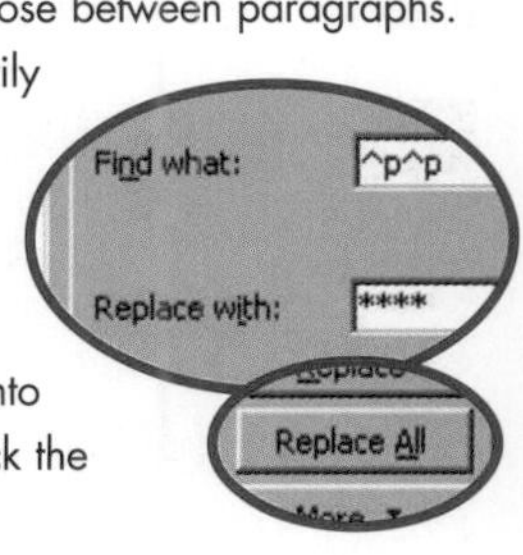

7 You'll see the text of the email message change and Word will tell you how many replacements it made. Click OK.

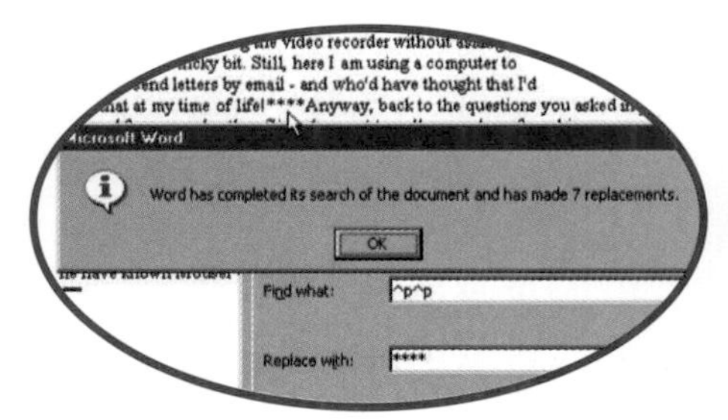

8 Now we want to remove all the single line breaks left in the document. Type ^p into the Find what box, and delete the four asterisks from the Replace with box, leaving it blank. Click the Replace All button. This removes all the line breaks.

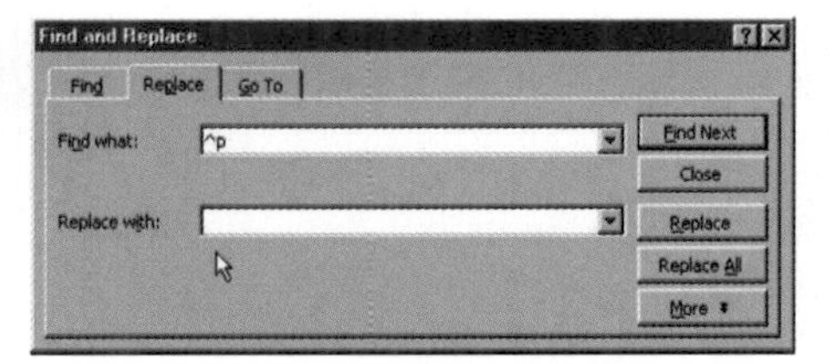

9 When the replacements have been made, you must now convert the temporary asterisks back into two line breaks. Type **** into the Find what box and ^p^p into the Replace with box, and click the Replace All button again.

10 Close the Find and Replace dialog box and you'll see that your email document is now properly formatted: the lines go across the page and Word wraps them as necessary. Click the Stop Recording button. Save the document as email.doc ready for the next exercise (opposite).

SPECIAL CHARACTERS

When you want to replace a line break in Word, it isn't possible to press the [Enter] key in the Find and Replace dialog box. So, in steps 6, 8 and 9 we used Word's facility for typing special characters into a dialog box. Word uses ^p to represent a line break. By using two in succession you can find the two line breaks that occur between paragraphs (one to finish a line and one for the blank line).

Customizing macro toolbar buttons

As well as placing macro buttons on a toolbar, you can even customize the way they appear. Here we look at how to give the shortcut button a name - and even an image - of your choice.

1 Open the neatly formatted document that you created opposite, then select the Customize command from the Tools menu.

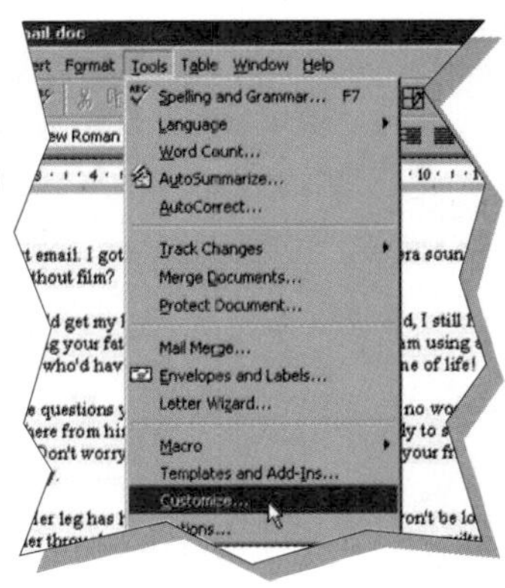

2 Click on the Commands tab of the Customize dialog box and scroll down the Categories list until you see the Macros entry. Click on it and then select the email.doc from the Save in list box. You'll see your macro appear in the Commands panel on the right. Word automatically gives the macro a prefix, showing that it has put it in the NewMacros Project. Press the Keyboard button.

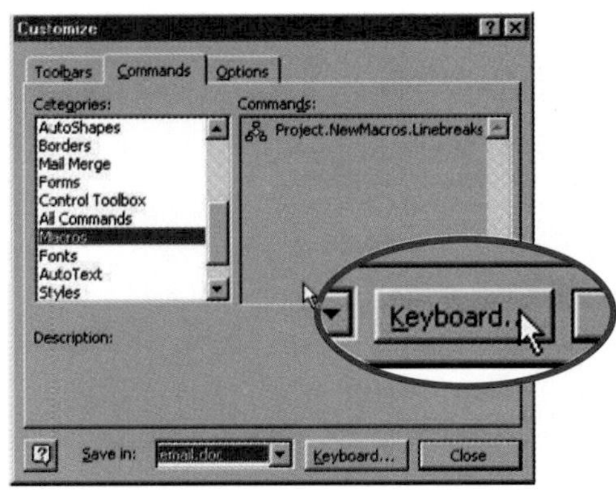

3 Follow similar steps in the Customize Keyboard dialog box: select Macros from the Categories list, email.doc from the Save changes in list box, and then click on the Linebreaks macro.

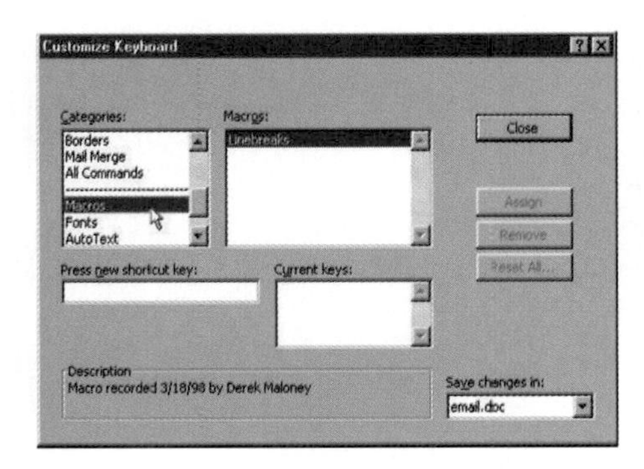

4 Click in the Press new shortcut key box and then press [Ctrl]+[8] together to indicate the keypress you want to use. You'll see Ctrl+8 appear. Press the Assign button and then the Close button. Our macro can now be triggered by this keyboard shortcut.

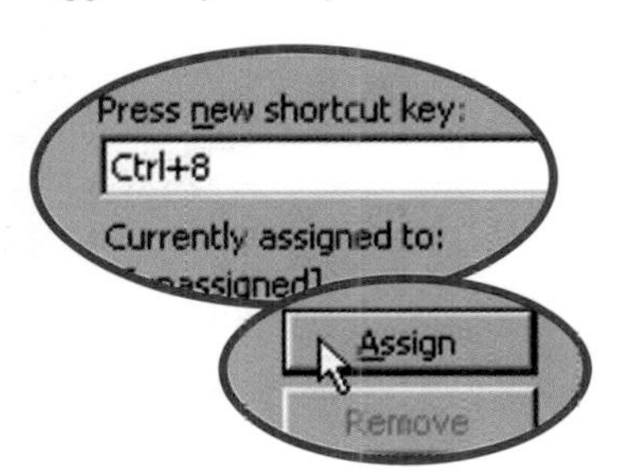

5 The toolbar button has the unwieldy name Project.NewMacros. Linebreaks. Let's get rid of it. Right-click on the toolbar button. You'll see a pop-up list of options. Give your macro a shorter name (Linebreaks), and press the [Enter] key.

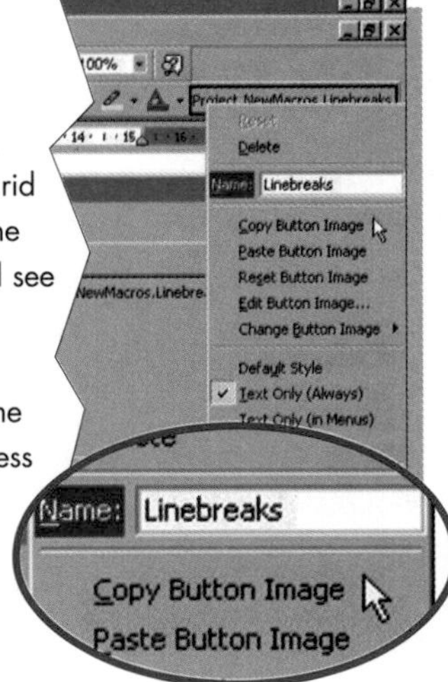

6 You'll see the button name change. You can give the button a more personal touch by adding an icon. Right-click on the button again and then click on the Change Button Image option. You'll see a panel of icons appear; click on one. Press the Close button on the Customize dialog box to get back to your document.

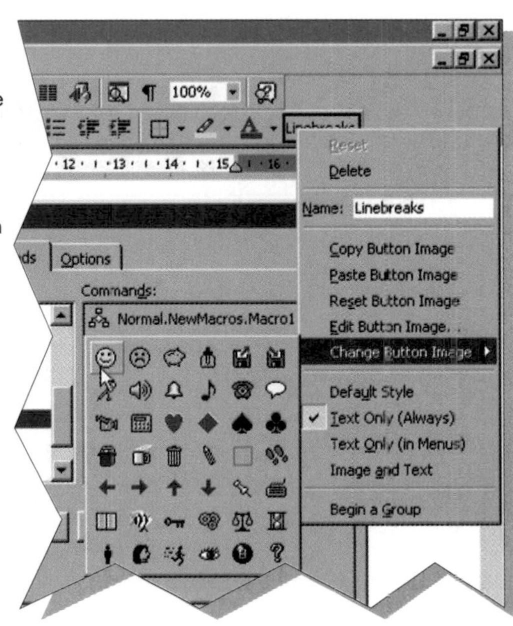

7 Your macro button is now in place and customized with a new name and icon. Don't forget, when experimenting make sure to save your changes in the document you're working on. As with all macros, don't save the Linebreaks macro in the Normal.dot template until you are sure that it works correctly.

PC TIPS

Macros and Toolbars

If you assign a macro to a customized toolbar and you want to copy it to another document via Organizer, copy the customized toolbar as well to avoid having to create a new macro shortcut. Make a copy of the target document as a back-up.

Using custom macros

Extend Word's capabilities by using the Organizer to install ready-made macros and to transfer styles and toolbars between documents and templates.

Any task that can be achieved by using keyboard or menu commands and/or mouse clicks can be automated by recording it as a macro. However, while this process covers most useful tasks, it certainly doesn't cover everything. There are some extra commands that can't be recorded but which you can add to your basic macro so that it becomes much more intelligent and more powerful.

For example, you might want your macro to perform a loop, making it repeat an action again automatically until whatever task it is carrying out is complete. This can be particularly useful for a search-and-replace macro, as a single search through a document might not be sufficient. For instance, in our first macro (see page 31), we replaced double spaces with single spaces. If our original document had three spaces together, the first pass would have reduced this to two but we would need to run the macro again to remove this 'extra' double space.

● Basic programming

Such functions cannot be achieved with the basic macro recorder. The macro needs to be programmed to ask itself questions and then to carry out its task according to the replies. In the case of the formatting macro, the instructions might be to keep running until no double spaces are found and then stop. Such commands can do wonders for a basic macro. However, in order to use the macro editing tools (see page 33), you would need to learn a little programming.

● Ready-made macros

A much simpler option is provided by the ready-made custom macros you can buy from developers who specialize in creating them for Word and other software (see Powerful macros box, right).

Some of these automate tasks to such an extent that they can appear to have added new functions to your programs. You can see what's possible without having to buy anything extra because Microsoft has included a few sample macros on the Office CD-ROM for you to try out.

Included are macros to find and replace symbols and to display header and footer panels. Opposite, we show how to install a useful example called the Multiselect Spike macro. This allows you to copy multiple items on to the Clipboard – a handy way of making notes on a document. Although you can download macros from the Internet, it is best to stick to established Web sites, such as the home page of Word guru Woody Leonhard (www.wopr.com/).

By programming a powerful macro or installing a ready-made one, you can soon have Word performing even weightier tasks.

POWERFUL MACROS

Many software developers have programmed powerful macros, or even suites of Word utilities, using Visual Basic. A range of such macros and utilities is available on the Internet, usually as shareware. Some of these add-ons have proved so useful that they've caught the attention of Microsoft itself and have been incorporated into later releases of the commercial software.

Copying a custom macro

Here we'll install the Spike macro included on your Office CD-ROM. Before you start, insert this CD-ROM into your computer.

1 Create a new Word document and save it with a suitable file name. From the Tools menu, go to Macro and select Macros.

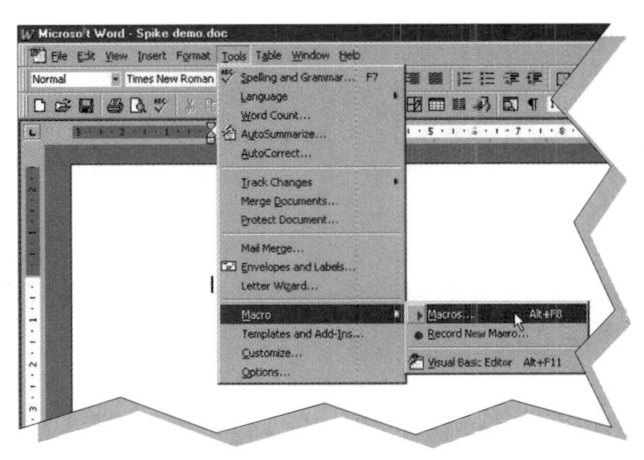

2 Click the Organizer button when the Macros dialog box appears.

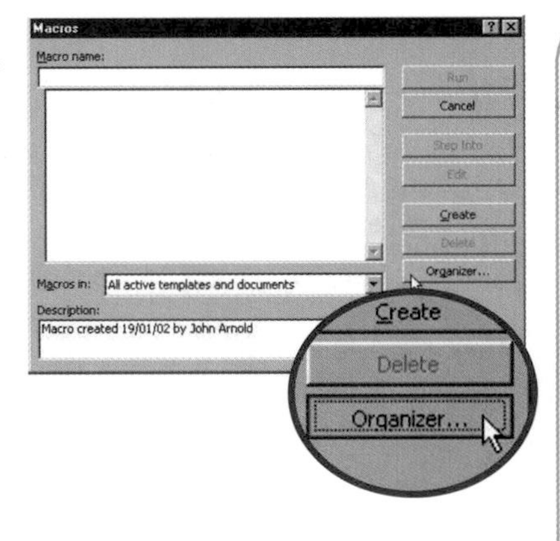

3 The Organizer shows the Normal.dot template on the right. Any macros you have created and assigned to the Normal.dot template will be held there in NewMacros. Your open document is on the left. Under the Normal.dot entry, click the Close File button, and then click again to open a new file.

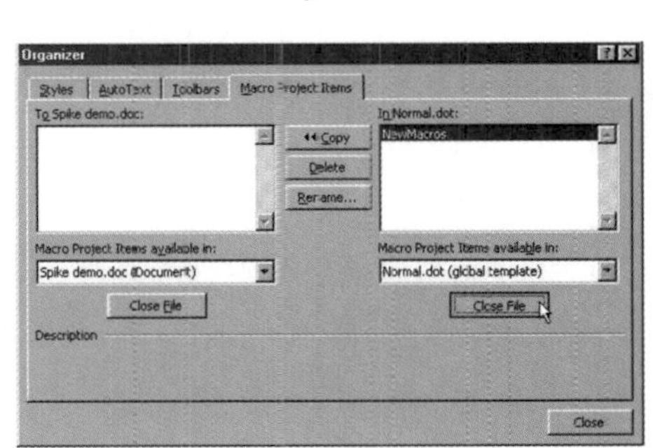

4 Find the Word macros template Macros8.dot (in the Office/Macros folder on the CD-ROM) and then open it.

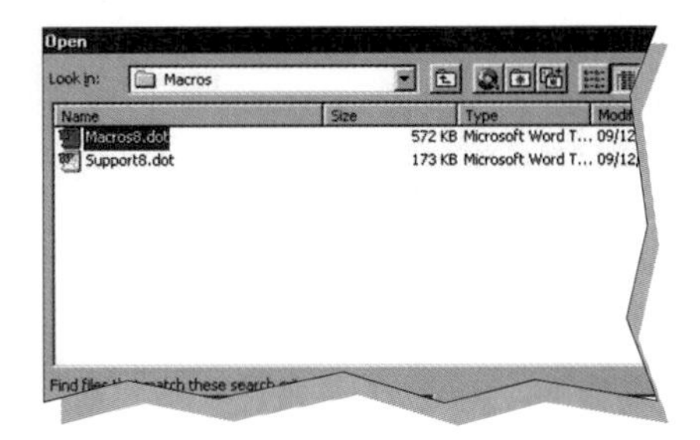

5 You will now see all the different macros contained in this template. Select the one we are after (called Spike) and click the Copy button. You'll see the macro appear in the panel on the left.

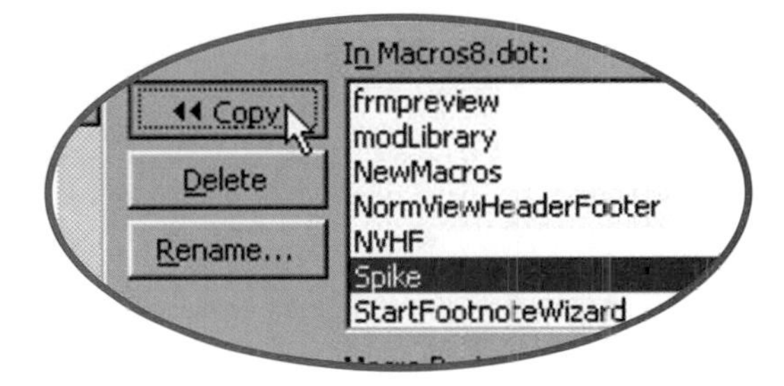

6 Now click the Toolbars tab. Select the Multiselect (Spike) toolbar and copy it to your active document, as in Step 5. Note that if custom toolbars and macros have been created together, they should be kept together. For example, if you copy the toolbar without the macro, it won't do anything.

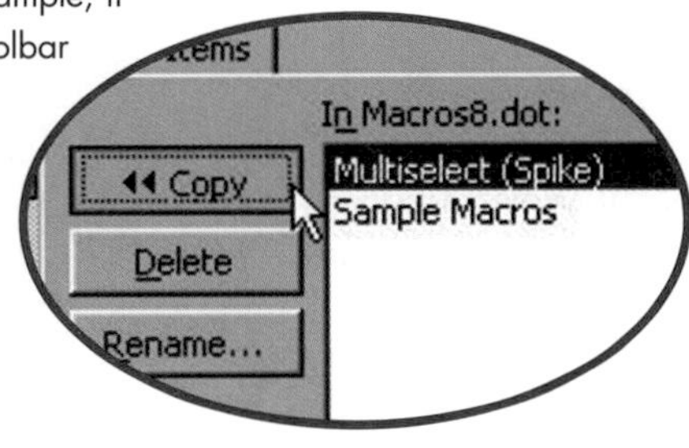

7 Now click the Close button. Bring up the Macros dialog box, as shown in Step 1. You'll notice that, rather than copying one macro, you have copied a macro project, which contains a number of macros. Press the Cancel button.

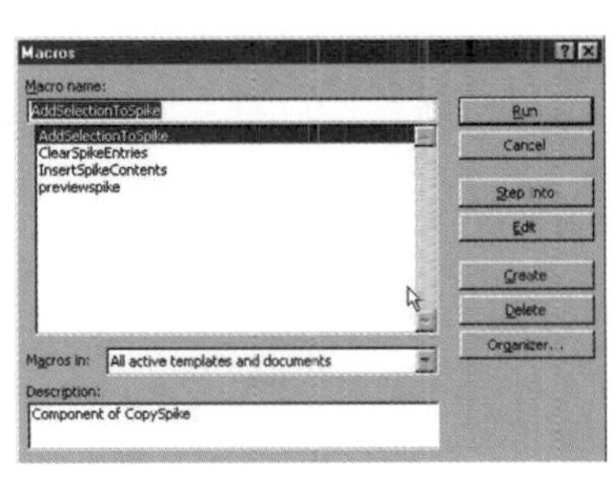

8 You also need to 'switch on' the toolbar: click on the View menu, then the Toolbars option and you'll see your new Spike toolbar listed. Simply select it to display it.

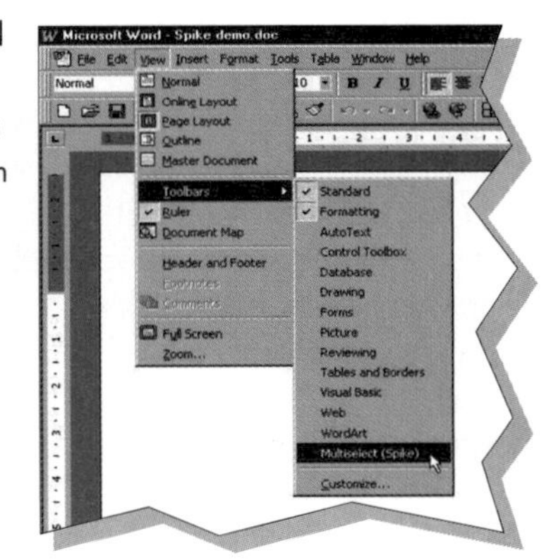

PC TIPS

Using the Multiselect Spike macro

After adding the macro and its toolbar to a document, you can easily copy several different chunks of text at once between one or more documents simply by pointing and clicking. Select the first piece of text and press the Add selection to Spike button in the Spike macro toolbar. Continue to select and add text to the Spike from anywhere in the document. Each successive block of text is added in order. Move the text insertion point to another part of the document – or even a completely new document – and press the Insert Spike button. All the items from the Spike are added to the document. Click the Clear the Spike button to remove all text from the Spike.

Using Word's sections

One of the handiest features for working with longer documents, Word's sections allow you to control the breaks between different parts of your document and choose different page settings for them.

Most of the documents you create with Word will consist of single pages – letters, fliers and short notes. These documents will naturally use the same basic page settings throughout, although you might change the type area or page orientation, depending on whether you are preparing a letter or a simple poster.

However, as you start to work on longer documents, you'll often find that they fall into natural sections and it can be very useful to be able to have different settings for each one.

For example, a book author would certainly want to make sure that each chapter started on a new page. Similarly, a student writing up a long project might need to break it up to make the organization of the work clearer. A club brochure could consist of several parts, each of which covers different activities, plus a membership form. While if you were creating a long questionnaire, you might like to separate the covering letter as well as the various sections of the main document.

● Basic page breaks

You might already be using manual page breaks to separate parts of longer documents. We showed the basic method in Stage 1, page 41, which is to position the cursor at the beginning of any line of text, select Break from the Insert menu and click on Page in the Break dialog box. This will then take the following line of text to the first line of the next page, which will greatly help to improve the clarity of a lengthy document.

● More control from sections

However, while the manually inserted page break works well enough, Word provides another option that will give you much more control and flexibility. This is to make use of Word's section breaks.

To take a simple example, imagine that you are preparing a report that needs to be printed on both sides of the paper. It would be very handy if the text could be organized so that each new chapter falls on a right-hand page, which makes the new section easier to spot for anyone flicking through the report. Word's section breaks allow you to do exactly this, since one of the options is to specify that each new section of your document starts on an even or an odd page.

PC TIPS

Page numbering in sections

When you add sections to a document, you gain much more flexibility with your use of page numbers. For example, you can make each new section of your document start from page one, or use a different numbering system for the notes at the end of a report. You're not restricted to one continuous sequence of numbers as you are with an unsectioned document.

This is clearly much better than using manual page breaks, where you might find you need to add an extra break to create a blank page if the previous chapter falls short. Worse still, if you add more text in the middle of a chapter that has been divided with manual breaks, the extra text might spill over onto another page, spoiling your careful planning.

Using section breaks overcomes this problem because, in effect, you're telling Word that whatever else happens, the following part of the document must start on a right-hand page. And, as we show on page 41, the page settings of each section can be controlled individually and are very flexible.

● Invisible sections

Sections aren't just useful for handling page breaks. Word also uses them when working in columns and, in certain circumstances, will even add the sections for you.

For example, to create a report with a title at the top and several columns underneath it, you highlight the main text and use the Columns button to specify how many columns you want put in (see Stage 3, pages 28-29). Immediately Word switches to Page Layout View and shows your newly organized page.

To separate the columns, Word adds two section breaks – one before and one after the text you highlighted. Both are Continuous section breaks (see Inserting section breaks, below). These breaks are invisible in Page Layout View, but if you switch to Normal View (click on the small icon in the bottom-left window corner), you will see them as lines separating the text, as shown on the right. You can even delete them if desired.

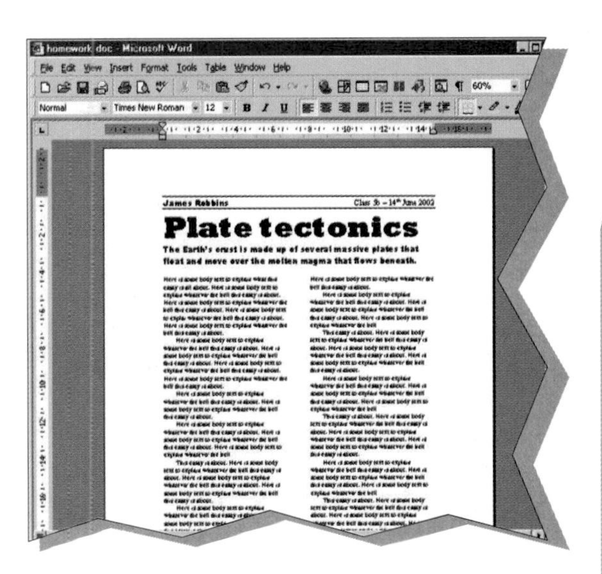

Word sometimes puts in section breaks automatically. The main part of the report above appears in two columns which Word has separated from the rest of the document by using Continuous section breaks. These are hidden in Page Layout View, but you can see where the breaks are inserted by switching to Normal View (below).

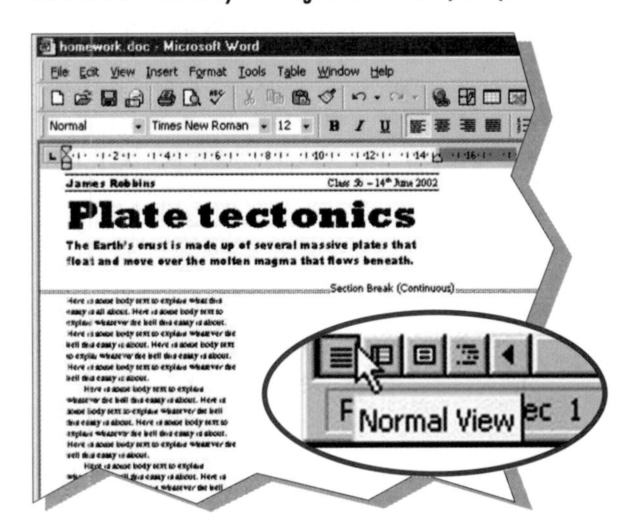

INSERTING SECTION BREAKS

You insert section breaks from the same dialog box that you use when inserting manual page breaks. Select the Break command from the Insert menu and you'll see the Break dialog box (right). One of the reasons why many people use page breaks is that it's the default option in the dialog box – if you press the OK button without making any changes, you'll get a page break. But Break has four more powerful options listed under Section breaks in the middle of the dialog box:

Next page
With this option – that is most similar to a simple page break – a section break appears at the text insertion point and the following text appears on the next page.

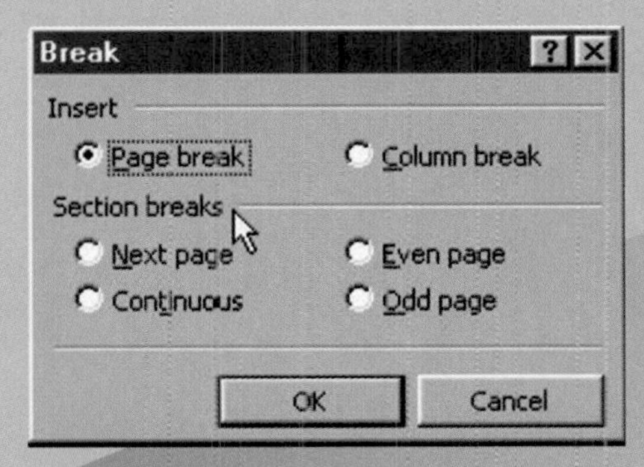

The main benefit, however, is that by starting a new section instead of a new page, you are given far greater flexibility. For example, inserting section page breaks enables you to use different page settings in each section (see page 41).

Continuous
You don't have to start a new page to start a new section. You can use this option to start a new section on the current page, for example, if you want to add a panel of text to a normal page.

Even page/Odd page
If you are working with double-sided print-outs and need to ensure that the next section starts on a left-hand or right-hand page, use this option. Depending on how you have set up the page numbering (see Stage 2, pages 34-35) and whether page one appears on the right or left, you can use either the Even or the Odd option to ensure that the new section starts where you want it to start.

Using sections

Adding and removing section breaks works just like adding and removing page breaks, but you can add extra options to control the structure of your documents.

1 We've started with the cover page for an imaginary holiday club brochure. This is going to be organized in five parts, as shown by the five headings, and we'll want a new section for each part.

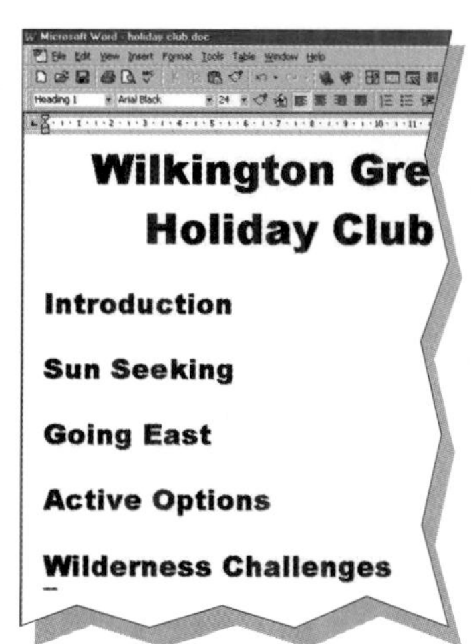

2 Position the cursor at the very beginning of the first heading, which says 'Introduction' and select the Break option from the Insert menu.

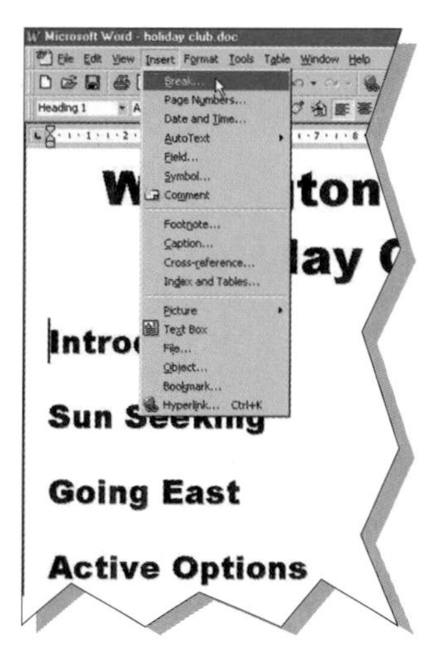

3 When the Break dialog box appears, select the Next page option below the Section breaks heading and press the OK button.

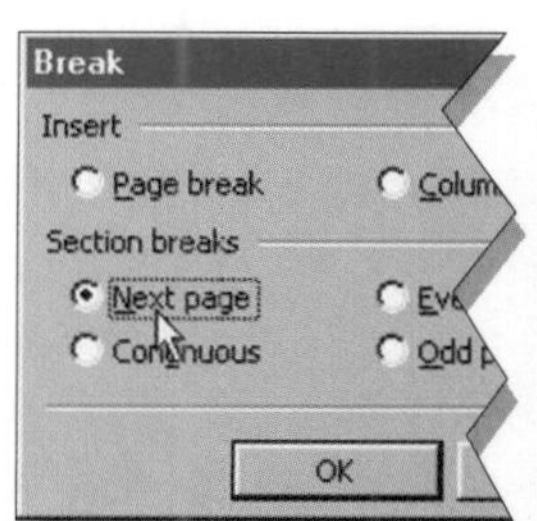

4 Word adds a double dotted line across the page, with the words Section Break (Next Page) centred within it.

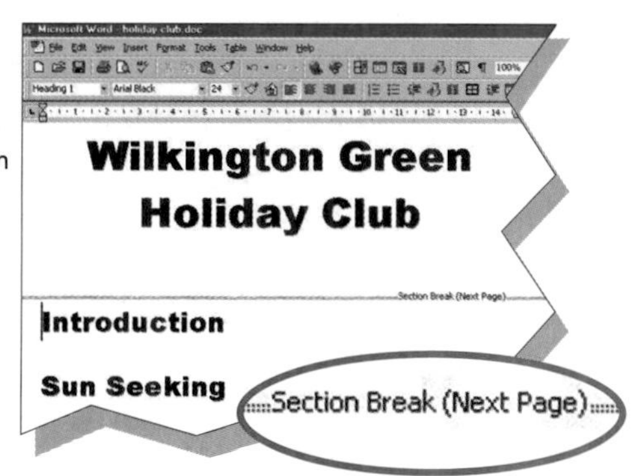

5 Select Page Layout from the View menu and then choose a zoom percentage (50%) which will allow you to see two pages side by side.

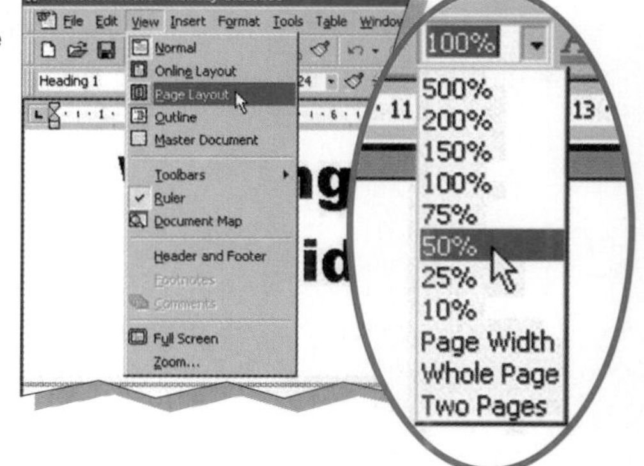

6 As you can see, the first heading now sits at the top of the second page. So far, this could have been accomplished with a manual page break. To see one of the advantages of using sections over page breaks, choose Header and Footer from the View menu.

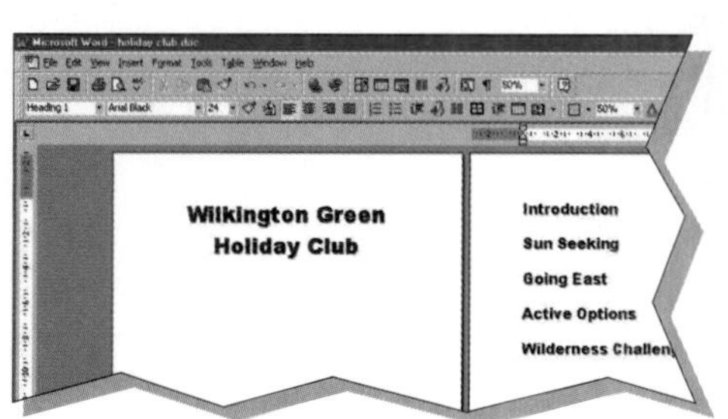

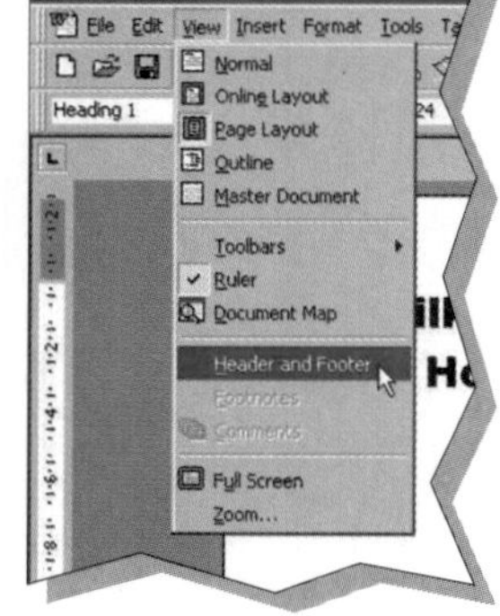

7 At the top of the second page you'll see that the header is labelled Header – Section 2 and Same as Previous. On the floating Header and Footer toolbar, press the Same as Previous button.

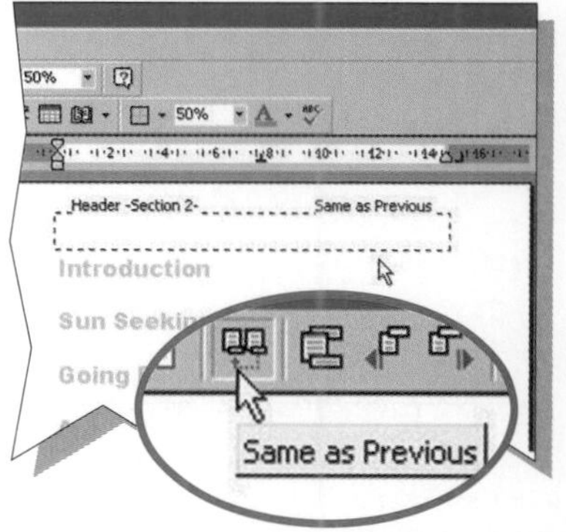

8 The header of the second section is now independent from the first. You can add different information for the first section (the title page) and second section. We've added a heading and page number for Section 2.

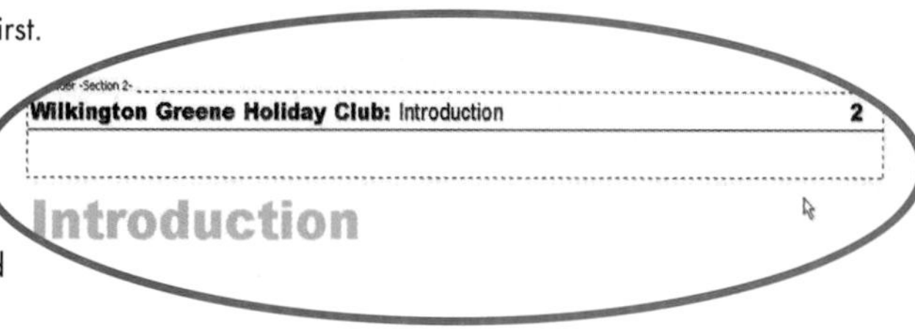

PC TIPS

Deleting a section is easy. Switch to Normal View and scroll through your document until you see the Section Break horizontal line. Move the mouse pointer over the double dotted line and click once to move the text insertion point to this line. Press the [Delete] key: the section break will disappear and the following text will run straight on from the previous section.

Sections and page settings

If you find a single page setup for a whole document too limiting, you can use sections to give yourself more options.

1 Here we've used the same document as opposite and have created sections for each heading and then added some text and pictures to each to complete the brochure. We've also added a new section at the end for a table of prices and information.

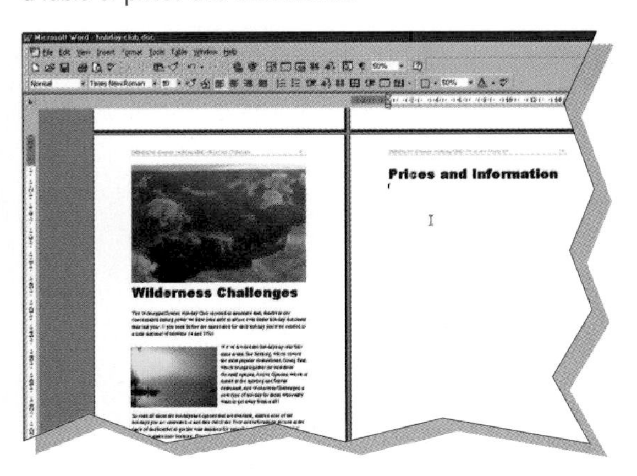

2 On this final page, we've zoomed in to add a Word table showing holiday bargains. As you can see, this needs several columns and the width of the page means that text wraps inside each cell – often causing ugly word breaks (inset).

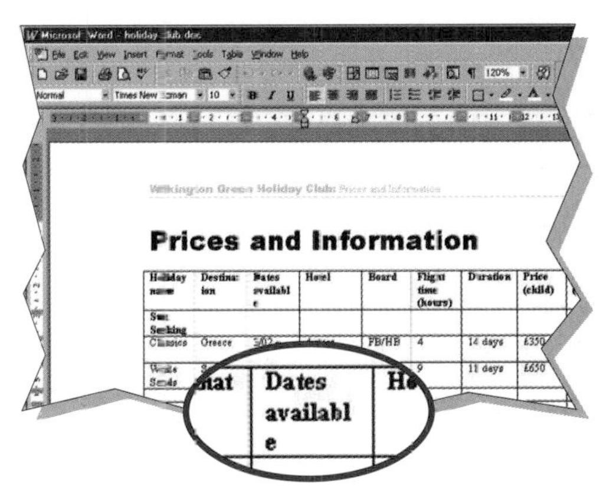

3 If we change this page's setup to landscape, the table can be much wider. As it is a separate section, we can alter it without affecting the rest of the document. Select the Page Setup option from Word's File menu.

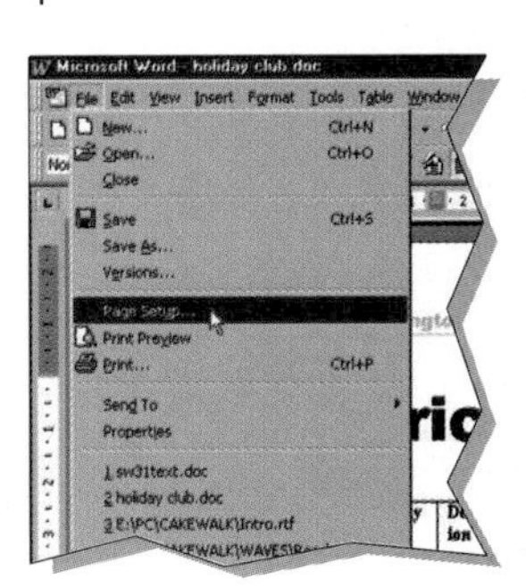

4 When the Page Setup dialog box appears, click on the Paper Size tab. Select the Landscape option. Note that Word knows we are working with a document that's divided into sections and, in the Apply to list box, suggests which part of the document – Selected sections – it will apply this page change to. Press OK.

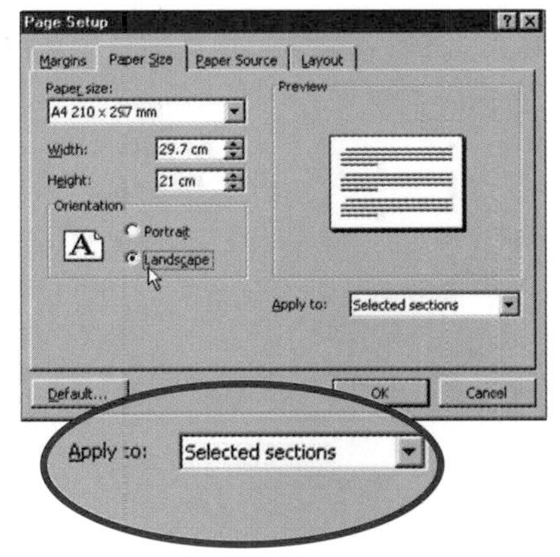

5 Zoom out a little, so that you can view the whole page. You'll see that there's much more space for your table on a landscape page.

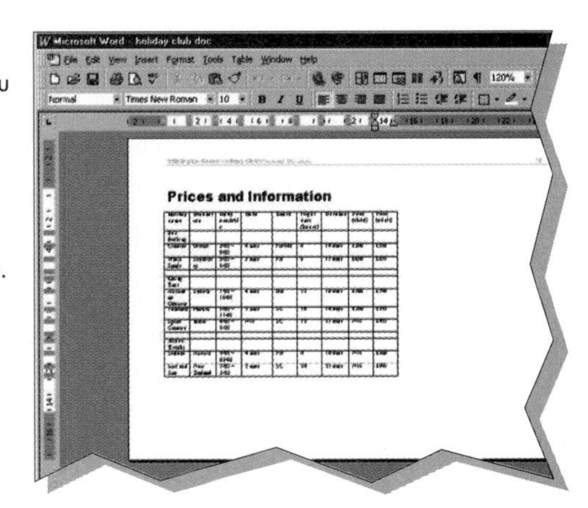

6 Now you can adjust the column widths for the table to take advantage of the extra space. As you can see, the information looks much better and the awkward text wrapping has gone.

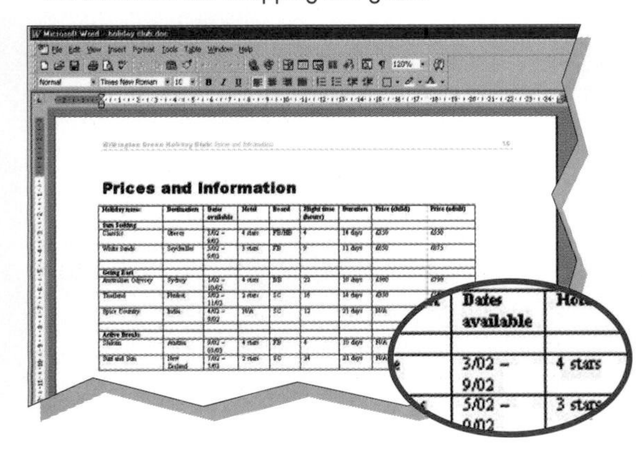

7 To see the overall effect of your section breaks, select Page Layout from the new menu and choose a low zoom percentage. Here you can see the layout of the whole document.

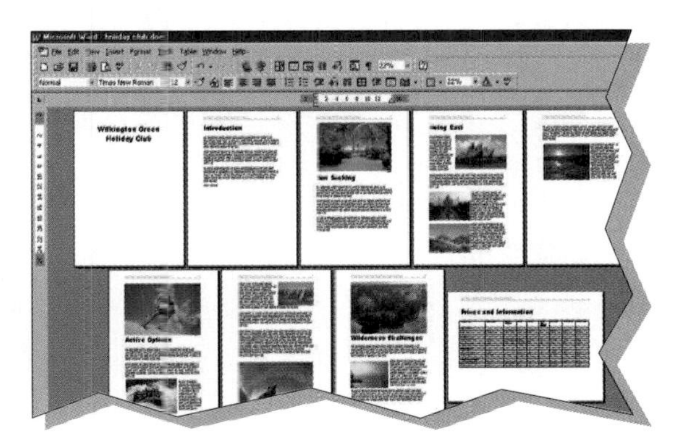

PC TIPS

You can use other page settings within your document. You can, for example, change the page margins for any section of your document, and even change the page size. However, try not to change more than is necessary in order to keep your document more manageable.

Creating a fax sheet

If you've installed fax software on your PC (see pages 26-27), all you need is a fax cover sheet and you're ready to fax documents anywhere in the world.

If you are planning to send documents by fax, the chances are you will have created them in Word, so why not fax them straight from Word rather than printing them out? Not only is it easy to combine a Word-generated fax cover sheet with a document, but you also get far more control over the look of the fax than you would if working with two different programs.

As you're probably aware, there is a certain amount of 'etiquette' to a fax cover sheet. It should show who the fax is for and their company, who it's from, the date, the number of pages (including the cover sheet), and a telephone contact number in case of an error in transmission. Such details typically appear in the top third of the cover sheet, along with a company or personal logo, if applicable, and an address. The rest of the page is left free for the message. This message could contain the fax message itself (in which case the whole fax is just one page long), or an introduction to the other pages, which were probably created in a separate document.

● Choose your style

All these fax elements are neatly covered by Word's own fax Wizard, or, more straightforwardly, by the fax templates. Both Wizards and templates offer the choice of three styles: Professional, Contemporary and Elegant.

The only problem with these fax sheets is that as Word is one of the most popular applications in the world, you can be sure that you won't be the only person using Word fax sheets. In other words, your fax sheet might well look unoriginal – indeed, identical to thousands of others. If this doesn't bother you, that's fine; if it does, you might want to make a few tweaks, such as adding a logo, to create a finished result that is noticeably different from anyone else's. In the following exercise, we show how to customize a Word fax sheet and save it as your own template.

When you send a fax in Word (or indeed any program, see pages 26-27), you will be asked if you want to include a fax cover sheet with the document you are sending. On some PCs, the choice offered refers to the basic cover sheets that come with Microsoft Fax, which are, if anything, more common than Word cover sheets and rather less smart. Consequently, we're going to show you how to make your faxes stand out by creating a customized Fax cover sheet. Then we'll demonstrate how to send your fax straight from your computer via your modem.

Even if you don't send faxes direct from your computer, you can print out smart-looking cover sheets to send through your ordinary fax machine.

Customizing a fax template

While there is a range of Word fax template styles to choose from, they are all very likely to be used by countless other fax senders. You can add a personal touch, however. Here we show you how to customize and save a template as your own.

1 Open Word and from the File menu select the New command to bring up the New dialog box. Click the Letters & Faxes tab, select Professional Fax.dot and click OK.

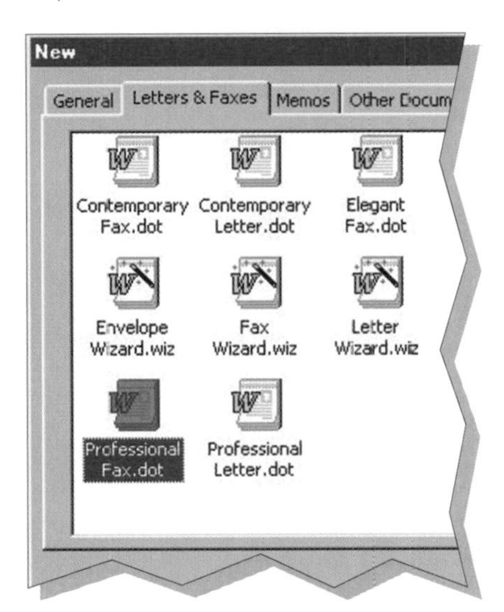

2 Click over the word 'here' next to the From field and type in your name (inset). Click on the 'here' in the top left-hand corner and type in your address plus your phone and fax numbers. Highlight 'Company Name Here' and type in your company or personal name. That's as far as you can go for a generic fax sheet because all the other variables are going to alter from fax to fax (see Step 3 overleaf).

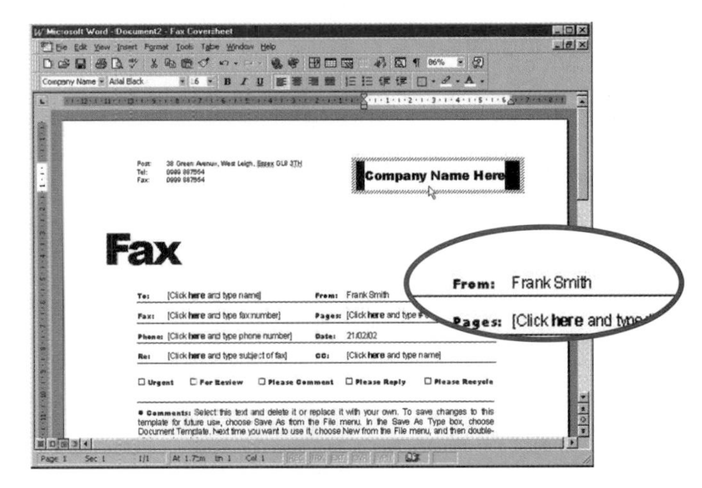

The choice of fax templates

THESE ARE THE three default fax templates included with Microsoft Word and they are really of quite high quality. Of the three, Professional is probably the most suited for the individual, or the small business: it's bold, clear and unfussy. The template named Elegant has an official look, if a little bit plain. The Contemporary design, as its name suggests, looks modern, clean and quite dynamic. Despite this, it's often better to try to make your fax template more individual.

You could happily use the Professional template as it is, but with the others – especially Contemporary – you should really take the trouble to customize. In fact it is relatively easy to enhance a template. For instance you could replace the Contemporary globe design, which may not be suitable for everyone, with another, more relevant piece of artwork. Then you could make a few other tweaks along the same lines as in our example and you would have a perfectly acceptable and, more importantly, unique-looking fax template to use.

The Professional (far left), Elegant (centre) and Contemporary fax templates.

3 We're now going to make a few tweaks to the fax to customize it. These are only subtle suggestions because the changes you decide to make will depend on your needs. Select the company name paragraph and from the Format menu select Borders and Shading. Click the Shading tab, change Style to Clear and click OK.

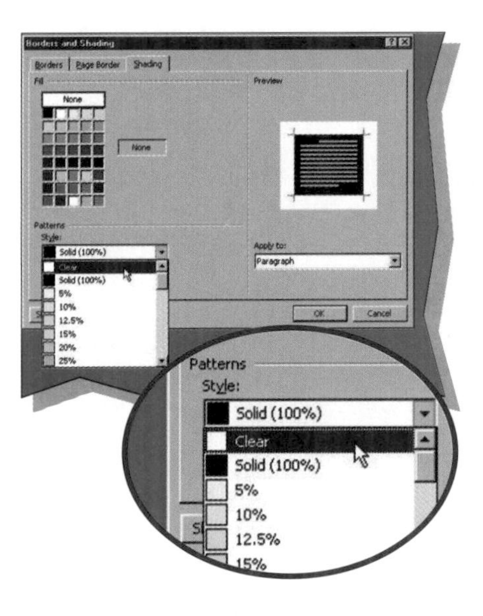

4 Next, change the font of the company to one that you like and have used, perhaps, in other documents, such as letterheads. We've chosen a font called CopperplateGothic; don't worry if you don't have that, just select an alternative. You might want to experiment with alternative fonts here. We've also increased the text size to 20pt, right-aligned it, put the company name in capitals and the 'INC' in a smaller size. We've also changed the font of 'FAX' to echo this.

5 You can add a simple piece of clip art to help your fax stand out. Bring up the clip art dialog box (see Stage 3, page 33) and select a suitable image. Remember that faxes are transmitted in black and white, so simple line drawings and silhouettes are best. Select a picture and click the insert button.

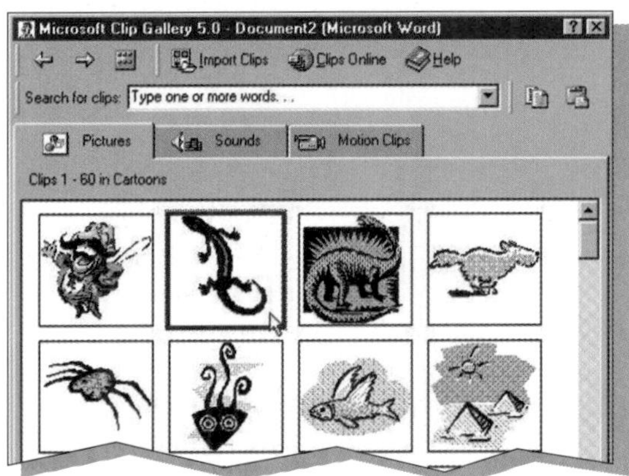

6 Resize the picture and drag it to the correct position beside your company name.

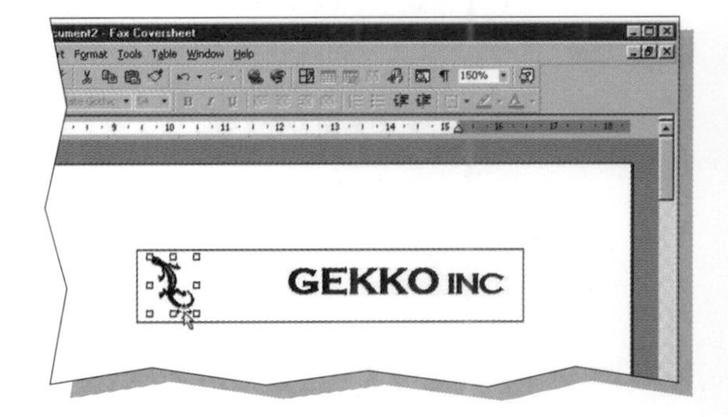

7 Next, delete the check boxes that sit just under the addressing sections. We've also changed 'Comments' to 'MESSAGE' and deleted the explanatory text below it.

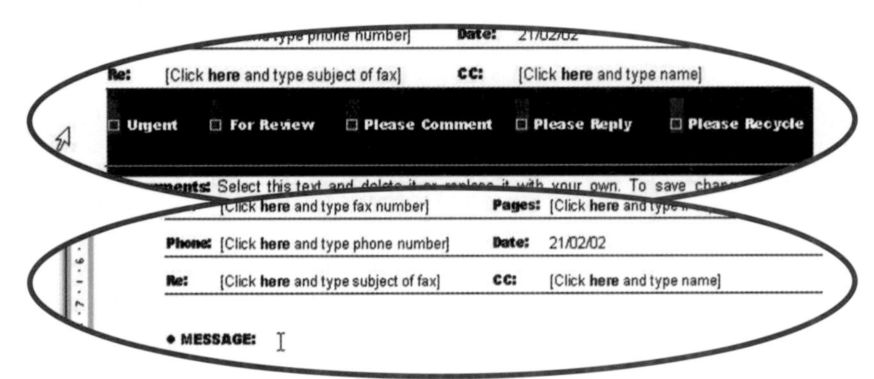

8 Now save the completed fax sheet as a new template. From the File menu select the Save As option. In the dialog box that appears, select Document Template (*.dot) from the Save as type drop-down list box. This will automatically take you to the Templates directory.

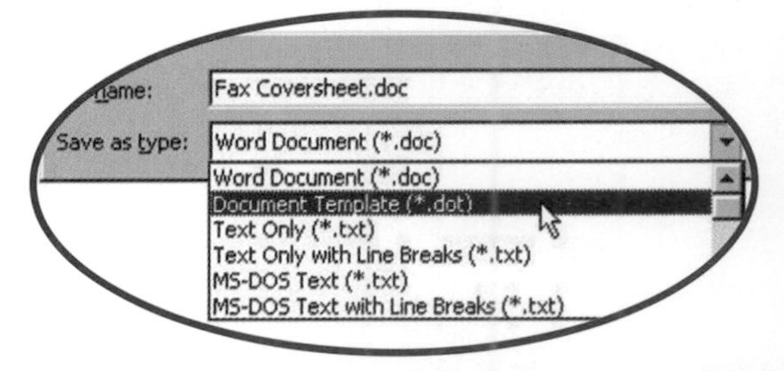

9 Change the file name to Mynewfax.dot and press the Save button. Your fax sheet will now be available to you whenever you select New, as in Step1.

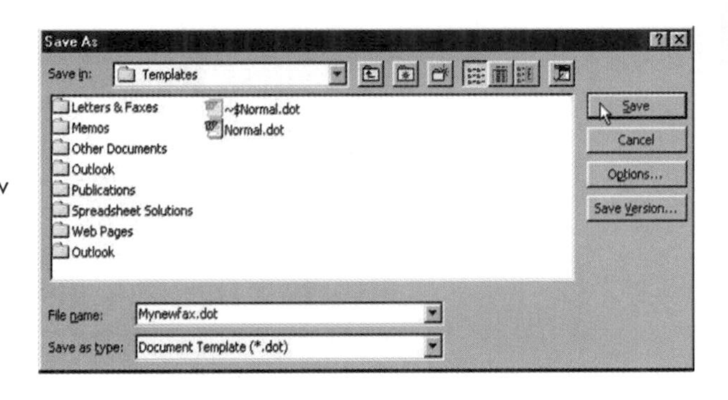

PC TIPS

Message at the bottom

It's usual on fax cover sheets to include a message at the bottom that says 'If there has been a problem in transmission please call...' with your contact number. Curiously, this is not included on the template used here, so you might want to add it. The easiest way to do this is to draw a text box and type the copy into it.

Sending a fax directly from Word

When you have created your fax, you could print it out and then fax it as normal. However, you can miss out this stage altogether and fax straight from Word.

1 Start Word and select New from the File menu. When the New dialog box appears, you'll see the Mynewfax.dot template that you created on the previous page. Double-click on it.

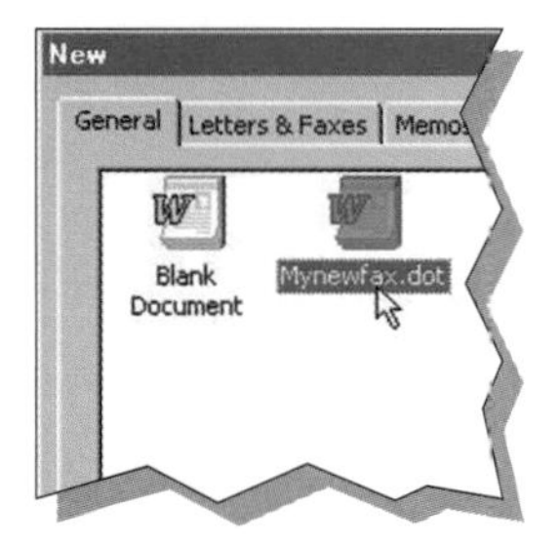

2 A new document will open, based on the template you created. Click on the To text and change it to the name of the person you want to send the fax to. Do the same for the other details, including the fax number and subject (Word will change the date automatically).

To: Charles Longbridge **From:** Frank Smith
Fax: 0999 123456 **Pages:** 1
Phone: 0999 123457 **Date:** 21/02/02
Re: Lizard Literature **CC:**

ADDRESS BOOK

With most fax software, you can enter names and fax numbers in a phone book. These are then ready for use and you won't have to key in a number each time you send a fax using your PC.

3 Then type the main part of your message into the area below 'MESSAGE:'.

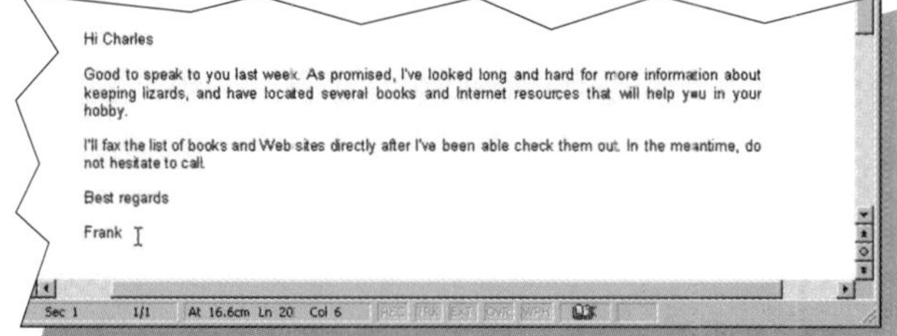

4 When your message is finished, save the fax. This time, you'll be saving a document rather than a template, so you'll be using the Word Document format and a .doc file extension. Word chooses this automatically, so you need only locate the folder in which you want to save the fax and type a name into the File name box.

File name: charles fax1.doc
Save as type: Word Document (*.doc)

5 Now the fax can be sent: press [Ctrl]+[P] to bring up the Print dialog box. Click on the Name drop-down list box and select your fax software instead of your usual printer. Press the OK button.

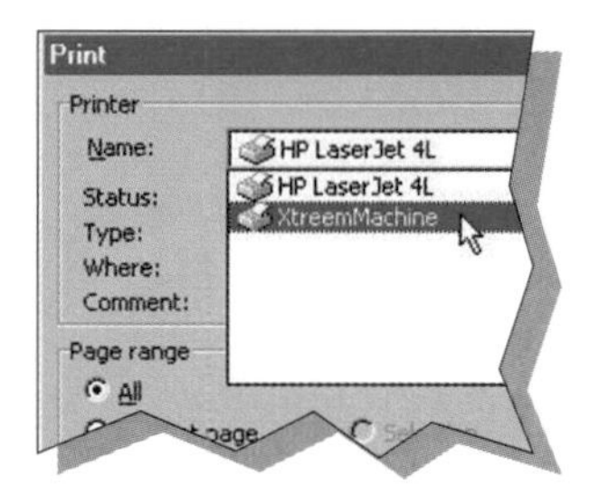

6 At this point your fax software asks for the details of the recipient: type in the name and fax number. Follow your fax software's on-screen instructions until you see a Send button. Click it to start the fax.

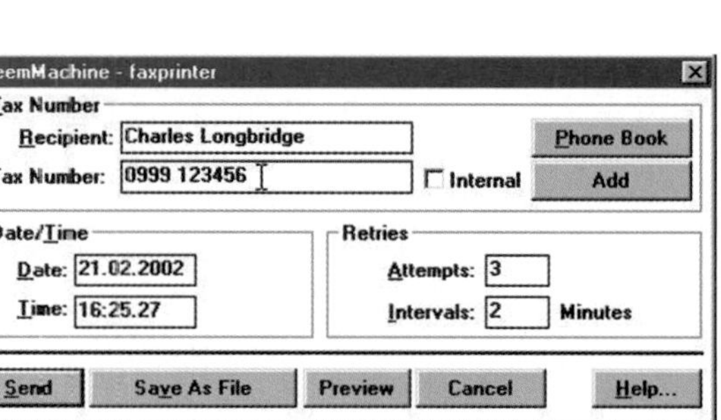

PC TIPS

Fax anything

Assuming you have fax software installed, the chances are that if you can print a document from an application, you can also fax the document from the application directly. As with the example shown on this page, you should be able simply to select the name of your fax software (instead of a printer) from the print dialog window to send the document as a fax via your modem. Be sure to save your document before faxing. You might also have to adjust the Page Setup settings.

7 Your fax software window appears and prepares the electronic document. It also sets your modem, so it is ready to send.

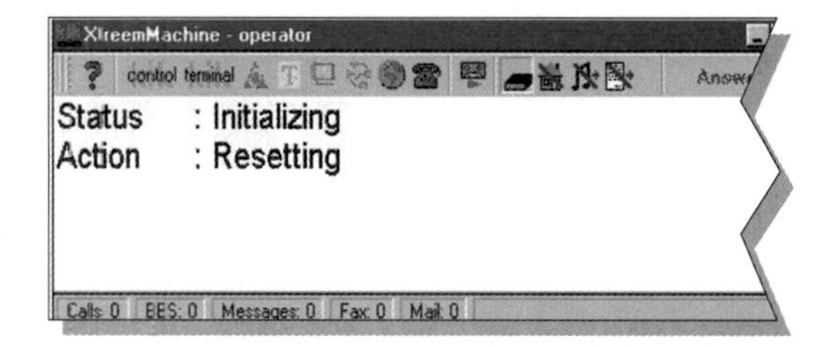

8 You will hear your modem dialling the fax number and see confirmation of the progress of your fax message on your screen. When the fax has been sent – in less than a minute for most one-page faxes – the modem hangs up and the status window closes.

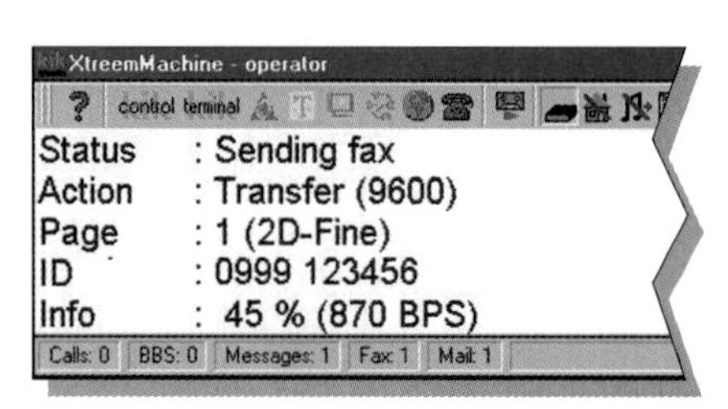

Working with multiple worksheets

If you've got lots of related spreadsheets that you want to keep in one place, Excel's workbooks provide you with a quick way of saving them all in one file.

Until now we've worked with spreadsheets that only have one page (or worksheet) in them. In fact, spreadsheets aren't called spreadsheets in Excel – they're called workbooks. They have this name because an Excel workbook can be made up of more than one worksheet. Think of each one as being like a separate page of figures in an accountant's book.

A simple workbook with one worksheet is fine for uncomplicated or ad hoc calculations with a few figures, but there will be times when you'll be glad of the extra power, convenience and organization of workbooks containing several worksheets.

● One book – one file

A workbook is saved as a single file, regardless of how many worksheets it contains. So, for example, if you keep a monthly record of figures, it can be much easier to keep each month's figures on a separate worksheet within one workbook. This is much simpler than having a separate workbook (and so a separate file) for each month's figures.

It's also a lot easier than keeping the figures for every month on one page because that makes it hard to move around the document and work with its contents. It also makes sense to keep related worksheets together in one workbook file because it helps avoid the risk of losing one section of information. Excel provides the tools to label individual worksheets within your workbook with real names. Each worksheet in a workbook has a tab at the bottom to identify it. To start with, the tab names are simply Sheet1 or Sheet2, but you can easily rename them to something more relevant by right-clicking on them, choosing the Rename option from the menu that appears, and typing in the new name.

These tabs make it easy to switch between worksheets within a workbook while you're working. Just click on the tab of the worksheet you want to see and Excel will bring it to the top of the pile.

● Adding new worksheets

Excel also lets you add new worksheets and remove out-of-date ones. You can also move worksheets around within a workbook and make copies of them, or even move or copy entire worksheets to another workbook. All these functions are available from the menu that appears when you right-click on a worksheet's name tab.

EXCEL 2000

Excel 2000 has most of Excel 97's commands, so whichever program you use, future Excel exercises in *PCs made easy* will work in both programs. Where there are any differences, we'll highlight Excel 2000's method with this type of box.

Setting up and moving worksheets

To demonstrate how to work on separate worksheets within a single workbook, we use the workbook we created to add up the total of a credit card bill (see Stage 1, page 61).

1 Start Excel, click the Open button on the toolbar and use the Open dialog box to locate and open one of your worksheets. Ideally, use one with monthly data, such as the credit card file we are using, although you can experiment with any worksheet.

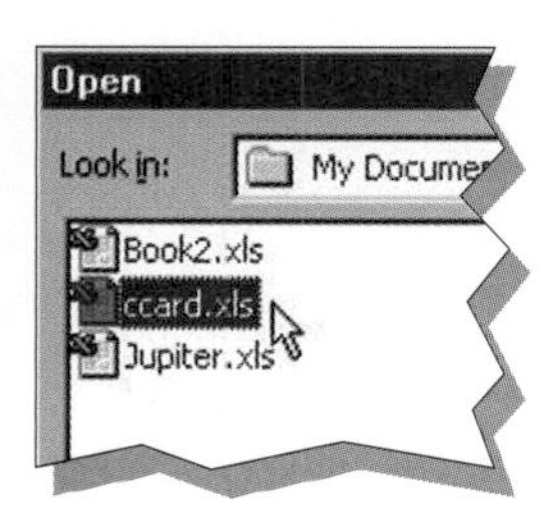

2 We'll use a different worksheet for each month's data, so we need to give the sheets meaningful names. Start by right-clicking on the Sheet1 tab at the bottom of the worksheet. Select the Rename option from the menu that appears (top). The word 'Sheet1' will be highlighted so just type 'January' over it as the new name for this worksheet (right). Press the [Enter] key when you've finished typing.

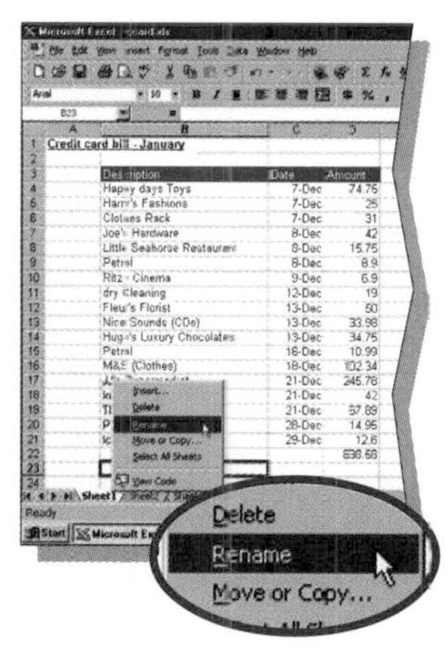

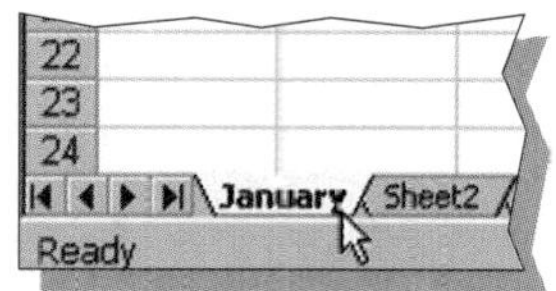

3 Now we want to type in the data for February on a separate worksheet within this workbook. Click on the tab labelled Sheet2 and a second empty worksheet comes to the top. Now you can type in all the data for the February bill. We should rename this worksheet 'February'. So, as in Step 2, right-click on the Sheet2 tab to call up the menu. Choose the Rename option and type over the highlighted word 'Sheet2' with the word 'February'. Press the [Enter] key when you've finished. You can then enter the data for March in Sheet3 and rename that sheet, too.

4 When you've renamed all the worksheets, you'll see all the tabs with their new names. If you are in the March worksheet and want to switch to either the January or February worksheets, simply click on the tab to view the worksheet you want.

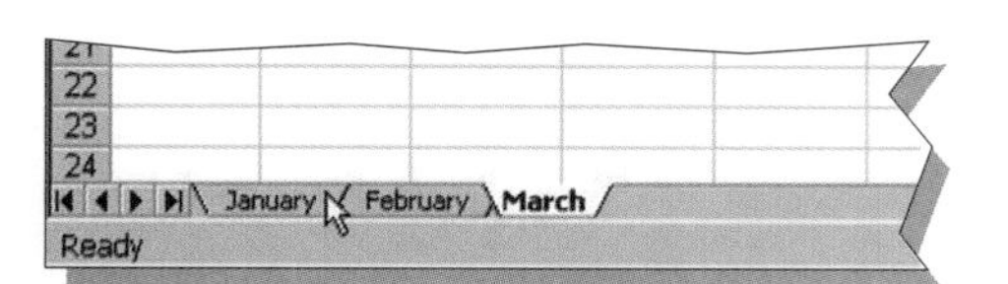

5 Let's suppose you've paid off the whole of the January credit card bill. Let's assume you don't want to keep your January worksheet. The quickest and cleanest way to remove this information from your workbook is to delete the whole January worksheet. To do this, right-click on the January tab and choose Delete from the menu that appears.

6 You'll then see a window which asks you if you're sure you want to delete the whole worksheet. Click on OK to delete the worksheet. Now we can save the work we've done by going to the File menu and selecting the Save option. This will save the whole workbook, including both February's and March's worksheets, in a single file.

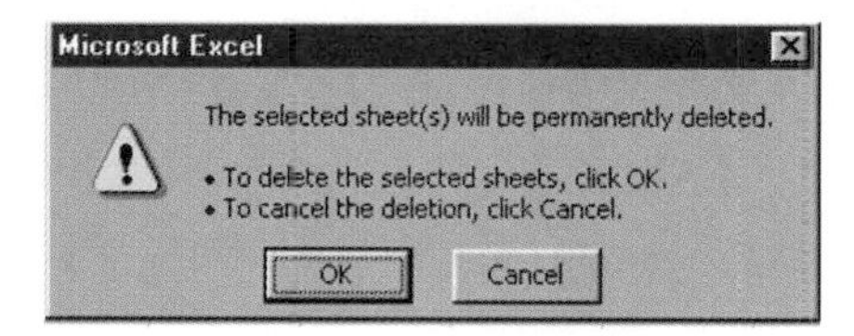

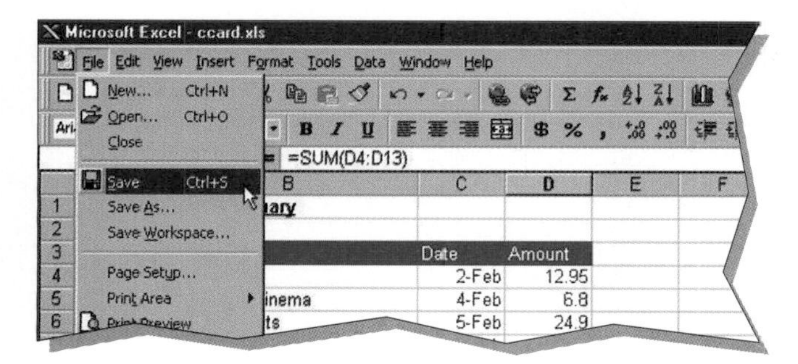

PC TIPS

Moving whole worksheets

You can move or copy a worksheet in the current workbook or even to a different workbook. Right-click on the worksheet tab you want to move and choose Move or Copy from the menu that appears. For example, highlight February in the Before sheet box (right) to put the March worksheet before February's. Click OK and the worksheets swap places (lower right).

If you want to copy a worksheet, right-click on the worksheet tab and select the Move or Copy option from the menu. Click in the Create a copy box (a tick appears) and then click on OK.

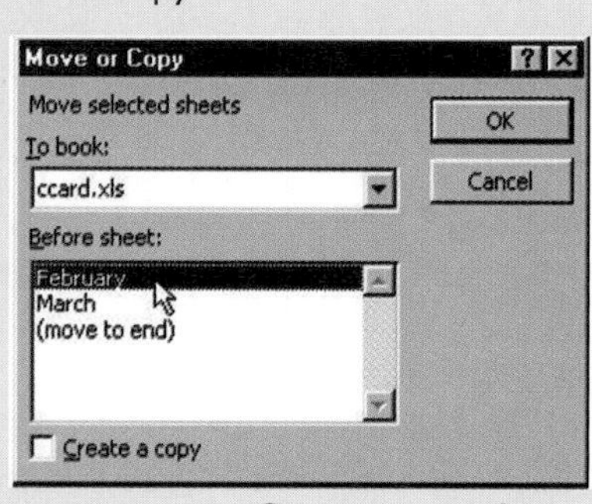

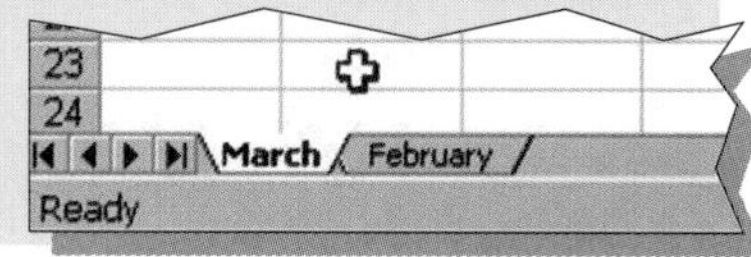

Transposing rows and columns

Copying and pasting saves time by re-using information you've already typed in. Here's a way to make these operations even more flexible.

We've already seen how to copy the content of one cell and paste it into another (see Stage 2, pages 54-55). Remember that when you do this, Excel copies and pastes more than just the data held in a cell, it copies everything to do with the cell, including its formatting and any formulae that are stored in it.

That is why Copy and Paste are great time-savers when you've got information you want to repeat several times in a worksheet. We've also seen that the process isn't confined to single cells, but can be used to move the contents of a whole group of cells in one go.

● Moving data more flexibly

So far, we've used Copy and Paste to move data from one block of cells to an identical block elsewhere in the worksheet – taking information a bit further across a row, for instance. However, it's sometimes useful to be able to transfer data that is held in a row into a column instead – or vice versa.

For example, suppose you are constructing a table of distances between towns to help you plan the mileage for a touring holiday. Once you have typed the towns' names across the top, you don't want to waste time retyping them down the side. Fortunately, Excel offers you a way to **transpose** cells when you copy and paste them, which saves all that trouble.

The first stage is the same as for ordinary copying and pasting. You start by highlighting and copying the cells you want to use. Then you select a cell to indicate where you want the data to go. But now, instead of using the Paste command, you need to choose Paste Special and tell Excel to transpose the data.

You use the same process whether you are copying cells from a column to a row, or a row to a column. And it doesn't matter how wide or deep the area of cells you choose to transpose is. The only constraint on transposing rows and columns is that the group of cells you copy from must not overlap the group of cells into which you paste them.

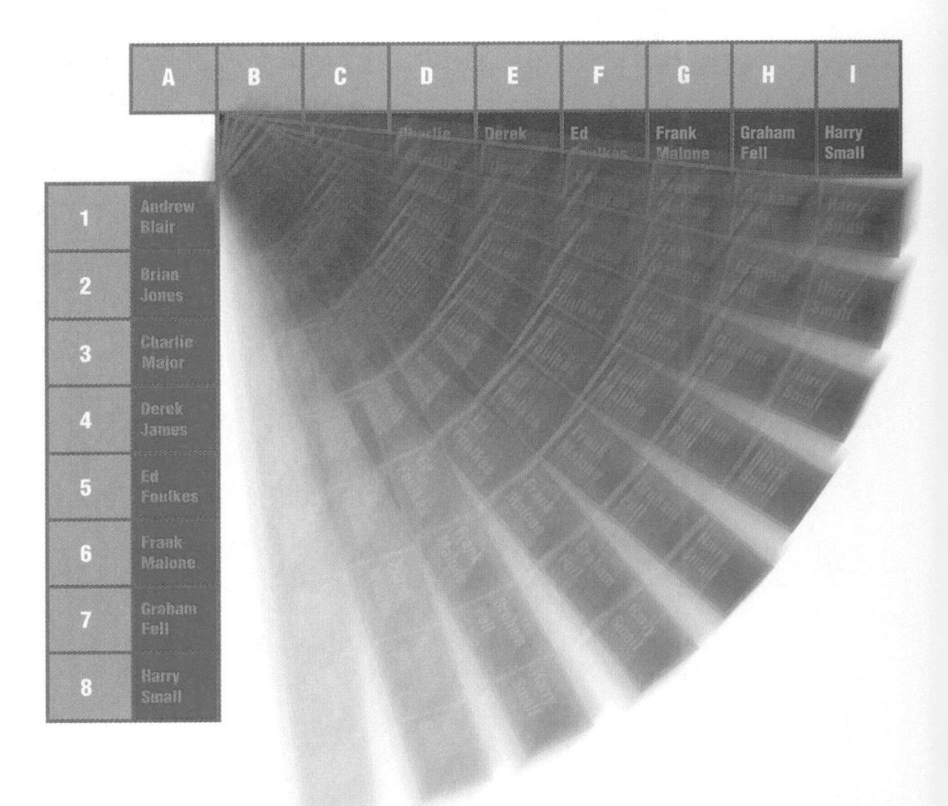

WHAT IT MEANS

TRANSPOSE

Transpose simply turns column references into row references and vice versa. When you apply Excel's Transpose function to a group of cells, it converts each row into a column and each column into a row. So if you were to copy and transpose a group of cells that was 10 columns wide and two rows deep, it would now become two columns wide and 10 rows deep.

	A	B	C	D	E
18					
19	Average test results - geography lessons - %				
20		Jeff	Sandra	Tracey	Ray
21	Jan	67	89	45	97
22	Feb	76	89	66	100
23	Mar	73	97	60	97
24	Apr	87	80	86	95
25					

Transposing groups of rows or columns has many uses. One valuable application is that if you realize a table would look clearer the other way round, you can simply copy and transpose the whole thing.

	A	B	C	D	E
10					
11	Average test results - geography lessons - %				
12		Jan	Feb	Mar	Apr
13	Jeff	67	76	73	87
14	Sandra	89	89	97	80
15	Tracey	45	66	60	86
16	Ray	97	100	97	95
17					

Making a simple transposition

Transposing data can be a real time-saver for all sorts of repeated information. We'll use this method in various ways to reduce the work needed to set up a fixture list for a squash-club league.

1 Start off by setting up a table with the names of the members of the club and the match dates. As each member will play each other, we need to repeat the names of the players down column A. We have started to type in Andrew's name, but it would save time to re-use the names we've already got in the top row. So highlight all the name cells except for Andrew and select Copy from the Edit menu.

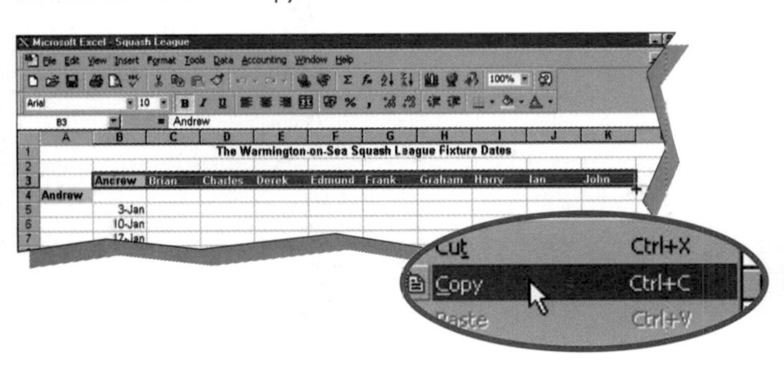

2 Now click on the cell below Andrew in column A, where we want the names to appear. This will be the first cell Excel will use when we paste the data we've just copied. Next choose the Paste Special option from the Edit menu.

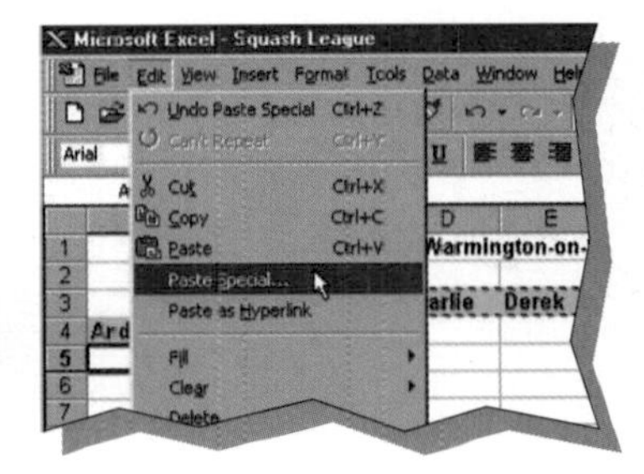

3 The Paste Special dialog box appears. Click in the Transpose check box in the bottom right corner to make a tick appear. Ignore all the other options and click on the OK button.

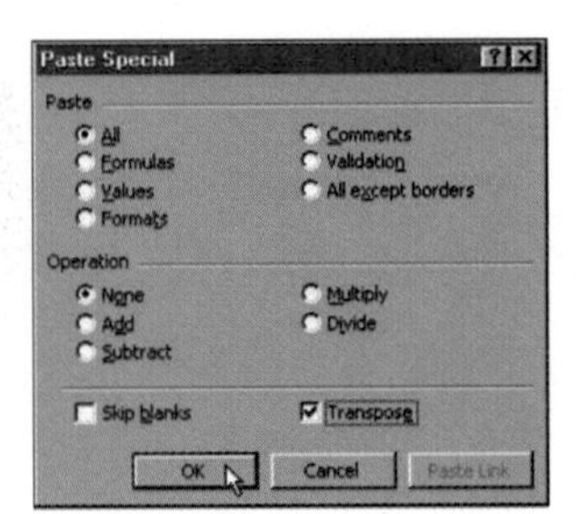

4 Excel will paste the cells you've copied into column A, resulting in a table that looks like this.

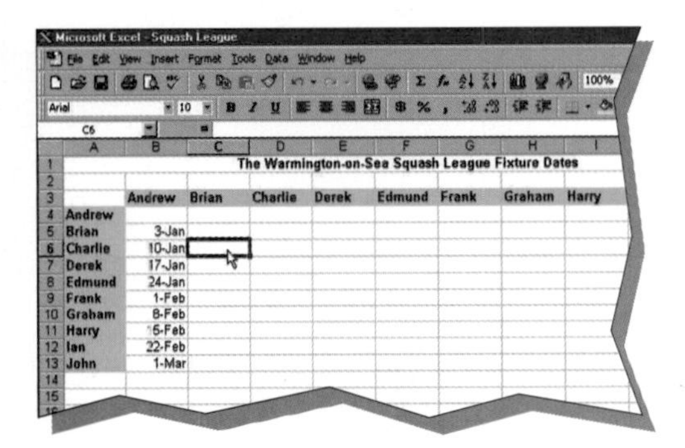

5 It's also possible to transpose cells from a column to a row. For instance, we want to copy the first column of dates in our fixtures table into the row alongside Andrew. Highlight the cells we want to copy. This time, we'll use the keyboard shortcut for copying by pressing the [Ctrl] and [C] keys simultaneously.

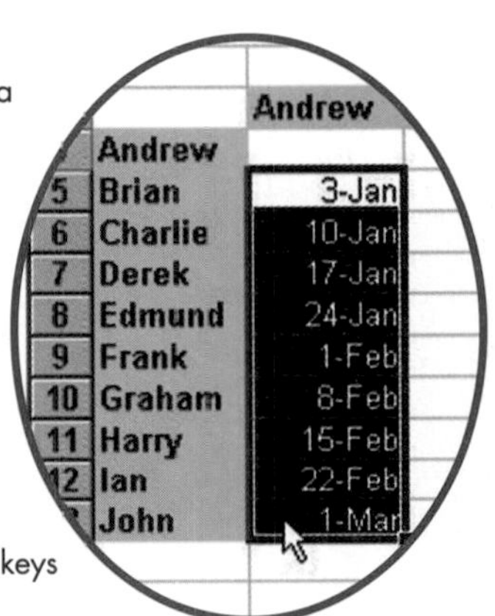

OVERLAPS

It's important to learn the restrictions on pasting transposed cells. The most important one is that you can't let the area of cells you paste into overlap the area of cells that you have copied from. We've tried to do exactly that here and Excel has given us a warning that we're not allowed to do it.

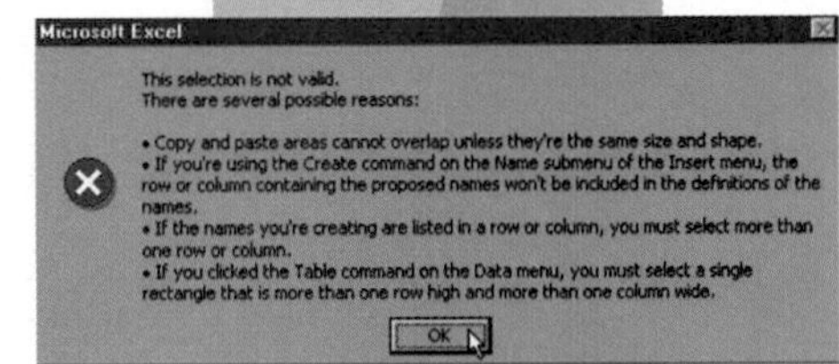

6 Click on the second cell in Andrew's row, under Brian. Choose Paste Special and tick Transpose in the Paste Special dialog box. Click the OK button: the result will look like this (below).

7 Now you can continue using a combination of normal Copy and Paste commands and transposing Copy and Paste commands until you have filled in the whole table with the dates of the fixtures. This method will complete the table much more quickly than if you typed in each date individually.

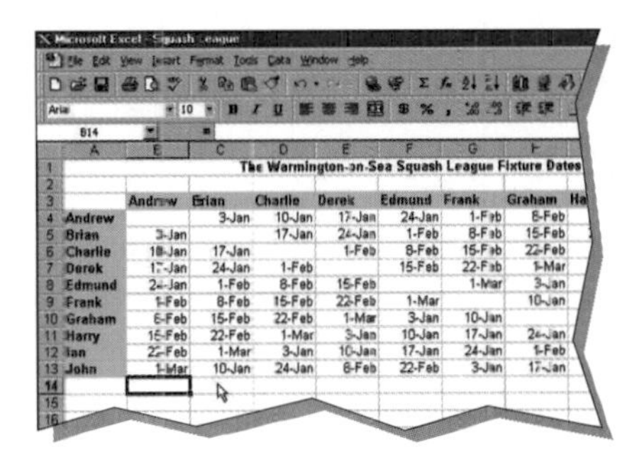

Adding up whole rows and columns

You already know how to add up several cells, but what happens if you want to add another one? Here's how to avoid rewriting the formulae that carry out the calculations every time you decide to include more data.

We learnt how to add up a range of cells by using the AutoSum button on Excel's Standard toolbar (see Stage 1, pages 60-61). More recently, we've also discovered that AutoSum works by using the SUM function (see Stage 4, pages 46-47).

The SUM function can work with a list of cell references, so, for example, the formula =SUM(A1,B2,C3) would add up the contents of cells A1, B2 and C3. But it can also work with a range of cell references, so you can add up all the numbers in cells A1 to A5 by using the formula =SUM(A1:A5).

AutoSum and the SUM function both work perfectly well when you have a fixed number of cells to add up. But what happens if you want to add more cells to the total? An obvious way to guarantee that your formula will include the new cells and work out the correct total is to modify it every time you add another cell. However, this would be a terrible waste of time because it means devising a new formula every time you add more data.

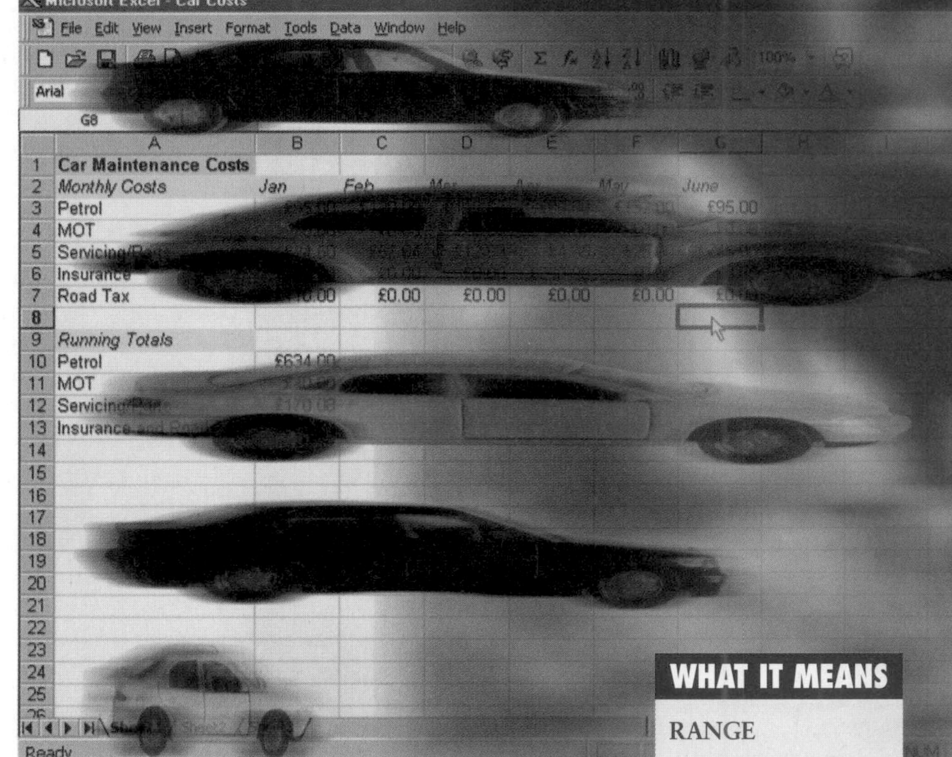

● **Adding extra data**

Experienced Excel users employ a neat trick to save time and avoid this problem. A simple modification to the SUM formula makes sure that Excel adds up all the cells in a whole row or column. That means that every time you want to include some extra data in the total, you just enter it in any cell in the same row or column as the other numbers.

You still use the SUM function to create the formula. But instead of entering normal cell references, you simply type the row or column reference twice with a colon in between. For example, the formula to add up all the cells in row 5 is =SUM(5:5). The technique works in the same way for columns so that column letters can be used to create a formula for adding up a whole column. For instance, the formula =SUM(B:B) adds up the whole of column B. You can even add up all the cells in more than one row or column (see opposite).

Finally, remember that Excel won't let you put this type of formula in a cell that is in the same row or column you wish to add up. This is because it would be trying to add itself to the total, creating what is known as a circular reference, which is impossible to calculate.

WHAT IT MEANS

RANGE

Many Excel functions, such as SUM, let you use a range of cells as arguments. A range of cells is all the cells between (and including) two specified cells. For example, the range A1:A10 means all the cells A1, A2, A3, A4, A5, A6, A7, A8, A9 and A10. Similarly, B2:C3 encompasses cells, B2, B3, C2 and C3.

Adding up a complete row of data

Excel worksheets are often used to record new data on a regular basis. We show you how to keep an accurate running total, no matter how much data you want to add.

PC TIPS

Quick formula to add up a whole row

You can create a formula to add up a whole row without having to type it in. Here's how to do it in three time-saving clicks for the Petrol running total in cell B10 of the example on this page.

Use the first click to select the cell B10 where you want to place the formula. The next click is on the AutoSum button.

The last click is on the grey row button at the left end of row three. Finish by pressing [Enter]. You can also set up a formula to add a whole column using this method.

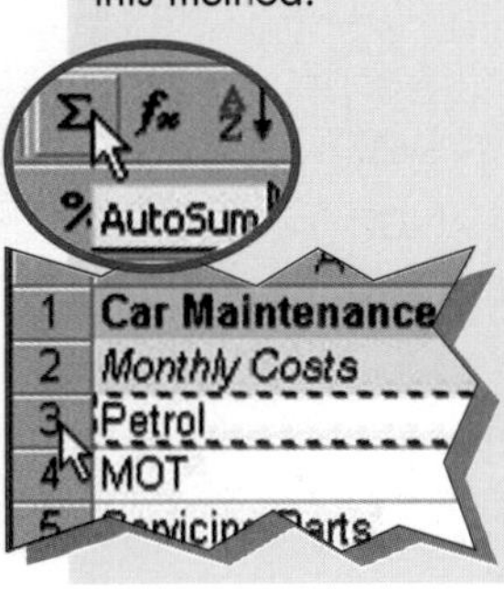

1 Let's imagine that you want to use Excel to keep track of your monthly car expenses. We've set up this worksheet to record your costs, with a separate row for each type of expense. The top part of the worksheet holds monthly costs and the bottom part is used to calculate the running totals.

2 We've already learnt how to add up a group of cells using the AutoSum button (see Stage 1, pages 60-61). Use this technique to create formulae in cells B10, B11, B12 and B13 to calculate the running total for the expenses from January to April. Note: in cell B13 the insurance and road tax in rows 6 and 7 are both added into one combined running total (B6:E7).

3 But a problem appears with this approach as soon as you need to add more data. We've added the May expenses in column F, but the running totals formulae don't take these new figures into account. The way that the worksheet has been set up means that every time you add a new month's expenses, you'll have to modify the running totals formulae to include them.

4 A better way is to add up whole rows so that whenever you type in a new month's figures, you don't need to update the formulae. Click in cell B10, type in the formula =SUM(3:3) and press the [Enter] key.

5 Now use the same technique to put the formulae =SUM(4:4) and =SUM(5:5) in cells B11 and B12. (Note that the same method can be used to add up complete columns as well as rows. For example, you could use the formula =SUM(D:D) if you wanted to add up all the numbers in column D of a worksheet.)

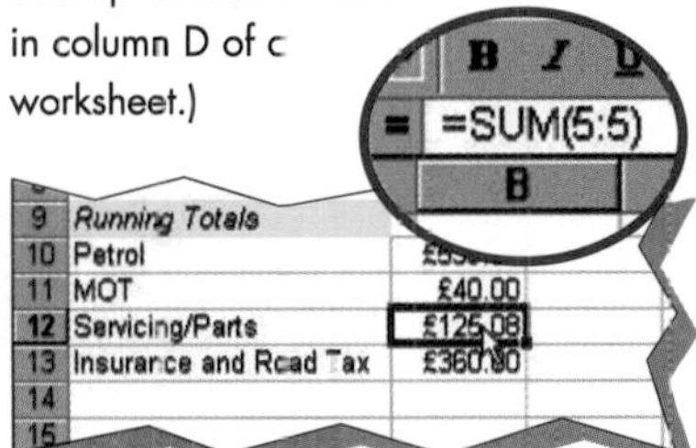

6 The insurance and road tax costs are combined in one running total in cell B13, so here we need a formula that adds up the numbers in two complete rows. To do this, replace the old formula in cell B13 with =SUM(6:7) to add up all the data in rows 6 and 7.

7 Now let's try adding the car costs for June. Watch cells B10, B11, B12 and B13 as you type in the figures for each item and you'll see the running totals update automatically to take account of the extra data.

Exploring Excel's IF function

Here's our guide to the secrets of Excel's IF function – a special function that automatically knows when to put different values into a given cell.

We've already seen how using Excel functions can make complex calculations easy (see Stage 4, pages 48-49). Simple functions, such as LOWER and CONCATENATE, can be applied directly to your formulae to do things quickly that would otherwise take a long time.

Excel also includes a special type of function that can be used to make your worksheets even more clever. For example, it can be useful to have a cell that contains a certain formula (or piece of text) depending on the contents of other parts of the worksheet. In this case, you might use an Excel worksheet to keep track of your bank balance. If you're in credit, you might want a particular cell to contain the text 'In Credit'. But if you're overdrawn, you might want the same cell to contain the word 'Overdrawn'.

● Formulae with conditions

Such formulae are known as conditional formulae in Excel. Conditional formulae have a lot in common with conditional formatting techniques (see Stage 3, pages 58-59), which make Excel automatically change the formatting of a cell, depending on whether or not a certain condition is fulfilled. The idea behind conditional formulae is similar: you can change which formula is calculated, depending on whether a certain condition is fulfilled or not.

The key to setting up conditional formulae is Excel's IF function. This uses three arguments: the first is the condition you want to test for; the second is the value (or the formula) you want in the cell if the condition is true; and the third is the value (or formula) to use if the condition is false.

So, in our bank balance example, the first argument would be a test to see if the value in the bank balance total cell was greater than zero. The second would be the text 'In Credit' and the third argument would be the text 'Overdrawn'. You can also nest conditions to create very powerful decision-based worksheets. By using multiple IF functions together, you can create conditional formulae that can cope with more than just two possible outcomes.

WHAT IT MEANS

NEST

Nesting allows you to put together a sequence of conditions. Here's an example in plain English of a nest of conditions that you can use with Excel: 'if cell A1 is less than zero, the balance is overdrawn; if cell A1 is greater than zero, the balance is in credit; if it is neither of these, the balance is zero'.

The IF function simply tests whether a condition is true or false, but this simplicity belies its power – especially when you 'nest' several conditions.

Using a conditional function

Here we make Excel work harder for its keep. Even a simple worksheet can benefit from the use of a conditional function, and Excel makes it easy for us to use this powerful facility.

1 Start with a fairly simple worksheet, such as the one here which is set up to record your budget for monthly expenses, together with the actual amount spent. Under the budget column, we've entered the monthly amount we are allowed to spend on each major outgoing.

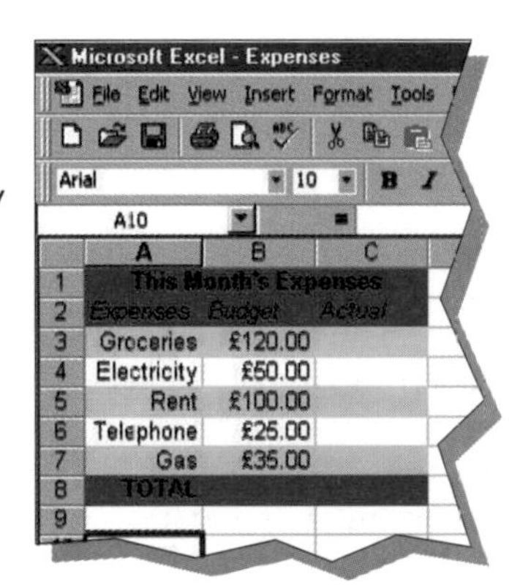

2 Next, we've typed in the actual amounts spent on each item this month. With these initial amounts, we'll stay within the budget figures we've just keyed in. Type in any numbers – just make sure they are not higher than those in Step 1.

3 Now we need to create formulae to add up the two monthly totals in cells B8 and C8. With this simple worksheet you will be able to work out whether or not you have overspent your budget.

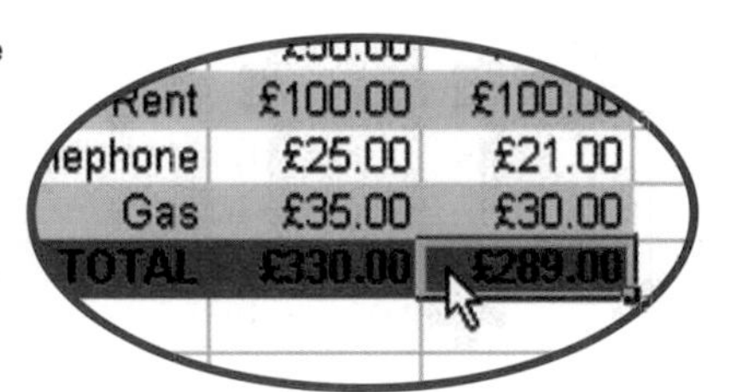

4 However, now we'll create a simple IF function that will tell us automatically if we've overspent or stayed within our overall budget. Click once on cell D8 and then click on the Paste Function button.

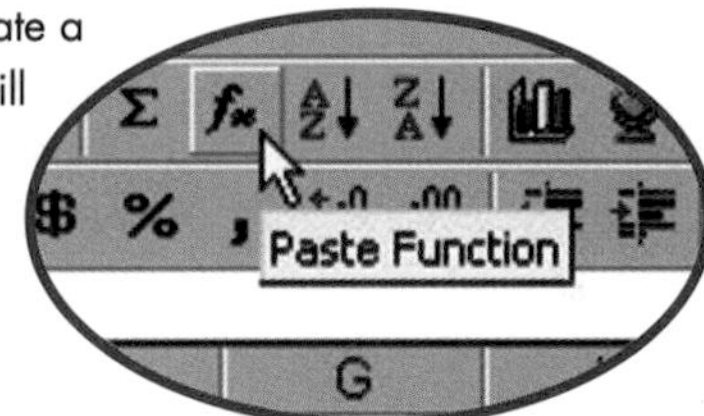

5 The Paste Function dialog box will appear. Select Logical from the Function category list on the left and select IF in the Function name list on the right. Then click on the OK button.

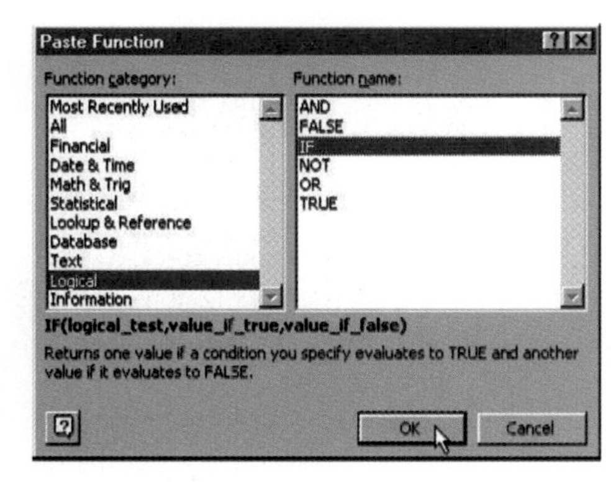

6 Now we can fill in the arguments for the IF function. The first one is the condition you want to test, which in our case is whether your actual expenditure is greater than the budget. Position the cursor in the Logical_test box, click on cell C8, then type > and click on cell B8.

PC TIPS

Putting no entry in a cell

You might want your IF function to put nothing in a cell, for example if the figures comply with the condition being true. To do this, type "" in the Value_if_true text box. If you want to put nothing in a cell when the condition is false, simply type "" in the Value_if_false text box.

7 The Value_if_true box is where you type what you want cell D8 to contain if expenditure exceeds budget. Type "Over Budget" and in the Value_if_false box type "OK". Finish by clicking the OK button.

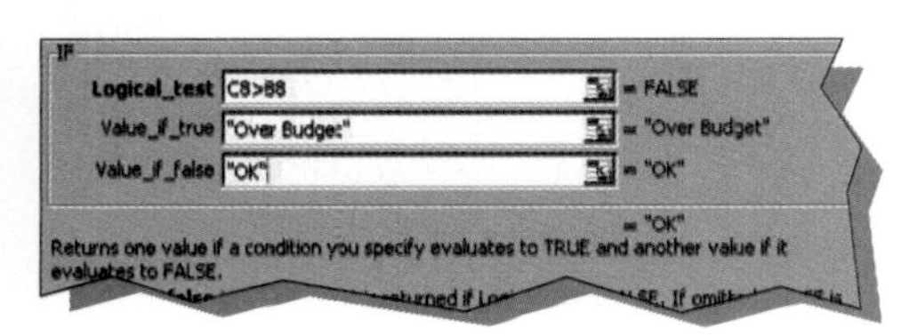

8 Now cell D8 contains the word OK because this month's expenses are within budget. Try changing the actual expense figures to make their total greater than the budget total and watch what happens in cell D8. Excel changes the text to warn you that you've gone over budget (inset).

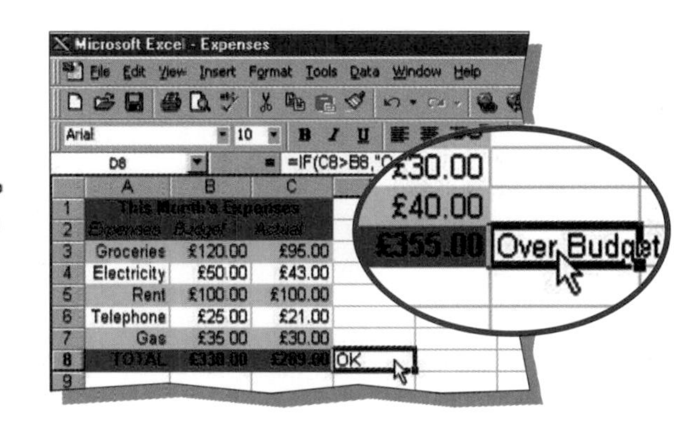

Creating easy-to-read worksheets

Many worksheets present a vast, often confusing, array of information. Here we give you some tips for ensuring that important points stand out clearly on your worksheet.

Creating a worksheet is a two-part process. First, you have to sort out the mathematics and logic involved in the data and formulae of the worksheet cells. Second, you have the often neglected task of making sure that the information in the worksheet being created is clear enough to digest quickly.

There's a natural tendency to spend more effort on the worksheet's content. After all, a computer worksheet that contains faulty formulae is worse than one done correctly with paper, pen and calculator. However, it's vital that you don't neglect the second task: presentation. It pays to make sure that your worksheets are easy to read as well as being fault-free.

A simple calculation shows why it's important to think about presentation issues: a worksheet of just 20 rows by 10 columns has 200 cells. With the right design and layout, the handful of cells that contain the most vital information can be spotted quickly.

Often, the right design will depend on the individual worksheet you are creating, but there are also tips and techniques that you can use to make all your worksheets clearer.

Microsoft Excel - tests.xls

Test	1	2	3	4	5	6	7	8	9	10	11	12	13	14	15	16	17	18	19	20	21	22	23
Ahmed	19	18	36	19	11	3	6	24	37	27	28	13	26	14	13	3	5	38	14	37	10	29	28
Cathy	10	24	34	30	31	35	21	37	15	7	36	36	14	15	26	1	38	40	24	27	31	23	6
Cindy	2	36	23	7	34	4	27	27	39	14	18	3	23	38	22	33	15	36	24	27	20	40	34
David	39	21	37	23	5	39	5	29	2	0	27	19	34	21	14	16	32	30	2	29	13	33	33
Gianni	14	27	7	39	22	0	38	32	4	16	8	19	32	35	35	31	16	28	33	1	25	26	30
James	3	28	26	37	15	24	7	21	3	19	31	4	9	24	40	20	6	21	37	10	7	40	18
Jenny	30	35	33	16	11	3	20	17	37	39	4	39	26	38	33	18	17	22	38	14	28	37	27
Jo	26	15	13	29	11	30	22	21	25	3	21	30	35	10	29	3	1	29	22	7	14	11	18
John	14	22	39	15	30	14	27	25	11	35	1	22	37	17	2	24	12	14	12	39	4	16	37
Katie	19	24	15	28	23	20	39	25	17	39	2	27	16	29	24	32	15	10	15	6	15	38	18
Keith	39	36	17	29	36	12	16	34	4	18	31	7	30	8	36	12	19	22	31	34	9	7	5
Lucinda	24	29	7	25	14	40	38	35	1	3	4	34	16	2	20	28	22	15	3	33	19	27	25
Michelle	2	2	19	12	16	7	7	19	40	8	37	25	23	24	24	27	8	25	22	6	15	39	25
Neil	11	35	10	26	20	6	40	20	38	10	10	20	21	4	6	17	24	6	20	11	24	24	22
Paul	6	36	32	27	29	8	7	29	17	30	26	5	7	26	10	21	33	13	4	32	2	13	27
Peter	12	9	32	20	29	28	23	38	24	10	34	2	13	39	0	38	16	36	13	37	3	11	28
Sandra	3	15	32	35	2	35	14	3	32	23	38	31	33	4	11	19	28	2	38	8	16	15	38
Simon	28	21	7	31	4	20	0	0	7	20	38	4	34	6	31	32	22	23	23	37	32	1	37
Siobhan	35	23	19	30	35	5	3	26	2	14	23	2	39	20	27	18	23	38	36	36	11	24	22
Wayne	29	9	12	0	21	36	25	26	23	10	17	29	19	24	6	8	27	8	28	35	2	31	24

Add alternating bands of colour to long rows or deep columns to reduce the chance of your eye accidentally slipping from one row or column to another as you scan across the screen.

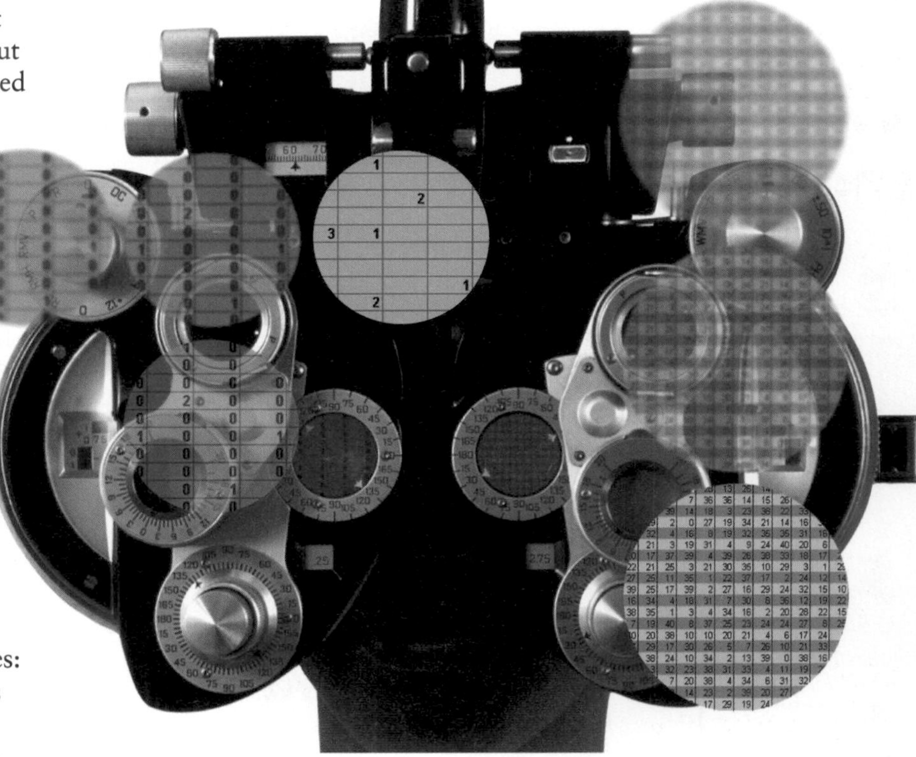

Worksheets can be made easier to read by the clever use of colour or through hiding unnecessary information.

● Using colour wisely

Sometimes, very wide or deep worksheets can be hard to follow. As your eye moves along a row or column, it can accidentally slip to the wrong line of information. Adding extra space between the rows or columns can help alleviate this problem, but there is a price to pay, namely an awful lot of scrolling because of the extra space.

A much better solution is to use alternating colours for any rows or columns that are tricky to follow. Simply by adding cell background colours to your wide or deep worksheets, you'll significantly reduce the strain on your eyes.

You probably know from looking at your bank statements that columns of financial figures are easier to follow if the numbers are

PC TIPS

If you find Excel's standard selection of 40 colours too restrictive for your needs, why not create your own?

Bring up the Options dialog box by selecting the Options command from the Tools menu. Click on the Color tab and use the Modify button to specify your own colours.

bills.xls

	A	B
1	Item	Amount
2	Electricity	9.86
3	Gas	2.75
4	Food	211
5	Loan	27.46
6	Insurance	15.75
7	Petrol	32.95
8	Total	299.77
9		
10		

To make sure important figures aren't lost in a column of less significant figures (above), line them up along their decimal points (below). Notice how much more obvious the 211.00 for food has become.

bills.xls

	A	B
1	Item	Amount
2	Electricity	9.86
3	Gas	2.75
4	Food	211.00
5	Loan	27.46
6	Insurance	15.75
7	Petrol	32.95
8	Total	299.77
9		

lined up vertically along their decimal points. When you type numbers into a blank spreadsheet, you'll see that Excel simply aligns them to the right of the cell. This is adequate for normal numerical usage, but often proves awkward for working with figures representing sums of money.

● Take your places

By telling Excel that you want to see the same number of decimal places for all the figures in the column(s), you can make sure that important numbers are easy to spot. In the example on the left, the figure of 211 is lost among all the much lower decimal amounts. By highlighting the column of figures and pressing the Increase Decimal button twice, all figures have two decimal places, so the 211.00 figure stands out.

● Currency symbols

You can also use Excel's Currency format to draw attention to the figures in your worksheet that are amounts of money. Select the cells that contain money figures and use the Number tab of the Format Cells dialog box to select Currency from the list of categories provided. Excel will add the symbol

	A	B
1	PTA newsletter	
2	Advertising income	
3	TGK Ltd	£500
4	Sun King	£250
5	TN Micros	£88
6	AutoRent	£250
7	SL Studios	£500
8	MacDuffs	£375
9	Soft Wear	£390
10	PDQ Copy	£450
11	Total	£2,803
12		

	A	B
1	PTA newsletter	
2	Advertising income	
3		£
4	TGK Ltd	500
5	Sun King	250
6	TN Micros	88
7	AutoRent	250
8	SL Studios	500
9	MacDuffs	375
10	Soft Wear	390
11	PDQ Copy	450
12	Total	£2,803

While it's helpful to be able to see which figures in a worksheet are amounts of money, too many currency symbols get in the way and can make numbers hard to read (above left). A clearer alternative is to use a single symbol at the top of a column of figures (above right).

in front of each number. Be aware, however, that too many £, $ or Fr symbols in your worksheet make it hard to browse your figures; the fact that every entry begins with the same symbol can work against legibility. Take a tip from most accountants – simply add a single currency symbol to the top of the column of figures.

Hiding zero values

To spot the patterns of data in tables that contain a large number of zeros, you can simply hide them from view.

MANY TYPES OF worksheet are tables that include a large number of cells containing zero. Once again, this makes browsing the worksheet for the real data – the non-zero values – very difficult. In cases such as these, it can be useful to simply hide the zeros from view. Once they are invisible, the table is able to reveal a real pattern in the data.

1 In this table of goal-scorers and games played, all the zeros not only make it very difficult to see who's doing well but they also make it hard to spot any trends in the figures.

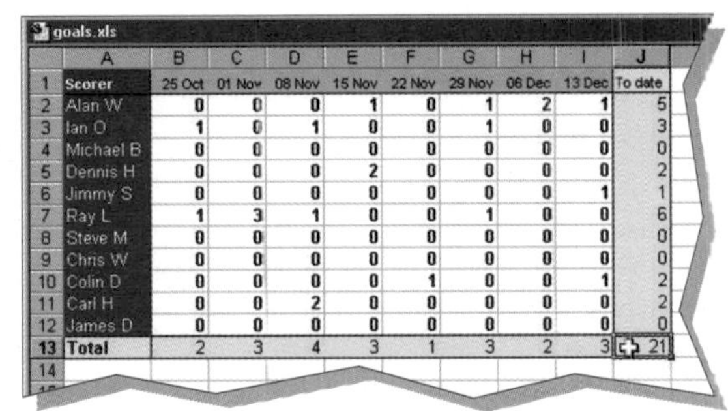

goals.xls

	A	B	C	D	E	F	G	H	I	J
1	Scorer	25 Oct	01 Nov	08 Nov	15 Nov	22 Nov	29 Nov	06 Dec	13 Dec	To date
2	Alan W	0	0	0	1	0	1	2	1	5
3	Ian O	1	0	1	0	0	1	0	0	3
4	Michael B	0	0	0	0	0	0	0	0	0
5	Dennis H	0	0	0	2	0	0	0	0	2
6	Jimmy S	0	0	0	0	0	0	0	1	1
7	Ray L	1	3	1	0	0	1	0	0	6
8	Steve M	0	0	0	0	0	0	0	0	0
9	Chris W	0	0	0	0	0	0	0	0	0
10	Colin D	0	0	0	0	1	0	0	1	2
11	Carl H	0	0	2	0	0	0	0	0	2
12	James D	0	0	0	0	0	0	0	0	0
13	Total	2	3	4	3	1	3	2	3	21
14										

2 Select Options from the Tools menu. When the dialog box appears, click on the View tab towards the top left of the menu.

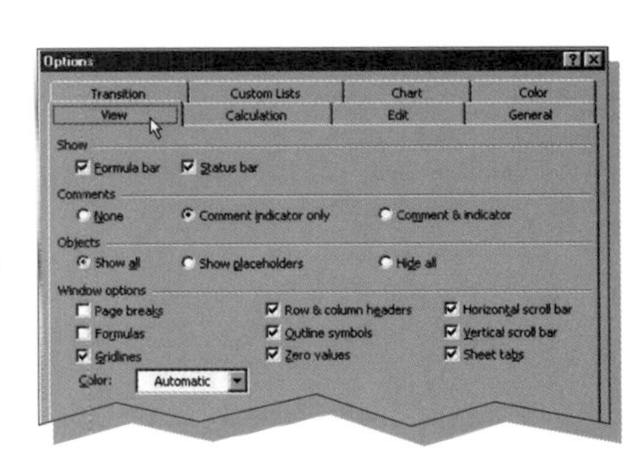

3 Untick the Zero values box in the Window options section of the dialog box, and then press the OK button.

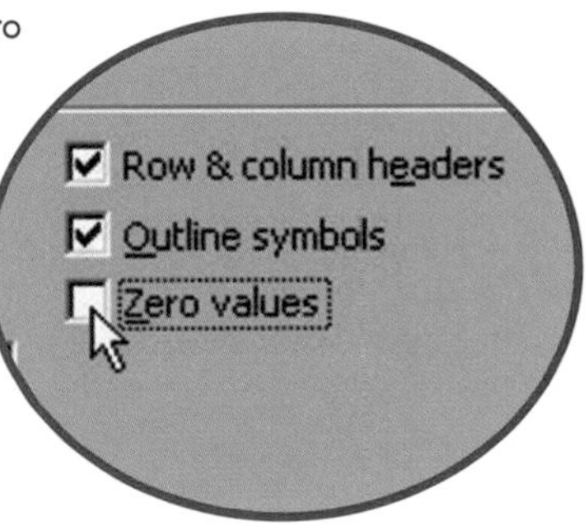

4 Now that the zeros have disappeared from view, the real data stands out. You can see the regular goal-scorers and the scoring trends at a glance.

goals.xls

	A	B	C	D	E	F	G	H	I	J
1	Scorer	25 Oct	01 Nov	08 Nov	15 Nov	22 Nov	29 Nov	06 Dec	13 Dec	To date
2	Alan W				1		1	2	1	5
3	Ian O	1		1			1			3
4	Michael E									
5	Dennis H				2					2
6	Jimmy S								1	1
7	Ray L	1	3	1			1			6
8	Steve M									
9	Chris W									
10	Colin D					1			1	2
11	Carl H			2						2
12	James D									
13	Total	2	3	4	3	1	3	2	3	21
14										

Tracking changes in your worksheets

If you share your worksheets with colleagues or members of your family, keeping track of who made which changes is hard work – unless you get Excel to track the changes for you.

Until now, we've always talked about the worksheets you create and work on with Excel as if you're the only person using them. Yet the real world is very different: people share information – especially computer files, such as Excel worksheets – with each other all the time. You might have business worksheets that you collaborate on with colleagues, or maybe you share worksheets about domestic finances, with your partner at home, for example.

● Visual reminders

So how can you keep track of all the changes made by different people using the same workbook? The usual solution lies in good communication – but conversations can be forgotten and notes are easily lost.

Excel offers you a much more reliable method in the form of Track Changes commands. With these, Excel stores changes and leaves a visual reminder (a blue triangle) to show you what's changed. Simply hovering the mouse over a changed cell brings up a note showing the most recent changes that have been made to it.

	A	B	C	D	E	F
1	Holiday budget					
2	Flight	490				
3	Hotel	250				
4	Taxis	100				
5	Misc	400				
6	Total	1240				

John Arnold, 10/04/02 12:17:
Changed cell B4 from '50' to '100'.

Once you've turned on Excel's tracking feature, changes made to the information in your worksheet are recorded. The new value is used in the calculation, but the old one is recorded in a pop-up note.

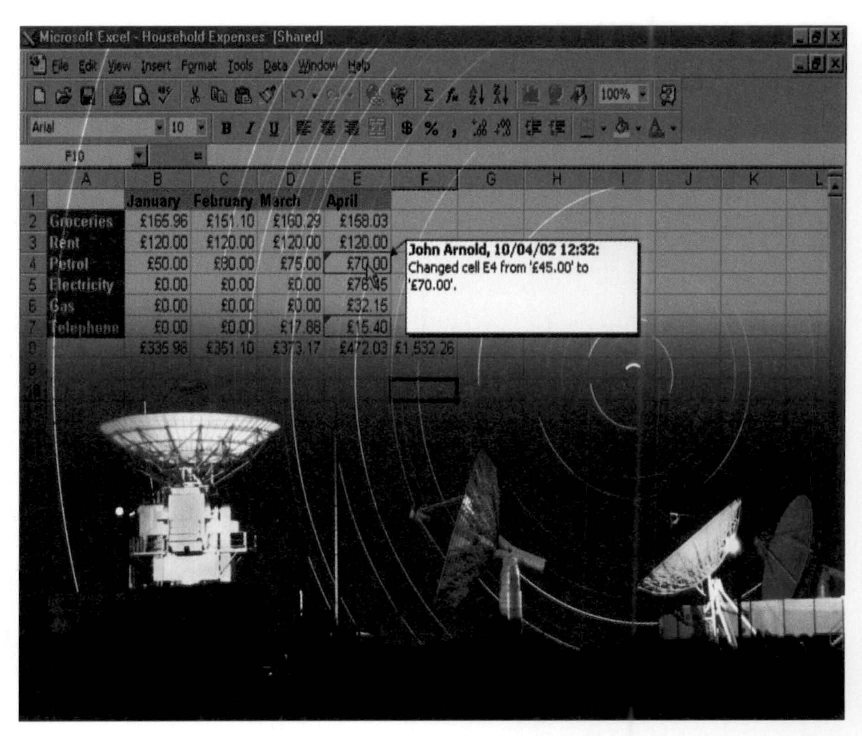

Getting Excel to monitor what goes on when you're not there is a good way of keeping up to date with changes made to a worksheet.

You can also run through all the changes made to a worksheet and accept or reject them one by one. This makes it easy to revert to the original values for some cells and accept changes made in others.

● Whodunnit?

For businesses where workers collaborate on a worksheet that's been shared over a network, being able to track changes is essential. At any time, a project manager will be able to see who has made which changes to what because Excel stores the change made, together with the name of the person responsible for it.

PC TIPS

Tracking options

You can decide what information you want to track. For example, you can track all changes; those made since you last saved the worksheet; those made since a specific date; or even those made by a specific person or persons.

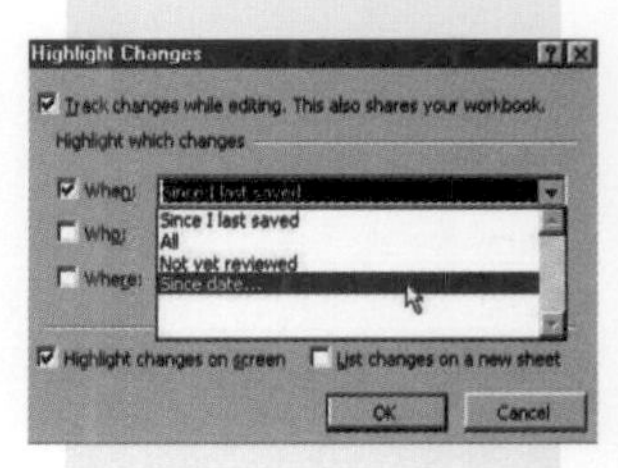

How to keep track

Here we show how the process of tracking changes works by making changes to an existing worksheet.

1 For this exercise, we've started with the monthly home accounts worksheet created in Stage 4, on page 63, although any worksheet will suffice.

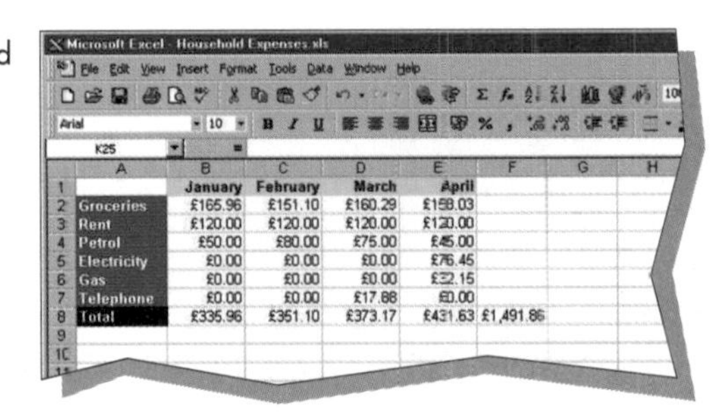

2 First we need to set up Excel so that it tracks changes. Select Track Changes from the Tools menu and then Highlight Changes from the sub-menu.

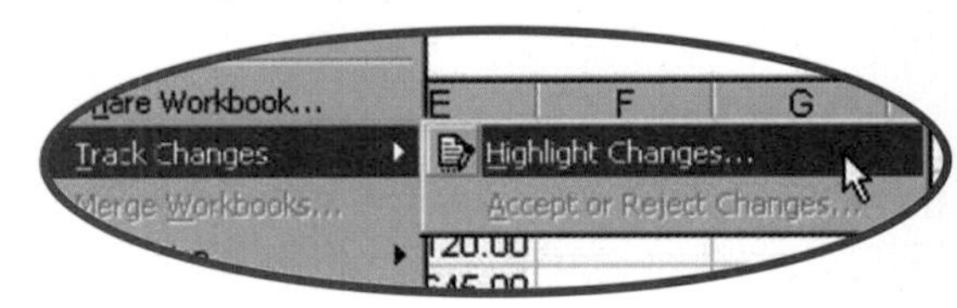

3 This will open the Highlight Changes dialog box. First tick the Track changes while editing box, then make sure that the When option is ticked with All selected from its list box, and that the Who option is ticked with Everyone selected. Click on the OK button.

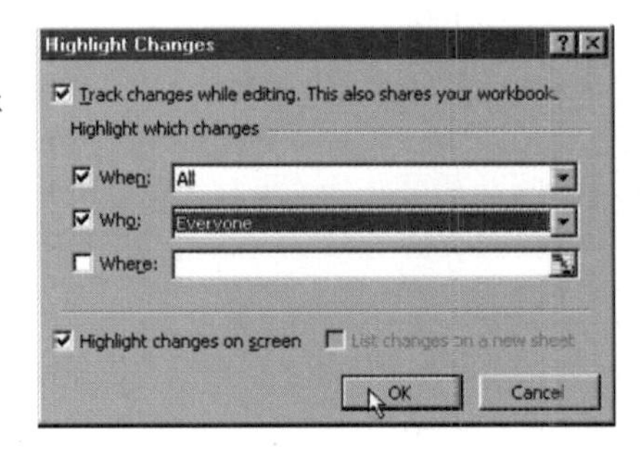

4 Now click on one of the cells in the worksheet and change its value by typing in a new one. Once you press the [Enter] key, Excel indicates that the cell has been changed by adding a blue outline and triangle.

5 To see the changes made to a cell, hold the mouse pointer over any cell with a blue triangle.

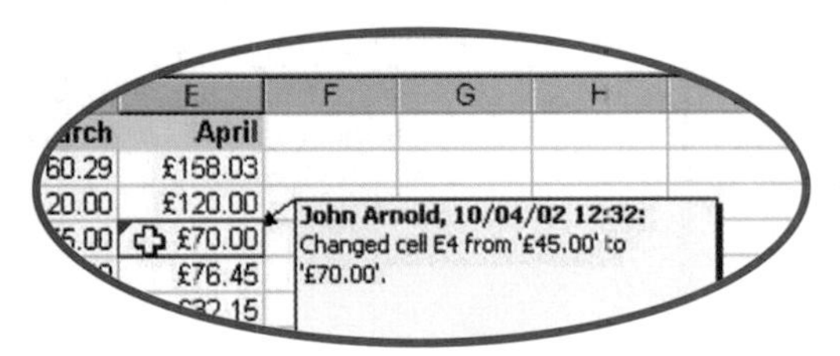

6 Make some other changes to the worksheet and then click on Track Changes in the Tools menu and choose Accept or Reject Changes from the sub-menu that appears. Excel needs to save the worksheet first. Press the OK button when prompted.

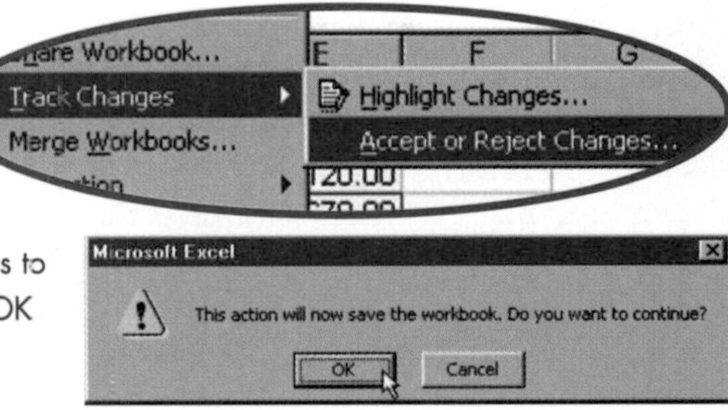

7 Next, Excel asks what sort of changes you want to review: leave its suggestions as they are and press the OK button to continue.

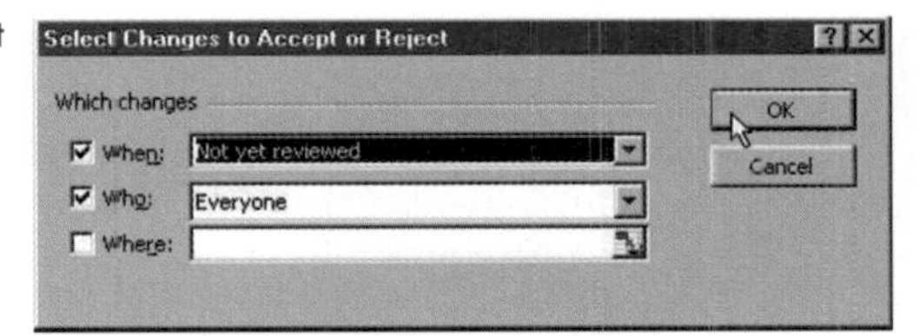

8 Now Excel lets you accept or reject each change in turn. The first change is shown and the relevant cell is highlighted with a dotted border. To keep the new information, click on the Accept button.

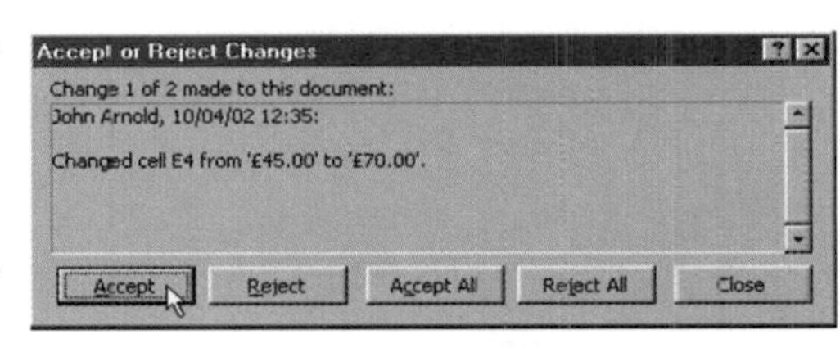

9 Now Excel moves on to the next change made to the worksheet. Press the Reject button and you'll see the cell revert to its original value (inset).

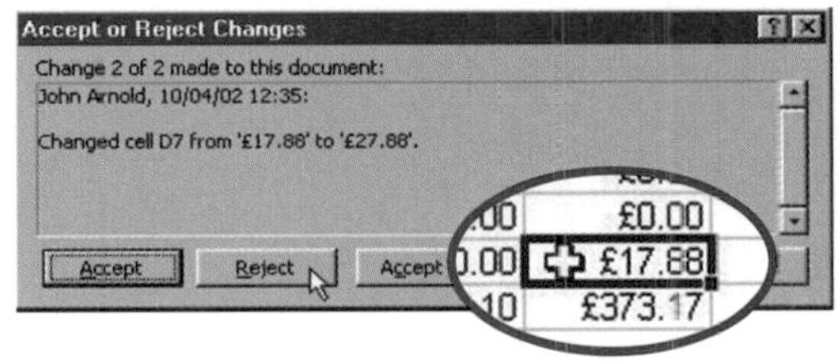

PC TIPS

Keeping a record of changes

You can keep a permanent record of the changes tracked in a special History sheet in your workbook. To do this, save your workbook, then open the Highlight Changes dialog box. Click in the List changes on a new sheet checkbox and then click OK. A tab for a new worksheet, called History, is added to the row at the bottom of the Excel window. Click on it to see the list of changes (below).

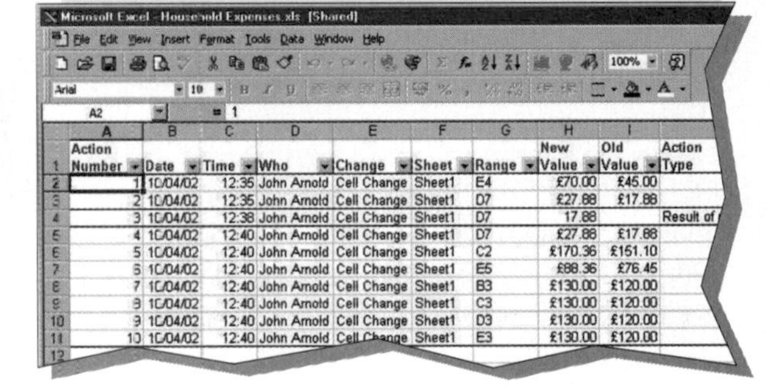

Adding objects from other programs

It can be extremely useful to include elements that have been created in other software in your Excel workbooks. Find out how to do this by using the powerful Windows facility, Object Linking and Embedding.

On many occasions in this series we've seen how handy it is to use Excel to make raw data easier to understand in Excel workbooks. For example, we can add formatting to cells, add text headings to explain the data or create graphs and charts to enhance the presentation and make it easier to read.

Sometimes, though, you might want to add material that has been created in other programs to your Excel workbooks. The easiest way to do this is by copying elements from one application and pasting them into Excel. The problem with this approach is that every time the item changes in the original file, you'll have to repeat the operation to ensure that the pasted version is updated.

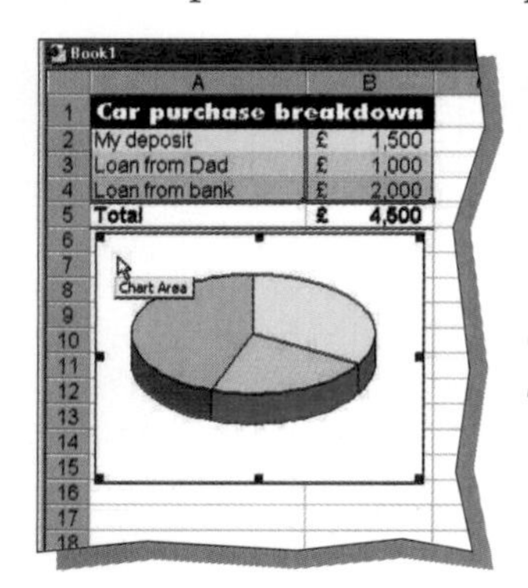

If you've created a graph or chart from data in a worksheet, you've already been using OLE. The chart (left) is actually a separate object floating in the worksheet.

You can get round this problem by using the Object Linking and Embedding (OLE) facility. This is a Windows feature that allows you to insert objects from one program into documents created in a completely different program. It's also the technology that lets you insert a graph into a spreadsheet (see above).

● Linking objects

You can use OLE to link elements created in another program to your Excel worksheet. Linking is useful if there are several people working on different parts of the same project. For example, you might be looking after the figures in Excel while somebody else is writing notes about the figures in Word. By using linking you can include the notes in your worksheet and ensure that they are updated automatically.

Embedding allows you to create elements within Excel by using other programs' features. For example, you could create a graphic of a company logo within Excel using the menus and toolbars of CorelDRAW drawing software.

OLE lets you add graphics to Excel worksheets. If you then change the graphic in the program it was created in, the changes are automatically updated in Excel.

PC TIPS

Editing embedded objects

You can return to an embedded object at any time and edit it with the same tools that you used to create it. All you have to do is double-click on the embedded object and Excel's menus and toolbars will be replaced with those relevant to the application used to create the object.

Embedding objects in worksheets

Use the full power of Windows and OLE by incorporating an object from another software program into Excel, and linking the object to the worksheet.

1 Here's a worksheet that holds the price list for a greengrocery business. Let's see how we can use OLE to create and embed a company logo straight into this worksheet.

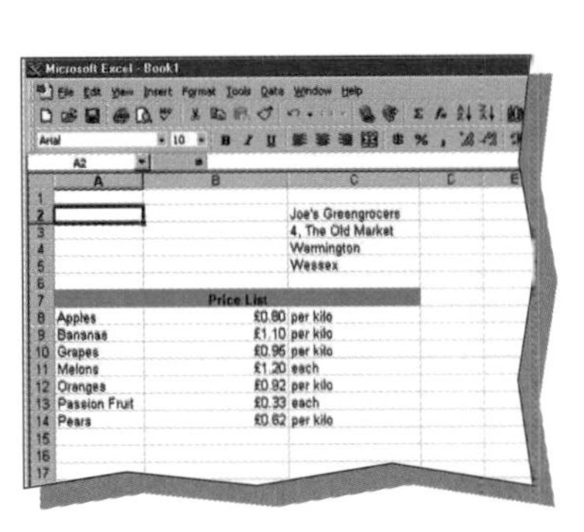

2 We want to include a graphic logo in the top left corner of our worksheet by adding an embedded object from CorelDRAW. We have to start by opening Excel's Insert menu and selecting the Object command.

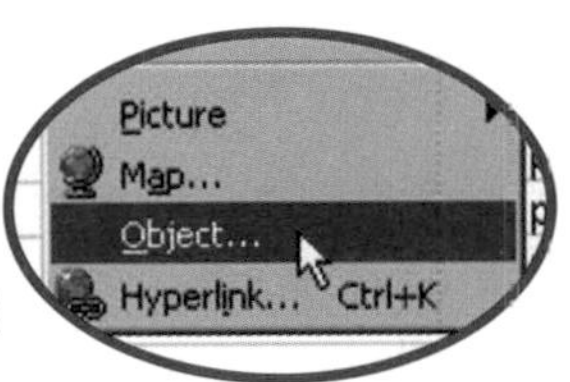

PC TIPS

Adding voice notes

Adding voice notes to your Excel worksheet is easy using Object Linking and Embedding. Ensure your sound card, speakers and microphone are set up (see Stage 2, pages 92-93) and choose the Wave Sound object in the Object dialog box (see Step 3). The Sound Recorder program pops up ready to record your voice note (see pages 20-23). The note is stored in the Excel worksheet as an icon (right). Double-click on it to hear it.

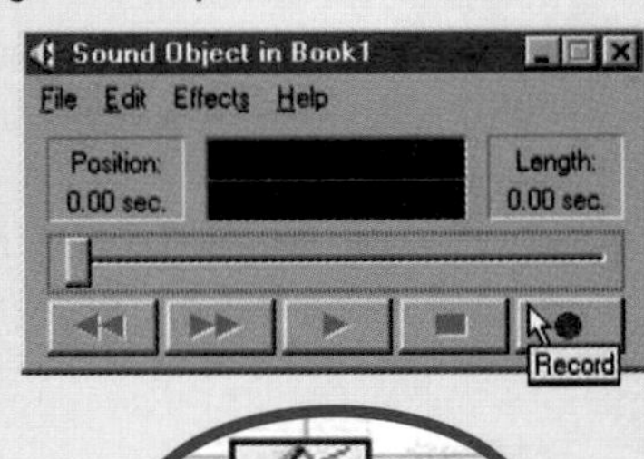

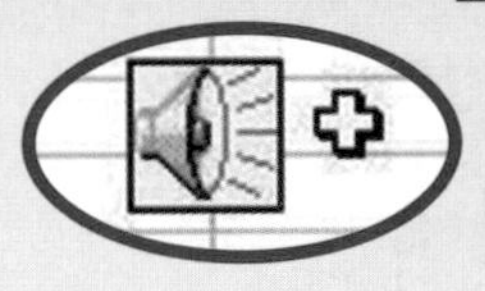

3 Excel opens the Object dialog box. Start by clicking on the Create New tab and then highlight CorelDRAW 9.0 Graphic in the Object type list. Make sure there's no tick in the Display as icon checkbox before clicking on the OK button.

4 You'll have to wait a few moments while your PC finds CorelDRAW. Then you'll see that the toolbars and menus from CorelDRAW will replace Excel's. A rectangular drawing area will also appear on the worksheet.

5 Before we create our logo, let's put the drawing area where we want the logo to appear. You can do this by dragging and dropping it to a new position. The drawing area can also be resized by moving its handles.

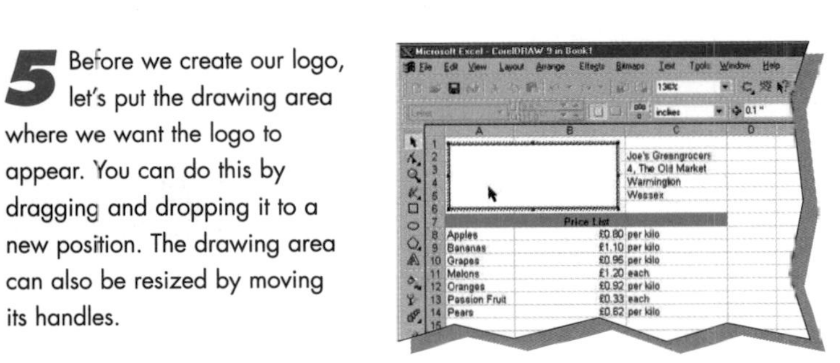

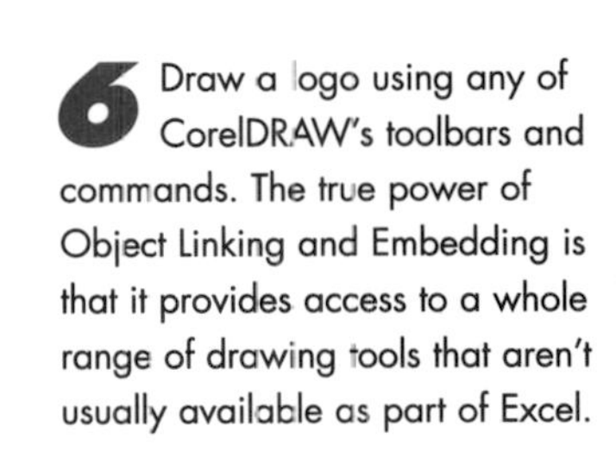

6 Draw a logo using any of CorelDRAW's toolbars and commands. The true power of Object Linking and Embedding is that it provides access to a whole range of drawing tools that aren't usually available as part of Excel.

7 Once you've finished creating your logo, click once anywhere on the Excel worksheet outside the drawing area. This will make the CorelDRAW menus and toolbars disappear and restore the original Excel ones. This just leaves the problem of the black border that we don't want around our logo.

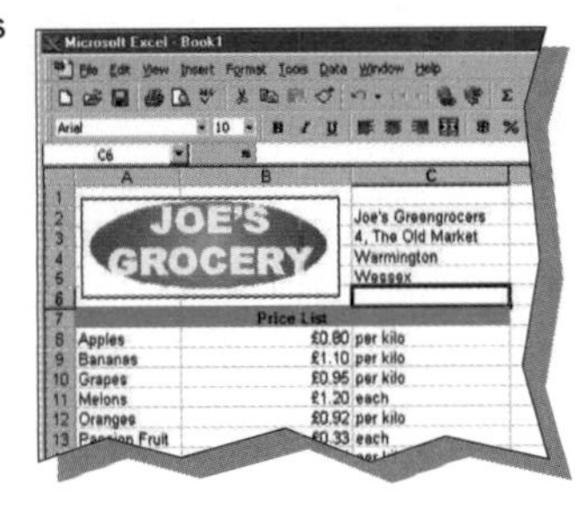

8 To fix this, right-click on the logo and select Format Object from the menu that appears. Click on the Colors and Lines tab in the Format Object dialog box and set the Line Color to No Line. Finish by clicking on the OK button.

9 Here's the finished logo in place in the Excel worksheet. When you save the worksheet, the logo is saved with it.

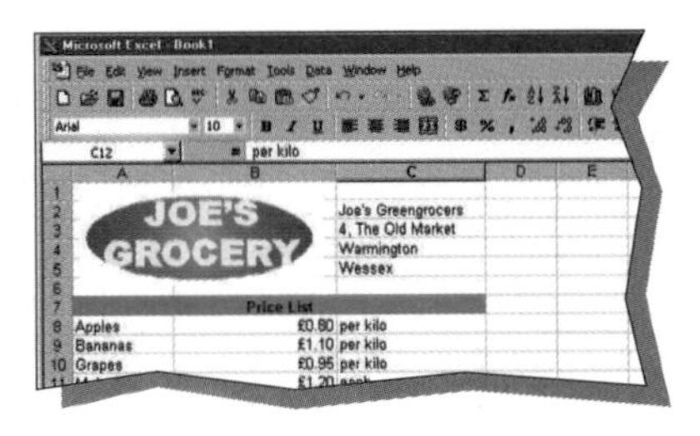

Concatenating cell data

Concatenation is a very useful function which can be used to take the information held in Excel cells and turn seemingly complex data into plain English sentences.

We have seen how functions can be powerful and useful tools for manipulating data (see Stage 4, pages 46-49). Most of the functions covered so far have dealt with numerical calculation, but concatenation provides a useful way of manipulating text.

Excel's own description does not really suggest how powerful the CONCATENATE function can be. It simply suggests that it joins several text strings into one text string. What this actually means is that you can instruct the CONCATENATE function to link several words or phrases to construct a longer, meaningful sentence. You do this by giving it a set of references called arguments, the term used for the instructions given to functions.

● A powerful function

One sort of argument is simply a piece of text. Suppose, for example, you type the formula =CONCATENATE("There are 10", " melons in stock") into cell A1; note that a space must be inserted after the second opening quote to create a sentence with spaces between the two arguments. The function reads the two phrases in double quotes – "There are 10" and " melons in stock" – as arguments, each consisting of a text string. It links the two and places the resulting text string, "There are 10 melons in stock", in cell A1.

This might not seem very useful, but the real power of the CONCATENATE function lies in the fact that it can also use cell references as arguments. Thus it can pick up text or numerical data from cells in your worksheet and use it as part of the sentence. For example, imagine that you're a greengrocer who uses an Excel table to keep track of fruit and vegetable stocks. If cell B1 contains the word "melons" and cell B2 contains the number of melons in stock, putting the formula =CONCATENATE("There are ",B2, " ",B1," in stock") in cell B3 will create a simple, clear sentence about your melon stock levels. If the value in cell B2 is 15, the resulting text in cell B3 would read "There are 15 melons in stock".

The only limitation of the CONCATENATE function is that Excel restricts you to using 30 arguments. In practice, this is unlikely to happen, as there won't be many occasions when you need to use more arguments.

● Extending the potential

On the rare occasions when you do need to concatenate more than 30 text strings and cell references, there is an ingenious solution. Simply use one cell containing a formula that uses the CONCATENATE function to join the first 30 arguments together. Then use an adjacent cell to hold a formula to join together the remaining arguments. Finally, create one more formula in another cell and use the CONCATENATE function to join the two parts of the whole string. Remember that you can hide the temporary cells if you don't want to see them using Excel's Hide and Unhide commands through the Format menu and sub-menus (see Stage 3, pages 64-65).

> **WHAT IT MEANS**
>
> TEXT STRINGS
>
> *A text string is any sequence of characters (letters, spaces, numbers or symbols) grouped together in a particular order. A text string can be as short as one character or word, such as the letter 'a' or the word 'apple', or it can be a whole sentence, such as, 'We have 12kg more apples than bananas in stock'.*

Using the CONCATENATE function

Here we add explanations to the mountain height table we created in Stage 3, on page 59.

1 Quite often, the raw data in a worksheet like this one (right) can be difficult to interpret. So let's use Excel's CONCATENATE function to turn the existing information into plain English sentences that will make the table easier to understand.

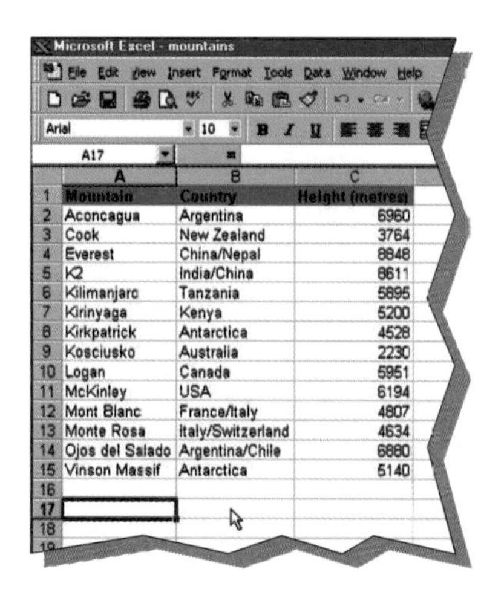

	A	B	C
1	Mountain	Country	Height (metres)
2	Aconcagua	Argentina	6960
3	Cook	New Zealand	3764
4	Everest	China/Nepal	8848
5	K2	India/China	8611
6	Kilimanjaro	Tanzania	5895
7	Kirinyaga	Kenya	5200
8	Kirkpatrick	Antarctica	4528
9	Kosciusko	Australia	2230
10	Logan	Canada	5951
11	McKinley	USA	6194
12	Mont Blanc	France/Italy	4807
13	Monte Rosa	Italy/Switzerland	4634
14	Ojos del Salado	Argentina/Chile	6880
15	Vinson Massif	Antarctica	5140

2 Let's start by creating a formula to make a sentence about Mount Aconcagua in Argentina. Select cell D2 and click on the Paste Function button in the Standard toolbar.

3 Excel will open the Paste Function dialog box. First highlight Text in the Function category list in the left window. Next, highlight the CONCATENATE function in the Function name list in the right window. Click OK.

4 A dialog box opens to take the arguments for the CONCATENATE function. Position the cursor in the Text1 box. Click on cell A2 to tell Excel to use its contents as a text string to start the sentence. Notice how the text in A2, "Aconcagua", is shown to the box's right and the formula builds up in the Formula Bar (inset).

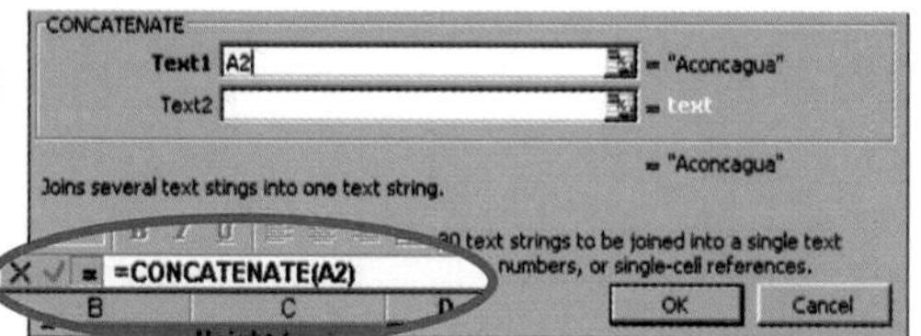

5 Now click in the Text2 box and type " is a mountain in ". This tells Excel to use these words as the next part of the sentence. Be sure to type a space before 'is' and after 'in' as you need these to appear in the final sentence. Next position the text cursor in the Text3 box and click on cell B2. Press the OK button to finish.

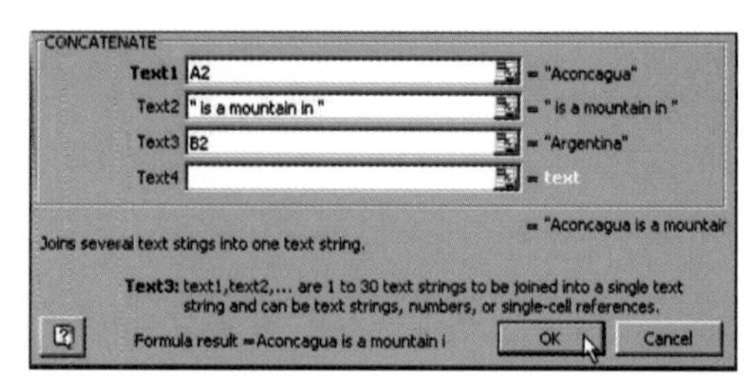

6 Here's what the completed sentence looks like. The formula in cell D2 uses the CONCATENATE function to link the text from cells A2 and B2, inserting the extra phrase in between.

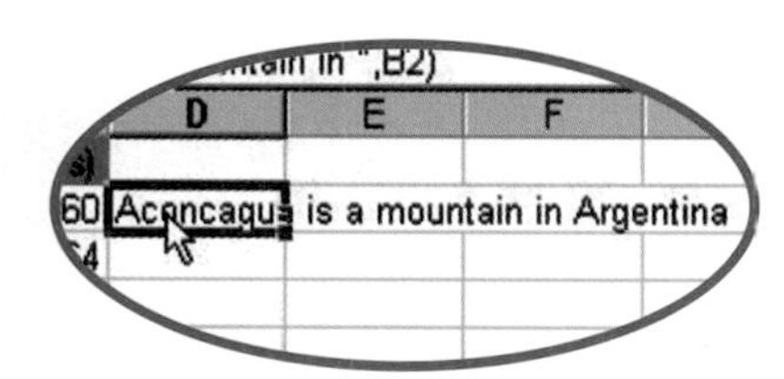

7 We can also include numerical data in the text of a sentence. Click on cell D2 and use the Formula Bar to add three arguments after the CONCATENATE function: the first is the text string ". It is "; the second is a reference to cell C2 (which holds numerical data about the height of the mountain); the last is more text that reads " metres high."

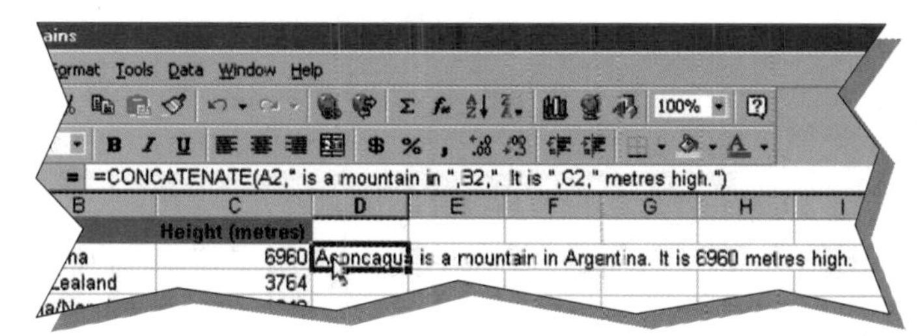

8 Of course, with a single example like this, we could have just typed the text straight into cell D2. But using the CONCATENATE function has two advantages: first, we don't have to retype the sentence if the data changes; and second, we can copy and paste the formula in seconds to complete our table using all the other data, as shown right.

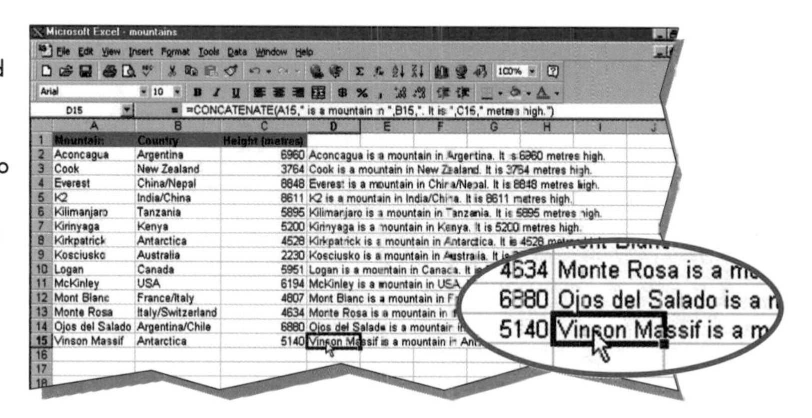

PC TIPS

Using the & operator

Another way to join text strings and cell contents together is to use the & operator. For example, the formula =A2&" is a mountain in "&B2 produces exactly the same result as the first formula we created using the CONCATENATE function as described in Step 6.

Publishing to the Internet

If you're an Internet user, you'll find that it's easy to share your artistic handiwork with the rest of the world, thanks to CorelDRAW's built-in Web publishing facilities.

CorelDRAW is great for creating pictures to illustrate everything from a community poster to your child's geography homework or a business plan. If you've got an Internet account and personal Web space, you'll find that it's also useful for creating graphics for the Web.

To do this, you should produce graphics in the usual way, using all of CorelDRAW's graphics tools. You then use a special command, Publish To Internet. This creates files that you can copy to your Web site. You can also view them from the hard disk to check what they look like.

● What's in a Web page?

If you've read pages 154-157 in Stage 3 on setting up your own Web site, you'll already have an idea about what's involved in creating Web pages.

Basically, each Web page is a text file. This comprises any text that you want to appear on the page, plus a series of commands – called tags – that describe what the page should look like and which graphics to place where. This combination of text and commands is called HTML (Hypertext Markup Language). You can type these commands in yourself, using an ordinary text editor such as Notepad. However, if you want more help, you can get assistance by using an HTML editor. Many of these allow you to construct a page by dragging text and pictures around with the mouse. The advantage of this approach is that it keeps all the HTML commands hidden away in the background.

● The CorelDRAW approach

Publishing to the Internet with CorelDRAW falls into the latter category – you needn't type in any HTML commands at all. With CorelDRAW you can create your page in exactly the same way as you would for any other purpose. When you then choose the Publish To Internet option, you are given several choices as to exactly how your Web page is saved.

One of CorelDRAW's neatest tricks is the way in which it can overcome one of the Internet's inherent display problems, which arises when visitors to your Web site do not share the same typefaces as the ones you used when you created your page. When this happens, their computers will normally substitute other typefaces and your neatly laid out Web page can end up looking awful.

CorelDRAW can save all the text on your Web page as pictures – thus removing the missing typeface problem altogether. Admittedly, you do need to check the size of the files that you create in order to make sure that they are not so large that they will take ages for your Web site visitors to download. However, CorelDRAW's technique offers a useful way of creating Web pages that you can combine with others, such as those set up in Word (see Stage 4, pages 42-43).

The power of CorelDRAW extends into cyberspace, helping you to produce great-looking Web pages. You can make your Web site look unique with custom-made artwork.

INTERNET OPTIONS

You can choose whether to publish your drawing as a page or as a single image. If you're not using other Web editing programs, choose the first option. CorelDRAW creates all the HTML for you. But, if you are also using a Web editing program to create your Web pages, select the second option. Once you've published a drawing as an image, you can insert it into your Web page, just like any other graphic.

Different ways of Web publishing

CorelDRAW offers you a range of options for saving your picture files to the Internet. Each has its pros and cons, but it is easy to select the one that suits you best.

WHEN YOUR WEB page or graphic is ready and you select the Publish To Internet command, it asks you to choose which way to save your graphic. There are many options, and although you don't have to choose which method you are going to use until your design is finished, it's always best to have one in mind as you work, so that you can tailor your efforts to its particular features.

● Publishing to bitmap format

This is the simplest of the three methods to use when you are creating Web pages in another program and just want to include an image created in CorelDRAW.

A CorelDRAW image is created as a vector-based graphic. This process converts the image into a graphics format that can be displayed on the Internet – a Web-compatible bitmap. The result is either a .JPG or a .GIF (for more details on these file formats, see Stage 4, pages 74-77). Once the image has been converted, you can place it on a Web site by incorporating it into HTML code created with Notepad or an HTML editor.

Note that the whole CorelDRAW image becomes a single bitmap chunk, which means that you need to pay careful attention to the size of the files being created (see page 65). A full A4 page of CorelDRAW images results in a very large bitmap file, which will take up a lot of space on your site and will also take a long time for visitors to download.

● Publishing to HTML

This is the primary way to create Web pages automatically with CorelDRAW. Unlike the bitmap method, which converts only the pictures, publishing directly to HTML lets you use Internet-specific functions, such as links to other Web pages. This makes it possible to create a complete Web site with CorelDRAW.

Choosing this option saves your graphic as an image and creates HTML files containing automatic links to it – plus a set of commands that link the pages together. You can even create an image map to make your graphics more interesting and more interactive for people who browse your Web site.

To do this, you assign different links to the various CorelDRAW objects in your picture so that your Web site can direct browsers to a choice of Web pages. For example, a site for an estate agent might display pictures of a floor plan for each of the properties on his books. Anyone who clicks on the living room would be taken to a page describing the room's size and its features; those clicking on the kitchen would see a list of kitchen appliances and fittings.

● Laying out with tables

If you decide to publish your drawing as an HTML Web page, CorelDRAW can make a Web page that uses a table for layout. The advantage of this is that almost all Web browsers will be able to display your pages properly.

CorelDRAW places the shapes, text and images you have used in your drawing into different cells in the table. It automatically makes small adjustments to the position, so it's vital to check the final layout. Fortunately, when you finish publishing your drawing to the Internet, CorelDRAW can immediately start your Web browser program and load the page for you to check.

Publish your own unique graphics on your Web site with CorelDRAW.

PC TIPS

Help is at hand

Whenever you convert one of your designs to a Web page, CorelDRAW checks it to see if there are any conflicts. If there are potential problems, CorelDRAW alerts you to them and lets you fix them. For example: if you have forgotten to mark some text as HTML-compatible, CorelDRAW spots it and gives you the chance to fix it before creating the final Web page.

WHAT IT MEANS

IMAGE MAP

This is a single Web graphic that works as a special type of link to other Web pages. If you click on one part of the image, you will be taken to one Web page; if you click on another part you will end up on a different page.

TYPES OF TEXT

If you use text in your drawings, CorelDRAW offers a number of ways to handle it when it comes to publishing on the Internet. The best approach is to let CorelDRAW treat Artistic Text and Paragraph Text very differently (see Stage 4, pages 78-81). Artistic Text, which can include text to which you've added effects, is best converted to a bitmap graphic – it then looks exactly as you drew it, no matter what typefaces are installed on the visitor's computer.

For Paragraph Text, however, such bitmap files can become very large and cumbersome, so CorelDRAW saves it as text within the HTML file. This may lead to slight differences in the text's appearance, depending on the typefaces the visitor has, but it is the best compromise.

Save your drawings as Web pages

You don't need to go to the trouble of typing any HTML code to create Web pages because, with the help of an easy-to-follow wizard, CorelDRAW can do it all for you.

1 Start CorelDRAW and design your own Web page. You can use any combination of text, shapes, clip art and photos that you need to ensure that the design works.

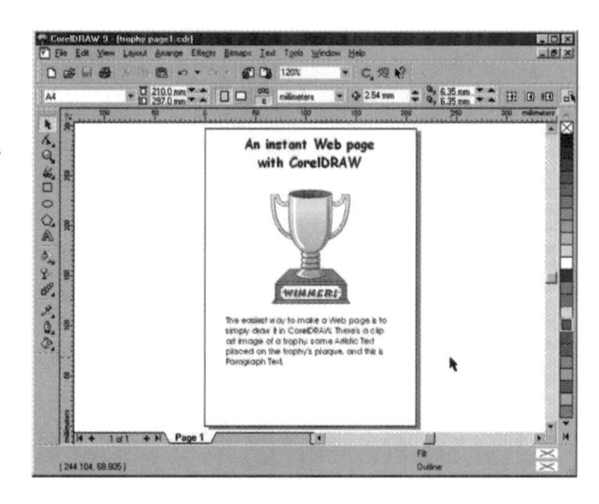

2 If you have used Paragraph Text (see Stage 4, pages 80-81), select the first Paragraph Text box in your drawing, then select Make Text HTML Compatible from the Text menu. Do this for each Paragraph Text box in turn until all the text is HTML compatible.

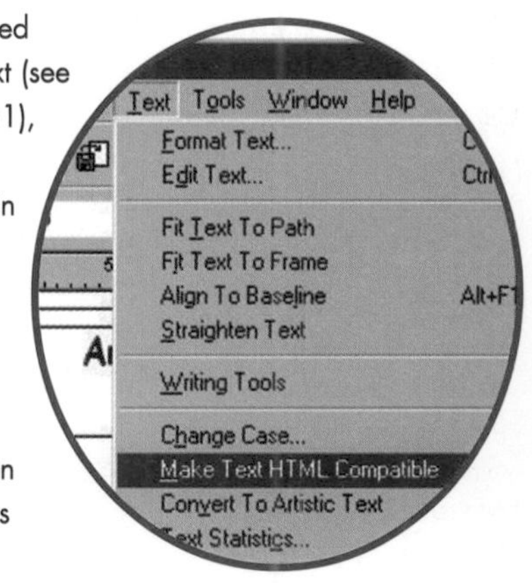

3 Select Publish To Internet from CorelDRAW's File menu. This starts a Wizard that leads you through the process step by step.

4 The first thing to do is choose a folder for your Web pages. Go into Windows and create a folder if you haven't already done so, then click on the Browse button to select it.

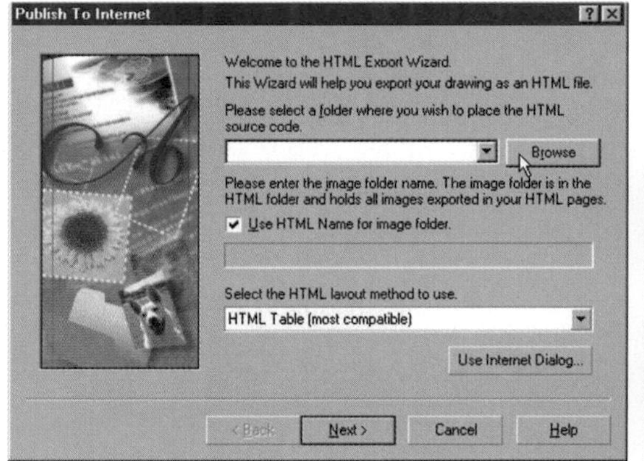

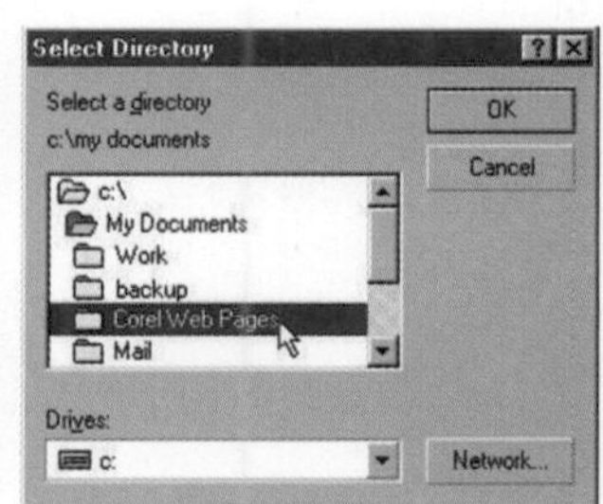

5 Make sure that HTML Table is selected as the HTML layout method, then click on the Next button to proceed.

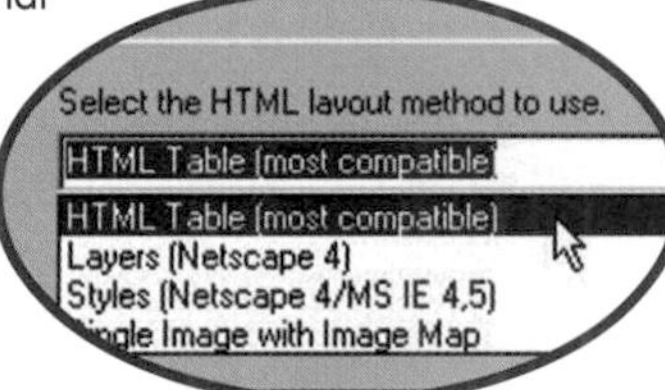

6 You can now tell CorelDRAW how to handle images in your Web page. Choose the GIF option if your drawing contains only shapes and text with a limited number of colours. If your shapes and text use many colours, choose the JPEG option. We've chosen JPEG because of all the colours we've used to create the shading on the trophy.

Please select how you would like your images exported:
JPEG
JPEG Options...
Interlace

7 It's best to leave the two bitmap settings ticked. This ensures that any scanned photographs you've included are displayed as well as possible. Leave the final option unticked and click the Next button.

8 In the final Wizard screen, make sure the 'View page in browser' option is ticked (inset) and press the Finish button. CorelDRAW starts your Web browser and loads the Web page it has created. Look very closely and you'll see that a few things look a little different, but on the whole it should be pretty much as you drew it.

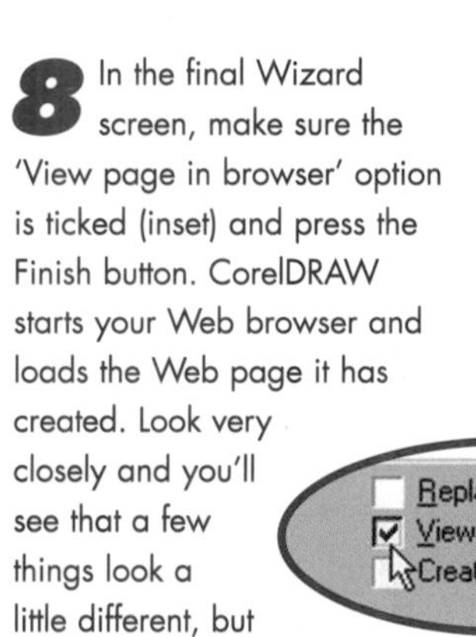

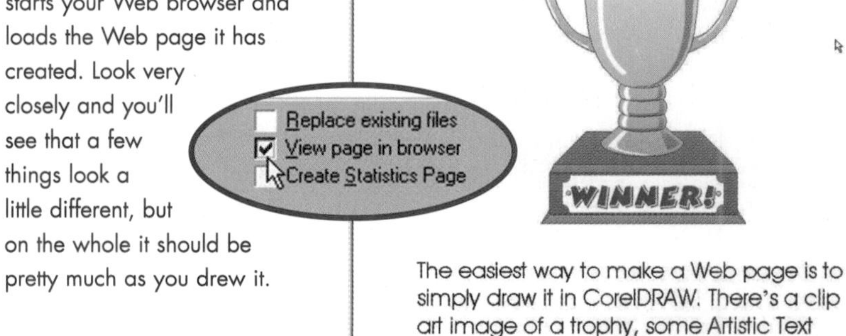

Make Web graphics with CorelDRAW

Use CorelDRAW's powerful vector graphics commands to make great images that you can turn into bitmaps and add to your Web-page designs.

1 Few Web authors want A4-sized images, so the first step is to create the graphic in the correct size: start CorelDRAW and select Options from the Tools menu.

2 In the dialog box that pops up, double-click on Document in the panel on the left. Then double-click on Page and finally single-click on Size.

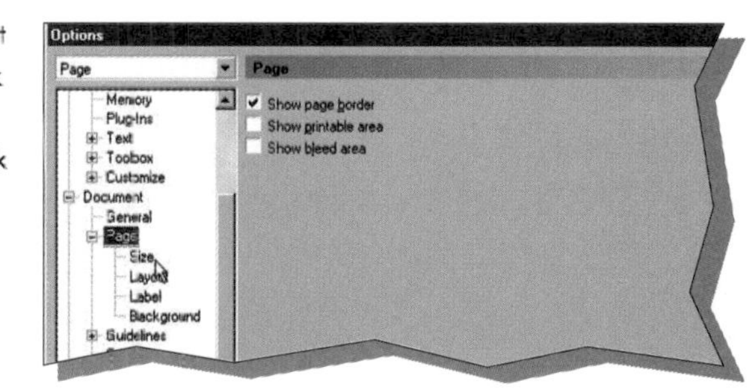

3 In the centre of the dialog box, select Custom for Paper and pixels for the units of measurement. Then choose the resolution – 96 works best for most computers. (CorelDRAW suggests using your printer resolution, but this will make the image too small.) Finally, type in the width and height measurements you want for your graphic, then click OK.

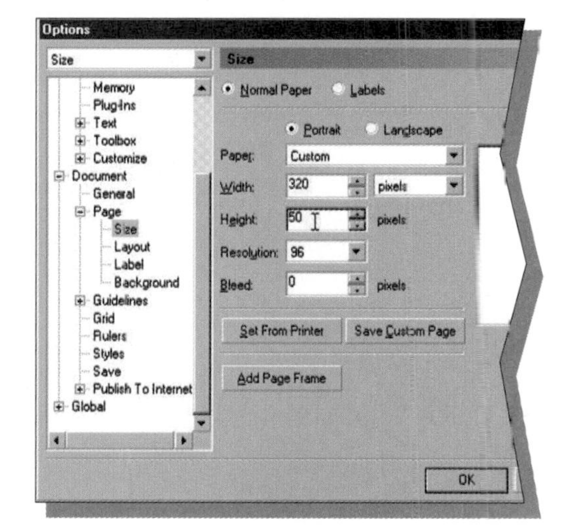

4 The drawing area is now much smaller, and CorelDRAW's Property Bar shows the dimensions of your image. The rulers are also marked in pixels.

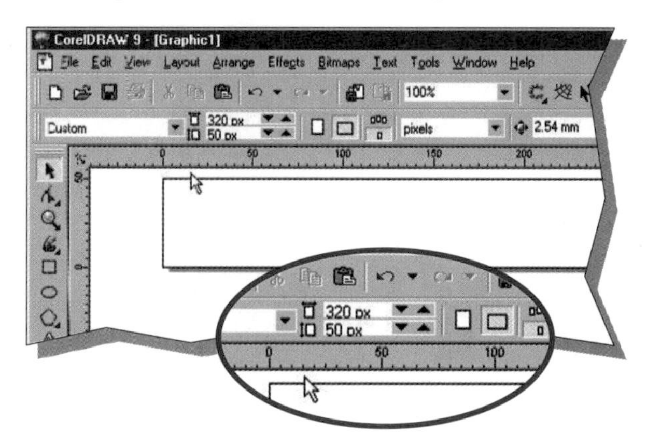

5 Design your picture using a combination of text, graphics and special effects.

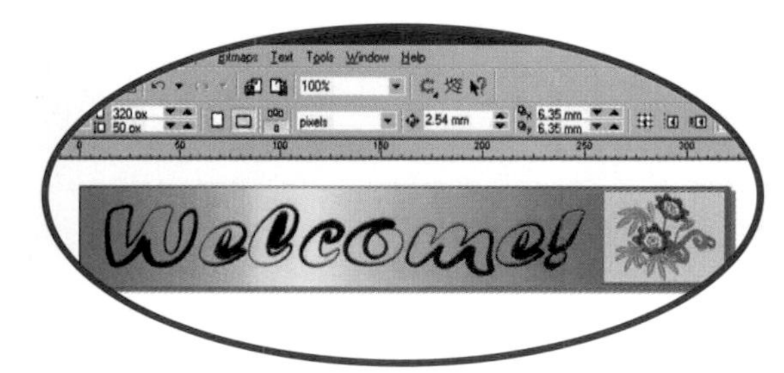

6 Save your design as a CorelDRAW graphic (CDR) and then select Publish To Internet from the File menu. Follow the instructions given in Steps 4-8 on the previous page, but this time select Single Image with Image Map in the first Wizard screen.

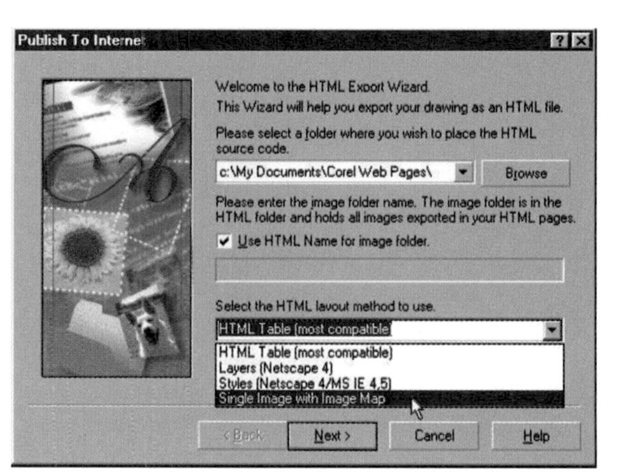

7 CorelDRAW saves the graphic file in the folder you selected in the Wizard and then previews it with your Web browser program. Now just open the Web page you want the image to appear in, and insert it.

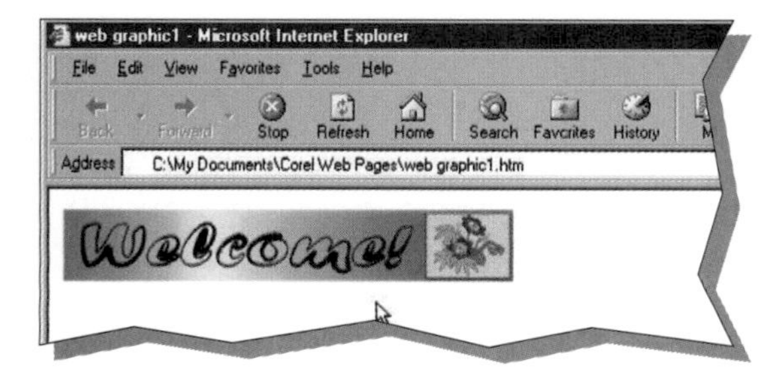

PC TIPS

Many Web authors create all their Web images at high resolutions, even if they plan to use smaller versions in their Web pages. This is because it is easy to make a good quality, smaller version of a high-resolution picture than vice versa. Use CorelPHOTO-PAINT to create a smaller version of any image by using the Resample command on the Image menu.

Customizing CorelDRAW

When you work with a program for an extended period of time, you develop your own way of getting things done, possibly without noticing you're doing it. CorelDRAW is no exception.

You can alter the appearance of CorelDRAW on your screen and have your favourite tools just a keypress away when you know how to customize.

With a complex program such as CorelDRAW you might be happy to stick to the main menus; or perhaps you might prefer to dip into the realm of the experienced user and memorize the many keyboard shortcuts available. There are many more things you can do to make yourself feel more comfortable within the CorelDRAW program and which will enable you to carry out your tasks quickly and easily.

In common with so much of CorelDRAW, the options for customization are both plentiful and varied. Making the effort to get to grips with them in the short term can pay off handsomely in the long run.

● Shortcuts to faster drawing

Assigning keyboard shortcuts to regular tasks is one of the most common ways of customizing any program, enabling you to work more quickly and easily. There are a lot of preset shortcuts already, but you might well prefer to assign your own – either because what you need is not covered or because you find the standard ones hard to remember. If you wish, you can set up numerous shortcut configurations, which you can use for certain projects or certain types of files.

It's always a good idea when assigning a keyboard shortcut to use a combination that's relevant, and therefore easier to remember. Some classic examples of shortcuts which are built into all Windows programs are [Ctrl]+[S] for Save, or [Ctrl]+[P] for Print. Whether or not you have assigned customized shortcut keys, you can print out the full range as a handy reference (see page 68, Step 7).

● Assigning shortcuts

You could make life easier by 'labelling' the keys that have shortcuts, although all but the function keys have too little space around them to allow this to be practical.

If you prefer using the mouse to the keyboard, you'll be pleased to know that CorelDRAW's menus are just as customizable as the keyboard shortcuts. You can change the position of menus, as well as adding and removing commands, menu separators and so on.

You can also customize toolbars by changing their size, position and appearance – deciding whether you want them to be floating or locked in position on one edge of the window. With the colour palette, you can move and remove colours and create custom palettes for specialist tasks.

The Customize options

Go to the Tools drop-down menu in CorelDRAW and you will find that one of the choices is Options. Click on this to bring up the Customize options, some of which we show you here.

There are five separate sub-sections to choose from in the Customize section of the Options dialog box (right). From here you can change several aspects of CorelDRAW to suit your own specification. For example, if you want to change the menus, click Customize and then Menus to see what the available options are.

The Color Palette is the most simple to customize, having just six options. You might find it easier to work with more colours visible (right) and to increase the size of the swatches.

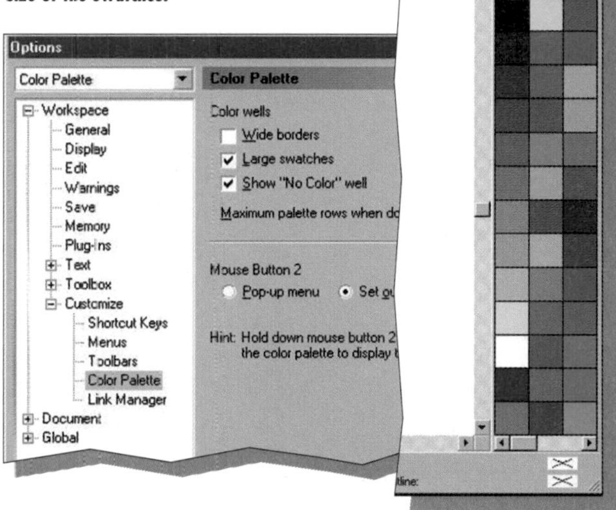

To place your favourite functions on the toolbar of your choice, simply click on the Toolbars sub-section and find the command in the list. Drag the icon (highlighted in the panel on the right) to exactly where you want it on the toolbar.

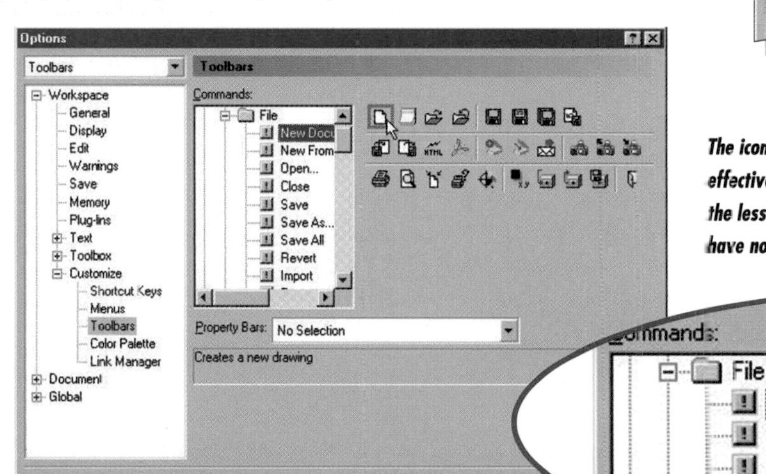

The icons that appear on toolbars throughout all Windows programs are usually quite effective at communicating the particular function they represent. However, some of the less common ones (inset below) might still leave you confused, especially if you have not used them for a while, so make a note of any shortcuts you add.

Adding a shortcut

Here we show you how to add a keyboard shortcut. It will save time if you add several shortcuts in one go.

1 Start up CorelDRAW and open a new document. Then, from the Tools menu, select Options.

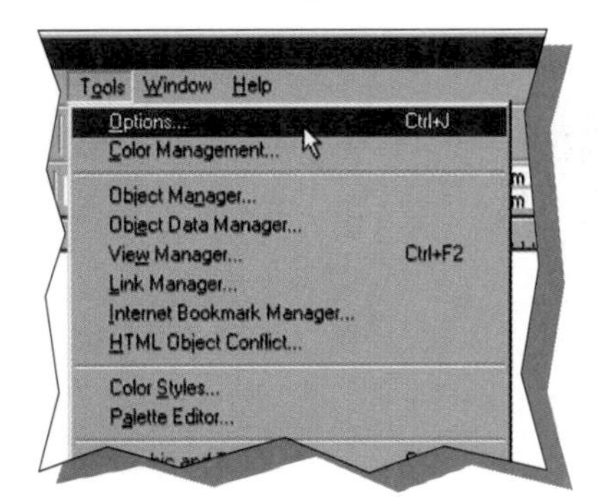

2 Click on Customize and then Shortcut keys. Use the Commands panel in the centre to find the command you want a shortcut for. We've chosen the Simple WireFrame command, which is in the Display Folder, found inside the View & Display Folder. Click on the Simple WireFrame command.

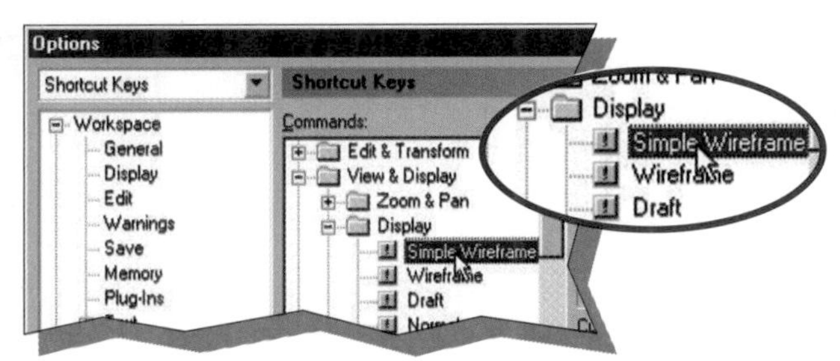

3 Click in the Press new shortcut key box, hold down the [Ctrl] key and press the [W]. CorelDRAW tells you that this combination is currently assigned to the Refresh Window command.

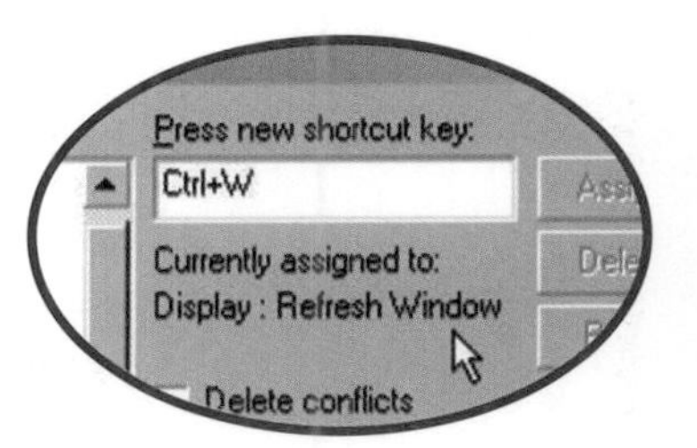

4 We could replace the original shortcut (see PC Tips box, right), but we'll try another combination. We still want to use the W (for WireFrame), so we're going to go for [Ctrl]+[Shift]+[W] together. Replace the [Ctrl]+[W] text you added in Step 3 with this new shortcut. Now click Assign.

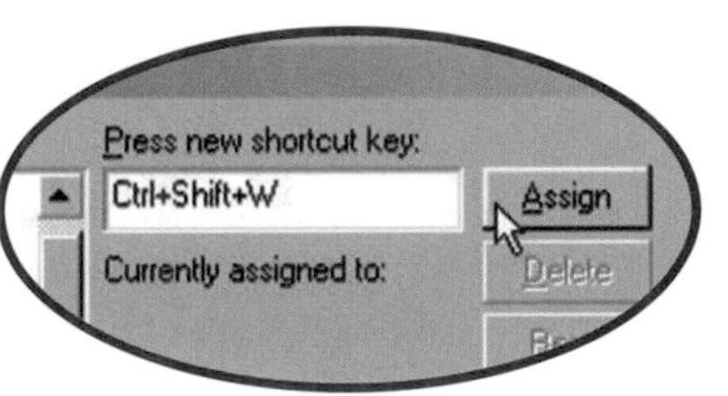

5 This new shortcut appears in the Current shortcut keys panel. Press the OK button.

6 You can try your new shortcut immediately. For this wireframe shortcut, open any CorelDRAW picture and press [Ctrl]+[SHIFT]+[W] to see it change into a simpler outline view.

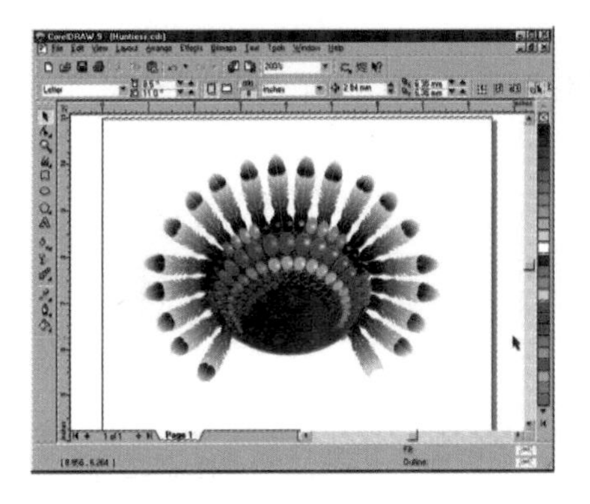

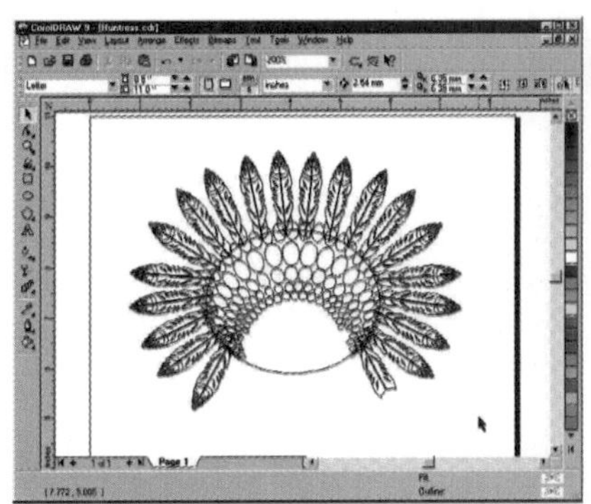

7 You can add as many extra shortcuts as you like by following the same process. If you want to see the full set of shortcuts, click the View All button in the Options dialog box. You can browse the list or click the Print button to make a hard copy reference.

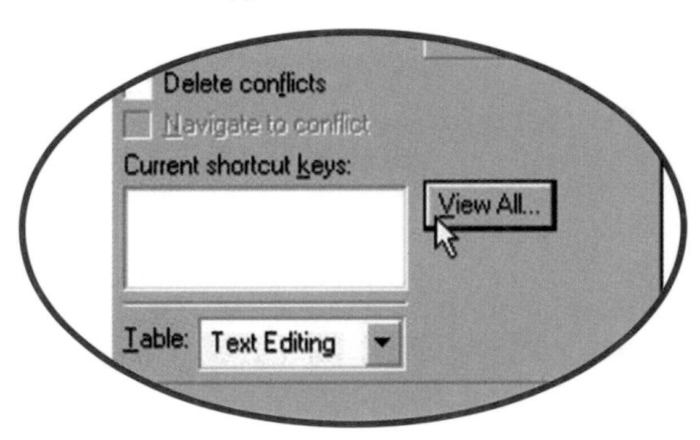

Shortcut Keys

Command	Table	KeyStroke	Description
Align & Distribute : ...	Main	B	Aligns selected obj...
Align & Distribute : ...	Main	P	Aligns the centers o...
Align & Distribute : ...	Main	E	Horizontally aligns t...
Align & Distribute : ...	Main	L	Aligns selected obj...
Align & Distribute : ...	Main	R	Aligns selected obj...
Align & Distribute : ...	Main	T	Aligns selected obj...
Align & Distribute : ...	Main	C	Vertically aligns the ...
Display : Full-Scree...	Main	F9	Displays a full-scree...
Display : Refresh ...	Main	Ctrl+W	Redraws the drawi...
Display : Toggle Di...	Main	Shift+F9	Toggles between t...
Dockers : Linear Di...	Main	Alt+F2	Contains functions f...
Editing Commands :...	Main	Ctrl+C	Copies the selectio...
Editing Commands :...	Main	Ctrl+Insert	Copies the selectio...
Editing Commands :...	Main	Ctrl+Shift+A	Copies specified pr...
Editing Commands :...	Main	Ctrl+X	Cuts the selection a...
Editing Commands :...	Main	Shift+Delete	Cuts the selection a...
Editing Commands :...	Main	Delete	Deletes the selecte...
Editing Commands :...	Main	Ctrl+D	Duplicates the sele...
Editing Commands :...	Main	Ctrl+V	Pastes the Clipboar...
Editing Commands :...	Main	Shift+Insert	Pastes the Clipboar...

Export to CSV | Print | Close | Help

PC TIPS

Replacing existing shortcuts

If you do want to change an existing shortcut to a new command (see Step 4), just put a tick in the Navigate to conflict box before pressing the Assign button. Then, when you do press the Assign button, CorelDRAW will immediately let you choose another combination for the other command.

Delete conflicts
Navigate to conflict
Current shortcut keys:

Making customized menus

Here we demonstrate how to generate your own custom menus by creating a new menu for zoom commands. This will enable you to access the commands directly rather than as a sub-menu off the View menu.

1 Bring up the Options dialog box and select the Menus section in the Customize group on the left. Open up the View & Display folder in the Commands list and then the Zoom & Pan folder.

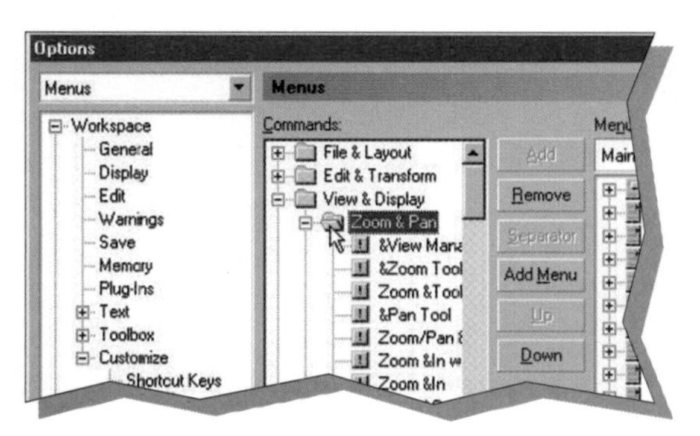

2 With the Zoom & Pan Folder selected, click the Add Menu button.

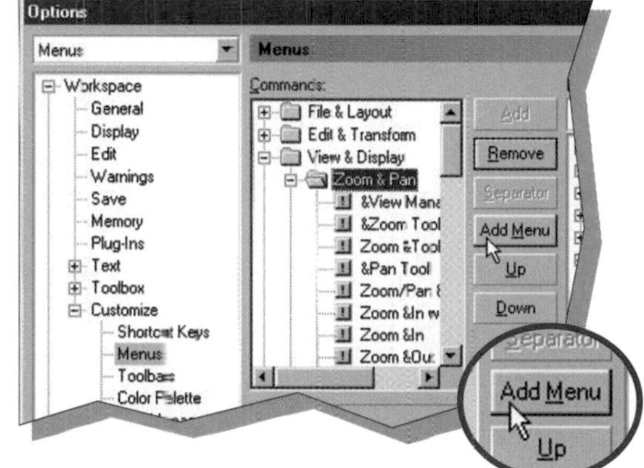

3 A new menu (called Menu) appears in the list on the right. Type in the name &Zoom. The ampersand (&) character is very important (see [Alt] key shortcuts box, right).

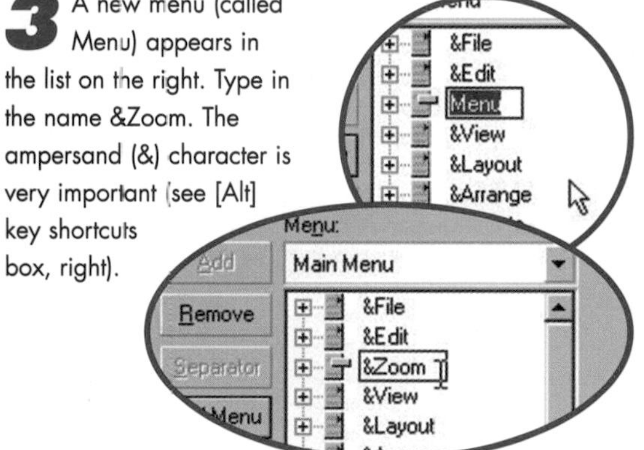

4 The menus are listed in the order that they will appear on the menu bar, from left to right. Move the menu into position by clicking the Down and/or Up buttons (you can move the other menu entries around this way as well).

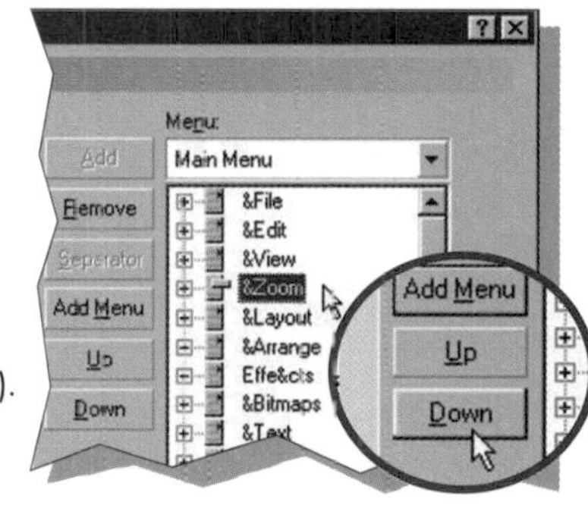

5 Open up the Zoom & Pan folder in the Commands panel, as in Step 1, and click on the first command, &View Manager. Click the Add button.

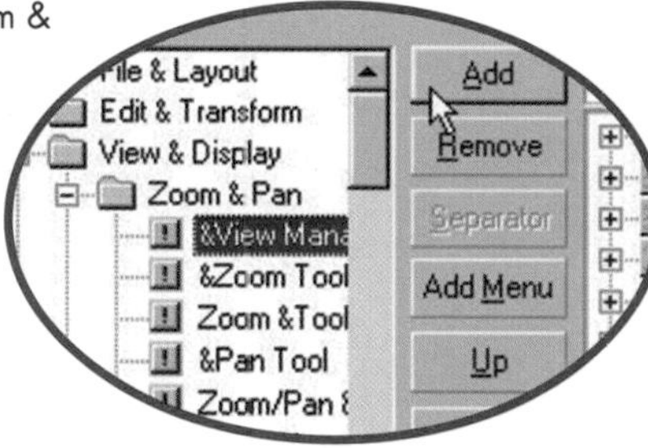

6 Click the Separator button to add a line between the View Manager menu entry and the subsequent menu commands.

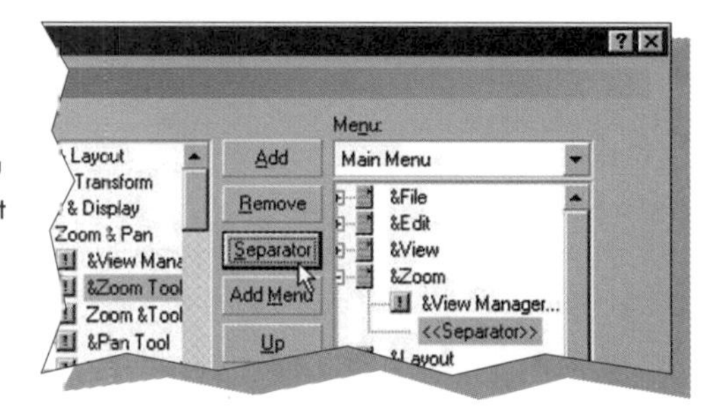

7 Click on each of the View and Pan commands in turn, pressing the Add button to include them in your new menu. Then click the OK button to return to CorelDRAW.

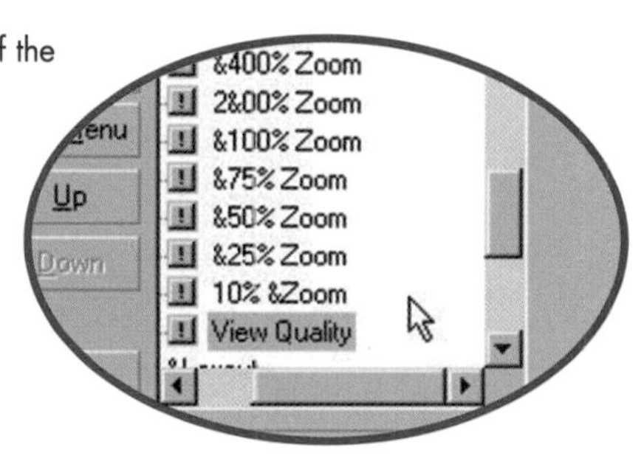

8 You'll now see your Zoom menu entry in CorelDRAW's menu. Click on it and you'll see the commands you added.

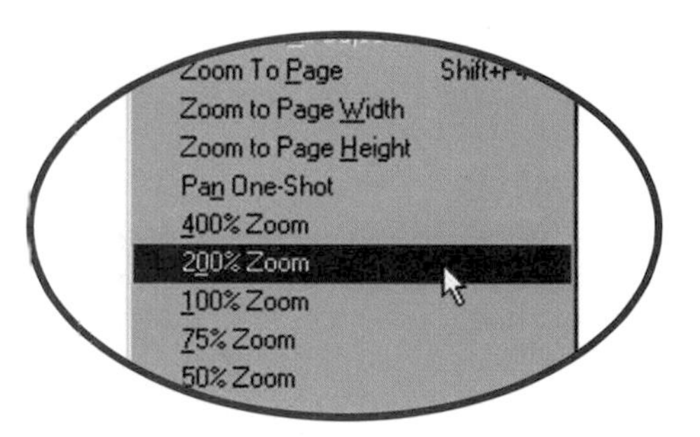

[ALT] KEY SHORTCUTS

You might have noticed that the menus and options in many programs have a line under one of the letters. The F in the File menu and the H in the Help menu are almost always underlined. Pressing the [Alt] key together with the underlined character selects that menu (or option), just as if you had clicked it with the mouse. Many PC users find this quicker than using the mouse, as their fingers can stay on the keyboard. Adding an & character to the shortcut (see Step 3) puts an underline below the character that follows it.

Creating a business card

CorelDRAW is perfect for creating professional-looking business cards. There's no need to commit yourself to a long print run, you can just print them out as needed, changing the details on them when you want.

Business cards are handy things – and not just for businessmen, either. They used to be called visiting cards and were usually carried by rather grand people who used them to pass on their personal details or to register a social call.

Given that most people have details that they want to pass on from time to time, whether personal or for business, at social or professional functions, a card can be very useful for practically everyone. It is certainly more efficient than writing your phone number on the back of an envelope.

● Creating a good impression

We're going to show you how to create a business card, although the same principles apply to personal cards. Your card is your public face and it's often all the person you give it to will have as a reminder of your meeting. It should display the essential information (see below) very clearly, but it should also possess a style that underlines the image you want to project. Obviously, that can vary enormously from person to person and company to company.

● Go with your logo

If you have a business, it's possible that you will already have a company logo, typeface and so on. If this is the case, creating a business card will simply be a matter of applying these harmoniously on the right-sized card. Doing this brings together many aspects of CorelDRAW that we have covered before. What's more, you can apply the same principles to other company stationery that you might need, such as a compliments slip, sticky labels or a company Christmas card.

● Important details

A business card should include certain essential information, which for most people means name, job title, address and telephone numbers (home/office, mobile and fax), clearly arranged underneath a corporate logo. Other information to put on the card might include Web and email addresses. The name of your company is also a good idea, if it's not clearly legible on the logo.

The design of a personal card can be much more flexible. You might even want to have more than one personal card, depending on the occasion. You might, for example, want to give out your telephone number, but not your address, or perhaps your email address and not your telephone number, and so on. There is rather less pressure to include a logo

You get only one chance to make a good first impression – and business cards are a great way of doing just that.

on a personal card, but a little artistic or possibly abstract imagery can work very well. However, choose the image carefully to ensure it gives the right impression. A picture of a large and powerful sports car, for example, might convey an inappropriate impression of yourself to others.

● Mean business

If you're self-employed, you might also have a business card (with or without a logo). However, if you do the occasional freelance work, you might want to keep your card much simpler and style it on personal lines, perhaps with a description of what you do (journalist, decorator or whatever). In the steps on the following pages, we take you through the procedure for creating a business card, making the most of a few new CorelDRAW tricks along the way.

We're going to start our design by opening up a sample file that is included with CorelDRAW. This will give us a few pointers and a basic outline to start working on. We'll then take it apart and begin to build it back up again as we want.

Once you've worked your way through our examples, you might want to do something similar but this time creating a unique card that is tailored to the needs of your business.

Printing your cards

Depending on the specific make and model of the printer you have access to, there will be different options for printing out your completed business cards.

Create a really great impression by making sure the smart card design you create is printed out as well as possible, using high-quality card.

ONCE YOU'VE gone to all the trouble of designing your business card, you have to print it out. CorelDRAW is extremely efficient for short runs: it will automatically print out ten copies on a single piece of paper. However, you don't really want a card printed on ordinary paper – you need something more substantial. There are a few printing options you can explore.

It might be possible to print straight onto a card of reasonable weight direct from your printer. Check your printer documentation – you might be surprised at what your printer can handle. The simpler your printer's mechanism, the more flexibility you have when it comes to card. Laser printers can have quite complicated paper paths, and paper often goes through several tight turns inside the machine. This makes thicker card a problem because it often jams. Inkjet printers usually have straight paper paths, so thicker paper and cards are less likely to get stuck. If there is a jam, inkjets are much easier to clear – simply pull the offending article out.

● Making cards

If your printer documentation recommends using only special lightweight paper, the result will be flimsy. To get around this, use some spray mount (a lightweight glue in an aerosol can), available from graphics stores. Spray the back of the printout and stick it to a backing of card. Cut them to size with a ruler and a scalpel or craft knife after you have stuck the paper on – don't try to stick the paper to cut-out cards one at a time. If you do it well – it might take a bit of practice – the finished cards will be perfectly acceptable. Another solution is to get your cards professionally printed.

Note that printing costs tend to be considerably more expensive the more colours you use. Most business cards use two colours: usually black plus one 'spot' colour for highlighting key details. That would be fine for the first card we create, but not the second. If you wanted to get the second card printed professionally without it costing a fortune, you would have to either convert the picture to monochrome (black and white), or to a duotone (involving one other, additional colour).

Designing a business card

We're going to open up an existing CorelDRAW business card and edit it for our own purposes, at the same time introducing you to a few of CorelDRAW's tricks. The card we're going to produce is for a fictional 'Bob Jensen', who sets up hi-fi systems and advises on sound and acoustics.

1 Start CorelDRAW and select New From Template from the File menu. From the CorelDRAW business card templates in the Template Wizard dialog box, select Litbcard. If a dialog box pops up saying that fonts are missing and others are being substituted, click OK.

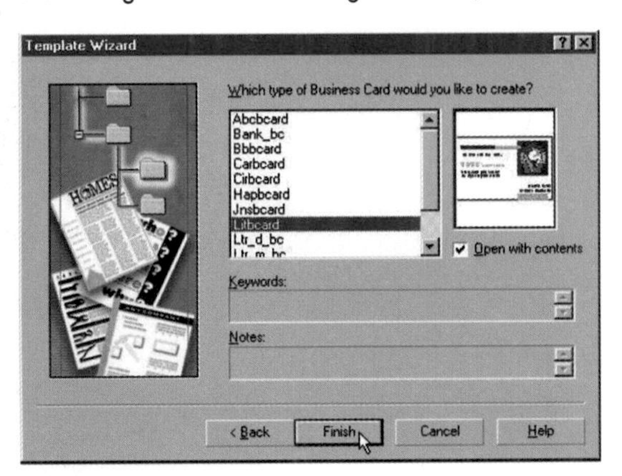

2 The file you've opened is a bright and breezy, but still reasonably formal, business card. The first thing we want to do is replace the main image on the right with something else. Click on it and delete it. Later we'll overtype the text with the new details.

3 We're going to use one of the symbol fonts that comes with CorelDRAW. Insert the main CorelDRAW disc (disc 1) in your CD-ROM drive and install the 'MusicalSymbols' font (see Stage 3, pages 16-17). You'll find this font in the Fonts\Symbols folder on the CD-ROM.

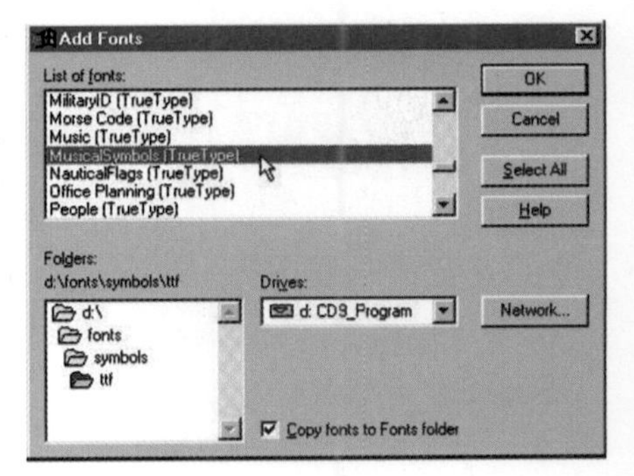

4 We want the bass clef symbol in the MusicalSymbols typeface. This is entered simply by typing a question mark using the Text tool (see Stage 2, page 74).

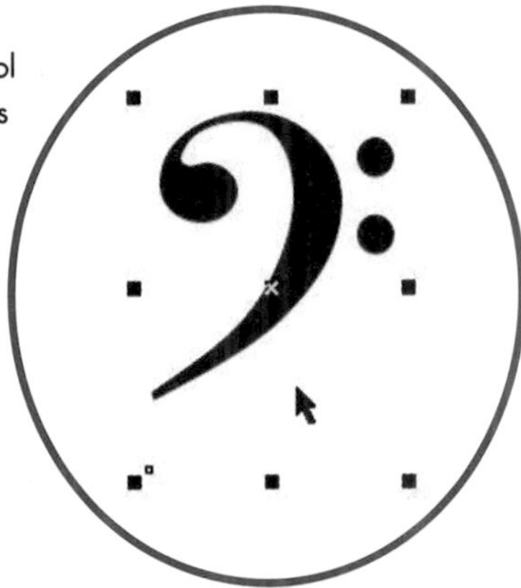

5 Click on the Interactive Blend tool button and then select the Interactive Extrude tool (selected in inset below). Click on the bass clef and drag the mouse slightly up and to the right. Move the 'X' handle to adjust the effect if necessary.

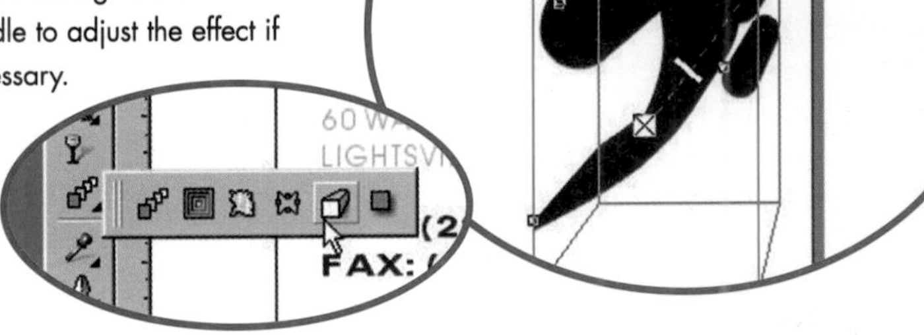

6 Notice that the bass clef now has depth. Click the colour wheel tab on the Property Bar. Select Use Color Shading, leave the From as black, but change the To to a different colour.

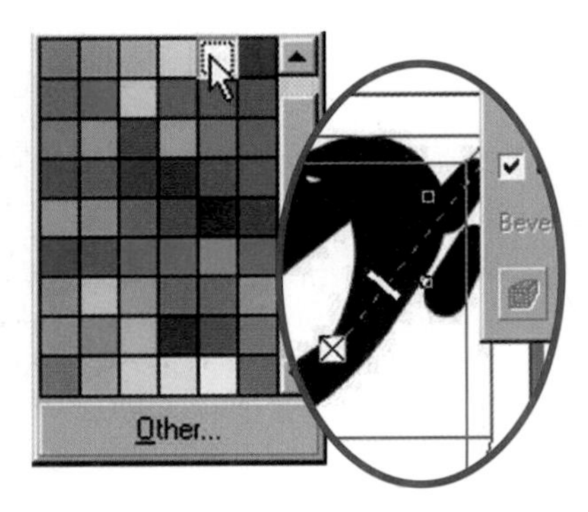

7 Now rotate the symbol. First, click on it twice (slowly so that CorelDRAW doesn't interpret the action as a double click), and then drag the rotation handles that appear around the symbol. When you're happy with how it looks, select the bass clef image and enlarge it by dragging the corner of the text box.

8 The rest is reasonably straightforward. We've edited the text, filling in the new information for Bob Jensen in place of the old. You'll almost certainly need to adjust the text size and spacing to make your information fit the available space. We've also changed the colours to suit the nature of the business. Now save your file.

Creating an advanced business card

Here we're going to create a more personal business card. While it shows less information than the previous card, it still enables this landscape designer to get her message across. A high-quality design is important in this instance as it conveys an impression of creativity to potential clients.

1 Open up the CorelDRAW file you created in the previous exercise, but save it with a different, relevant name and delete everything on the page. On this card, we're starting from scratch. The most interesting part of this exercise is putting the graphic across the top. Insert the photos CorelDRAW CD (disc 2) in the drive, then, from the File menu, select Import and open up Natur12l (it's in the Tiles\Nature\Large Folder).

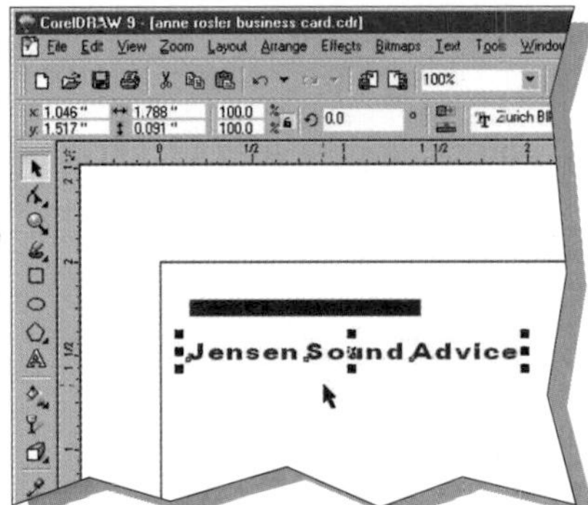

2 Grab hold of a corner of the picture with the Pick tool and expand it until it's a little wider than the width of the card.

3 Use the Shape Tool to crop the picture so that it sits along the top of the card, with a depth of 2cm or so. Pay attention to the group of flowers you are selecting.

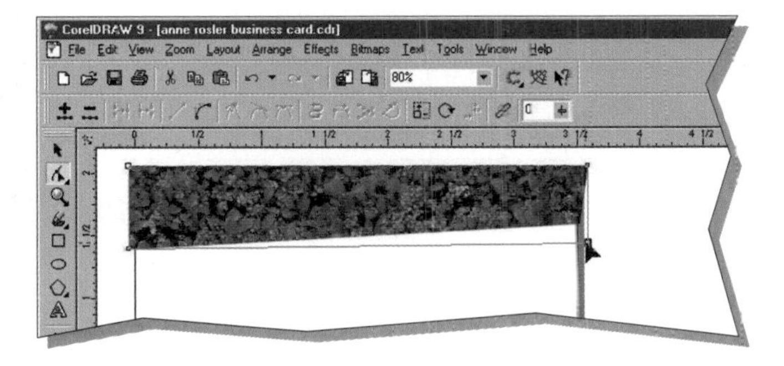

4 From the Tools menu, select the Interactive Transparency tool. (We looked at the Transparency tool in Stage 2, pages 84-87.)

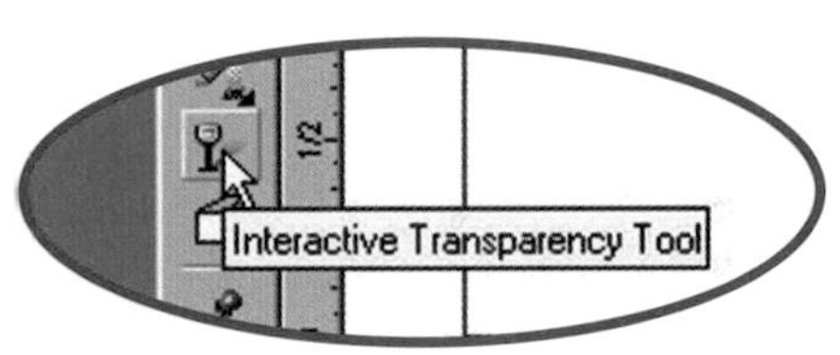

5 Click and drag from the top left to the bottom right of the flower picture so that it starts solid in the top left and fades out in the bottom right.

6 Click on the first node (the start point) and set the transparency on the slider bar to around 20 (solid). Click on the second node (the end point) and set the transparency to 100 (totally transparent).

7 You now have a pale area on the right-hand side so that any text that runs over the picture will be clearly legible. Now you can add your text: we've used repeated text in different colours to improve our overall design (see Stage 3, pages 70-73). Note how the colour we have chosen for the repeated text matches the colour of the flowers in the picture.

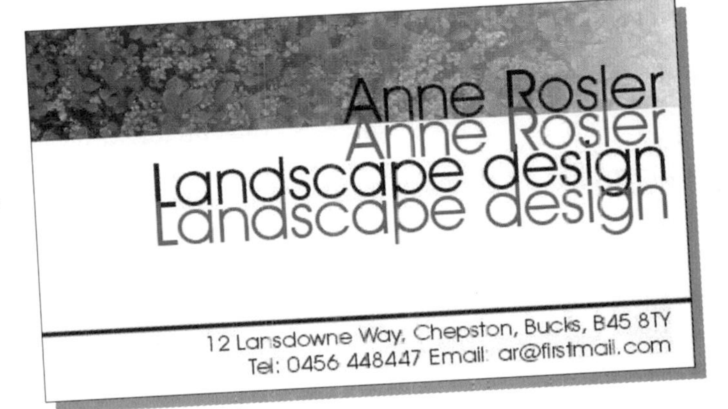

PC TIPS

Less is more

When designing, follow the 'less is more' rule. Keep it simple and try not to get too carried away with colours and fonts.

Colour and CorelDRAW

Apart from drawing skills, an important technique to master in CorelDRAW is the selection of colours. This will enable you to show your drawings off to best effect.

Don't be fooled simply because CorelDRAW shows you only 100 colours in its palette. There are, in fact, millions to choose from. Obviously, a full palette of millions of colours is impossible to show on a screen.

If you use only the colours shown in the basic CorelDRAW palette, you might already have struck limitations in making your pictures look realistic. You might have found that the exact colour or tone of your work is hard to achieve.

● The basic palette

The basic palette has a fair number of greys, slate blues, greens, browns and a smattering of bright, saturated colours, but for practical purposes there's a distinct lack of reds, yellows and creams and very few blues. If you were limited to using just these few colours, many styles of drawing would be impossible. Fortunately, CorelDRAW provides several ways of adding extra colour flexibility.

CorelDRAW lets you see the full range of colours available for a shape if you right-click on it and select Properties. If you click an Edit button to bring up the Uniform Fill dialog box, this gives you access to all the possible colours (see Colour choice box, right).

● Choosing and adding colours

You can choose new colours as and when you use them, or you can add them to the basic CorelDRAW palette. The latter option makes sense if you want to use, say, sets of three or four matching or contrasting colours consistently for a range of designs – letterheads, business cards, compliments slips and so on. This means that they're never more than a single click away. However, the danger of doing this is that you can 'lose' them in among the basic colours. After a while, you might forget which are yours and use the wrong ones, thus risking inconsistency from one design to the next.

● Multiple palettes

To overcome this, you can set up your own palettes of colour, creating different selections for different types of drawing or design. This is the best way of selecting colours when working on very different types of picture. For example, use a Web-orientated palette of colours that display clearly on-screen to make graphics for a Web page and a palette of soft, natural tones for illustrations of landscapes.

Apart from CorelDRAW's basic palette, there are dozens of ready-made palettes for tackling different types of design. For example, a selection of green and red shades is ideal for Christmas designs, while another packed with bluey-greys is great for simulating metallic sheens on objects in technical drawings. You can also work with several palettes at the same time, picking and choosing colours from any of them. If you find a drawing full of useful colours, you can save its palette for use in your own designs.

COLOUR CHOICE

The Uniform Fill dialog box lets you choose colours from the many millions available. You can either type colour values into the Components boxes, or use the square and vertical slider on the left to choose a colour by simply pointing and clicking.

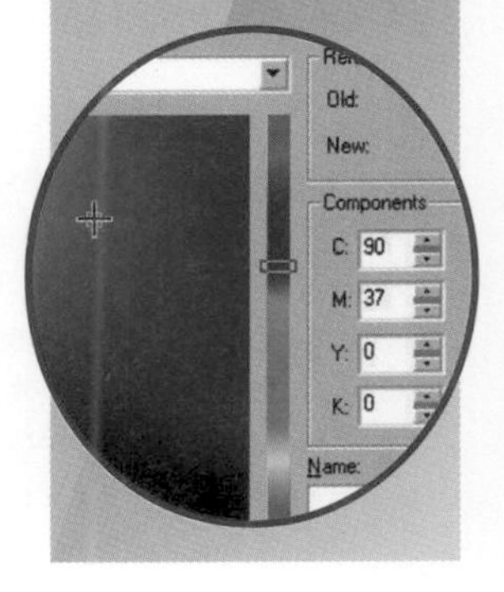

Choosing colours

There's more to choosing colours than just picking something that looks good on the screen. Here are the factors to consider.

ALWAYS BEAR IN mind the eventual purpose of your drawings and designs – what might look good on screen can look very different on paper. Your hours of designing can be ruined by poor colour reproduction. But there are ways to avoid such problems.

● Colour models

The main reason why colours look different on screen and on paper is that the two ways of creating colours are very different. On the computer screen, colours are made by combining different amounts of red, green and blue (RGB). By contrast, colours on paper are made up of dots of cyan, magenta, yellow and black (CMYK). These systems are known as colour models. CorelDRAW lets you use whichever type of colour model that suits the ultimate destination of your images. (It also has more models than RGB and CMYK for different types of professional graphics output.)

● Light and colour

There's another reason why colours that look great on screen might translate badly to the printed page. The colours you see on a page depend very much on the colour of light striking the paper. A page viewed under fluorescent lights looks different from the same page viewed under natural daylight because daylight tends to be slightly bluer than artificial lighting.

By contrast, the dots of colour on a computer screen transmit light. Although they are still somewhat susceptible to the colour of ambient light in a room, there's less scope for drastic differences.

Professional graphic designers treat on-screen colours with suspicion. Many use screen colours merely as a guide and place their trust instead in colour-sample books. These contain hundreds of colour swatches with their CMYK colour values printed next to them. By choosing a colour from a book and typing in the CMYK colour values to make a CorelDRAW colour, designers can be sure of how their designs will look when their documents are finally printed.

The home user can't afford colour books, however, as they are very expensive and work only for professionally printed pages. But you can make your own colour swatch pages using your own printer (see page 77).

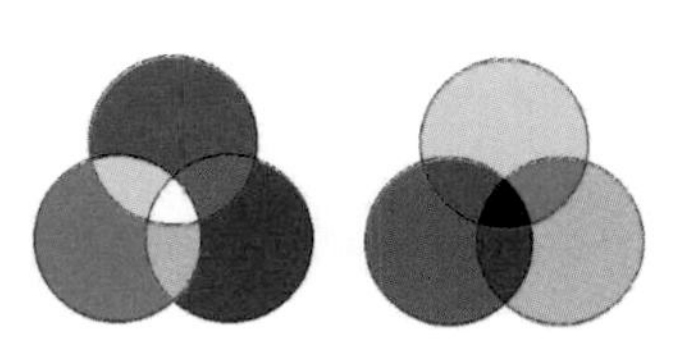

The two most-used colour models are RGB, for screen-based images (left), and CMYK, for printed pictures (right).

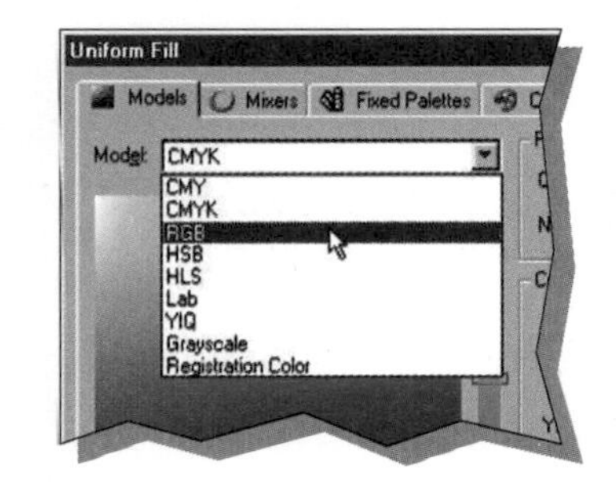

Choosing the right colour model is a vital but often overlooked part of the design process.

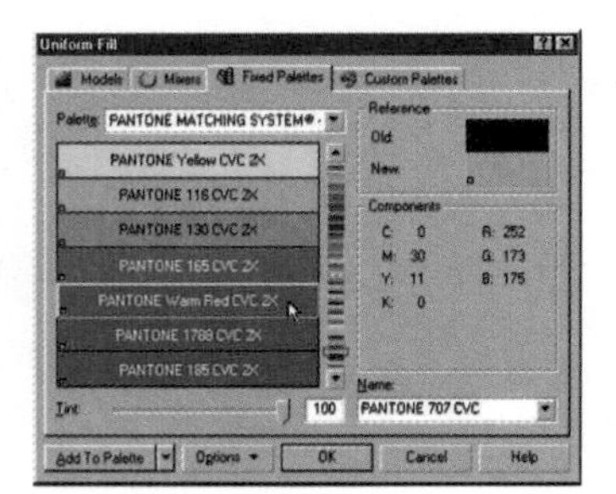

For 100 per cent guaranteed colour matching, professional designers and printers use Pantone colours – a massive range of solid inks that are uniform across the world.

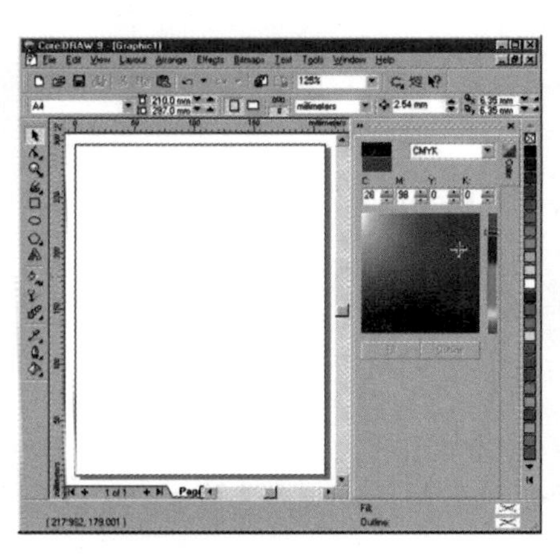

You can also use the different colour models from the Color Docker: click the Window menu, then Dockers and finally Color (see Stage 3, pages 74-75, for an explanation of Docker).

PC TIPS

Palette positioning

CorelDRAW palettes are usually locked to the right side of the CorelDRAW window and arranged in a single column of colours. To make it more convenient to select colours, you can turn any palette into a floating window: click the grey area at the top of the palette and drag it into the main part of the CorelDRAW window. The palette can also be enlarged by dragging its corner out so that you can get at all its colours without scrolling.

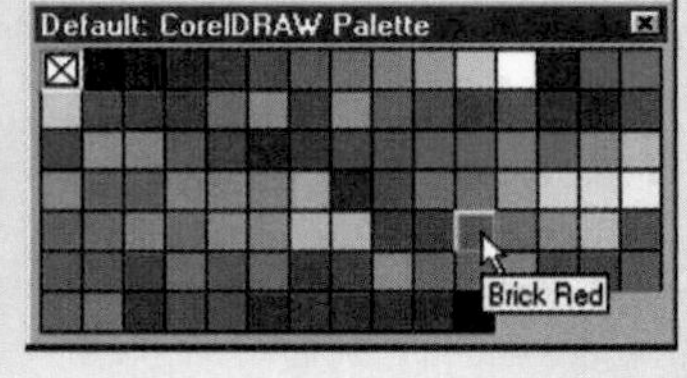

Working with palettes

CorelDRAW's basic colour palette gets you started, but add or create your own for better drawings.

1 Start CorelDRAW and click the Window menu. In the Color Palettes menu, select Palette Editor.

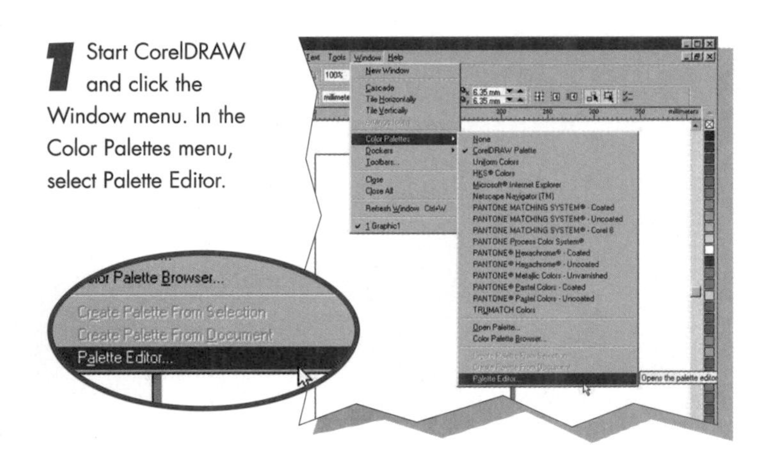

2 The window that pops up shows the limited range of colours in the standard CorelDRAW palette. To see what other palettes are available, select the Open Palette option from the list box at the top of the dialog box.

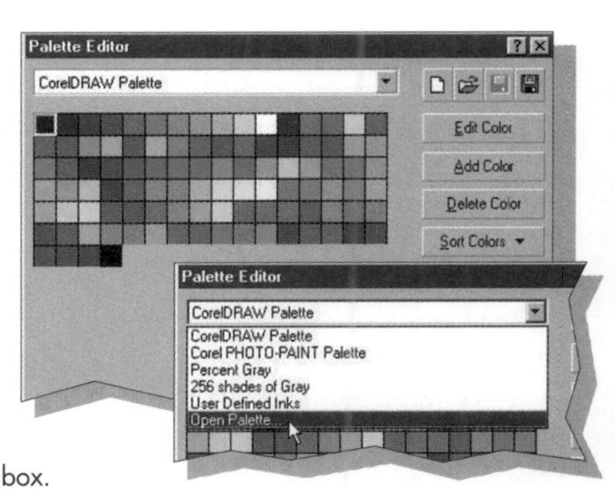

3 Use the Open Palette dialog box to choose a palette from CorelDRAW's Palettes folder. We have chosen cBlues.cpl in the Misc folder (located in the Palettes folder's CMYK folder).

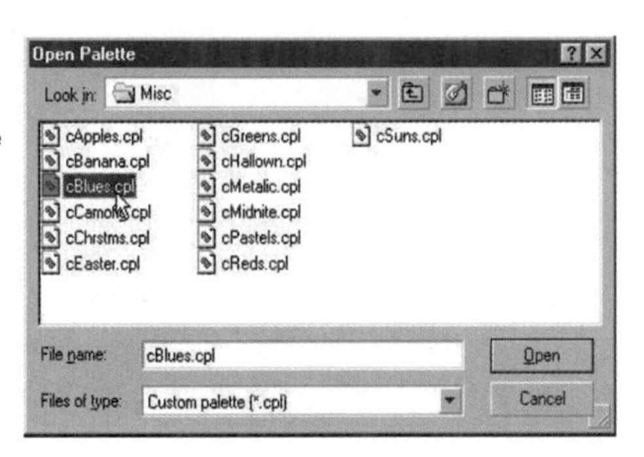

4 This palette contains dozens of blue tones – many more than the standard CorelDRAW palette. Click on a colour and the bottom of the dialog box shows the values that make up the colour.

5 If you want to create your own palette, click the New Palette button at the top of the dialog box. Give your palette a name.

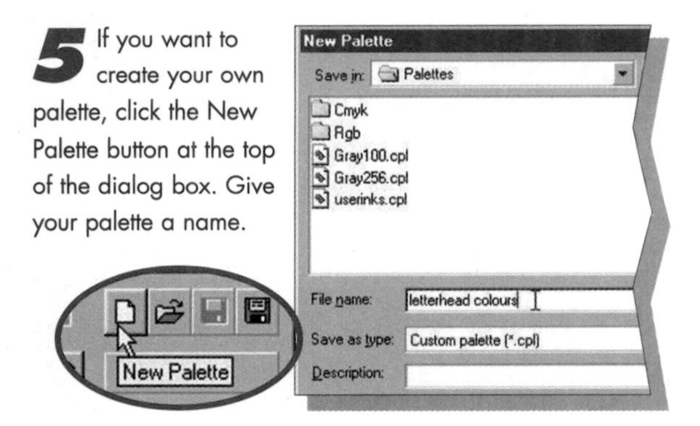

6 The palette starts off empty: click the Add Color button and then use the slider and pointer to choose a colour. Click the Add To Palette button. Repeat the process to choose more colours and click the Close button when finished.

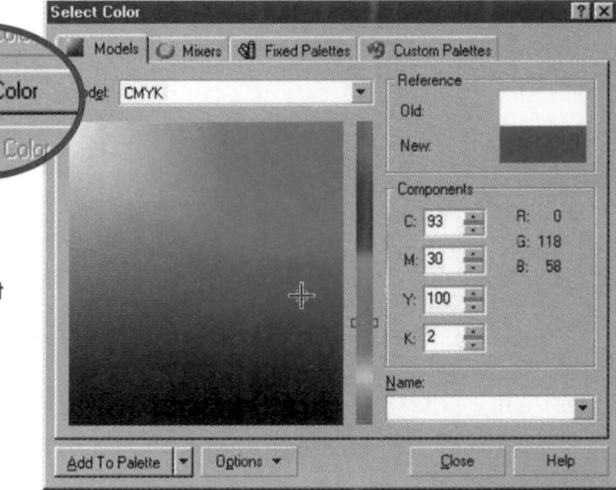

7 You can create palettes with as many or as few colours as you like. Click the Save Palette button when you've finished and then close the Palette Editor window.

8 To use your palette, click the Window menu, then Color Palettes and Open Palette. Select your palette and it appears just to the left of the standard palette; you can now use these colours in your drawing.

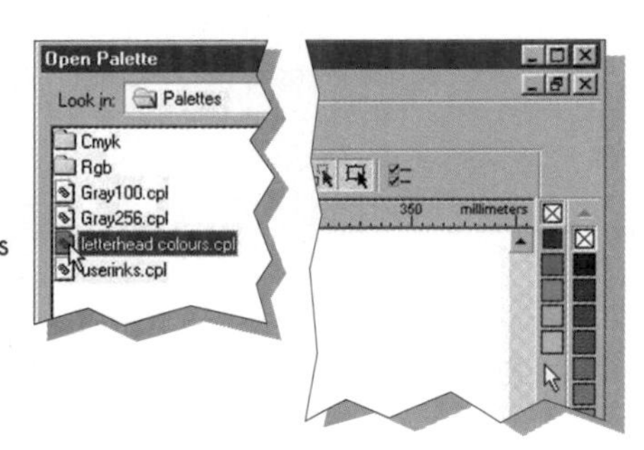

PC TIPS

Instant palettes

If you open a document – some CorelDRAW clip art or a drawing downloaded from the Internet, for example – and like the colours, there's a one-click method for creating a palette of the colours contained within it: click on the Windows menu and then Color Palettes. Choose the Create Palette From Document command.

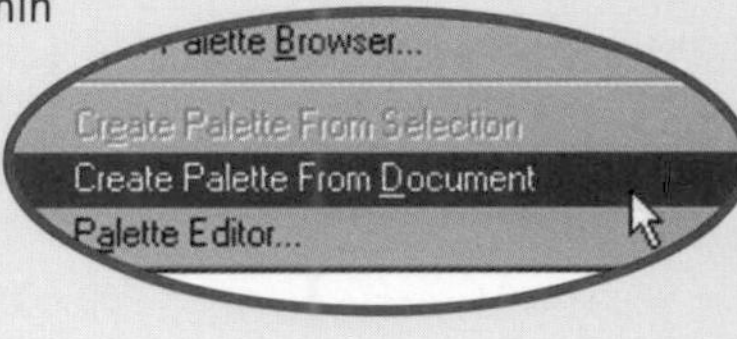

Print out your own colour swatches

If you want your drawings to print well, it's vital to check how different colours print out. Here's how to save time and paper by preparing some samples beforehand.

1 Start a new drawing in CorelDRAW and begin your colour swatch page by drawing a small square – approximately 1cm each side – at the top left of the page. Then right-click on the square and select Properties from the pop-up menu.

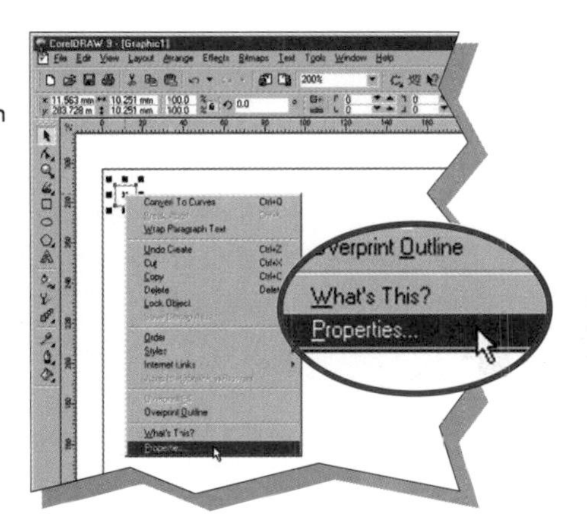

2 Click the Uniform Fill button on the Fill tab and then click the Edit button.

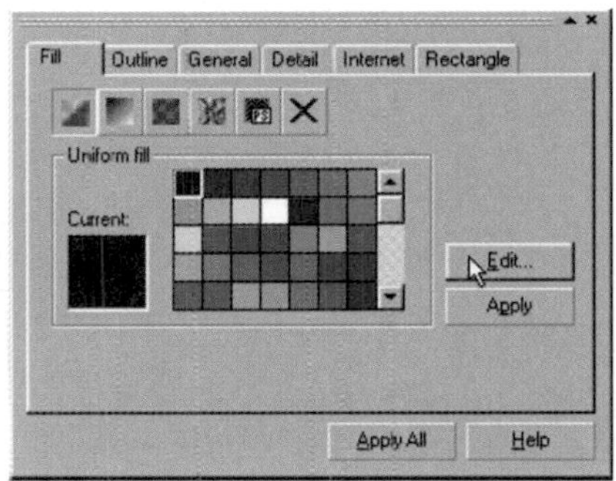

SPOT THE DIFFERENCE

Don't be misled by on-screen colours. Some squares on the screen might seem identical, but a paper printout will reveal subtle, but important, differences between them. Make a hard copy of the colour palette for reference. This will help to ensure your chosen colours are 'true'.

3 Use the Uniform Fill dialog box to select a start colour for your swatch. Here we want to make a printed swatch for medium-to-light, reddish-green colours, so we've opted for 0, 90, 90, 0 in the CMYK colour model. Click the Add To Palette button, then the OK button, and finally the Apply button to change the square's colour.

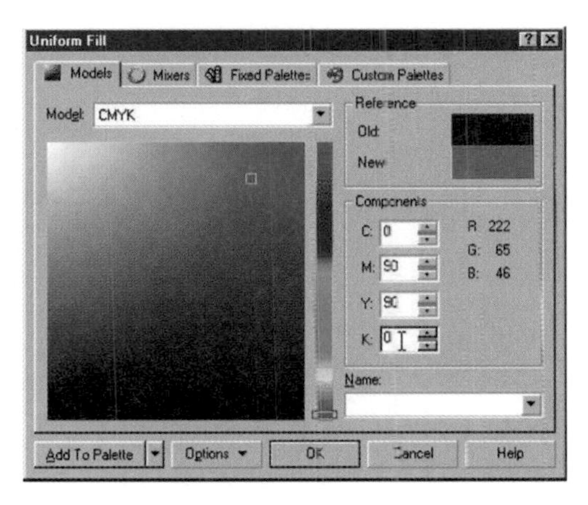

4 Duplicate the square and drag it over to the right side of the page, making sure it's at the same vertical position.

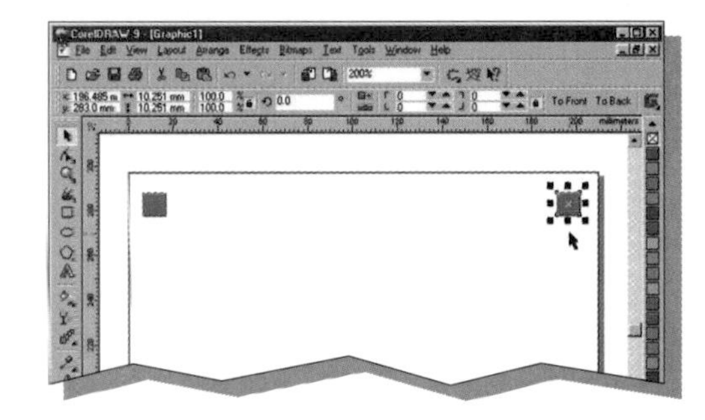

5 Select the second square and use the Edit button and Uniform Fill dialog box to select another colour; we've opted for 90, 0, 90, 0 in the CMYK model.

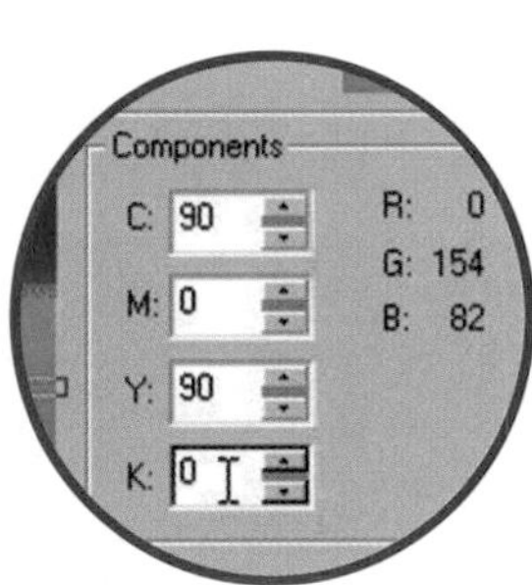

6 Now use the Interactive Blend Tool to create squares that blend from one colour to the next. You can get nine or 10 intermediate squares across a portrait A4 page and more if you create a landscape page.

7 Select all the squares and then press [Ctrl]+[D] to duplicate the row. Drag it under the first row and change the colours of the first and last squares. We've opted for lightening each row successively – decreasing the CMYK values equally. Notice that CorelDRAW automatically re-blends the colours with each change. Repeat for as many rows as you want and then save your swatch page. You can now print out the page to help you choose colours accurately.

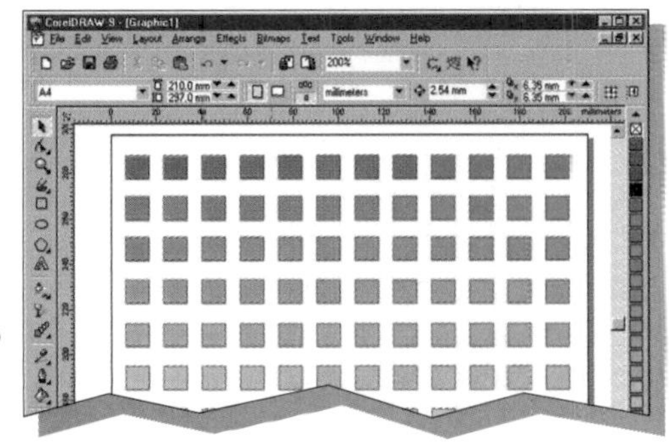

8 To use a colour in one of your drawings, open the swatch document and use the Eyedropper Tool to click on the colour you want. Then switch back to your drawing and use Color Docker's Fill button to colour any shape.

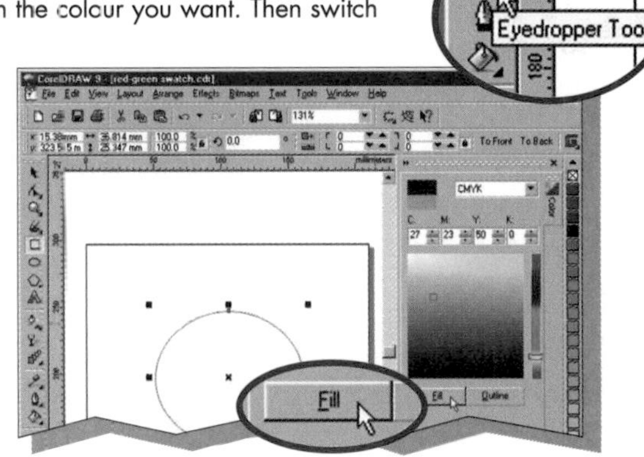

CorelDRAW™

Using Intersect and Weld to create complex shapes

We have now reached an advanced level in the CorelDRAW section of PCs made easy. Here we look at how to make the most creative use of everything we have learned so far.

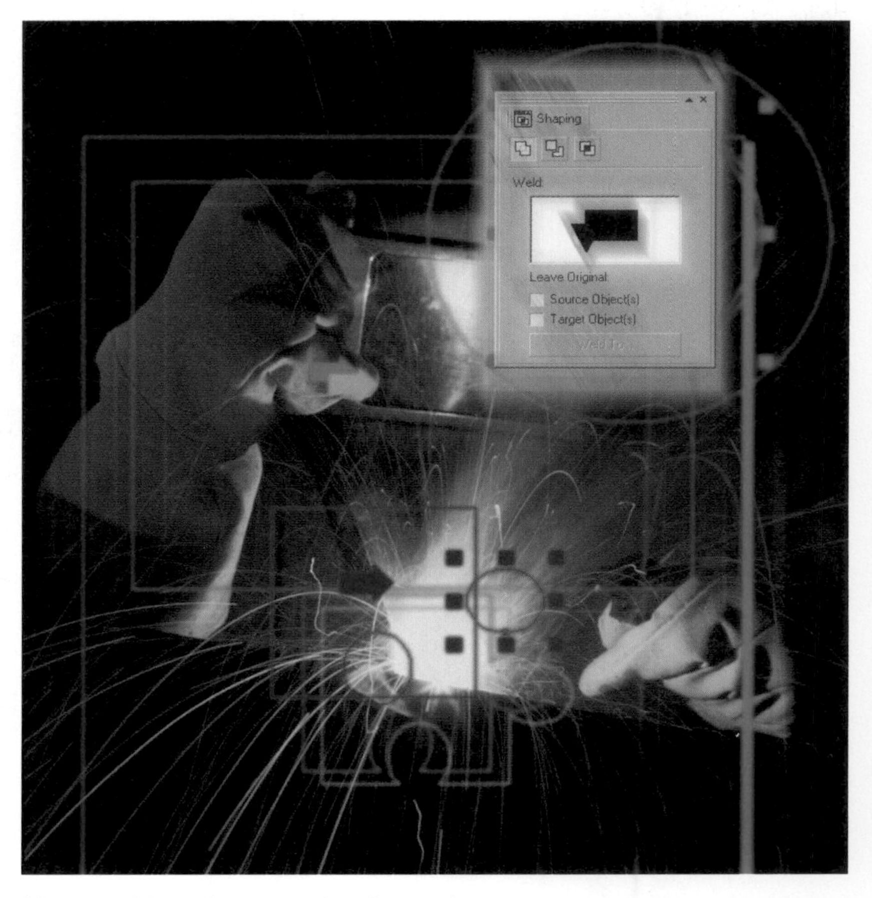

Make shapes in CorelDRAW do what you want by using the Intersect and Weld options.

If you've worked your way through all our CorelDRAW tutorials, you should have developed enough confidence with the program to embark on an advanced exercise. The CorelDRAW techniques described here aim to bring together much of what you have learned and also to add a few new methods for working with shapes.

We're going to show you how to use techniques called Intersect, Weld, Trim and Contour. Then we'll apply these techniques to create a smart cover sheet, ideal for situations where presentation is important, such as a dissertation or short story.

All these techniques are concerned with taking basic shapes and combining them, or adding to them in various ways to get more complex effects.

● Multiple object commands

Intersect, Weld and Trim are all available on the Properties bar when you select two or more, typically overlapping, objects with the Pick tool. Alternatively, you can call up the relevant dialog boxes from the Arrange menu. Their names give you some indication of what they do, but it's not always entirely clear which is the correct one to use at any given time.

Weld allows you to join together selected objects to create a single object. If the original objects overlap, this will leave you with a single outline. When you combine two or more objects, the newly welded shape takes on the fill and outline attributes of the target object. This is an important aspect to consider: if the formatting of two objects differs – perhaps one is red and the other is blue – welding them together forces the new shape to use one colour only. In order to preserve the different properties, you should use the Group command (see Stage 2, pages 88-89).

With the Intersect command you can create a new object that consists purely of the overlapping area between two or more objects (you can also choose whether to delete or keep the original shapes). Again, the new intersected object takes the fill and outline attributes of whichever of the originals you specify as the target. Trim is a sort of inverse of Intersect as it removes the area where objects overlap.

● Contours

The Contour command isn't, strictly speaking, a multiple-object command like those outlined above. Instead it creates an object composed

WHAT IT MEANS

TARGET

The target object is the last object you select before choosing one of these multiple-object commands. If objects have exactly the same properties, it doesn't matter which order you select them in. But, if they are different, think before selecting.

of several shapes based on a single original. In essence, it allows you to create concentric outlines outside or inside a shape. A simple way of describing the effect this creates is by comparing it to the contour lines you see on a map. You can specify the number of contours and the distance between them. It's ideal for creating numerous concentric lines spreading out from the original object (see right), such as ripples around a stone that has been thrown into a lake. But working out which command to use can be confusing.

● From basic shapes to complex objects
The Intersect and Weld commands let you use any number of basic shapes to create almost any shape you want. You'll often find that using these commands with simple shapes is an easier way of achieving complex geometrical figures, compared to using the Bezier curve tool (see Stage 2, pages 76-77). In the first exercise, we'll introduce the basic techniques and in the second, we'll use and combine them with other techniques to produce our finished illustration.
Along the way we will demonstrate just how easy it is to achieve effective and complex-looking results.

Which is the right command?

With a complex program offering as many tools, options and commands as CorelDRAW, it can sometimes be hard to know which option to use. Here we compare the most useful commands.

IT CAN BE A confusing business working on a number of objects simultaneously in CorelDRAW. What's the difference between the Group and Combine commands, for example? And what about Ungroup and Break Apart? Where does Separate fit into the equation? We've introduced some of these commands in an earlier stage of *PCs made easy* (see Stage 2, pages 88-89), but here's a comparison.

Grouping
This allows you to bind objects together so that you can move them as one, thus keeping their relative positions. You can have different fill and outline characteristics for different objects in a group (although you can also apply colours, fills and outlines to all objects in a group simultaneously if necessary). You group objects by selecting Group, and ungroup them by selecting Ungroup.

Combine
The Combine command sounds very similar to Group, but has very different results. When you Combine two shapes, CorelDRAW creates a single object that has clipping holes where the two shapes overlap. You can see through the clipping hole to view objects beneath the Combined shape.

Weld, Intersect and Trim
These commands work in a similar way to Combine. This means that they create a new shape with uniform fill and outline characteristics. However, unlike the Combine command, Weld, Intersect and Trim actions will always create solid shapes, without the clipping holes typical of combined objects. Unlike the Combine command (which also has a Break Apart command) Weld, Intersect and Trim do not allow you revert to the original shapes unless you use the Undo command (and the Undo command is only really suitable if you spot that you've made a mistake almost immediately).

Separate
The Separate command applies only to objects that have had the Contour command applied to them. If you add a Contour to an object, the new contour shapes remain attached to the original. The Separate command breaks this attachment.

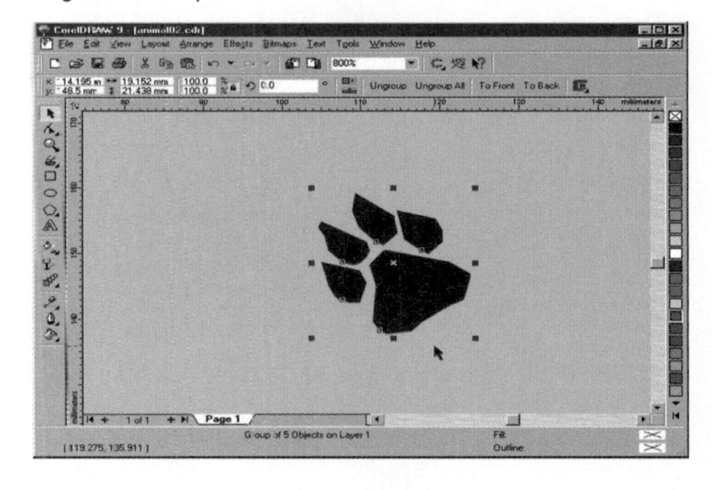

Using the Group command is extremely useful when you want to move several objects at once but keep their relative size and position. Here the five shapes that make up the animal paw print are grouped to make them easier to move.

Complex objects from simple shapes

The Weld and Trim commands are perfect for turning very basic shapes into objects that would otherwise be difficult to draw.

1 Start by drawing a square in a new CorelDRAW document. Then use the Ellipse tool to draw two circles that just clip the square, as shown below. Select Weld from the Arrange menu's Shaping sub-menu.

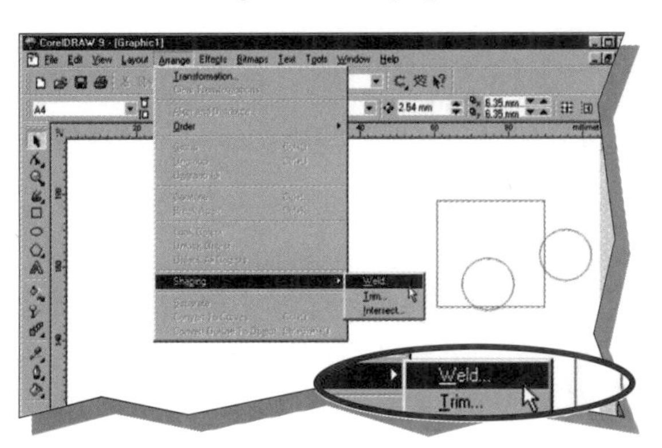

2 In the Shaping docker's Weld dialog box, ensure that both Leave Original options are unticked, then select the circle and click the Weld To button. The cursor changes to a different arrow. To weld the circle to the square, click once on the square.

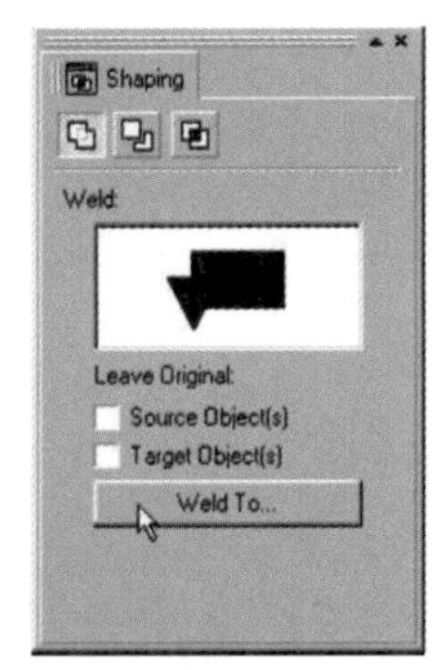

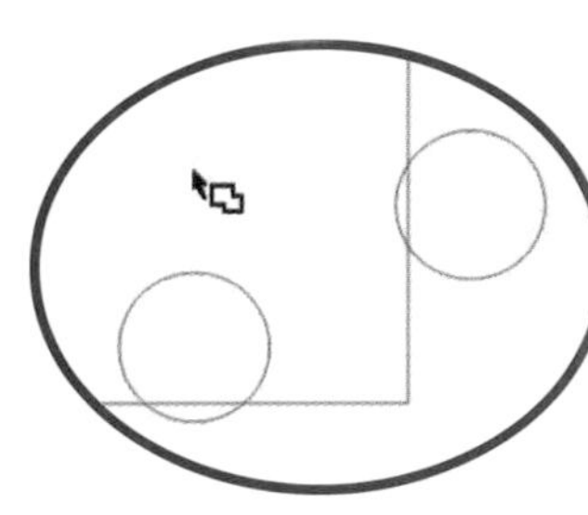

3 You'll see the circle and square become one object. Now click the lower circle and then the Trim button in the top part of the Shaping docker window (see PC Tips, right). Untick the Source Objects option, press the Trim button and click the square. You will now have an object that looks like a corner piece of a jigsaw puzzle.

4 Draw a circle above the jigsaw piece and select the Interactive Contour Tool from the Toolbar.

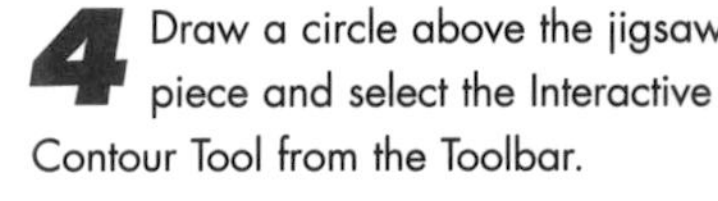

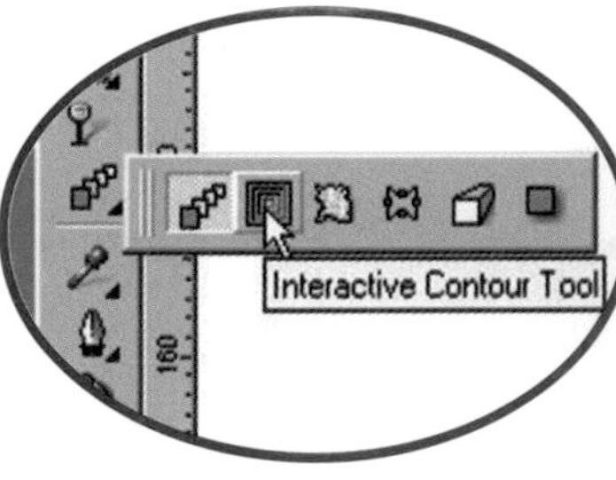

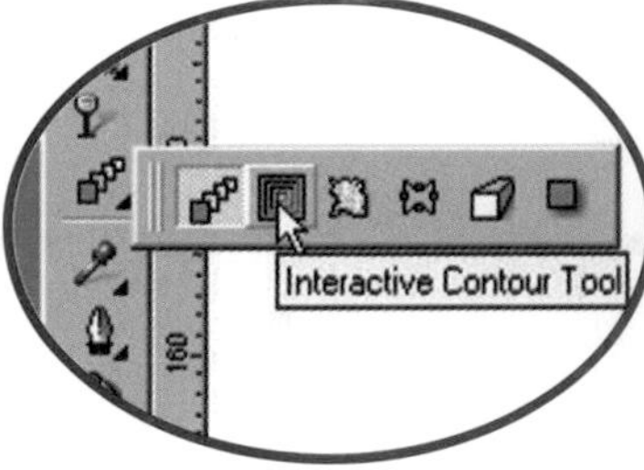

5 Click and drag the mouse from just inside the circle to just outside. As you move the mouse, CorelDRAW shows the contours you are adding. You can now release the mouse.

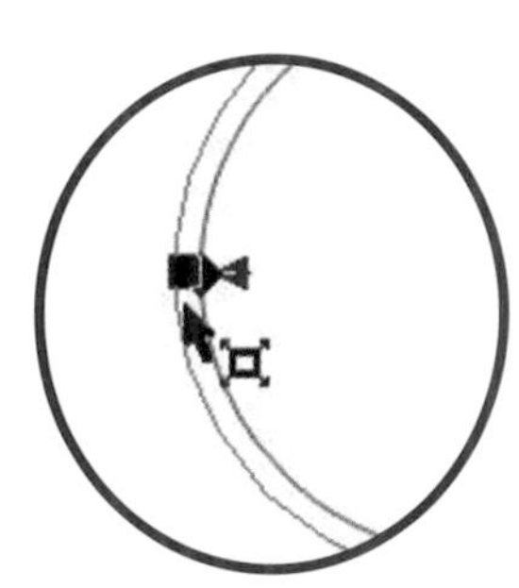

6 The contour action creates a single concentric circle that is now part of the original circle object.

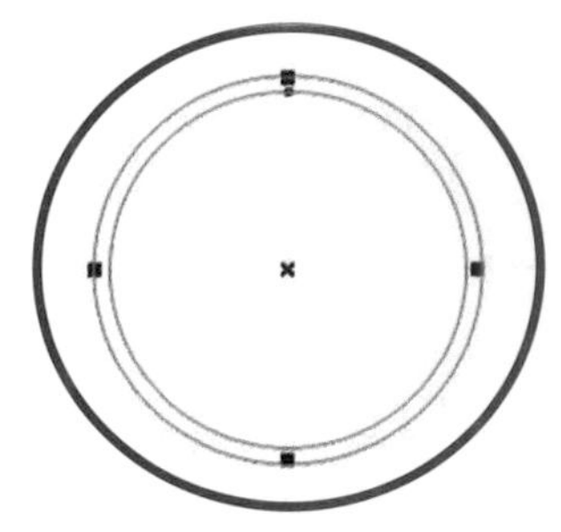

7 To add another concentric circle you can use the Contour command again. Before that, however, you must separate the circle objects. First, use the Pick Tool to drag an outline around the circles, then select the Separate command from the Arrange menu.

8 Now the two circles are independent shapes. Select the outside circle and add another contour. This time, use the Property Bar to change to an Offset of around 23mm before using the Interactive Contour Tool. Save this document as you will need it for the exercise opposite.

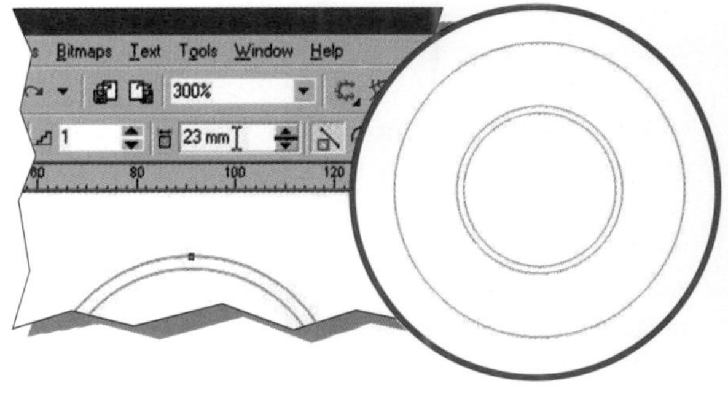

PC TIPS

The Shaping docker

Once you have brought up the Shaping docker window, you can use the three buttons at the top of the window instead of the CorelDRAW menu. Simply click on the appropriate command and the lower part of the dialog box changes to reveal the options applying to that tool.

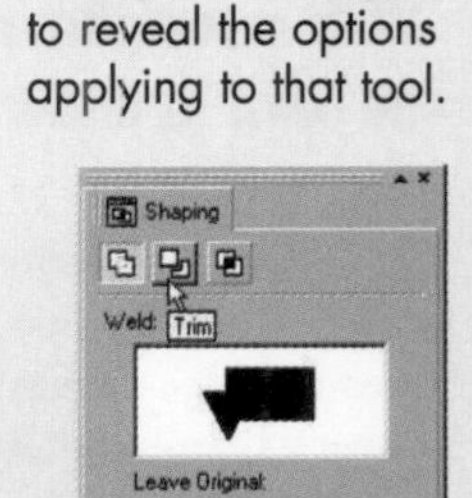

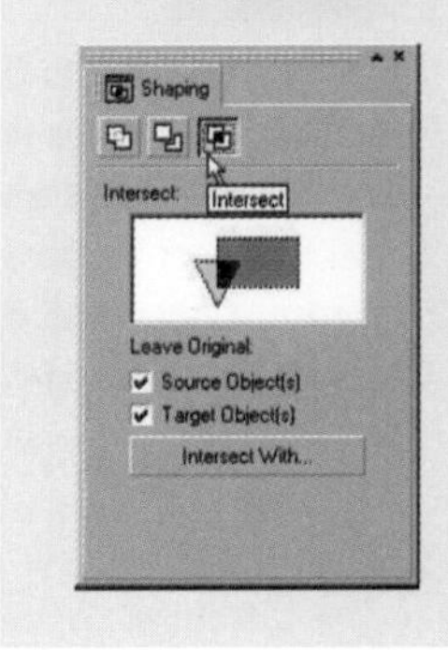

Using the Intersect command

Here we use Intersect to clip the circles we made in the previous exercise and add a few more basic objects, plus various fills, to create our finished picture.

1 Open up the document you created on the opposite page. Select the circles and drag them up to the top right of the page. Draw a rectangle across the top half of the page so that it cuts across the three circles, as shown here. With the rectangle still selected, go to the Edit menu and select Copy.

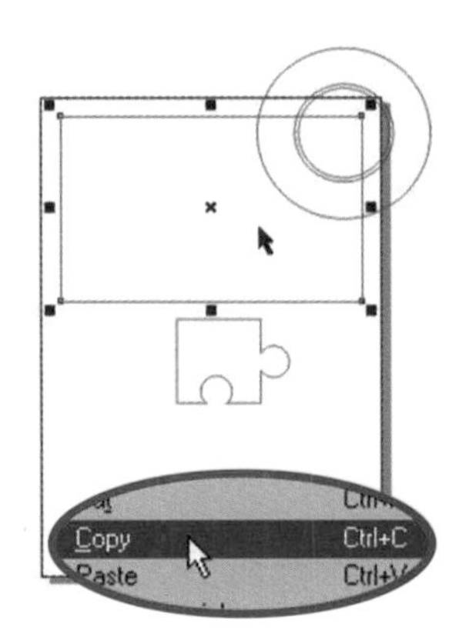

2 Use the Shaping docker window to bring up the Intersect options. Ensure that the Leave Original boxes are unticked and click on the inside circle. Then press the Intersect With button and click on the rectangle with the large arrow.

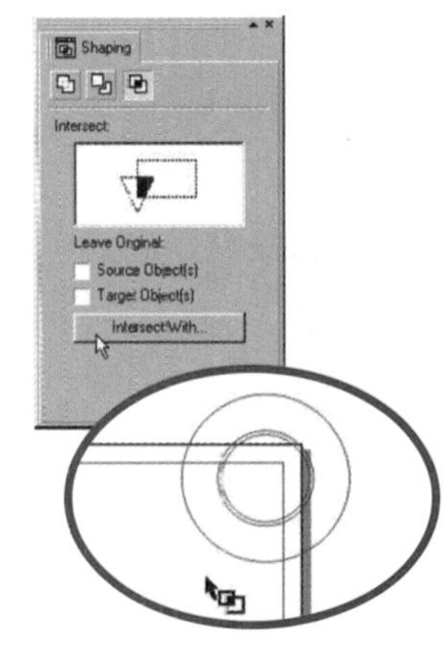

3 Both rectangle and circle disappear, leaving only the area that overlapped as a single new object. Press [Ctrl]+[V] to paste a copy of the rectangle back onto the drawing and repeat Step 2 for the other two circles. After pasting the rectangle back one final time, your drawing will look as shown on the right.

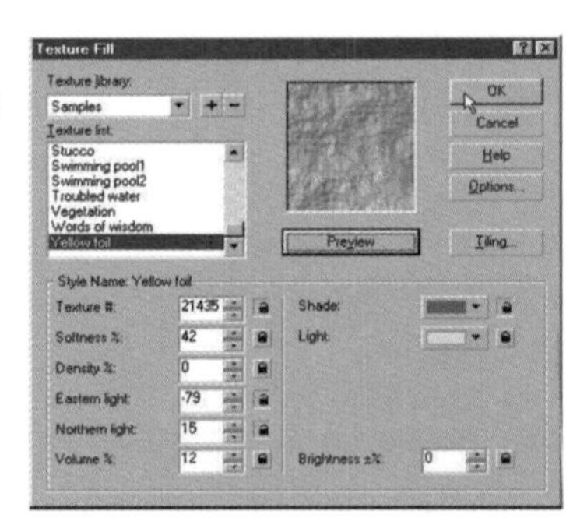

4 You can now use CorelDRAW's normal object fill and texture commands to colour in your picture. Click on the innermost circle quadrant, and then press the Texture Fill Dialog button located on the Fill tool.

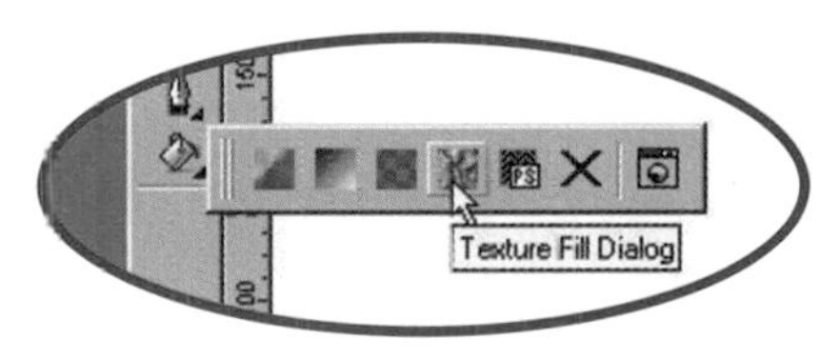

5 From the Texture library section, select Samples and then scroll down the list until you get to Yellow Foil. Use the shade button to select a colour, then click the OK button when you have chosen your combination.

6 Repeat the process with another colour and/or texture for the middle circle quadrant. We've opted for Solar Flares2. Click on Preview repeatedly (see Texture fills, below right) until you get a suitable design appearing in the preview box. Click OK.

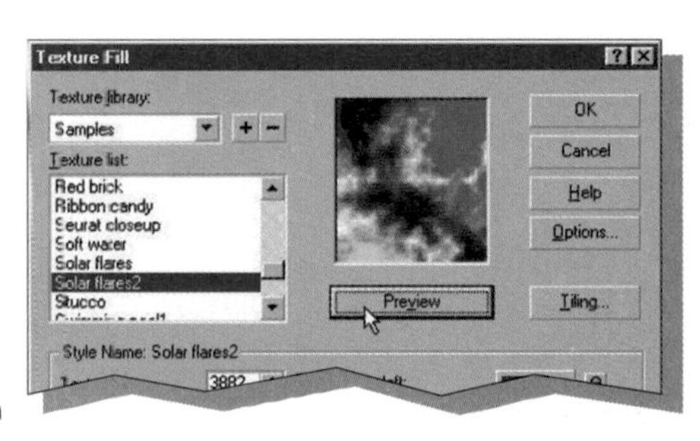

7 For the outermost quadrant, call up the Fountain Fill dialog box (located on the pop-up Fill tool toolbar), choose a Radial fill and select a deep red colour for the To colour. Also experiment with the Edge Pad and Mid-point settings, which let you change the positions at which the colour shift starts and stops. Fill the rectangle with solid black to be able to fine tune the way the red fades into the black.

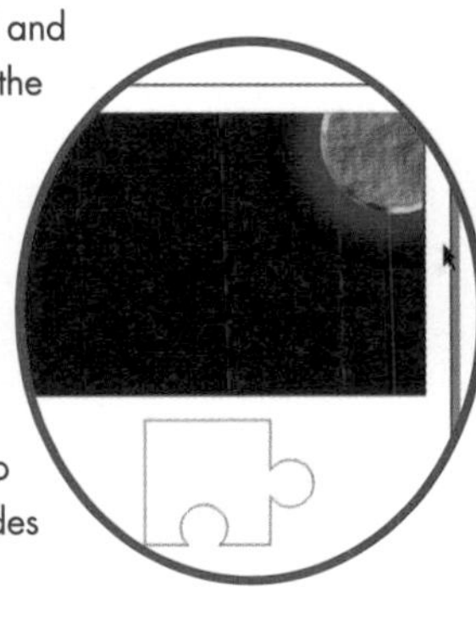

8 To complete our artwork we've added more textured and filled circles at the bottom of our black rectangle. We also added extra tags to our jigsaw shape before completing the overall effect with some appropriate lines of text.

PC TIPS

Remove outlines

In the final step shown here, the distracting black outlines for all objects have been removed to show the picture at its best. It is possible to create your drawing using objects with no outline, but then it becomes too easy to lose them on the page. The best approach is to start with black outlines and simply remove them when your picture is finished.

TEXTURE FILLS

When working with textured fills, don't be afraid to experiment with the variables, which can differ depending on the texture you use. By repeatedly clicking on Preview, you will see different versions of each texture.

Creating scripts

You can get CorelDRAW to perform many monotonous tasks that you might otherwise have to do by hand. While macros do this in Word and Excel, CorelDRAW uses scripts.

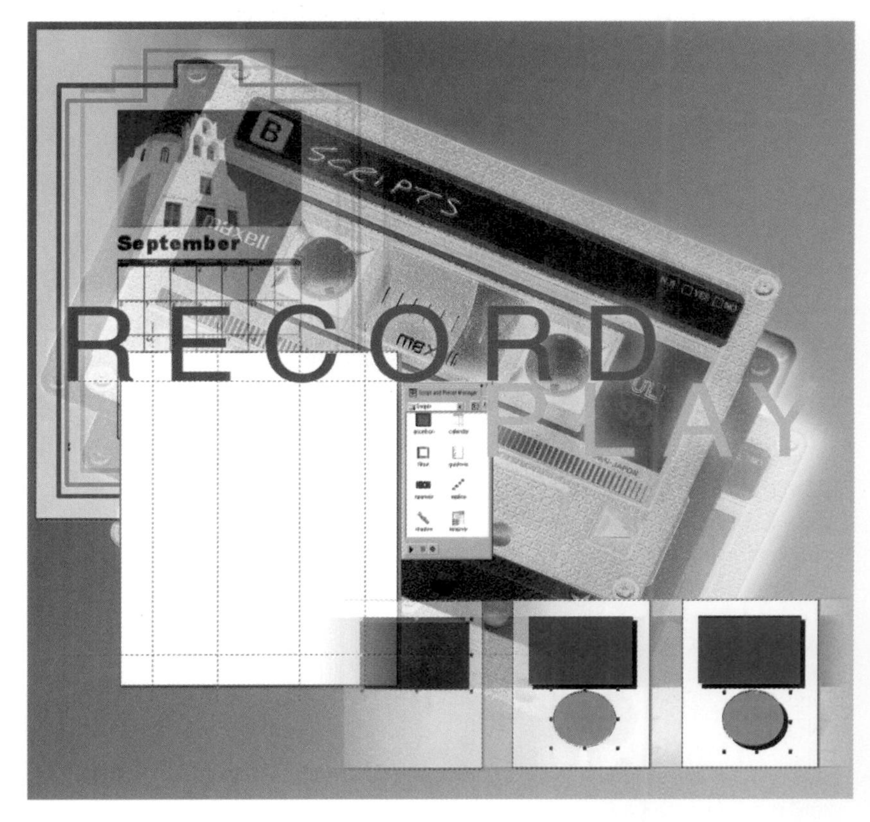

CorelDRAW can do some of the work for you – even quite complex drawing – when you use the script function.

Most major programs have an ability to record and play back commonly repeated tasks – thus saving you time and hassle. CorelDRAW is no exception. Typically, these task recordings are called macros (see pages 30-37) but in CorelDRAW they are called scripts. Other than this small difference, macros and scripts are identical.

CorelDRAW scripts are recorded and played back from the Script and Preset Manager. As you'll see in the exercise opposite, recording your own script is, at the simplest level, just a case of clicking the record button, carrying out the tasks you wish to automate and then pressing the stop button. The program will then ask you to save the script, give it a name and assign it to a folder, from which it will then be available. To activate your script, you simply find and select it, click on the play button and it will then carry out the work.

● Example CorelDRAW scripts

CorelDRAW includes some example scripts of its own, which can be quite complicated but still useful. There are scripts to add jazzy effects to text and/or objects, and some that take care of entire documents for you – for example, the Calendar wizard, which asks you a series of simple questions and then creates a calendar for you.

● Complex scripts

Clearly, there's more to scripts than simply playing back a number of recorded tasks: these more complex scripts ask for input from the user and then react accordingly.

In order to take advantage of this, you need to use CorelDRAW's SCRIPT editor, which, in common with the macro editors found in other programs such as Word and Excel, can be quite daunting. But there are plenty of useful things that you can do with simple scripts, for example, you can experiment with the scripts provided (see Example scripts box, below) to create eye-catching effects.

However, do be aware that some scripts require certain circumstances to run properly. For example, while one script might draw an object from scratch, another might edit an existing one, in which case you need to have selected an object for it to edit.

EXAMPLE SCRIPTS

CorelDRAW's Presets folder contains a number of scripts to create specific effects, usually to some text or a simple object. Each one has a preview to give you some idea of what it's going to do. 3dplaque, for example, creates this effect from a simple piece of text in a text box (below).

The Scripts folder has fewer files, but more variation and complexity. For example, the Calendar script asks you a number of Wizard-style questions, such as what date you want the calendar to start, what font you want to use, and whether you want a picture and/or a border. When you click Finish, it rapidly performs the necessary tasks, giving you the result shown far right.

Recording and playing back

In this exercise we show you how to create and play back your own simple scripts. Scripts can be extremely complex, so it's a good idea to follow through the steps here to ensure you have a good understanding of the basics.

PC TIPS

Fun scripts

You can run some useful and fun scripts from the CorelDRAW CD-ROM 1. From the Scripts submenu, select Run Script. Make sure that the CorelDRAW CD-ROM is in your PC's CD-ROM drive, then go to the Scripts folder on the CD-ROM. The scripts include an animal guessing game, a CD player (below) and a financial planner.

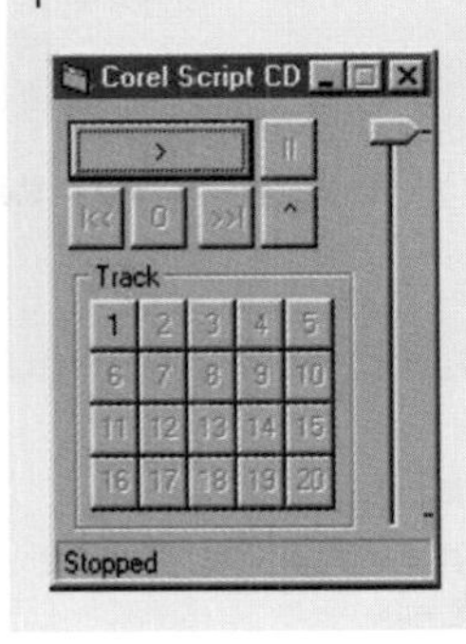

1 Open a new CorelDRAW document. From the Tools menu, select the CorelSCRIPT submenu and Script and Preset Manager.

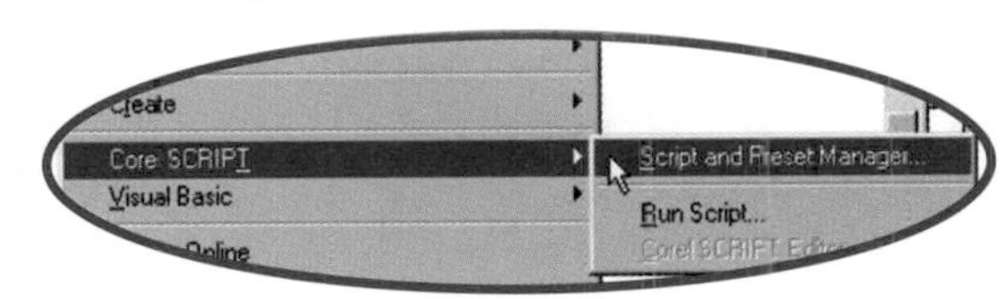

2 In the Script and Preset Manager window, click on the Record button.

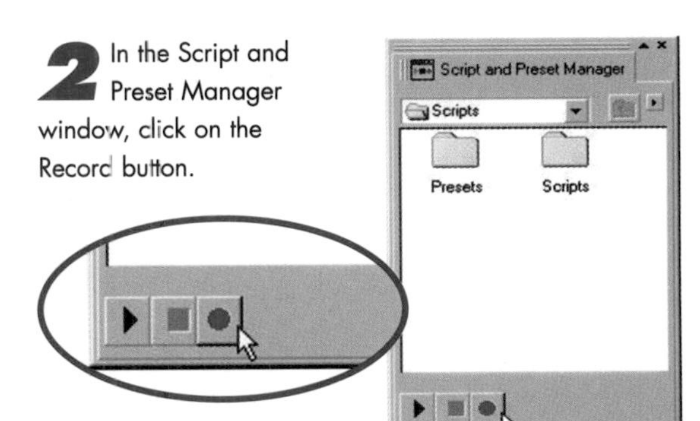

3 Select the Rectangle tool. Draw a rectangle and colour it blue, then click the Stop button in the Script and Preset Manager dialog box.

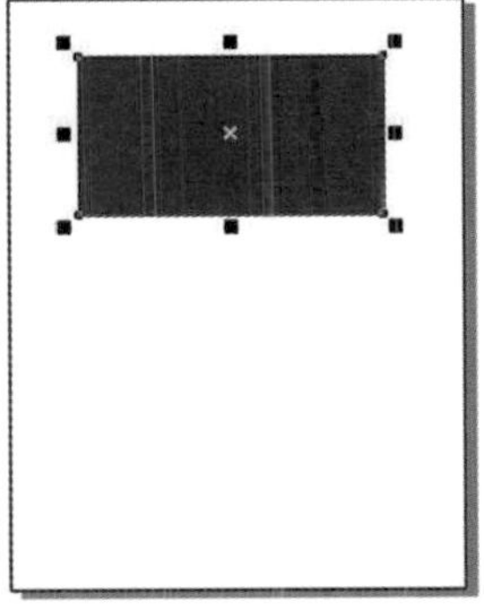

4 The Save Recording dialog box pops up. Create a new Custom folder, give the script a name and press the Save button.

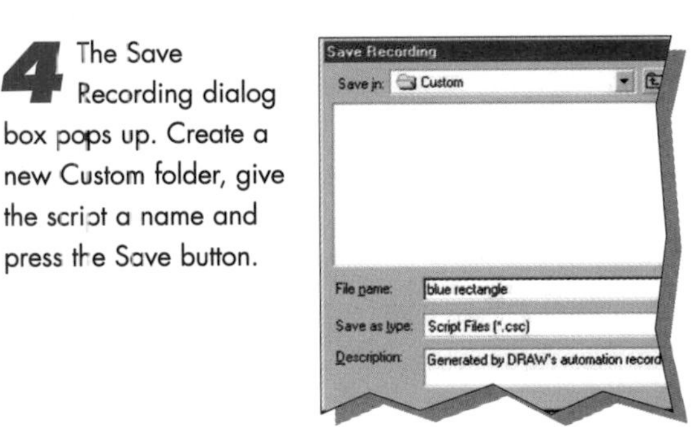

5 Open up a new document, click on the script you have just saved and click on the Play button. CorelDRAW will automatically draw your blue rectangle in the same location you did in Step 3.

6 Now we're going to create a script that edits an existing object. Click on the rectangle and then click on the Record button.

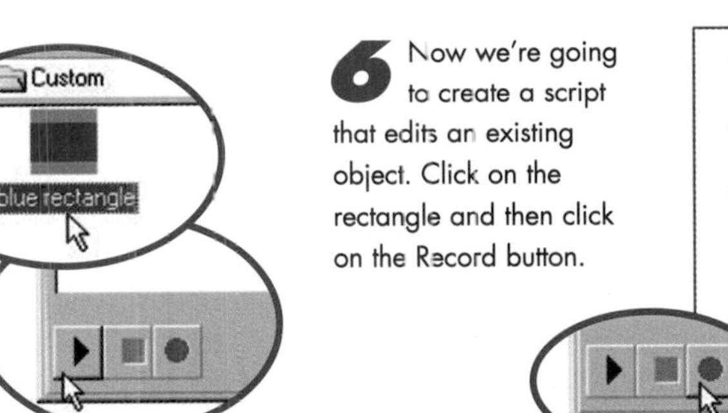

7 Press [Ctrl]+[D] to duplicate the rectangle and press the right and down arrow keys on your keyboard five times each to offset the duplicated rectangle down and to the right. Colour it black and click on the To Back button on the Properties Bar (see inset). Click the stop button on the Script and Presets Manager dialog box. Save the script in the Custom folder, as shown in Step 4.

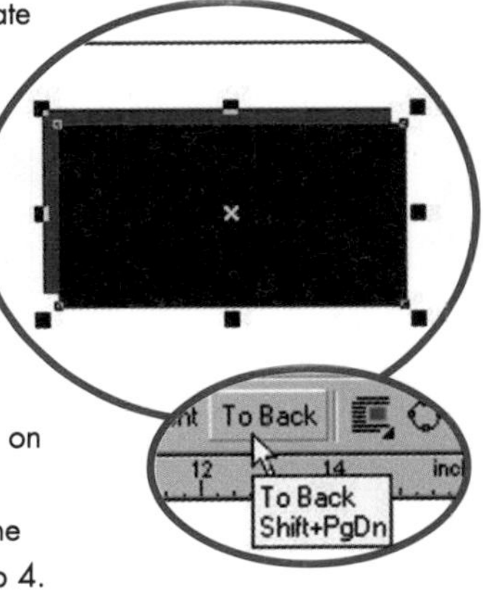

8 Draw an ellipse and give it a colour. Click on the drop shadow script you have just recorded and click the Play button. Your script will now give the ellipse a drop shadow.

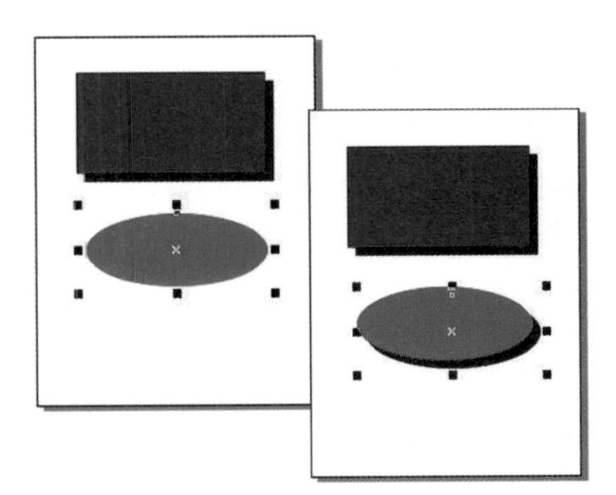

Getting started with Quicken

Making the most of your money can be time-consuming, but with Intuit's Quicken, it's fast, accurate and easy.

Use Quicken to help manage your finances and watch your fortune grow (or shrink), depending on how much you earn and spend.

Using a computer to manage your money allows you to keep track of all your various financial records. The right software can both help you record the way in which you spend and receive your money and let you plan your financial future. You can try out different scenarios to help budget for expensive purchases or to reduce a debt. Financial software can also provide sound financial advice and can analyze your current arrangements to check whether you are funding your pension plan, managing loan and credit card repayments and making the best use of your tax allowances.

A popular money management program is Intuit's Quicken range of software. New versions are released each year, with the core of the program being its account and transaction handling. For the exercises that follow, we've used Quicken Deluxe 2000, but you should still be able to follow our examples with newer or older versions.

● Recording transactions

Like any money management software program, Quicken holds records of all your transactions. These transactions include not only day-to-day payments from your current account and debits from your credit card, but also regular payments such as the mortgage and any pension contributions. It also keeps a record of income such as pay cheques. If you do not enter all of your transactions, you will find that the software does not reflect the correct bank balance and does not have a complete history of your spending habits.

You should therefore set aside a time each week or month to enter the cheques that you have written and to record money received. The best system is to enter all the new transactions as soon as your new bank statement arrives, or ask for a mini-statement at the end of each week to keep up to date with your account.

● Online banking

Many banks are now providing online services that let you check your bank balance from your computer. The new range of money management programs, including Quicken, supports these banks, allowing you to

WHAT IT MEANS

TRANSACTION

All of the events affecting your account balance are stored as deposit or withdrawal transactions in Quicken. You can think of your Quicken account as being like an all-encompassing version of the paper statements your bank sends you.

use the software to manage your money and instruct the bank to carry out any necessary actions. Linking your computer to an online bank also ensures that you always have up-to-date financial records on your PC.

The Internet also has an important part to play in any financial system. There are Web sites that contain financial information, for example, up-to-the-minute share prices, pension advice and interest rates, to name but a few. With the newer, more sophisticated money management tools, such as Quicken, you can directly access these Web sites from within the software and transfer price information to your computer automatically. If you have a portfolio of shares, this is a great way to track their prices and total value. Once you have the data, the financial software analyzes it to help make the most of your money. For example, it may advise you about minimizing capital gains tax on your shares.

● Setting up Quicken for the first time

After you have installed the program, you will need to create your first account (see page 86). When you have done this, you can add new accounts to contain details about different financial areas, such as transactions or paying your salary. We also cover other topics, such as printing from Quicken, in this volume.

Installing Quicken on your PC

Insert the Quicken CD-ROM into your PC and the software will install itself directly.

1 When you insert the Quicken CD-ROM, a message box pops up asking if you want to install the software. Click the Yes button. Click your way through the subsequent installation screens, using the Next button to go forward and the Back button to go back to previous screens.

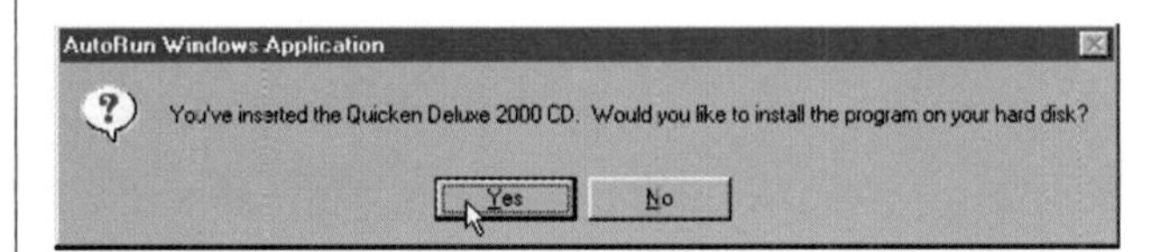

2 It's best to stick to the setup program's suggestions throughout. For example, if you choose the Express setup option, the most commonly used features of Quicken will be installed on your computer.

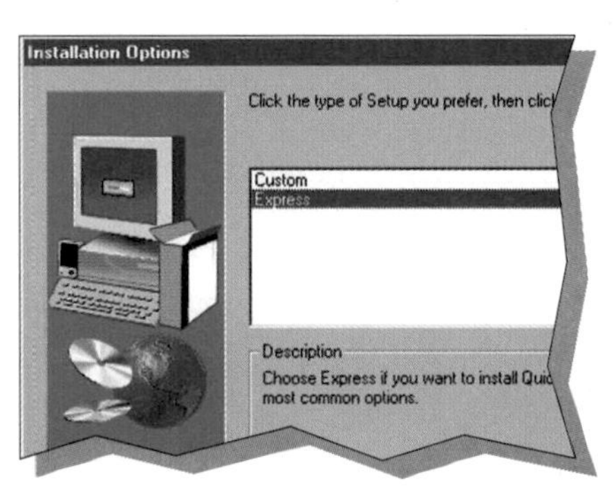

3 After the final Check Settings screen, the installation copies the Quicken files to your hard disk.

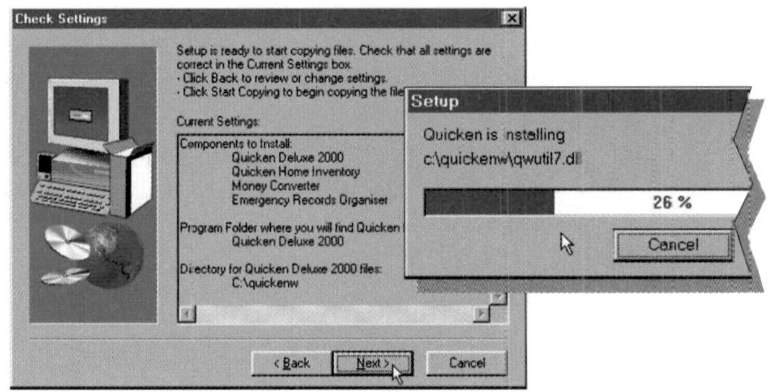

4 Finally, after restarting Windows to complete the process, Quicken is ready to run. You will see that there are two new icons on your Desktop.

5 Before you can start to use Quicken, you need to register the program. You can do this by telephone or via the Internet. Follow the steps in the on-screen wizard.

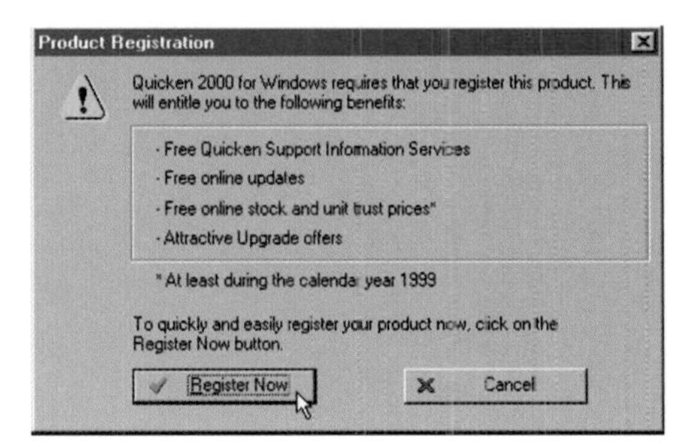

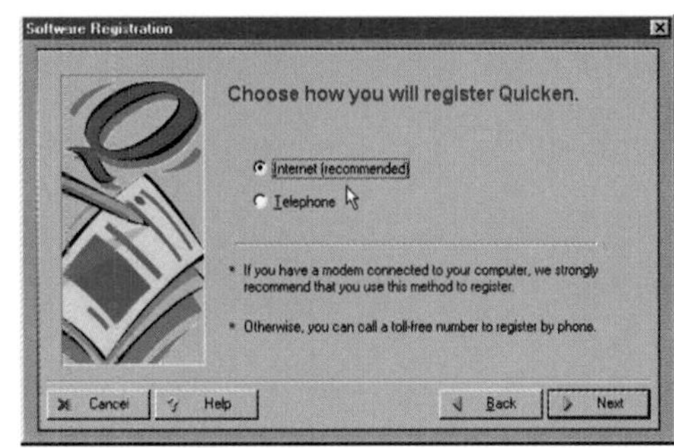

Creating your first account

The first time you get Quicken up and running, you'll need to spend a few minutes typing in some very basic information from your most recent bank statement.

1 The New User Setup wizard starts the first time you run Quicken. Press the Next button.

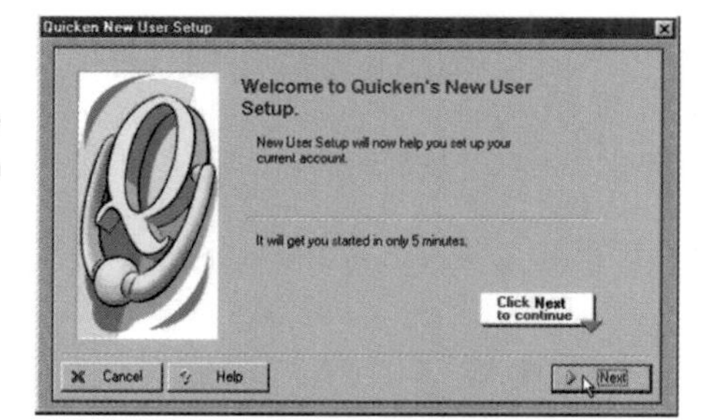

2 You need to answer four simple questions about your status so that Quicken sets up the right accounts. In the next screen you need to give your current account a name before pressing the Next button.

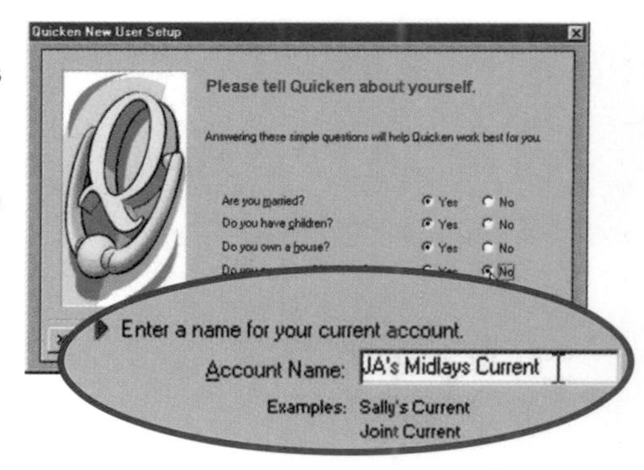

3 If you're self-employed and VAT-registered, you can track your VAT in this account. Otherwise, select the No option before pressing the Next button.

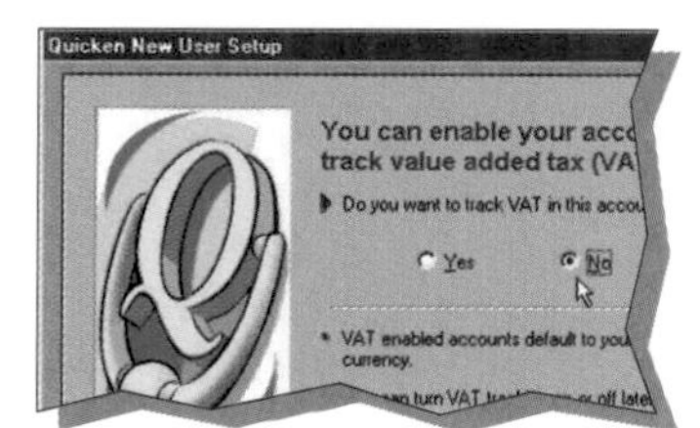

4 Quicken checks your Windows setup for details of your country and its currency. If it gets it wrong, select the correct currency values from the drop-down list box.

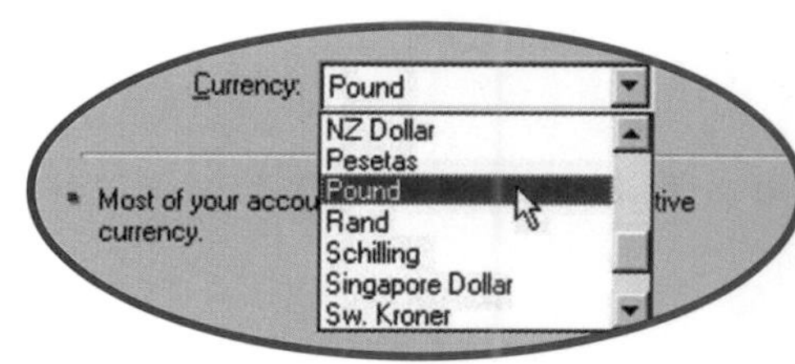

5 Quicken can use your most recent bank statement. Enter the statement date and closing balance. Press the Next button.

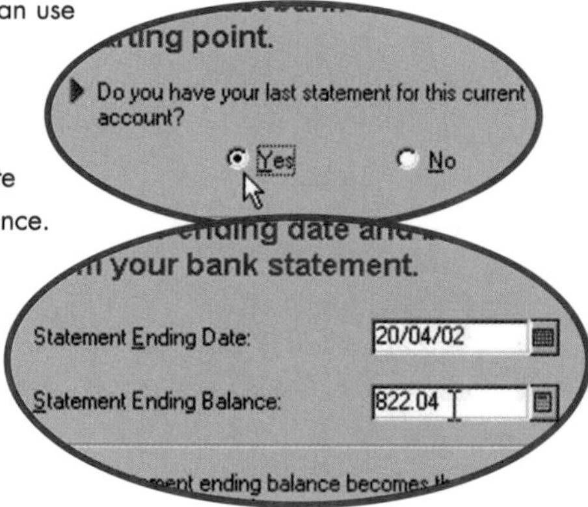

6 Quicken asks you to check the details you have selected. If all is correct, press the Next button. Otherwise, correct the information first.

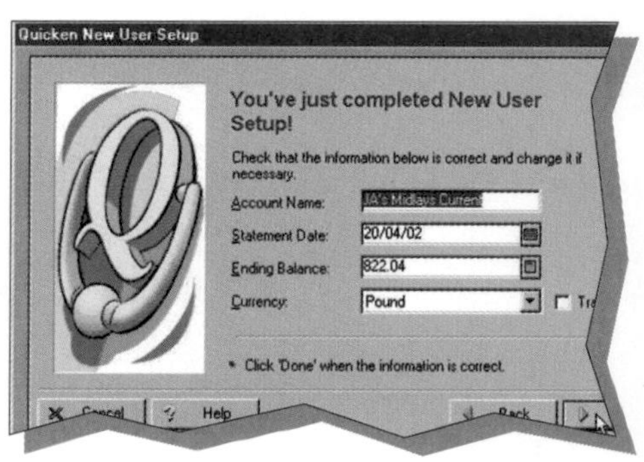

7 To see your account in Quicken, press the Done button in the final New User Setup screen. The Quicken window shows the account in an accounting ledger format. Your opening balance is shown at the top right-hand corner of the window.

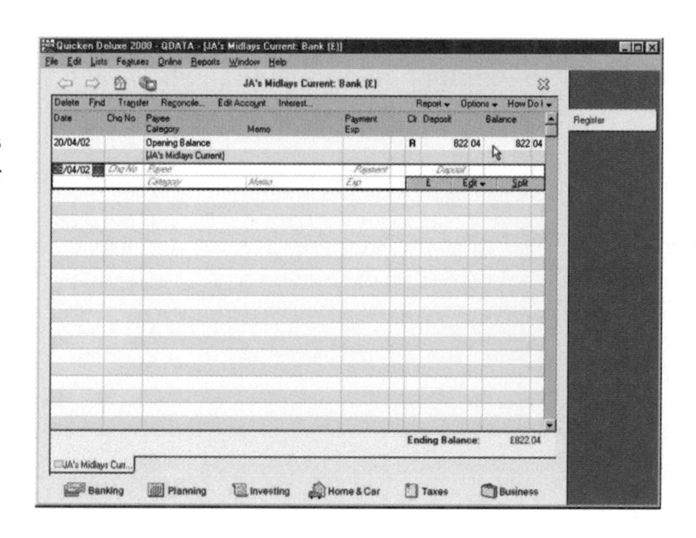

PC TIPS

Adding new accounts

Many people have more than one current account. To add another, select New from Quicken's File menu and then select New Quicken Account in the dialog box that appears. In the next dialog box, select the Current option, press the Next button and follow the stages shown in Steps 2–6.

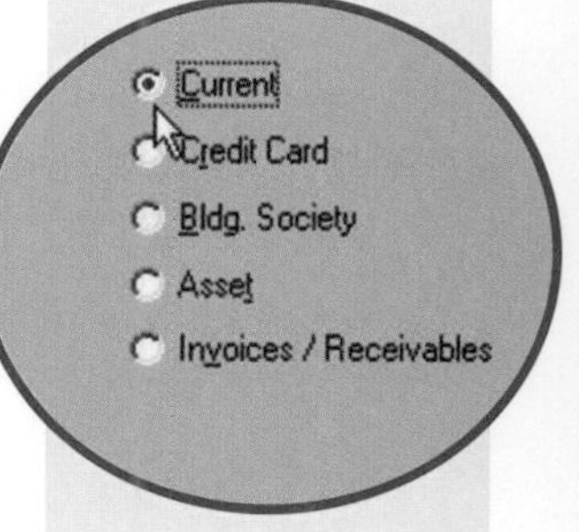

A tour of the Quicken window

To demonstrate the way Quicken's window is organized, we've added extra accounts to the one created previously. This adds extra tabs to the main part of the window.

QUICKEN IS AN easy, friendly program to use and it offers plenty of on-screen help. The How do I? function (see below) addresses the frequently asked questions Quicken users might have. There are even audio and video clips to help you (you will need to insert the Quicken CD-ROM in the CD-ROM drive of your PC to access these). When you have followed the New User Setup sequence (shown opposite), the final screen includes an Overviews button for a tour of Quicken's features. You can also see Overviews at any time by clicking on it in the Help menu (right).

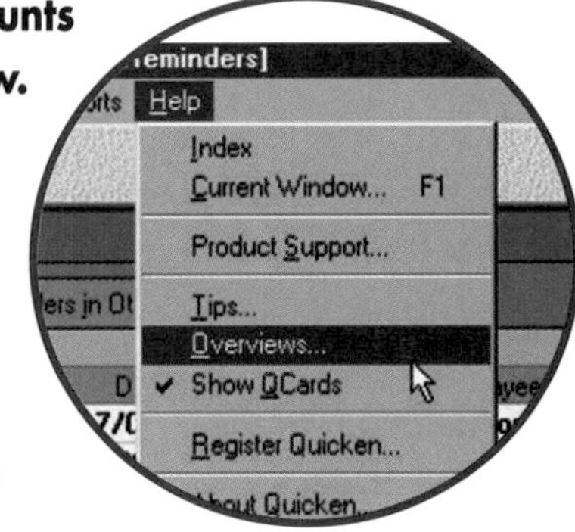

Toolbar
These four buttons let you navigate from one part of Quicken to another and update share values and exchange rates from the Internet.

Title bar
This tells you the program name, together with the name of the account you are working on.

Menu bar
This provides access to all the Quicken commands via drop-down menus.

How Do I?
Click here to see a list of frequently asked questions and the answers. These hints change to reflect the information that you are viewing.

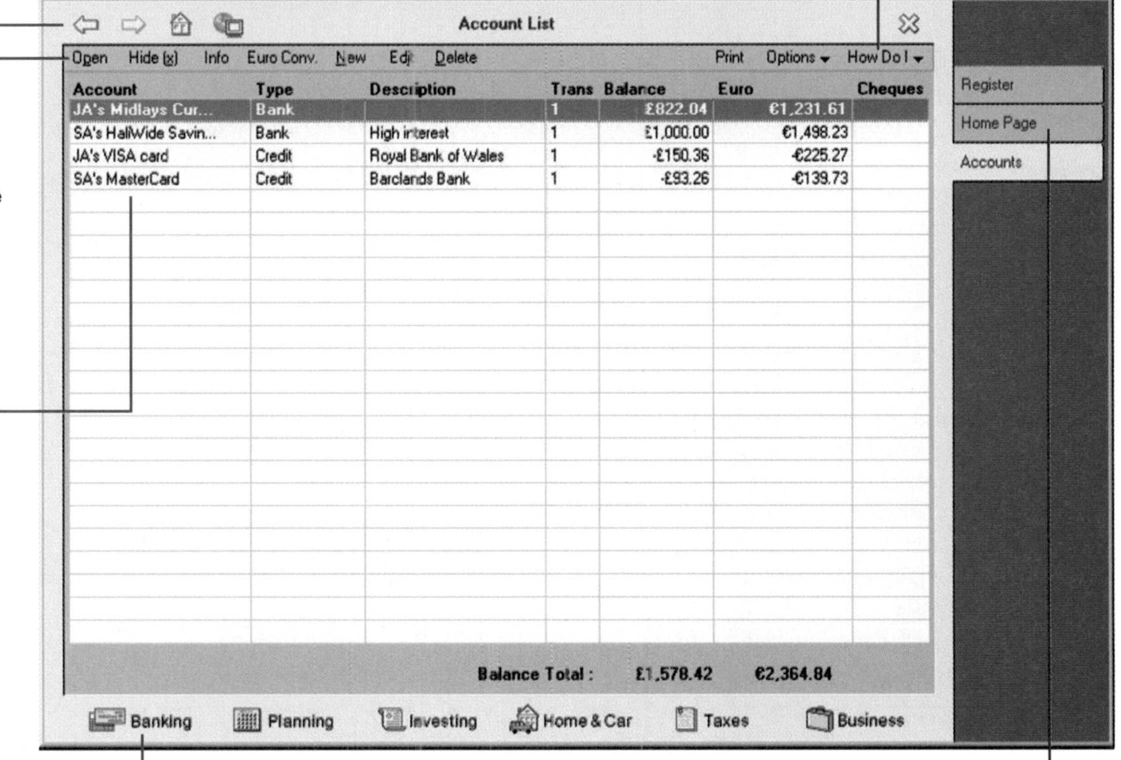

Button bar
The text buttons let you change the setup for your accounts. Click once on an account and then use the buttons to configure the account. For example, you can temporarily hide accounts from view.

List of accounts
Quicken lists all the accounts it is managing. You can add new accounts at any time or view accounts by their type. This opening display shows you the balance of each account, with a total shown at the bottom of the screen.

Toolbar
Six icons display more information about their subject. Move your pointer over an icon and you will see a list of options available. These organize information, commands and options by category.

Window tabs
You can set up different views of your account details: the main list of accounts; a Home Page that summarizes all accounts; and a Register for full, detailed information about the accounts. Each one appears here as a new vertical tab.

Adding transactions

Keep track of your bank balance by using Quicken to record your financial paying-ins and outs.

Working with your new account in Quicken shows the power of the program to keep your finances under control.

On pages 84-87 we showed how to set up your current, or cheque, account. Once you've typed in all the relevant details, you'll see a screen that shows your opening balance at the top of the page.

As you key all your new transactions into this window, they will start appearing under the initial opening balance in chronological order.

● Electronic bank statement

Quicken automatically does the maths on your account for you. Each deposit you make is added to the preceding total, and each withdrawal or cheque you write is subtracted. In this way, you keep an electronic version of your bank statement.

Unlike the bank statement you get every month, however, the Quicken account shows more information for each transaction. In particular, you can assign a category to each transaction which allows you to see at a glance what it was for. With categories, Quicken can also do analyses of your transactions.

● Making payments

Each time you add a new cheque, Quicken automatically uses the next number in sequence. This built-in intelligence ensures that you can keep track of any uncashed cheques. This is very useful as cheques don't appear on the statement that your bank sends you until the payees deposit them into their own bank accounts. But, by entering the details on screen when Quicken asks for each cheque in sequence, you can see the effect any outstanding cheques will have on your cheque account balance.

● Automatic saving

Quicken uses a database to store all your account details. One of the benefits of this is that you never have to remember to save the account information you type – it's saved automatically as you enter each transaction.

PC TIPS

If you share your computer, you will probably want to keep the financial details you record through Quicken confidential. The best way to do this is to add a password to any file you might use. Open Quicken, select Passwords from the File menu and select File from the sub-menu. Decide on a password and type it into the two text boxes in the dialog box (right). Now, anyone who tries to open your Quicken accounts won't be able to access them without the passwords.

Set Up Password
Password: ******
Confirm Password: ******
OK
Cancel
Help

Entering individual transactions

It's time to start doing some serious personal accounting by entering transactions in your new Quicken account. Below we show how to do this, including how to date and categorize the transaction and enter the payee information.

1 Open the account you created in the first Quicken exercise (see page 86). Quicken is waiting for you to enter your first transaction into this new account.

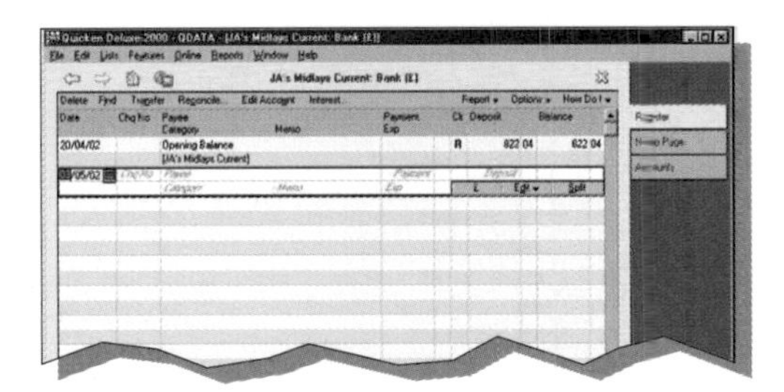

2 Before you start, assemble your bank paperwork – cheque book, deposit slips and so on – and sort it chronologically. Start with the first transaction (the one with the earliest date). To enter it, click on the little button to the right of the date field.

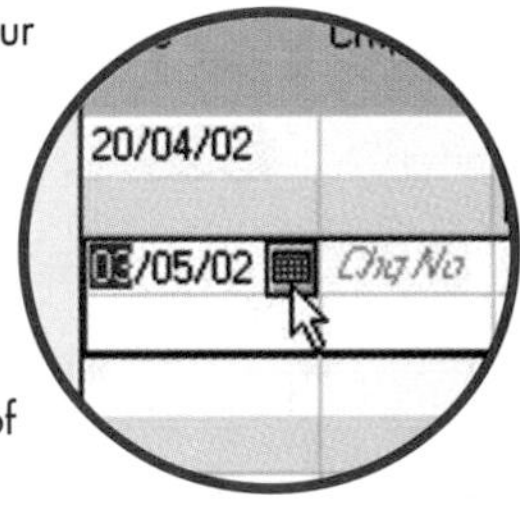

3 Quicken displays the current date by default, but you'll need to change this to the actual date of the first transaction by selecting another date from the pop-up calendar.

4 Press the [Tab] key to move to the next part of the transaction. Quicken displays a list of common types of transactions but, for your first cheque payment, just type in the cheque number.

5 In the Payee field, type the name of the person or organization to whom the cheque was made.

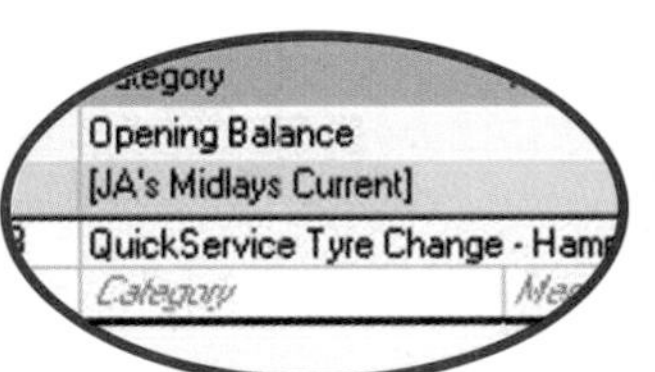

6 In the next field (the Payment field), type the amount of the cheque. For deposits, see Entering deposits box, right.

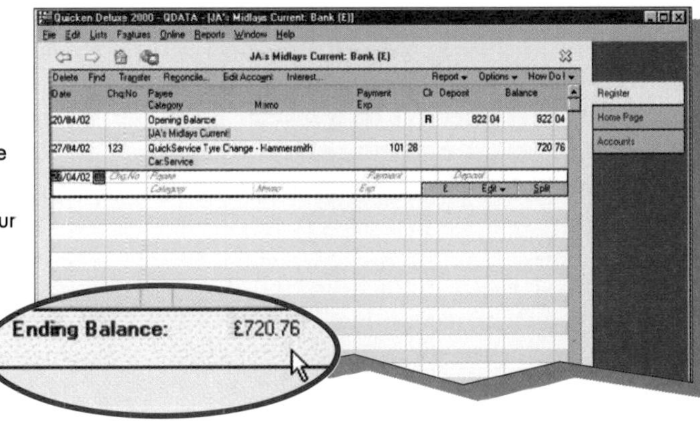

7 Press the [Tab] key again to select the Category for this transaction. Quicken's categories cover most common household jobs. Our first cheque is to pay for two new tyres for the car. Scroll down to the Car category and select the Service sub-category.

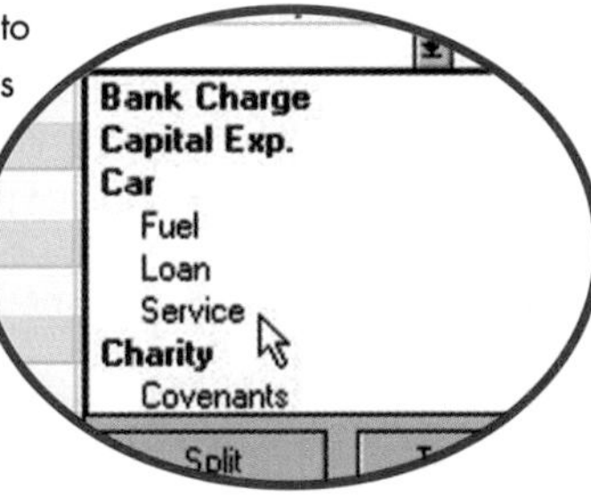

8 To complete the transaction, move the pointer to the £ button just to the right of the Category field and click it to store these details.

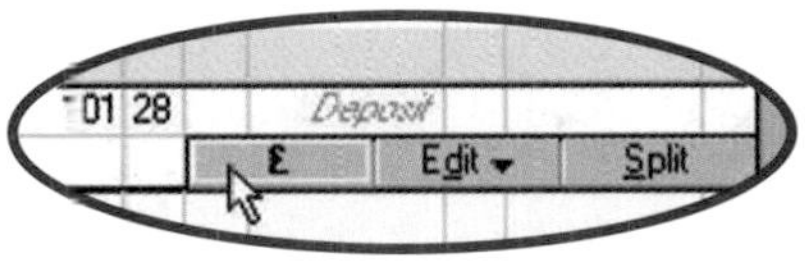

ENTERING DEPOSITS

Deposits follow the same general process as the cheque payment made here. Instead of typing a cheque number in Step 4, select Deposit from the list box (below). As you use the [Tab] key to move through the fields, you will automatically be taken to the Deposit column, where Quicken will add the amount to your balance.

OTHER TYPES OF TRANSACTIONS

We've shown how to add one-off cheque and deposit transactions to your account, but Quicken also allows you to set up regular payments and deposits, such as a regular salary transfer from your employer. We will cover these transactions on pages 90-91.

9 You have now entered your first transaction. If you take a look at the main Quicken screen, you will see that the new cheque transaction (a debit or payment out of your current account) has been entered and the new balance for the account is displayed at the bottom of the screen.

Paying in your salary

Now that you've set up your account and started to update your spending details, we show you how regular income items can be automatically accounted for by Quicken.

It might not be fun, but managing personal finances shouldn't be something that you just keep putting to the back of your mind. Quicken helps you keep on top of your money.

So far in this section about Quicken, we've seen how to create a current, or cheque, account and how to add individual expense and deposit transactions to keep the balance up to date. While you can enter every transaction as and when it becomes due, many will, in fact, be regular payments into or out of your account.

● Pay day

One of the most important regular transactions will be a monthly salary. This would normally be transferred directly into your bank account by your employer. Other regular deposits of money can include interest payments from a savings account, child benefit payments, perhaps, or payments from a trust fund.

You could enter each of these transactions as a one-off deposit each month, but this would be a time-consuming task. You would find it much easier to set these up as regular, scheduled transactions. Salaries are usually paid weekly or monthly, and Quicken makes it easy to add transactions on a regular basis, whether it is weekly, monthly, quarterly or even yearly.

● Regular bills

Once you have typed in the information, Quicken keeps track of the income from this source, and will even prompt you for details of when future salary payments are due.

Just like monthly salary deposits, other regular transactions can also be entered. You can, for instance, add details of regular bills or payments that are debited directly from your current account, such as gas and electricity. This relieves you of the almost impossible task of trying to remember every one. It's also the key to making sure that the Quicken data file doesn't become out of date. If you were to forget to enter a mortgage deduction, for example, the Quicken records would give you a misleadingly optimistic idea of your balance.

PAY SLIPS

To ensure that the current account you've already created (see pages 88-89) is up to date, you should have to hand any salary slips that you have received since you set up the account so that you can then enter the details.

Adding your salary details

If your employer transfers your pay directly into your bank account, Quicken can add it to your calculations automatically.

1 Open your current account and click on the Features menu. Select Set Up Pay Cheque from the Banking sub-menu. Click the Next button when the Welcome screen appears.

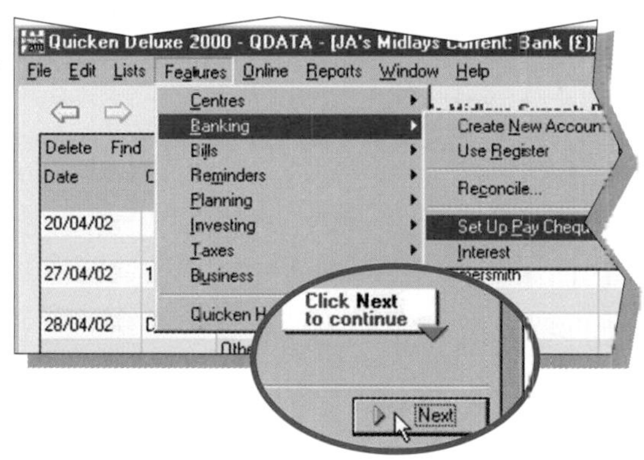

2 First, type a name (usually your employer) and enter how often you are paid. Click the Next button and, in the next screen, use the date of your last pay slip and select the Quicken account in which the deposit is placed.

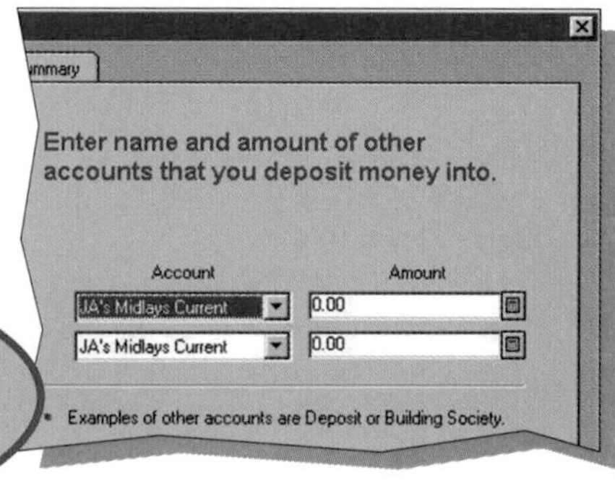

3 Enter the amount from the pay slip into the two fields, both before (Gross) and after (Net) deductions. Quicken automatically selects the Payment: Salary & Wages Category for this transaction. Click the Next button.

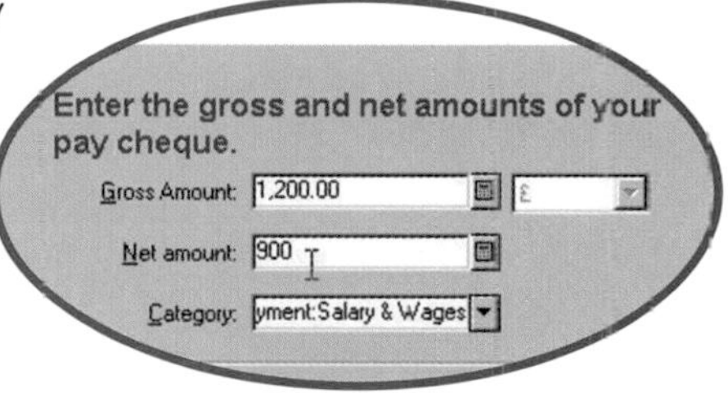

4 For this exercise, there are no other sources of income for this pay cheque, so select the No option and click the Next button.

5 Type the figures listed on your pay slip for all tax, insurance and other legal deductions into the amounts deducted section on screen. Click Next.

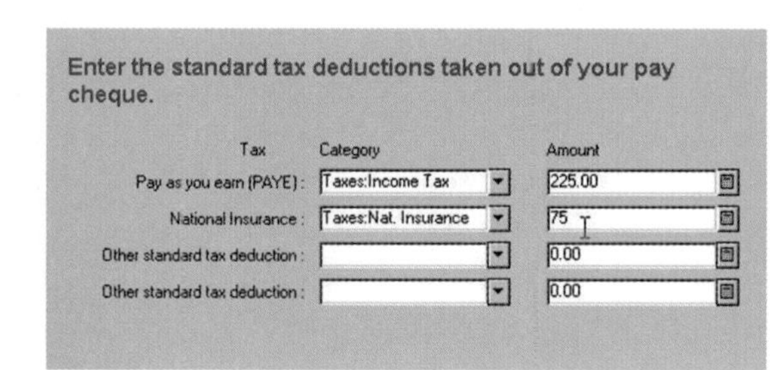

6 The next two screens let you enter information about other accounts in which you deposit money from your salary and any other types of deduction. Click the relevant options according to your pay slip.

7 That's all you need to do for this pay slip, but select the Yes option when Quicken asks if you want to be prompted for future salary payments. You'll then see a summary of the salary information that you have entered: check the details and click the Done button.

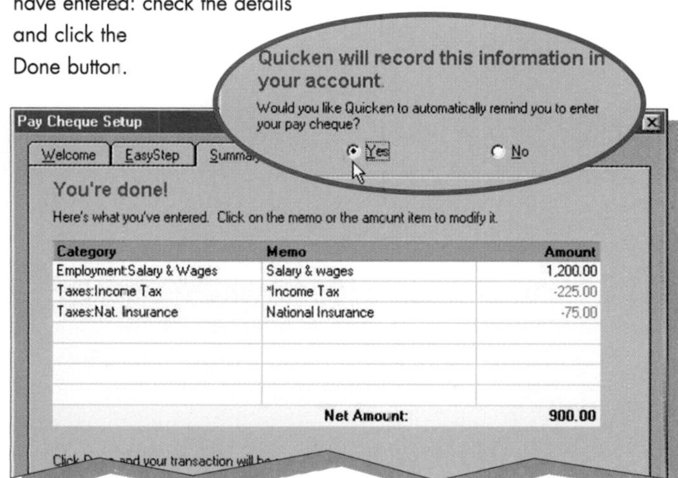

8 Quicken records the salary income as a Standing Order, so click the OK button. Look at your account and you can see your salary and any other transactions.

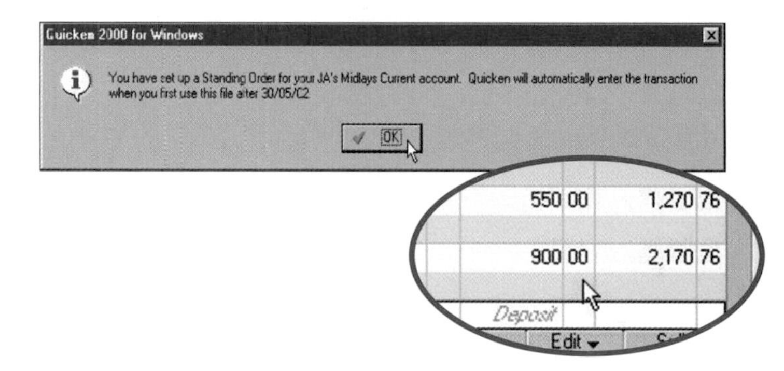

Printing from Quicken

It's great to have all your financial details stored on a computer, but often it is useful to have a printout to hand. Here we show how you can control both the amount of information you print with Quicken and what it looks like when printed.

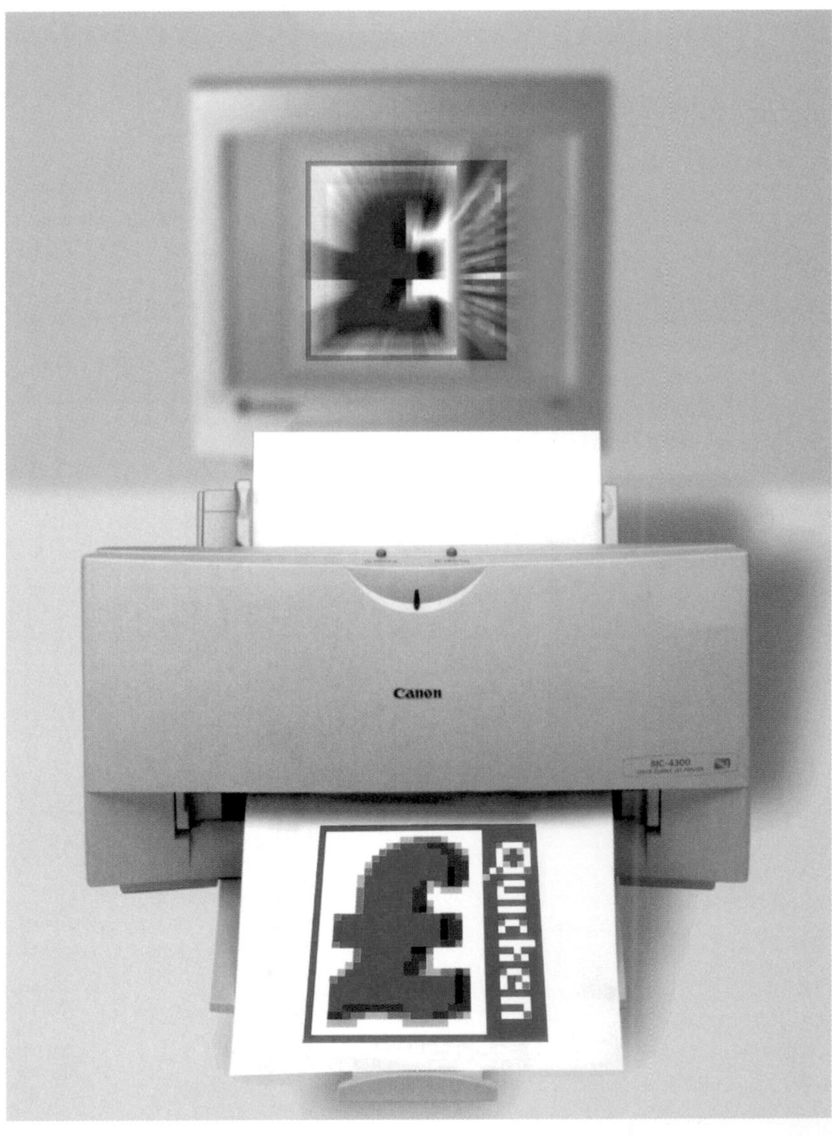

It would be hard to run a bank account efficiently without receiving regular statements, so make full use of Quicken by printing out your banking transactions regularly.

Once you have started to build up your account transactions and to keep track of your finances with Quicken's current account or Register, you'll find it useful to print a copy of the transactions. Here we will start by printing out a simple sheet. It looks just like an ordinary bank statement that we are all familiar with and gives details of both income and expense over a period of time.

At its simplest, printing from Quicken is as easy as it is from any other Windows program. All you have to do is select the Print Register command from the File menu and you get a printed copy of the information for the current account displayed on screen.

● Simple formatting

Quicken doesn't have all the text formatting tools of Excel or Word, but you can change the typeface and size for both the heading and main body of your printout. If you want more flexibility, you can transfer an electronic version of the printout into another program to fine-tune it further (see Printing to a file box, below).

Quicken also helps you to get the most from your information. For example, a simple monthly bank statement is useful and it is able to show how your bank balance changes after each transaction. However, this is not always suitable. You might find it much more useful to use Quicken to print out a statement summarizing the last quarter's or six months' account transactions. This facility is a particular boon for those who are self-employed, as they will be able to print out their yearly accounts to help with their income-tax returns.

PRINTING TO A FILE

Quicken includes options that let you send the print job to a file stored on your hard disk instead of your printer. If you do this, you can open the file in another program, such as Excel. You can then use Excel's extensive formatting and charting tools to improve the presentation of the Register before sending it on to the printer.

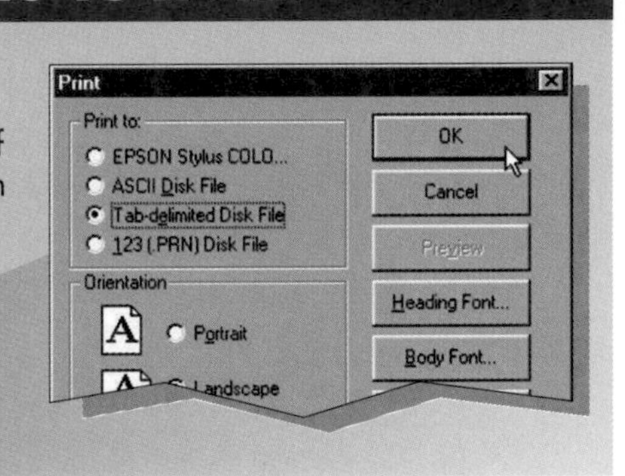

Simple printing with Quicken

Here we print out the details stored in the Register, Quicken's current account. The output is just as professional as a bank or building society statement.

1 Select your main current account by clicking on the Register tab on the right of the Quicken window.

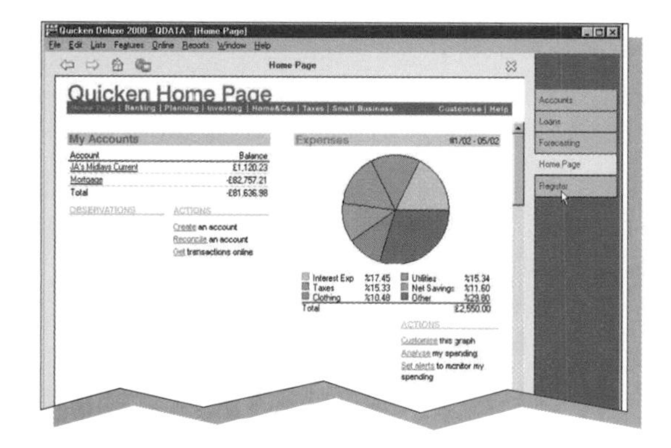

2 Select the Print Register option from the File menu. In the dialog box that pops up, type a Title. We have opted for 'Six month report'.

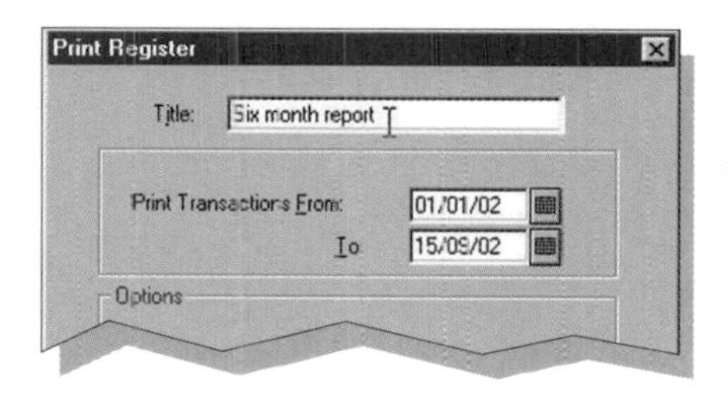

3 In the next two fields, enter the start and finish dates for the period. Click the Print button to continue.

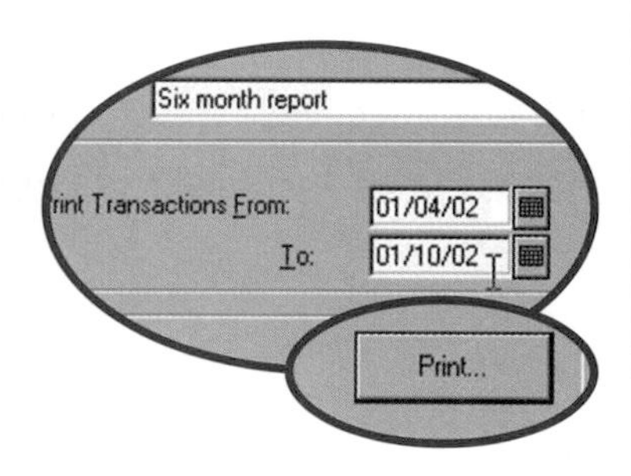

PC TIPS

Some transactions, such as income, which has several deductions, are split into several parts. To see how these affect your finances, tick the Print Split Transactions option in the Print Register dialog box (under the File menu) for the printed Register to show them.

Print Split Transactions

4 The Print dialog box appears. For a straightforward printout you do not need to make any changes to these settings. However, you can choose appropriate typefaces to make sure that the information on the page is easy to read. To start the process of selecting typefaces, click the Heading Font button.

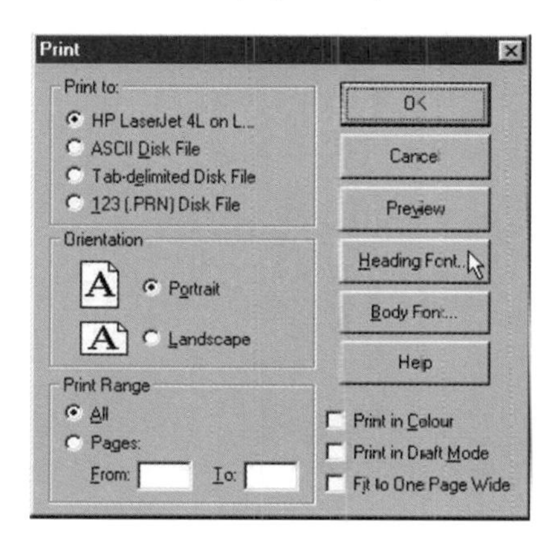

5 By scrolling up or down you can change the font, the font style and the size. Any changes you make appear in the Sample window. Click OK when you have finished.

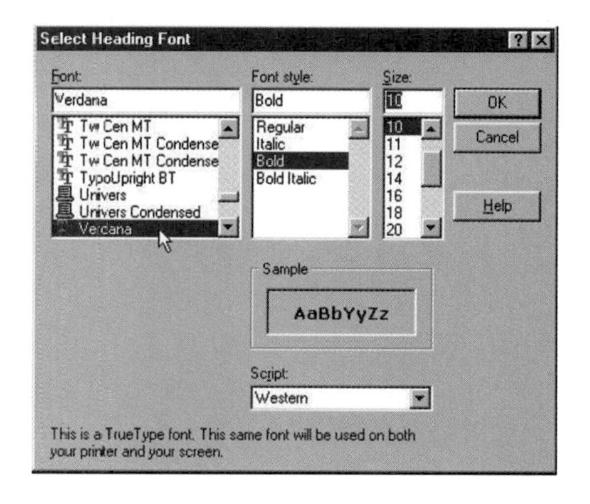

6 Do the same for the main part of the text on the page by clicking the Body Font button.

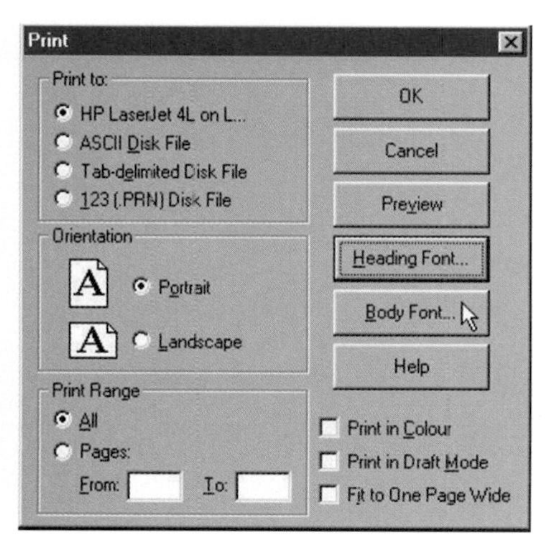

7 To check how the information will be printed on the page, click the Preview button on the right of the Print dialog box. If all looks well, click the Print button at the top left of the Print Preview window to send the page to the printer.

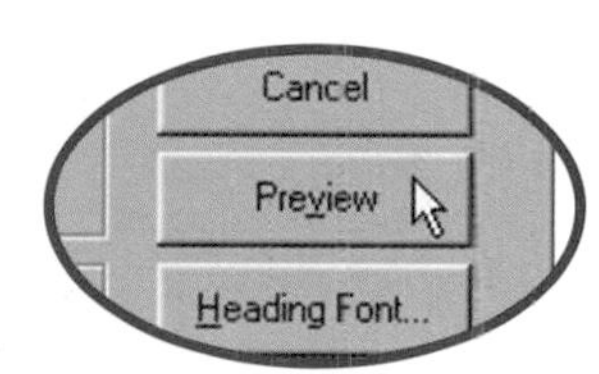

Six month report

JA's Midlays Current
30/05/2002

Page 1

Date	Num	Transaction	Payment	C	Deposit	Balance
20/04/2002		Opening Balanc cat: [JA's Midlays Curren		R	822.04	822.04
23/04/2002	DirDet	AAR Grou cat: Subscription memo Professiona	135.00			687.04
27/04/2002	123	QuickService Tyre Change - Hammer cat: Car:Servic	101.28			585.76
29/04/2002	Switch	C&Ds Fashion cat: Clothing	267.24			318.52
30/04/2002	DEP	ABC Consultant cat: --SPLIT- memo ABC Consultant			900.00	1,218.52
01/05/2002	124	Total Telecor cat: Utilities:Telephon	203.53			1,014.99
01/05/2002	125	Post Office cat: Car memo car tax	85.25			929.74
02/05/2002	Cash E	cat: Shopping	100.00			829.74
02/05/2002	126	SG&S Solicitor cat: Other Expense memo Survey fe	154.00			675.74
07/05/2002	127	Forman Smitl cat: Home Repai memo fit security light	95.00			580.74
09/05/2002	DEP	XYZ Ltc cat: Employmen			450.00	1,030.74
09/05/2002	DirDel	Natcester Mortgag cat: --SPLIT-	579.65			451.09
12/05/2002	128	East Riding Electricit cat: Utilities:Electricit	87.35			363.74
15/05/2002	129	Four Valleys Wate cat: Utilities:Wate	100.24			263.50
15/05/2002	130	Westchester Borough Coun cat: Taxes:Local Ta	91.00			172.50
19/05/2002	Cash E	Cash For Dinne cat: Entertainmen	50.00			122.50
20/05/...	...32	JA's VISA Car ABC Con...	39.35			83.15

Hardware

Home networking

As soon as you have two PCs in the same house, letting them talk to each other and share peripherals becomes a necessity. That's when you need a home network.

Linking PCs in a home makes it easy to share printers and scanners, as well as data files.

Home networking is easy and relatively cheap. Even with just two PCs, it's not hard to see the advantages of networking, whether in the small office or in the home.

First of all, it means that transferring files is simply a matter of moving the file over to the other PC, which is represented by an icon on the Desktop. Second, networking enables all users on the network (whether two or 200) to have access to important data stored on any given PC. So both partners in a household could access the home finance spreadsheet stored on a single machine. Setting 'access privileges' by means of passwords allows you to specify who can and cannot view certain folders or files.

Finally, networking allows you to easily share peripherals, such as printers, faxes and scanners. Sharing these devices is obviously cheaper than having one for each user. But it's also more efficient, saving both space and time.

● How to network

What makes home networking a serious option for many is the arrival of cheap, home-networking kits, based on the same ethernet cabling technology as that used in offices. For around £100, you can get all the hardware and software you need to set up a simple network around your home yourself.

Doing this requires the confidence to open up the PC and insert new expansion cards; if you're not happy about doing this, get help from someone who is. But don't forget to take into account the extra cost, if you do decide to pay for help.

A typical home networking kit offers a 'peer-to-peer' setup. In the package you will get a number of Network Interface Cards (NIC) with connectors, one to be fitted in each PC; cabling; a hub (the box through which all the cabling is routed); and any software for installation.

One choice you will have to make when buying is whether to go for 10Mbps or 100Mbps hardware.

WHAT IT MEANS

PEER-TO-PEER

In a peer-to-peer network all the PCs share resources with each other. This is different from a network where a PC is designated as a server and others link to it as clients, as is often the case in larger offices. In a home or small office you don't want to tie up a PC as a server, so a peer-to-peer set up is used where PCs act as both clients and servers.

The latter is 10 times the speed, and the extra cost is so low that it's only worth considering the 10mbps hardware if you're really strapped for cash. Buy a kit so that you can be sure that all parts are fully compatible. Hardware installation involves opening up each PC, inserting the network card, and then connecting the cabling connector on the card. Each cable then needs to be connected to the hub, which has its own power supply and often displays network activity on an LCD panel. As long as your PCs are in the same room, and you are confident of opening the PC and installing the cards yourself, it's easy.

More problematic, however, would be installing a home or office network when the PCs are in different rooms, or even on different floors. This is where you really should consider getting professional help. If you do want to network PCs in this way, make sure you get a clear idea of the cost of installing the type of network you want before going ahead.

MRI's £89 SoHo Network Start-up Kit contains the ethernet hub, interface cards and cabling to link as many as five PCs quickly and easily.

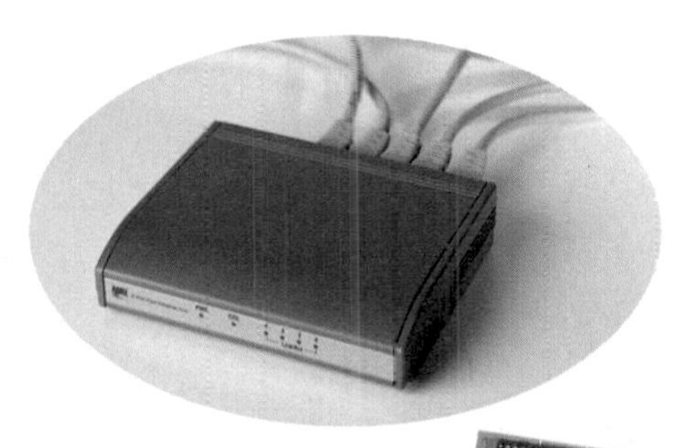

MRI's ethernet hub (above) is a box that is used to route all the cables coming from the PCs. The cables are plugged at their other end into Network Interface Cards (right) which give the PCs ethernet capability.

CONTACT POINTS

SoHo Network Start-up Kit
Network cards, cabling and ethernet hub to connect up to five PCs.
MRI
Tel: 020 8200 4422
Prices from: £89.99*
www.mri.co.uk

*UK prices

Software set up

It doesn't take long to set up your computers ready for network use.

THE NETWORK CARDS supplied with a home networking pack will work without your having to install any software. But you still need to do some work to tell Windows how to set up your PCs for network use.

1 Double-click on the Network icon in the Control Panel to bring up the Network dialog box (below). Here you can set up each PC as a Client for Microsoft Networks so that its files and resources will be available to other PCs in a network.

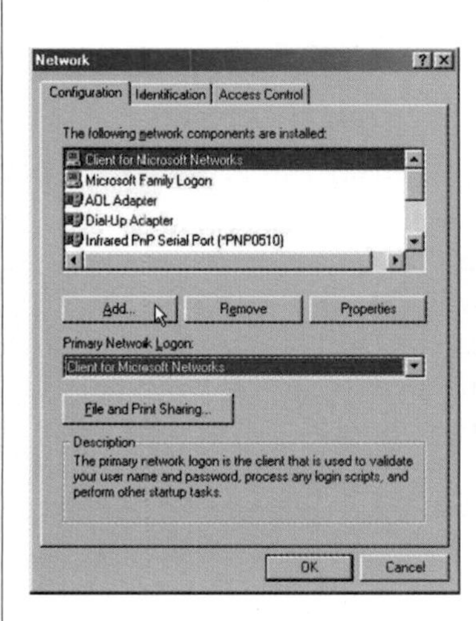

2 Click on the File and Print Sharing button and check both tick boxes in the File and Print Sharing dialog box that appears. This allows everyone access to the files on the PC and the printers to which it is connected. Click on OK to return to the Network window.

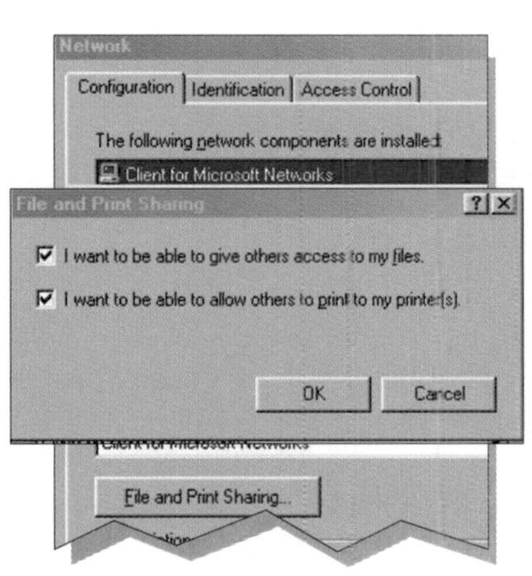

3 You have to identify each computer on the network, as well as the workgroup (sharing the network). Click the Identification tab and give each PC a different Computer name and Computer Description, but make sure that the Workgroup name is exactly the same on each one. When you've finished, click OK. Restart the PC for the changes to take effect.

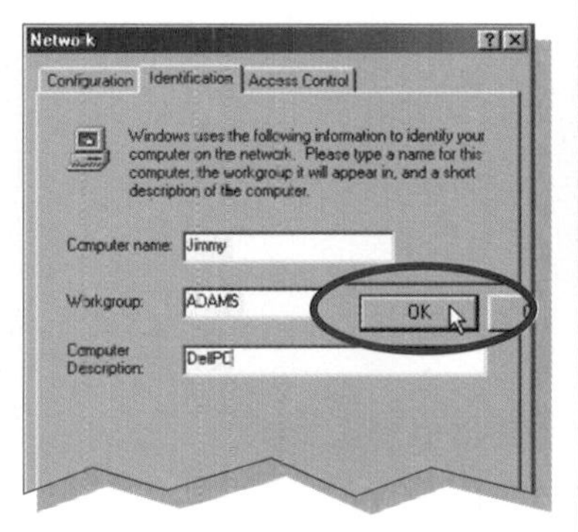

PC TIPS

Windows Me & home networking

If you are using Windows Me, you can take advantage of its Home Networking Wizard to guide you through the process of setting up the software once the hardware is installed. Click on the Start menu, then on Programs, then Accessories, Communications, and then the Home Networking Wizard.

Ergonomic accessories

Using your computer can be fun, but it can also be tiring. As well as making sure you have a comfortable work position, you can also buy accessories to help you avoid joint aches, pains and strains, and eye fatigue.

Even if you have an expensive monitor that looks great, you might benefit from an anti-glare screen.

Are you sitting comfortably? Almost certainly you're not. And if so, the chances are that you're not in the optimum position when typing at your keyboard or looking at your monitor. In fact, it's actually pretty hard to get your computer set up exactly right to maximize comfort and efficiency.

That's where ergonomics comes in. To put it simply, ergonomics is the science of designing machines and working conditions so that humans can work efficiently and comfortably. Since the invention of computers, industrial designers have come up with ideas to improve the way we interact with computers in terms of our comfort, health and safety.

● Designing for comfort

While computer design has come a long way in the past 20 years or so, it is still far from perfect. There are currently two main concerns about using computers. Both of these can be helped by using ergonomic accessories. The first concern is that using a keyboard for prolonged periods might cause RSI (repetitive strain injury) and long-term damage to your forearms, wrists and hands (see RSI – are you at risk? box, opposite). The second is that looking at a poorly set-up computer monitor for similarly prolonged periods can cause severe eye strain and headaches. But there are measures that you can take to make your own workspace more ergonomic, and there's a huge range of ergonomically designed accessories to help you.

The Microsoft Natural Keyboard is designed so that your hands fall on the keys in a comfortable position.

● A pain in the wrist

There's no question at all that typing for a long period of time can cause aches and pains – not just in the wrists and forearms, but also in the neck and shoulders. Much of this can be avoided by following a few simple rules. It helps if you can touch-type, as the technique will encourage you to keep your head and neck at the correct and most comfortable levels; if you have to hunt for each key, then the chances are that you will be hunched over the keyboard in an uncomfortable pose. If you do make the effort to learn touch-typing, you'll work faster and make fewer mistakes. But, even if you can't touch-type, you can still make sure that your

Wrist rests provide support for your forearms and wrists at a comfortable level, minimizing strain and greatly reducing the risk of RSI.

keyboard is in the best possible position. For example, if you have to bend your wrists upwards when you type, your keyboard is too high. Just adjust your desk or chair accordingly. The correct position to aim for is one where your wrists are at an angle of about 15 degrees.

If you can't get to the right level by adjusting your chair or desk, then you might need to invest in a wrist rest. These are simple, inclined pieces of plastic or foam which push up against, or are inserted under, the keyboard. As the name implies, you rest your wrists on them and they allow you to type at the correct angle. You can buy a simple wrist rest for as little as £6, although a smarter one costs about £15–20.

● The right key

You might also consider swapping your keyboard for one of the newer, ergonomic models. These are radically different in design to traditional keyboards. Most have a curved shape and the front of the keyboard extends towards the user, supplying a built-in wrist rest. The keys themselves are separated into two slightly angled banks so that your wrists slope in towards the keys.

There are many of these keyboards on the market and, although they cost rather more than a standard keyboard, they are still surprisingly affordable. For instance, you can buy a Microsoft Natural Keyboard for under £30.

● Eye level

Looking at a computer monitor for lengthy periods can cause eye strain, dry eyes and even, sometimes, headaches. The simplest way to avoid this is to take frequent short breaks, turning away from the monitor and focusing on something further away. But there's plenty more you can do.

As with your keyboard, you want your monitor at the optimum height – your eyes should be just a little higher than the top of the monitor screen. If you're the only person using the computer, this is arranged easily enough by adjusting seat and desk height. But if the computer is shared, especially in a family where the individuals are likely to vary substantially in height, then you need to think again.

The solution might well be to get an adjustable monitor arm. This is clamped to your desk or table and supports your monitor on a platform. You can then move the monitor up, down, around and even out of the way when it's not in use. There's a wide range of such monitor arms available, from budget models at around £30 to sophisticated devices costing up to £150.

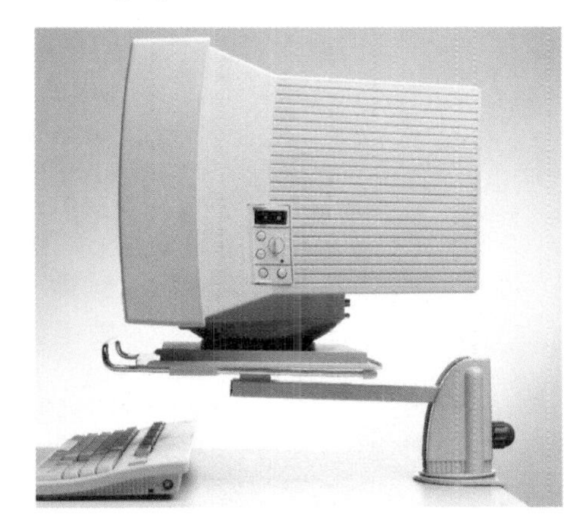

A monitor arm (above) allows the screen to be moved to a comfortable viewing level. It also creates more space on your desktop and allows you to swing the monitor out of the way when you don't need it.

RSI – ARE YOU AT RISK?

The answer, almost certainly, is no – at least, not from using your PC at home. RSI (repetitive strain injury) has received a lot of publicity in recent years due to a number of high-profile law suits in which keyboard users sued their employers for damages, claiming they had suffered serious long-term damage as a result of their work. Many of these cases were successful.

The average PC user should bear in mind that these are people whose entire job was entering data via a keyboard – the equivalent of typing at 100 words per minute for seven hours a day. It's not hard to see how, over a number of years, this could lead to the specific kind of RSI damage known as carpal tunnel syndrome, in which the nerves connected to the tendons of the forearm and wrist become inflamed and extremely painful.

If you're an average home PC user, you are most unlikely to contract such a serious complaint. Nonetheless, to avoid problems, you should always take sensible precautions.

● Anti-glare screens

You can further reduce eye strain by using an anti-glare screen. This clips to the front of your screen and cuts out as much as 99 per cent of glare. They're also anti-static and so help to prevent dust build-up on your screen.

Most anti-glare screens (sometimes called filters) are made of very thin sheets of coated glass. Budget filters are about £15 for a 15-inch monitor, while better-quality alternatives cost around £60. Expect to pay around £130 for a 21-inch monitor.

SITES TO @ VISIT

Learn more about the Natural Keyboard at the Microsoft site:
Microsoft
www.microsoft.com

For details about anti-glare screens try visiting:
GlareGuard
www.glareguard.com

Organizing a home workspace

Whether your home computer is for occasional use in the evenings and at weekends, or whether you've embarked on the adventure of working from home full time, organizing your work area is essential.

It's not hard to organize a home office efficiently, although it does require a bit of forethought and planning. Even if things are in a mess now, it's well worth making the effort to sort them out. You will almost certainly gain in terms of the pleasure you get from your PC and the quality of your work.

It needn't take too much trouble or expense to bring order to the work area. There are just a few key points to get to grips with: safety and security (both of users and of PC hardware, software and data); ergonomics and tidiness (an efficient and comfortable arrangement of the area around your computer); and the creation of a pleasant working environment.

● Safe and secure

A proliferation of cabling grows around most computer systems. Nearly every device you buy has its own power supply, as well as a cable connection to the PC's system box. All too often the result is a veritable spaghetti of wiring. This is not just ugly, but confusing and potentially dangerous. The profusion of cables makes adding a new device complicated – especially working out which cable belongs to what device. Adults as well as children can easily trip over floor cables, endangering themselves and possibly wrenching the cable from its connection. This could result in loss of data, or, even worse, you might severely damage your hardware. The solution is simple: keep cabling out of the way.

Make home computing more productive by organizing your workspace as efficiently as it should be in a busy office. Suitable furniture, such as this desk and chair from IKEA, is often inexpensive.

Few homes have enough power sockets, but try to avoid running your PC or other hardware off plug-in adaptors. Not only can these prove unreliable (they are easily knocked), but you end up with lots of trailing cables. Plug all the leads into one, good-quality extension lead with a multi-way socket block on the end. For about £20, you can buy one that includes a built-in surge breaker or 'spike protection' to guard against blips in the power supply that might cause your computer to crash.

● Cable management

Run floor cabling around the walls of the room and attach it safely to the skirting board. If this is not possible, the next best thing is to invest in cable bridges. You run the cabling through a cavity in these broad but shallow rubber strips, which sit neatly, flat on the floor. The bridge is deep enough to protect the cable but shallow enough not to trip you up.

A cable tidy will not just improve the appearance of your work area, it will also help to prevent any accidents caused by the leads that accumulate around a PC.

For wires running between the PC and its peripherals, use cable tidies to hold them together. These plastic ties often have tags for naming the cable, to help you avoid unplugging the wrong device. Considering the improvements they bring in safety and tidiness, cable bridges and ties are good value. A 1.5m length of single cable bridging costs as little as £9, and a pack of 100 releasable cable tidies costs about £12.

● Data safety

The safety of your data is as important to you as the safety of your PC hardware. If the power is suddenly cut off, everything you haven't saved could disappear at a stroke. Most offices with a large installation of PCs guard against this eventuality by fitting uninterruptible power supplies (UPS), which switch to battery power if the main supply goes down, and also guard against spikes. These are available for around £100. Although that is quite a lot of money for home users, it may well be a price worth paying if you are doing serious work at home – especially if you live in an area prone to power glitches.

With the cables neatly out of the way, you will want to turn your attention to organizing your desk space. We also looked at this topic as part of ergonomics on pages 98-99. If you can afford it, a special PC desk with areas and levels for each

To protect valuable CD-ROMs and keep them close to the computer, use inexpensive music CD storage cases.

component of your system is a good idea. Using adaptable shelving units to house your PC helps to make good use of small spaces in the home, but you must ensure that the monitor is positioned at the correct height in relation to the keyboard. Always go for practical working conditions over good looks.

Also invest in desktop storage for disks and CD-ROMs (they are more fragile than you think) and your papers and books. Many offices have implemented a clean desk policy, whereby you are not allowed to have papers or any unnecessary material floating around.

The workspace should be pleasant and comfortable. How you achieve this depends on your preference, but some points are worth remembering. First, find a comfortable, adjustable chair with good lower back support; you'll be sitting in it quite a lot, so choose carefully. Second, make sure your desk is at the right height for you and that you can use your PC keyboard comfortably. Third, look at lighting. Try to achieve an even brightness from multiple sources of light.

CHILDREN AND THE COMPUTER

Children are drawn to the PC as a source of education and recreation, so much so that it can sometimes be difficult to keep them away. That's no problem if you've bought your PC largely for the kids' sake, but if you want to do some serious work on it yourself, you need to lay down clear ground rules about when they can or can't use the PC or disturb you.

It's a good idea to set up your PC to allow different users to have their own settings or User Profiles, each accessed by a password. You can keep your programs and files in your own part of the computer, and the kids can have their own user profile from which they access their programs, files and games.

Ensure that your important data is safeguarded by regularly backing up your files to removable media, such as floppy disks or Zip disks. This will give some peace of mind. Password protection of key files and folders will also help.

There's also software designed to help you manage time on a shared PC. You can also set time limits on use so that, for example, a child might be allowed only one hour of PC time between 6pm and 7pm. Programs such as WatchDog allow you to monitor PC usage and set access privileges to programs, files and folders, and to set up different user profiles. Visit www.sarna.net to download a demo version of this program.

How processors work

The power of your processor is the key to your computer's performance. The amazingly rapid leaps that are made each year in processor technology are barely matched in any other industry. Here we look inside the processor.

Processors are more powerful each year due, in part, to their rising numbers of transistors. This Intel Pentium 4 has 42,000,000.

At the centre of your computer is an incredibly fast processor, made up of millions of tiny transistors. On their own, these transistors work as simple on/off switches – perfect for a digital computer where data is made up of binary 1s and 0s.

To get the transistors to do useful work, they are designed in complex arrangements made up of several thousands of transistors. The trick is to arrange these transistors into functional blocks. By doing this, chip manufacturers can make a processor understand instructions. Processors typically have an instruction set of several hundred or so instructions, which can be used by almost any type of program, and each of which plays its part in running your software and working on your documents and data.

● Software actions

When you type information into a Word document, you see it appear almost instantly on the screen. Likewise, when you type a sum into an Excel spreadsheet, you see the result appear when you press the [Enter] key. The PC's processor (usually a Pentium III or Pentium 4 chip) knows nothing about how Word or Excel actually work. Because they are written in a code that is directly understandable by the processor, Word and Excel translate your actions and commands as a large number of simple instructions, which are in the processor's instruction set, and it then carries them out.

● Hardware arrangements

While your software – Windows or Word, for example – is running, the functional blocks inside the processor work together: one part fetches instructions and data from memory on the motherboard (see pages 104-105); others execute the instructions and store the results inside the processor.

You can think of the processor as being arranged rather like a factory. Central to the processor are the machines (instruction execution units) that do the work. But equally important are the delivery of raw materials (data and instructions) to the machines at the right time and the removal of finished work (results) so that the next instruction can be executed. This function is built into the processor and defines its blocks and the way they are organized. Some blocks are highly specialized to enable particular operations to be carried out at maximum speed: for example, one is dedicated to carrying out complex mathematical operations.

There are three main groups of functions inside the processor: fetching, storing and executing. The block diagram (opposite) illustrates the basic arrangements.

WHAT IT MEANS

INSTRUCTION SET

Each processor is designed to execute a relatively low number (several hundred) of instructions. These instructions are usually simple, such as 'add these two numbers'.

● Fetching instructions and data

To start, instructions must be fetched from memory. First, the cache (a very fast, but small, amount of memory inside the processor) is checked to see if it contains this information. If it doesn't, the processor must fetch it from the memory on the motherboard.

Data is also fetched in a similar process – the data cache is checked and data to be worked on passed on to the chip's storage registers, awaiting an instruction.

● Instruction execution

The instructions pass to the decoder, which breaks up any complex instructions into a series of simpler ones. These then travel on to the execution units that actually carry out the instruction. There are two types of instruction execution units: integer units and the floating point unit (FPU). Integer units can handle many instructions easily, but they are very inefficient at some types of calculation, particularly those that involve numbers with decimal points. These are passed to the floating point unit instead, which is an area of the processor that is designed to calculate complex mathematical operations exclusively.

● Temporary storage

The instructions are then sent to the processor's storage registers where any necessary data is stored. Now the instructions actually operate on the data: the clock ticks and the results are stored once more in the processor's registers. Because the whole process runs as a pipeline, the next instruction is right behind and waiting for execution, having been fetched ready for use.

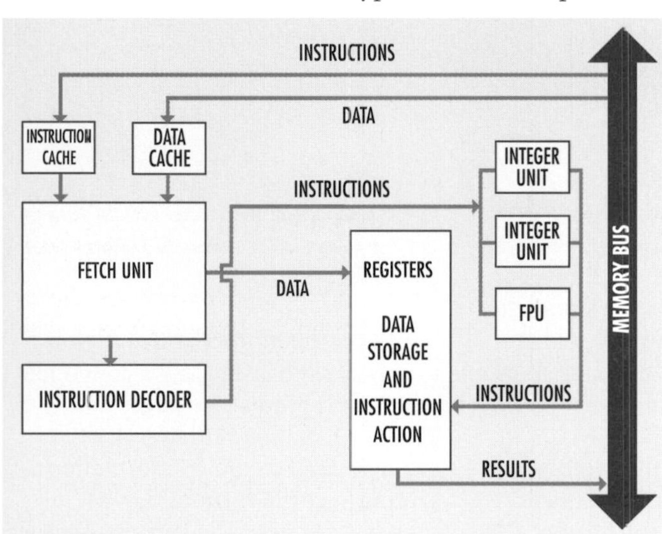

The millions of transistors in a processor are arranged into functional units. These work together to execute the instructions contained in computer software.

While a factory might speed up and slow down, according to the time of day and/or demands of work, the processor works at a constant pace, its speed governed by the computer's internal clock. The more ticks per second there are, the faster the instructions are executed.

There are several stages to an instruction's execution. With each clock tick the processor moves on one step. Clocks – even those that are employed in home computers – tick very fast, millions of times a second, and are measured in MegaHertz (800MHz, for instance, is 800 million ticks per second).

This processor is actually two chips in one: the processor itself and a very large cache. Combining them in one package helps to maximize performance.

● The production line

Modern processors can work on several instructions in parallel. This is rather like a team of cooks in a burger restaurant working on different parts of a meal at once. Instead of one person preparing all the parts of a meal in sequence – first the burger, then the chips, next the hot apple pie and finally the drink – several work at once in a parallel pipeline, making the whole meal much more quickly.

Processor evolution

Processor technology is developing at a phenomenal rate. With each new version of processor, more transistors are used to help execute instructions more quickly than before. Also, every update sees new instructions added to the instruction set, as when Intel introduced the MMX version of the Pentium, which had more Multimedia instructions.

Processor clock speeds continually improve as well. They have risen from around 5MHz, when the IBM PC first appeared, to 1,000MHz and more today. That's an amazing improvement. Chips of 1,500MHz are already appearing in reasonably priced PCs. One effect will be that games with extremely realistic graphics will have a cinematic quality.

Processor	Introduced	Transistors	Top speed (MegaHertz)
8086	1978	6,000	10
80286	1982	130,000	12
80386	1985	275,000	33
80486	1989	1,600,000	100
Pentium	1993	3,200,000	200
Pentium Pro	1995	5,500,000	200
Pentium MMX	1997	4,500,000	233
Pentium II /Celeron	1997	7,500,000	800
Pentium III	1999	9,500,000	1000
Pentium 4	2001	42,000,000	1500

The motherboard

A section of your PC – the motherboard – has one of the hardest jobs: handling all the incoming and outgoing signals from every other component. Discover how it works.

Modern motherboards have to cope with the demands that high-powered CPUs, such as the Pentium 4 (above), place on them.

Sooner or later most of us take the casing off our PC, perhaps to add extra memory or an expansion card (see Stage 3, pages 94-95). Inside your computer, you will see a large brownish-green circuit board, lying flat and occupying most of the available space, and covered with a fine tracing of thousands of thin golden lines.

This is your PC's motherboard, and even a cursory glance will show you that just about every part of your computer is connected to it. The golden lines are the equivalent of wires, which carry data and control signals around the board to and from the chips and sockets mounted on it.

● At the centre

In the past, we've used the analogy of the processor as your PC's brain. To extend the analogy further, you can think of the motherboard as the PC's central nervous system, the bit that carries the nerve impulses around the body. After all, a brain is useless on its own; it needs a nervous system to transmit and receive messages to and from the limbs and organs, which in the case of the PC are the monitor, keyboard and input/output devices.

The Central Processing Unit, or CPU, is by far the largest chip to be found on the motherboard. Its job is to process the instructions contained in your programs (see pages 102-103). It then relies on the motherboard to move information around – in the form of digital signals – between the various parts of the PC, as and when needed.

Future directions

The trend in overall motherboard design is towards combining more functions in fewer chips. A simplified design means a smaller motherboard that can be more easily and cheaply manufactured, and also means a smaller box for your PC.

This trend can be seen very clearly in notebook and hand-held computers. In notebook PCs, the PCI and ISA slots (see opposite) have been replaced by PCMCIA slots, which take expansion cards the size of a credit card. The development of faster processors, however, conficts with this down-sizing trend. Pentium III and Pentium 4 processors are large compared to the simple Pentium of the early 1990s and generate much more heat, needing bulky heat sinks and fans to cool them. In future, faster processors might not necessarily be bigger, but they'll be hotter. You can expect to see special Freon-based CPU cooling systems in newer computers soon.

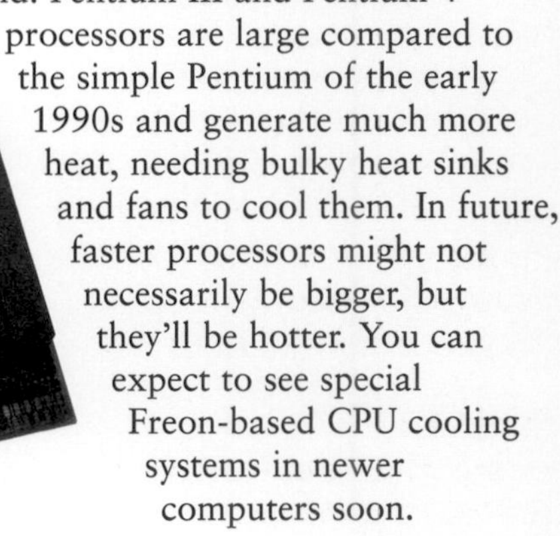

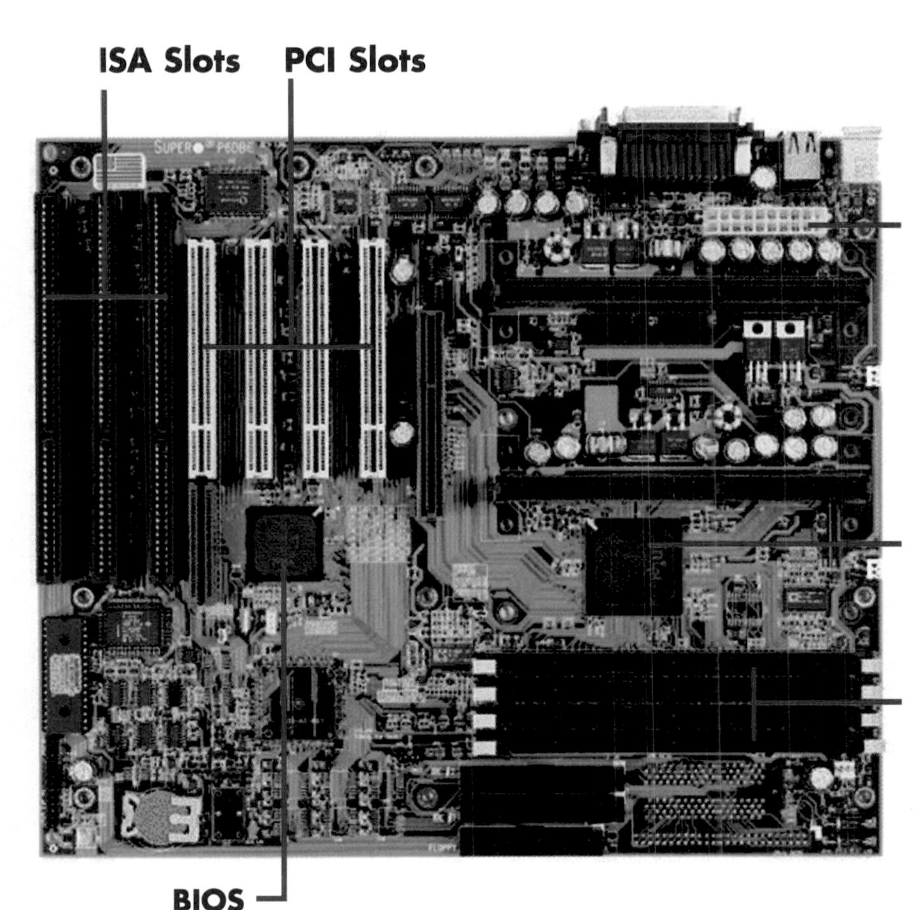

This typical motherboard – the P6 DBS Pentium II 440BX – is powerful enough to tackle most tasks required by the average desktop PC user.

● BIOS

Another very important chip on the motherboard is the BIOS. This is often located near to, or even in between, the expansion slots. BIOS stands for Basic Input/Output System, and this chip handles much of the basic work of the PC. For example, it determines how disk drives fetch data, and it's the first computer component to react when you press a key on the keyboard.

The BIOS also performs other crucial functions. When you switch on your PC, you see a text screen (which often seems to contain gibberish). This shows the BIOS carrying out memory and other checks to ensure all the computer hardware is working correctly. Once these are finished, the BIOS starts the operating system, at which point Windows takes over. Without the BIOS, your PC would never start.

● The chipset

The third major chip – or group of chips – on your motherboard is known as the chipset. This is a rather confusing term: it implies that a chipset comprises many chips, but this is no longer the case. The name arose because a few years ago the many functions that the chipset controls were shared between multiple chips on the motherboard.

However, if you bought your PC in the past year or so, the chipset is likely to be just one single chip. As chip and motherboard design have developed, more and more of these functions have been integrated into fewer and fewer chips.

Whether it consists of one or many chips, the chipset defines most of the crucial properties of the motherboard and, therefore, the computer. The type of chipset will first of all determine what type of processor can be used – Pentium III, Pentium 4, and so on.

The chipset also determines basic functional matters, such as the speed at which the data can be moved around the motherboard, the type of memory chips that can be used, and the kind of mouse or keyboard controller required.

● Expansion slots

Apart from the chips, the most prominent features on the motherboard are the arrays of expansion and memory slots. Modern PCs have two kinds of expansion slot: ISA (Industry Standard Architecture) slots, which are used for slower speed cards, and the shorter PCI (Peripheral Component Interconnect) slots, which can transfer data much more quickly than ISA slots.

The computer's graphics card is usually an AGP (Accelerated Graphics Port) card, which plugs into a single AGP slot next to the PCI slots. The AGP slot looks a little like the PCI slot, but uses the latest technology to work even faster.

Memory slots are much smaller than expansion slots. There are typically three of four on a motherboard. The number of slots occupied depends on how much memory you currently have installed. As with installing an expansion card, adding extra memory will compel you to open up your PC and get to grips with the motherboard. See Stage 3, pages 94-95, for details on how to upgrade your PC's memory.

OTHER COMPONENTS

There are many other less obvious, but no less vital, components on your motherboard. The battery and the CMOS (Complementary Metal Oxide Semiconductor) memory chip, for example, work together to store the setup configuration used by the BIOS when starting up your PC. The CMOS chip stores the data, while the small mercury or alkaline battery keeps it supplied with the necessary power. Other prominent features include the ribbon cables that connect the motherboard to peripherals such as the floppy and hard disk drives.

How the hard disk works

The hard disk is one of the key components of your PC. It is a huge storage device that holds programs and data in a quickly retrievable form.

Few components of your PC work quite as hard as your hard disk. From the moment you switch on your computer to the moment you turn it off, it toils tirelessly away – performing the vital tasks of fetching and carrying the data needed to run your software and load your files. And when your PC is not being used, the hard disk is just as important, since for most users it is the computer's only large-scale data storage device.

Hard disks have improved enormously in terms of speed and storage capacity since they were first introduced into PCs in the 1980s. However, the fundamentals of hard disk technology have changed little.

● Platters of information

Hard disks store information on flat, circular disks called platters. These platters are rigid and have a magnetic coating on both sides in which the digital data is stored. They are called 'hard disks' in contrast to floppy disks, whose casing encloses a flexible platter.

Hard-disk platters have a hole in the centre and are stacked on a motor-driven spindle that spins them fast – anywhere between 5,000 and 10,000 rpm, depending on the size and cost of the disk (faster is dearer). The higher the speed at which the platters spin, the faster data can be read from, or written to, the disk – and the faster your programs and files can be loaded into memory or saved.

● Reading and writing

The job of reading data from the disk, or writing data to it, is taken care of by the read/write heads. Each platter has two of these devices, one above and one below. To store data on the hard disk, the read/write heads convert bits of digital data into magnetic pulses, and then reverse the process to read data from the disk.

The read/write heads are mounted on head arms, which are very thin, triangular pieces of metal extending over the surface of the platter. These head arms are in turn connected to an actuator that moves them over the surface of the platter to locate the data elements being sought. The heads don't actually touch the surface of the platters when the disk is in operation, but ride over them on a cushion of air that is as little as 25 millionths of a centimetre thick. The delicate platters and arms are sealed inside an airtight case to protect them from dust particles – potentially dangerous to these precision-built, fast-moving items.

The operations of these components are controlled by a circuit board mounted inside the disk casing. This

Data stored on a hard drive's platters is accessed by read/write heads on movable arms.

FORMATTING

When you want to use a new floppy disk you have to format it; that is, run a program which prepares the disk for reading and writing information. This is also the case with a new hard disk. But with a hard disk, some formatting – known as low-level formatting – will almost certainly have been carried out at the factory. This low-level format determines certain physical properties of the disk, such as how the sectors are arranged (or 'interleaved'). There's a very strong possibility that the manufacturer will also have carried out a high-level format, which tests the disk to make sure that it is reliable and creates sector address tables (used to locate stored data).

circuit board governs a number of things, including the speed at which the spindle motor turns and the actuator controlling the movements of the head arm.

The hard disk needs to link in with the rest of the PC's circuitry; hence, there's also a hard-disk controller acting as the interface to the rest of the PC system. With older hard disks, such controllers took the form of a card occupying one of the PC's expansion slots. These days hard-disk controllers are generally integrated into the motherboard (see pages 104-105).

● Tracks, sectors and clusters

The data on the hard disk's platters is stored in a number of concentric circles, known as tracks. A track is divided into smaller areas called sectors, each one of which can store 512 bytes of data: a 4GB hard disk thus contains around 8 million sectors. However, if your data were stored in 512-byte chunks it would make the hard disk's job of finding it, reassembling it and loading it into your PC's memory an extremely inefficient one.

Instead, the File Allocation Table (FAT) file system used by Windows assembles sectors into larger blocks called clusters, which can contain as few as 8 sectors up to as many as 64 sectors.

The sectors in a cluster occupy a continuous block of space on the hard disk, making it easier for the read/write heads to find these larger chunks of data in one sweep. The clusters themselves can be located anywhere on the surface of the platters; they are not continuous. In order to load a file, your hard disk has to find all the clusters of which it is comprised in the right order.

Windows keeps track of these clusters with entries in the FAT, marking each one with a unique number and then marking the final cluster in the sequence with an 'end-of-file' marker. When they are instructed to load a file, the hard disk's read/write heads move across the platters at very high speed, finding each cluster as they go along and loading the file into memory.

● Capacity and progress

Hard disks have developed rapidly. In the late 1980s, an expensive PC might have a hard disk capacity of 40MB; now hard disks with 500 times that capacity are the norm. Not only are they bigger and faster, but they are cheaper; it's reckoned that there has been a 100,000 per cent improvement in the price-performance ratio in the last 15 years. This is just as well, since for every rise in hard disk capacity there has been an equal increase in the size of the files that need to be stored for today's program versions.

Fragmentation/defragmentation

A single file can be stored in many clusters located on different parts of the disk, but this is inefficient. Because hard disks are mechanical devices with moving parts, they are necessarily much slower than the electronic parts of your PC. Ideally, each file's clusters should be positioned one after the other on the disk; in other words, they would be 'contiguous' (meaning end to end), so minimizing the need for these 'slow' mechanical parts to move about looking for them. In fact, your PC's file system begins life with most of the files contiguous. But as time goes by and files are added and deleted, the disk becomes fragmented – the clusters for some of the files are no longer next to each other nor even near each other. Obviously, this leads to slower loading of files.

You should defragment your hard disk periodically so that the clusters are rearranged in more contiguous positions. This will speed up the loading time of programs and data files. Windows is supplied with the Disk Defragmenter program, which defragments disks (see Stage 3, page 10). There are also many commercial programs that claim to do this, notably (right) the Speed Disk module of Norton Utilities (see pages 10-13).

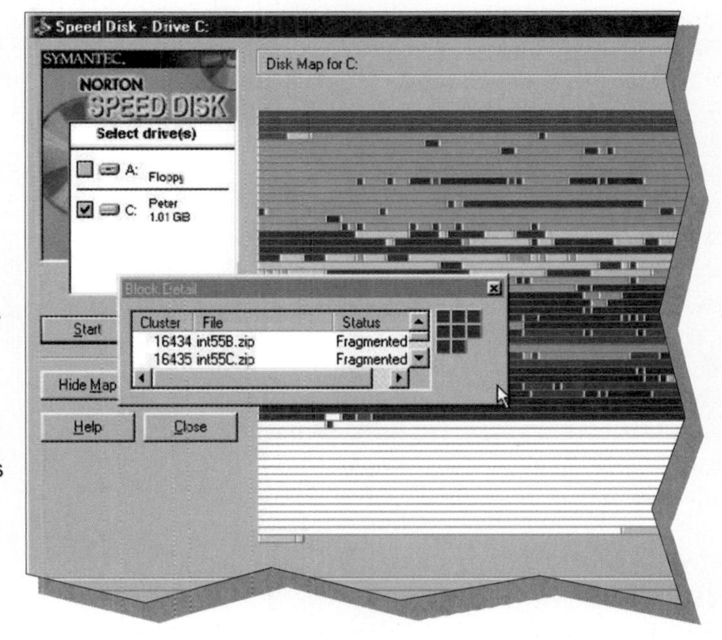

Understanding memory

The ability to store data in memory and recall it is one of the most important factors that make the modern desktop computer possible. But, in fact, a computer has several types of memory, used in several different ways.

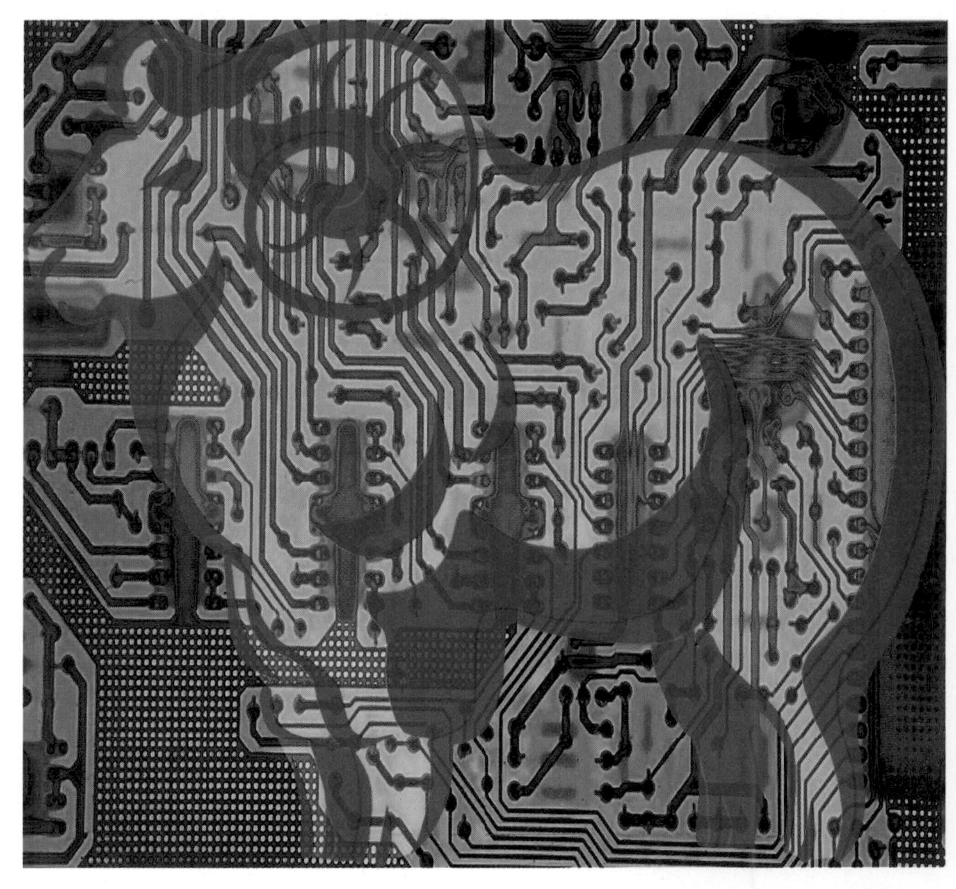

The different types of computer memory are known by their acronyms. These include RAM, ROM, DRAM, SDRAM, DIMM, PROM and EPROM. While initially confusing, you'll soon be able to recall what they all mean.

More than any other factor, such as disk space or processor speed, it is a computer's memory that determines how efficiently and how reliably it works. Even if you have a PC with a very fast processor, your software will still run slowly if you don't have enough memory installed. But what exactly is a computer's memory?

Computer memory is actually a pretty loose term. First of all, memory can refer to several different kinds of computer chip, each with its different uses. However, there is also a distinction between physical memory and virtual memory.

Virtual memory does not consist of real computer chips at all. Instead, it is simply a way of getting the software to pretend that it is using physical memory chips when, in fact, it is using part of your hard disk as a form of temporary storage. This provides a short-term way in which to increase the available memory without having to install any extra chips.

● The computer's main memory

Physical memory chips come with various setups, designed to be installed inside your PC and other computer equipment, such as printers. These fall into a small number of different types, of which the most important is RAM (Random-Access Memory). RAM is what people are usually referring to when they ask 'How much memory has your PC got?' Also known as main memory, RAM comes in the form of strips of computer chips that slot into the PC's motherboard. These are distinct from the processor's very high-speed cache memory chips.

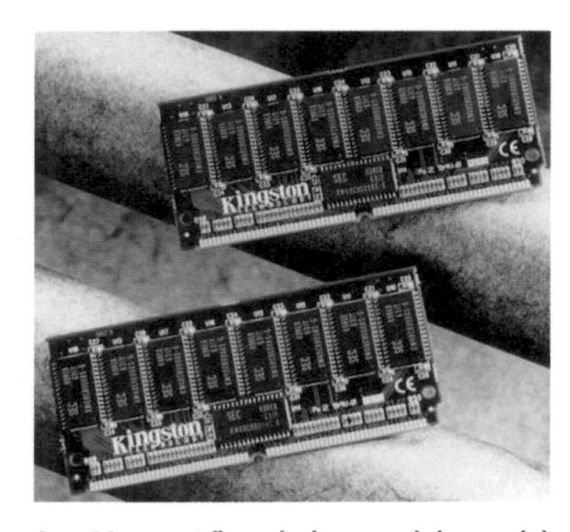

Some PCs – especially notebooks – can only be upgraded with more expensive, non-standard size memory boards.

You might expect memory to be a permanent quality, in the same way that humans will always remember the answer to two plus two, once they have learnt it. However, although devices such as your hard disk provide long-term storage for this type of data, RAM is continually being overwritten and re-used by new data. RAM is more like the short-term memory we use to remember a phone number we have just been told, until we can write it down.

RAM is used as a temporary storage area for all the information that your PC is dealing with from second to second. Although your hard disk is used for long-term storage of all the data needed by your programs, it takes a while to find data on the disk and load data from it. It is quicker if all the data you use is placed in RAM and accessed from there.

You can both read and write to RAM. This means that, as well as calling up the information held there, you can also put data back into it. However, this form of memory is what is known as 'volatile', meaning that it will be erased when you switch off your PC or if there is a problem with the power supply. This is why it is vital to save your work periodically, thus transferring the data you have just created and placed in RAM to permanent storage on the hard disk.

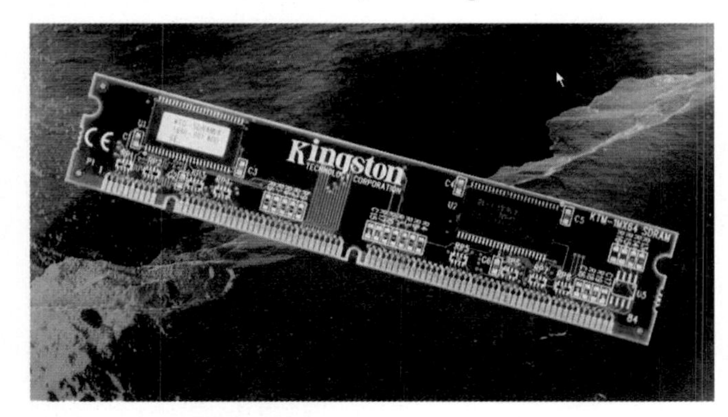

Synchronous Dynamic RAM (SDRAM) DIMMs give fast memory access in new PCs. SDRAM could soon be superseded by RDRAM (see New speed standards box).

● Other types of RAM

Nowadays, it's not just PCs that use RAM. Many internal add-on devices (such as sound cards and graphics cards) have their own memory. RAM chips are also commonly fitted to external hardware, such as printers.

The reason for adding RAM to all these devices is just the same as the reason for adding it to the PC itself – to increase performance and to minimize the time spent reading the hard disk. For example, if a printer has its own RAM, this can be used to store a lengthy document while it is being printed, with no need to take up any further computer time. Also, faster versions of RAM, such as Synchronous Dynamic RAM (SDRAM), have made memory access, and hence the PC, faster.

● Other types of memory

Although RAM is the only kind of memory that you are ever likely to want to change, it's still useful to know what other kinds of memory exist. These form one or more types of ROM (Read-Only Memory). All PCs and most external devices have a small amount of ROM: in fact, a PC must have it in order to work.
As the name suggests, any data held in ROM can only be read, not added to or altered. The important point is that ROM is non-volatile (retaining the information it stores, even when the power is off). For this reason, a PC uses ROM to store the essential instructions it needs to start up. The only problem with this is that ROM is not very fast. However, as it is only used briefly when the PC is switched on, its speed doesn't matter.

● Special ROM

PROM (Programmable Read-Only Memory) is a special type of ROM. It is rarely used in home PCs but is fitted widely in devices that depend on embedded applications, such as supermarket tills. PROM is basically a blank memory chip on which you can store the kind of program used to run such devices.

Remember that you can't erase a PROM chip after you've filled it, so it's not reusable and the only way to update any equipment that contains it is to change the chip. However, EPROM (Erasable Programmable Read-Only Memory) is pretty much the same as PROM, except that it's possible to wipe it by exposing the chip to ultraviolet light, and then it can be reprogrammed.

● EEPROM

EEPROM (Electrically Erasable Programmable Read-Only Memory) is similar to EPROM, except that it can be erased by an electrical charge. This type of memory is starting to appear in external hardware, such as modems and printers. The advantage of using a programmable ROM is that such devices can have their internal programs updated as new drivers and software become available.

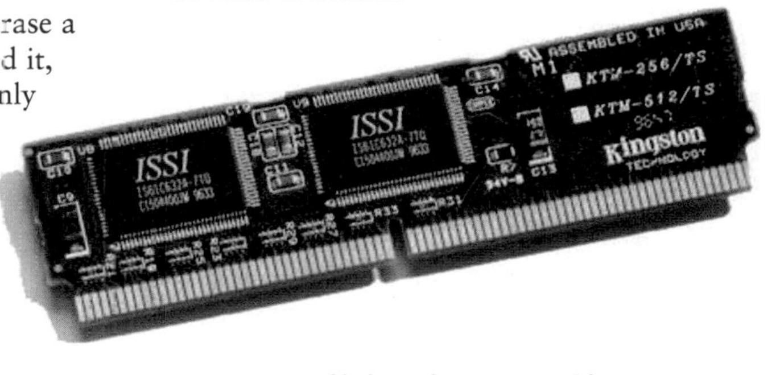

Special high-speed memory is used for a processor's very fast cache memory.

CHEAP MEMORY

One good thing about memory is that it's cheap. It wasn't always this way, but with a dip in the price of silicon and other physical materials, purchasing extra RAM is nowadays pretty inexpensive. It's still not easy to work out what kind you need (see Stage 3, pages 94-95), but as long as you consult a computer dealer, there's little reason for your PC not having the optimum amount of RAM. Prices vary, with 64MB of RAM costing between £25 and £35, depending on the manufacturer and retailer.

NEW SPEED STANDARDS

A few years ago, the fastest widely available type of RAM was DRAM – Dynamic Random Access Memory – (see Stage 3, pages 94-95). But things change quickly in the PC world and another breakthrough has put an even faster type of RAM on general release. Called SDRAM (Synchronous DRAM), this is an advanced version of the DRAM standard. The 'synchronous' tag means that it can run at the same speed as the PC's processor, making it about three times faster than conventional RAM. Of course even SDRAM's status won't last and faster types of memory, such as RDRAM (Rambus DRAM) and SLDRAM (SyncLink DRAM), have already been introduced. As yet, however, they have not caught on in a big way, and SDRAM is still the most widespread fast memory.

How keyboards work

As the main interface between you and your computer, the keyboard is one of the PC system's most vital components. So it's worth giving a little thought to what goes on every time you press a key.

Working with an ergonomically styled keyboard can be kinder on the fingers, hands and arms.

No single item of your PC hardware takes as much of a hammering in the course of its lifetime as the keyboard. No matter what software you're using (with the important exception of some games that use a mouse or joystick), the keyboard is still the main means of entering data and commands. Given that the keyboard itself contains over 100 moving parts – and that they have to operate reliably many thousands of times – the keyboard has to be built to very high standards.

Fortunately, most keyboards are built to last, using tried-and-tested technology that has changed little since the first IBM PCs appeared in the early 1980s. That's not to say that keyboards shouldn't be treated with due care and respect – cleaning and looking after your computer's components will increase their efficiency and lifespan.

It's worth emphasizing how important it is to keep liquids as far away as possible. It's extremely easy to knock over a drink while you're working at your desk, and if any liquid gets in your keyboard, it could cause irreparable damage. If you shake the drops out immediately and leave the keyboard to dry, this might spare it, but often spillage means having to buy a new keyboard.

However, a replacement keyboard is one of the more affordable PC components; you can pick up a perfectly good one for less than £20 – but you shouldn't need to (barring spillages) as your keyboard should go on working for many years. Replacement keyboards are also worth considering if you're not happy with the existing one. If you decide to fit a new keyboard, there is a range of alternatives available (see Alternative keyboard layouts box, right).

A computer keyboard has a tiny circuit board linking it to the PC's system unit.

ASCII CODES

Your PC's processor deals only in binary numbers. You, however, work with the letters, numbers and other characters on your keyboard and those displayed on screen, so the computer has to have some way of connecting the numbers it processes with the characters you see. This is called ASCII (American Standard Code for Information Interchange), which represents English characters as numbers, with each letter assigned a code from 0 to 127. As well as codes for upper and lower case letters, other ASCII numbers are used for numerical characters and special functions, such as accents or symbols that don't appear on your keyboard.

● How your keyboard works

When you press a key, you trigger a change in the amount of current that flows through a circuit attached to it. Embedded in the keyboard (or installed on the PC motherboard) is a specialized microprocessor (often an Intel 8048 chip), which scans each of the circuits connected to the keys, detecting fluctuations in the current as a key is first pressed and then released. The processor runs several hundred scans per second.

Each key is assigned a code, which the embedded processor can identify. When it receives a signal from a key, it generates a scan code. Each key has two of these; one for a press and another for a release.

The processor not only stores the scan code in the keyboard's memory area, but also sends it to the computer's Basic Input/Output System (BIOS) (see page 105). A signal known as an **interrupt** is then sent to the computer's main processor to let it know that a scan code is awaiting its attention. Afterwards, when the computer has finished reading the scan code from the keyboard, it sends back a message telling the keyboard that it can delete the code from its own memory.

● Interpreting your commands

Reading the keyboard is a complex, relatively slow process, but as it happens much faster than you could possibly type, this doesn't affect you. A complication is that each scan code has to be changed to the ASCII code (see ASCII codes box on the opposite page) for a character, or changed to a control code. The BIOS puts the resulting code into its memory, from which your application program, or Windows, collects it. The software then takes action. Depending on the code it finds, the software will display your keystroke as a character on the monitor screen, or operate the controls specified by that keystroke or combination of keystrokes, such as [ALT]+[S] for save.

WHAT IT MEANS

INTERRUPT

An interrupt is a signal telling a program that an event has occurred so that the software can take a specified action. Every single keystroke that you make generates an interrupt signal.

Alternative keyboard layouts

FOR ANYONE who's discontented with their existing keyboard, there is a host of alternatives. For example, there are various different 'ergonomic' keyboard layouts, all designed to make the act of typing more comfortable than on a conventional keyboard. Most of these curve to follow the natural movement of your hands and incorporate some type of wrist rest to help obviate the complaint known as RSI (Repetitive Strain Injury), which can afflict some people who type a great deal. Some of these keyboards even come in modular blocks (keypad, function keys and so on), which can be taken apart and reconfigured to suit the individual.

Another alternative keyboard aims to improve on the QWERTY key layout that has been around since the invention of the manual typewriter in the 19th century. QWERTY was designed not as an aid to speed up typing but as a means of slowing down the typist; on early models, if the user typed too fast, it caused the machine to jam repeatedly. Few of us care too much about the speed element, since we are unlikely to want to type at 130 words per minute. But apart from slowing you down, QWERTY is also inherently inefficient and uncomfortable – you are constantly stretching to reach the most frequently used keys.

The best known of several alternative keyboard systems is the Dvorak layout, in which (among other changes) the letters ASDFG on the 'home row' are replaced by AOEUI. Enthusiasts for this system claim it makes for faster, more accurate and much more comfortable typing. You can easily try out the Dvorak keyboard in Windows. Open the Control Panel, then open Keyboard. Click the Language tab, highlight your installed language, then click Properties. There's a keyboard layout selection, among which is US Dvorak (as well as options for left- and right-handed versions).

For more on the Dvorak keyboard go to www.mwbrooks.com/dvorak/index. html where there is a good selection of links to other Dvorak-related sites, together with an extensive array of information about the history and use of the Dvorak layout.

It looks like a normal keyboard, but examine it closely and you'll see the arrangement of the letters on the keys of this Dvorak keyboard is different from a conventional one. Dvorak devotees claim it is faster and more accurate.

Home Learning & Leisure

Geography

Learning about every aspect of landscape, climate, population and natural features – and the effects these things have on us – is a daunting task, but your Multimedia PC can help.

Geography is a big and complex subject, and the two Multimedia CD-ROMs that we take a look at here approach it from very different angles. Dorling Kindersley's *Test For Success Geography*, now published by GSP, is aimed squarely at GCSE revision and filling gaps in the student's knowledge, while Granada Learning's *Changing Environments* is based on a 1990s TV series called *Geographical Eye*.

● Test For Success Geography

Test For Success Geography is a series of questions and tests covering National Curriculum Key Stage 3 geography and is aimed at the 11-14 age group. The structure of the software is easy to grasp, allowing the student to get down straightaway to the serious business of finding out how much they have (or haven't) learned. To start you simply choose a level, from Foundation, Intermediate or Higher, then a subject, then a section, and finally a topic. You might, for example, select Physical Geography as the subject, Geomorphological Processes as the section and Rivers as the topic.

Once you've made these decisions, you simply answer the illustrated multiple-choice questions. Click the wrong button and you hear a nasty noise; answer correctly and, in addition to a tick, you receive a clear explanation of the answer. The 750 questions are accompanied by relevant and attractive images, such as maps, diagrams and satellite photos, helping to reinforce the principles involved. Once you've completed a test you can view your results.

Test For Success Geography is a good example of Multimedia software that is relatively narrow in scope but does its job effectively, simply and attractively. It will certainly make the chore of revision more pleasurable for the reluctant student, and its varied tests, either based on one particular section or chosen at random across the syllabus, will keep learners on their toes. Completing a few sessions with this software should make any student feel more confident in taking their exam – and more interested in the subject.

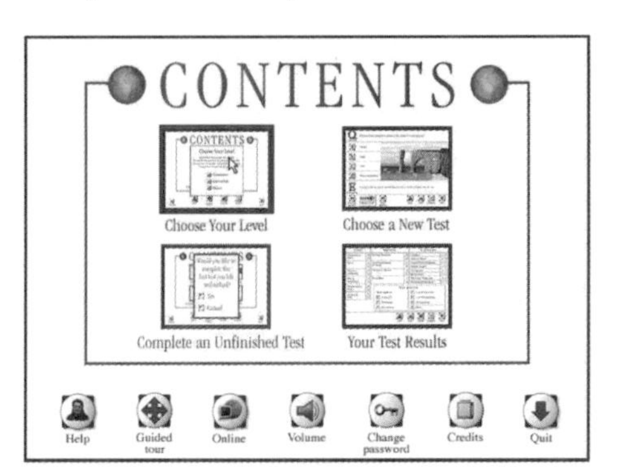

Test For Success Geography ***lets the student start at a comfortable level, which helps to increase confidence.***

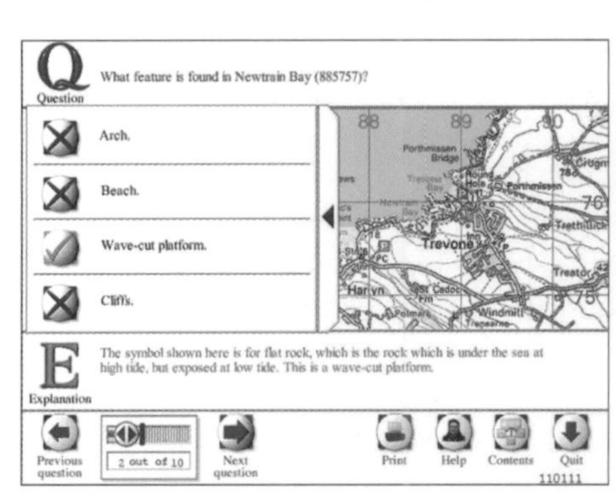

Details from Ordnance Survey maps are displayed with great clarity in **Test For Success Geography.**

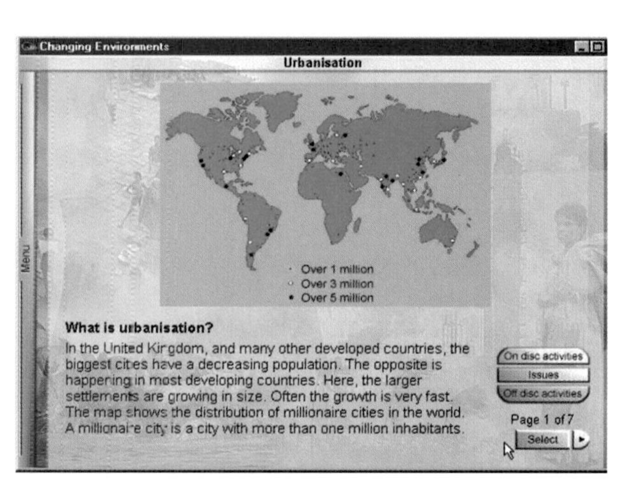

***Changing Environments* includes six case studies of European regions. Each one features extensive video footage, as in the case of the Doñana National Park in Spain (left). The video gives links to clear explanations, such as this one on the growth of urbanisation worldwide (right).**

● Changing Environments

As Granada Learning's *Changing Environments* is based on a geographical TV series, it is no surprise to find that the CD comes with a generous 30 minutes of video footage, not to mention the 300 or so colour images.

The video is no mere distraction, however. It is fundamental to the aim of the CD, which is to show how and why a given environment changes over time, and what – if anything – can be done about it if the changes are for the worse.

A typical screen from* Physical World*, showing how a text explanation is backed up by colourful and helpful graphic representation. Many diagrams are also linked to animations.

● Case studies

The core of *Changing Environments* is formed by the six case studies from around Europe. These include the pollution and overfishing of the North Sea, the flooding of the river Loire in France, the danger to the wetlands of Doñana in southern Spain, and an examination of the effects of lignite mining in a remote corner of Greece. In each case the video footage and commentary give a clear and engaging presentation of the factors that have changed the environment.

Each case study is linked to both on-disc and off-disc activities. The on-disc activities are learning modules directly related to the subject matter covered in the video. There are well-illustrated tutorials on a wide range of topics, each one tested thoroughly. Off-disc activities are issues that can be explored with further research; as such they may be of more use if carried out as group work in the classroom, which the teacher can help to organize, rather than in the home.

● Physical World

The significant factors examined in *Changing Environments* are a combination of the man-made and the natural. *Physical World* (also from Granada Learning) concentrates more on the work of nature, showing how the planet we live on has been shaped by the elemental forces at play for hundreds of millions of years.

As a result, this CD-ROM has a more textbook-like feel to it than *Changing Environments*. It also has far less video footage, but to compensate for the lack of video, there is a larger number of explanatory photographs, diagrams and animations.

The CD has three main areas: Features and Processes; People and their Environment; and Natural Hazards. The first section clearly illustrates the benefits of Multimedia technology for certain areas of knowledge: while a book can only show a static diagram, here the animated graphics can clearly show the effects of physical processes over time. Examples shown are the formation of river meanders and the movement of tectonic plates.

Both of these Granada Learning CDs are thorough explorations of their subject matter, and both offer plenty of ways for the student and/or teacher to expand on what has been learned. In conjunction with a program like *Test for Success Geography*, which really can find out if the user has taken it all in, they should help to produce a much richer understanding of the forces of nature and the consequences of mankind's interaction with them.

CONTACT POINTS

Dorling Kindersley
Test For Success Geography
GSP
Tel: 01480 496600
Price: £19.99*

Physical World
Price: £49.00 single user, £10.00 per additional user*
Changing Environments
Price: £49.00 single user, £10.00 per additional user*
Granada Learning
Tel: 0161 827 2912
www.granada-learning.com

*UK prices

20th-century history

Mankind has undergone every extreme of triumph and tragedy during the last century. Now you can learn about them with your Multimedia PC.

The 20th century was arguably the most momentous 100 years since human history began. Yet the very diversity of achievement, disaster, triumph and tragedy – together with the accelerating pace of change – make it a difficult period to appreciate in any kind of perspective.

However, the study of 20th-century history lends itself well to the Multimedia CD-ROM. There is a wide variety of discs available for both children and adults, with a full range of material giving either an educational or entertaining slant.

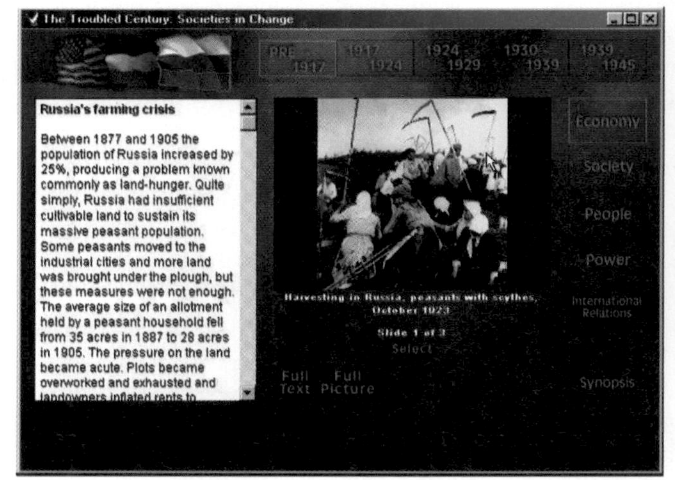

***The Troubled Century** CD-ROM from Granada Learning (above), which supports the National Curriculum (Key Stage 4), looks at the effect of conflict on society. The **Societies in Change** section (left) is typical of the presentation; the user can select the USA, Germany or Russia, and investigate the rise of capitalism, fascism or communism.*

● Times of trouble

The Troubled Century from Granada Learning is primarily intended for schools and is linked to Key Stage 4 of the National Curriculum.

This CD-ROM investigates some of the important events and people who shaped the century and is divided into three sections: The Struggle for Peace; Societies in Change; and Superpower Relations. These, respectively, look at war, the rise of political movements and the motives and actions of major world leaders.

The source material used in the compilation of the CD-ROM is excellent, with detailed contributions from well-established authors and a wealth of archive material. This would provide a very useful source for anyone studying Modern World History at GCSE level. Overall, it forms a good package, especially for classroom use. Teachers will no doubt find the accompanying educational paperwork valuable, too.

● Real lives

How We Used to Live: 1936-1953, which also comes from Granada Learning, is aimed at children between the ages of seven and 11 and is linked to Key Stage 2 of the National Curriculum. It is the third CD-ROM in the *How We Used to Live* series, based on the long-running educational television programme of the same name. Previous titles explored the Victorian period, but this CD-ROM features the lives of the Hodgkins family and their friends in the pre- and post-World War II periods. Using an extensive database of historical material, it looks at life in the home, at work and at play, tracing changes in technology and transport, as well as Britain at war.

● The good, the bad and the ugly

Makers of the 20th Century, from Linton Healey Multimedia, takes a different approach to studying the period. This CD-ROM tells the user about the events of the past 100 years through the biographies of 200 people who, for one reason or another, are widely regarded as having changed or

The colourful and innovative main screen of **Makers of the 20th Century** *(below) leads to fascinating information about the people behind the events of that era.*

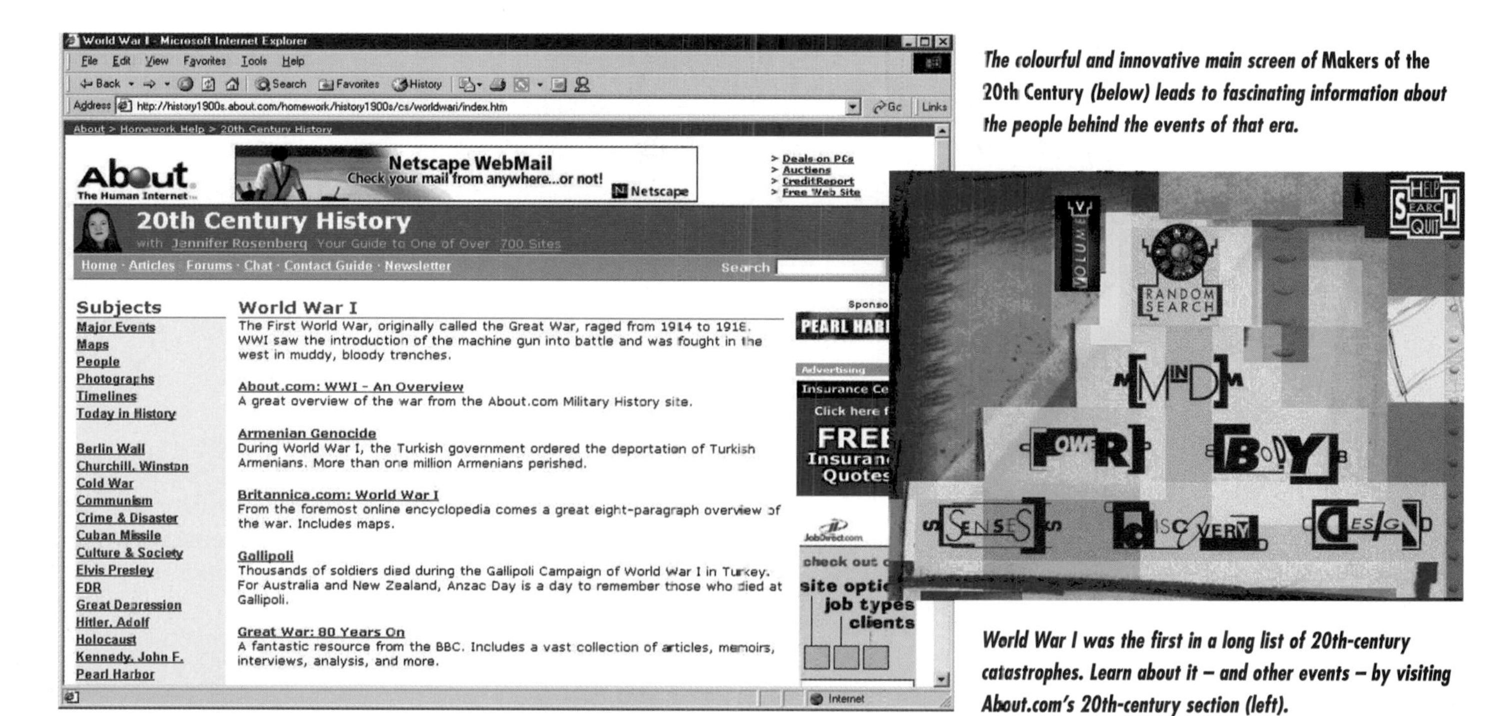

World War I was the first in a long list of 20th-century catastrophes. Learn about it – and other events – by visiting About.com's 20th-century section (left).

otherwise influenced our times. The people featured come from all areas of society, from the worlds of entertainment, science, philosophy and social reform. This makes the biographies diverse – ranging from Fred Astaire to Professor Stephen Hawking. *Makers of the 20th Century* incorporates pictures, movies and sound, so, for example, you can watch Astaire dance or listen to Professor Hawking explain his theory of the cosmos.

The CD-ROM also forms an historical archive, including many original documents that vividly bring to life contemporary events. The CD's earliest newspaper story features an attempt in 1901 to send a wireless signal across the Atlantic; the period is captured atmospherically and explained in an interesting and informative way.

● Studying specific events and people

There are several CD-ROMs which are devoted to significant events, such as World War I. Others look closely at individuals, such as Albert Einstein, or discuss specific incidents, such as the sinking of the *Titanic*. One such disk in *The Times Perspectives* series from Linton Healey Multimedia is called *Women's Rights*. It traces the history of female emancipation through the stories that were published in *The Times* newspaper.

Although mainly focusing on the 20th century, the CD-ROM uses the closing years of the 19th century to provide a backdrop to the changes that have taken place during the past 100 years.

One of the earliest reports features the 'auction' of a wife. Other stories cover the working conditions of women. The CD-ROM also traces the story of the suffragettes and those who have taken up the equal rights banner in the modern age.

Perhaps the only weakness of telling history through the reports of just one newspaper is that the stories reflect the political bias of the paper. This is what makes *The Times Perspectives* so different from CD-ROMs portraying past events through the eyes of those experiencing them.

● Looking forward

The computer has probably been one of the greatest forces for change in the 20th century, and there is endless speculation about the future of the technology, so it's refreshing to see that technology can bring the past to life as well as look to the future.

CONTACT POINTS

The Troubled Century
Price: £49.00*
How We Used to Live: 1936-1953
Price: £49.00*
Granada Learning
Tel: 0161 827 2927
www.granada-learning.com

Makers of the 20th Century
Price: £44.99*
Women's Rights
Price: £39.99*
Linton Healey Multimedia
Tel: 01525 852 813

*UK prices

SITES TO @ VISIT

The Internet can be extremely helpful for projects involving historical research.

American Cultural History
www.nhmccd.edu/contracts/lrc/kc/decades.html
This fascinating site is all the work of the librarians at Kingswood College in the USA. Using their own family photos as illustrations, they give you the story of American life in the 20th century, a decade at a time, with lots of key facts.

About.com
history1900s.about.com.
This site is interesting and well-organized, with information and links to many other sites on 20th-century history.

Holmes and Watson speed to the scene of a crime in the 1892 Conan Doyle story 'Silver Blaze'.

Classic literature

From Chaucer and Dickens to H.G. Wells and Bram Stoker, CD-ROMs can turn your computer into a library of classic literature.

It goes without saying that the book will never be replaced by the literary CD-ROM. After all, there is precious little pleasure to be found in reading a lengthy story on a PC screen, compared with curling up in bed with a good, old-fashioned book: a computer isn't really quite the same. However, for many people, there are plenty of other practical reasons for having classic literature available on CD-ROM.

● Elementary, my dear reader

The CD-ROM book really comes into its own as a study aid. For example, let's say you want to know in which Sherlock Holmes story the following lines were uttered: 'When you have eliminated all which is impossible, then whatever remains, however improbable, must be the truth.'

To look through the complete works of Sir Arthur Conan Doyle would take days, perhaps even weeks. However, with a CD-ROM such as *Great Works of Literature*, from Focus Multimedia, it takes a matter of seconds to search the computer text (also known as E-text, for electronic text) to find out that it was in the short story 'The Blanched Soldier'.

● Quotations

Similarly, you can discover the origins of Holmes' classic line 'The game is afoot' (from the short story 'Abbey Grange': 'Come, Watson, come!' he cried. 'The game is afoot. Not a word! Into your clothes and come!'). It actually comes from Shakespeare's *Henry VI Part One*: 'Before the game is afoot thou still let'st slip.'

Another advantage of the CD-ROM is that quotations such as these can easily be copied over to Word and then reproduced in essays or reports.

A single CD-ROM can hold a very sizeable collection of books. For example, *Great Works of Literature* contains almost 950 works by over 100 authors – from Aesop to Mary Wollstonecraft – and embraces everything from works of fiction to factual and historical documents.

● Classic works

Great Works of Literature's collection of novels includes such 'ripping yarn' classics as Henry Fielding's *Tom Jones*, Daniel Defoe's *Robinson Crusoe*, Jane Austen's *Sense and Sensibility*, Charlotte Brontë's *Jane Eyre* and Emily Brontë's *Wuthering Heights*.

You will also find Chaucer and Shakespeare alongside popular classics, which include most of the Sherlock Holmes stories and several renowned tales of horror, such as *Dracula* by Bram Stoker, and *Frankenstein* by Mary Shelley.

● Poetry please

Great Poetry Classics is just what it says: a selection of more than 1,000 of the world's classic poems. At its simplest level this is a very straightforward way of acquiring a poetry anthology: just click on an author and then select one of the poems to display it on screen, printing

Charles Dickens' Mr Pickwick is caught under the mistletoe by the ladies.

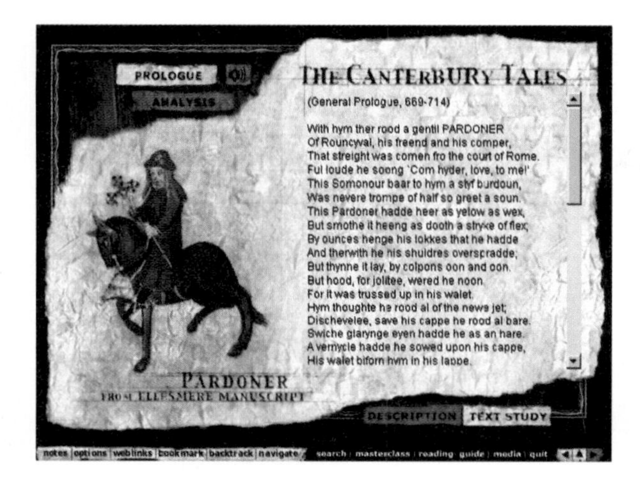

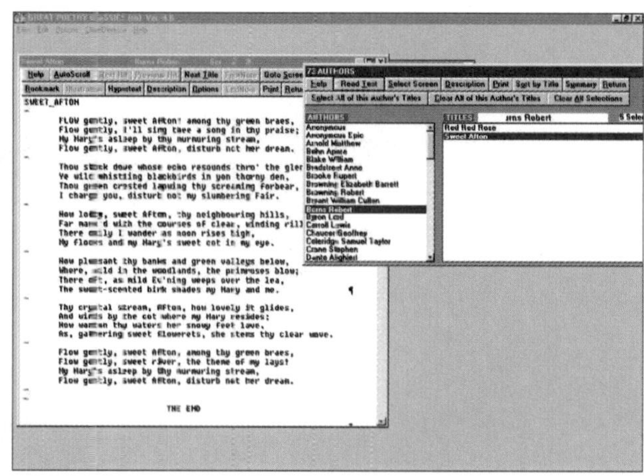

Get the experts from The Everyman Millennium Library (far left) to guide you through English literature, from the days of Chaucer to the modern day. Great Poetry Classics (left) brings over 1,000 poetry texts to your screen.

it out if you prefer to have a hard copy. But there is more to it than that. There are 45 poems available in audio format, enabling you to listen to them through your PC's speakers. The poems are intelligently and clearly read, with the result that those less used to poetry might well find these oral versions a welcome introduction to the expressiveness and power of verse. This is an excellent example of Multimedia computing in action.

The CD-ROM also has useful search and cross-referencing facilities. For example, you can very quickly find all instances of the word 'melancholy' in the generous selection of Keats' poetry. You can also sort the poems by age, type, phrase and so on.

SITES TO  VISIT

There is a host of classic literature to be downloaded from the Internet. In fact, the aim of Project Gutenberg at www. promo.net/pg is to make thousands of works of great literature available to anyone and everyone via the Internet.

The On-Line Books Page digital.library.upenn.edu/books/ lists thousands of books by author, title and subject. It also provides new listings.

Classics At The Online Literature Library at www.literature.org has many books by the expected writers, such as Dickens, but also includes the Oz titles by L. Frank Baum, Edgar Rice Burroughs' Tarzan series, plus the sci-fi works by H.G. Wells and Jules Verne.

● Focusing on Shakespeare

Another example of the CD-ROM's use as a reference guide is Focus Multimedia's *The Complete Works of William Shakespeare*.

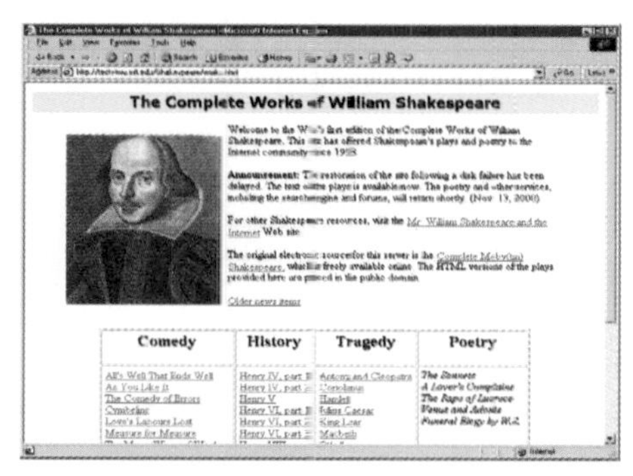

The Internet is also a rich source of literature. The complete works of Shakespeare are freely available on http://tech-two.mit.edu/Shakespeare/works.html

This has all the search features of *Great Works of Literature*, which is useful if you want to find the context of a famous Shakespearean quote. However, as well as the complete works, it also contains a Shakespeare study guide, plus selected book notes. Once again, this is a great-value title, which sells for under £10.

● The Everyman Millennium Library

If you're serious about the history of English literature, then look no further than Anglia Multimedia's *The Everyman Millennium Library* series of CD-ROMs. An ambitious project launched with Millennium Commission funding, this chronological series of CDs aims to show how literature has developed from Chaucer right through to the present day. The whole library consists of seven discs, but you can buy single discs that consist of one literary 'age' at a time.

The series was launched with a roll-out of Everyman classics to all secondary schools in the UK. Rather than concentrating on the text of the literature itself – which is better read off the page than off the screen – the project uses the Multimedia material to capture the attention, and to encourage the study of the classics.

Heavyweight contributors abound, with Master Classes from eminent professors of literature and input from Poet Laureate Andrew Motion. The Who's Who section allows you to see biographies of 700 key literary figures, and an interactive timeline helps to put the literature into cultural and historical perspective.

The CD-ROMs use a 3D stage metaphor for navigation, with each stage appropriate to the era the CD-ROM covers – such as Drury Lane for the 19th century. A Literary Companion supplies relevant information including reader notes and the glossary of terms and themes.

CONTACT POINTS

Great Poetry Classics
Price: £9.99*

Great Works of Literature
Price: £9.99*

The Complete Works of William Shakespeare
Price: £9.99*
Focus Multimedia
Tel: 01889 570 156
www.focusmm.co.uk

The Everyman Millennium Library
Price: £49.00* each
Anglia Multimedia
Tel: 0161 827 2927
www.anglia.co.uk

*UK prices

Discovering classical music

From school music lessons to TV commercials, classical music is everywhere. You can use your PC to learn more about why the works of the major composers are still part of our culture after hundreds of years.

The rich world of classical music has experienced much benefit from the introduction of Multimedia technology. Classical music CD-ROMs are widely available – and provide the bonus of being able to teach you something about what you hear.

Attica's *An Introduction to Classical Music* is a good Multimedia starting point for exploring this vibrant world. The CD, with four hours of playing time, contains excerpts from 207 pieces of classical music spanning several centuries. If you want, you can simply set these to play and enjoy background music while you carry on with your work. But there's much more to this CD than the musical extracts alone. The program kicks off with a comprehensive introduction that tells you just what classical music is and when it started. This brief history is extremely interesting, particularly when it explains how people listened to music in centuries past – whether chatting during the quiet bits or singing along with the more rousing or well-known tunes.

The main focus of the program, though, comes in the sections covering composers and compositions, and in the performances themselves. All the major composers of classical music – from Bach to Wagner and beyond – get a screen to themselves. These include a brief musical biography, a picture of the composer and a generous selection of extracts from

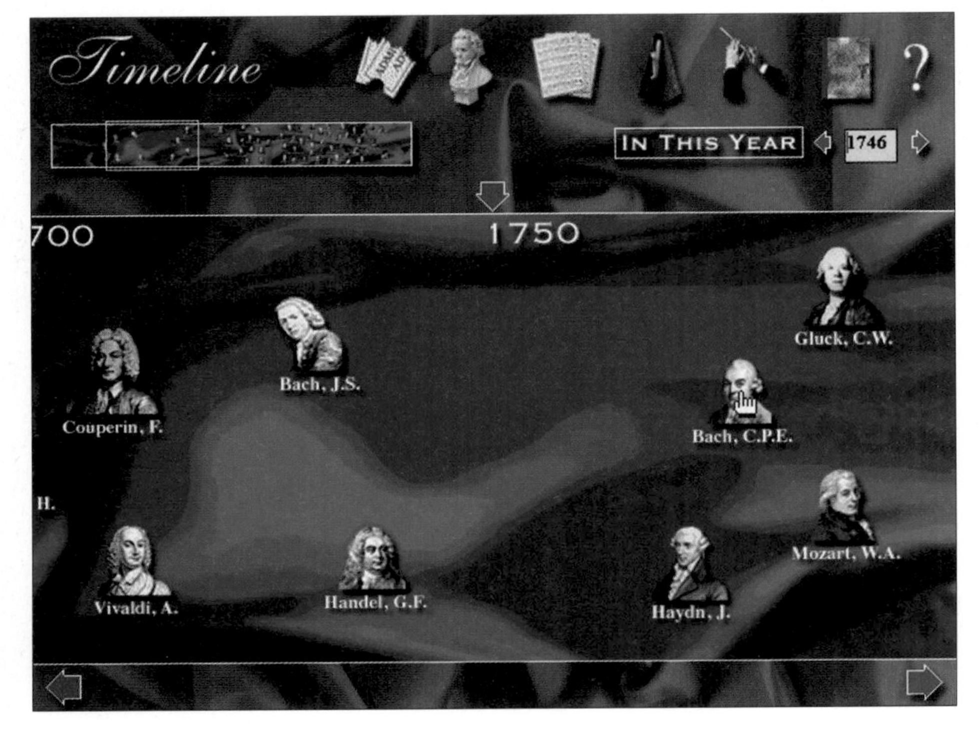

***An Introduction to Classical Music** provides an at-a-glance guide to which composers were working at any given time. Click on the In This Year button to get more detailed information.*

his works for you to listen to; usually there are at least four pieces, which is sufficient to give you an idea of their particular style. The Composition section takes a detailed look at a single piece by each of the composers, pointing out its musical attributes and character so that you can listen to it with newly informed ears.

● Timeline

There is also a useful Timeline section, which puts each individual composer into an historical context. You can then click on the In This Year button to get more detailed information on what was happening then in the world of classical music.

The software is clearly intended as an easy introduction to classical music for younger people; and they will find it an entertaining and user-friendly entry into that world. But older and more knowledgeable users will also find much that will be new to them. And, when you've taken in the information, you still have those four hours of great music to listen to over and over again.

Guide to the Orchestra, also from Attica, takes a different and much more focused approach to the subject. This CD is subtitled A Personal Guide with Sir Simon Rattle, and features the conductor taking us through a single piece of music, Benjamin Britten's *A Young Person's Guide to the Orchestra.* Because Britten's piece was not scored for the whole range of instruments, there is also additional original music commissioned from Judith Weir, the contemporary composer.

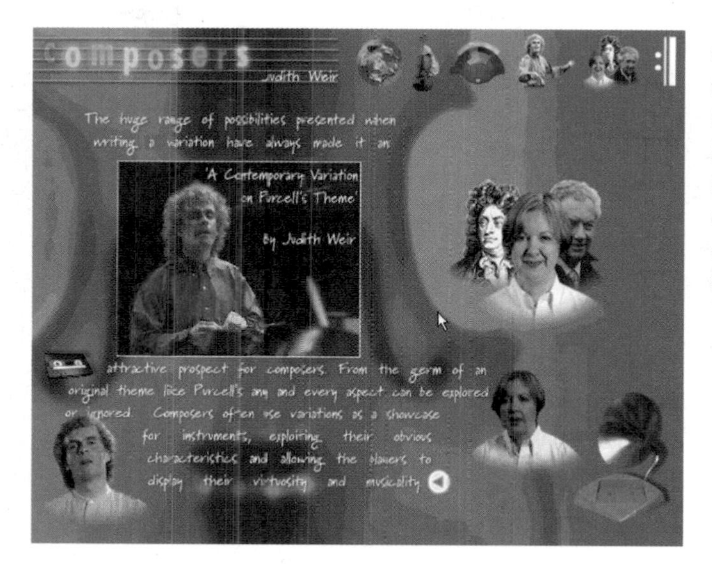

***Guide to the Orchestra* features quite a bit of video from animated talking heads. Here, Judith Weir talks about the thinking behind her composition. You can also click on Simon Rattle to hear him talking about the piece.**

● A living orchestra

As with Britten's piece, the aim of the program is to demonstrate, in an accessible and exciting way, how the instruments in the orchestra work – separately and together – to produce the massive range of tones, colours and moods available.

As well as video sequences and voice-overs from Sir Simon, there are also interviews with, and comments from, both Judith Weir and various members of the Birmingham Symphony Orchestra who play the music. In this way we build up a vibrant picture of how the orchestra interacts to produce the sounds the composer had in mind. We also learn about the different instruments and their roles, the physical layout of the orchestra, and something of the conductor's role in bringing it all together in performance.

Guide to the Orchestra is a rather more demanding Multimedia experience than *An Introduction to Classical Music* as there are fewer opportunities to simply listen to the music. But, with little effort, you will be rewarded by a much deeper understanding of making music.

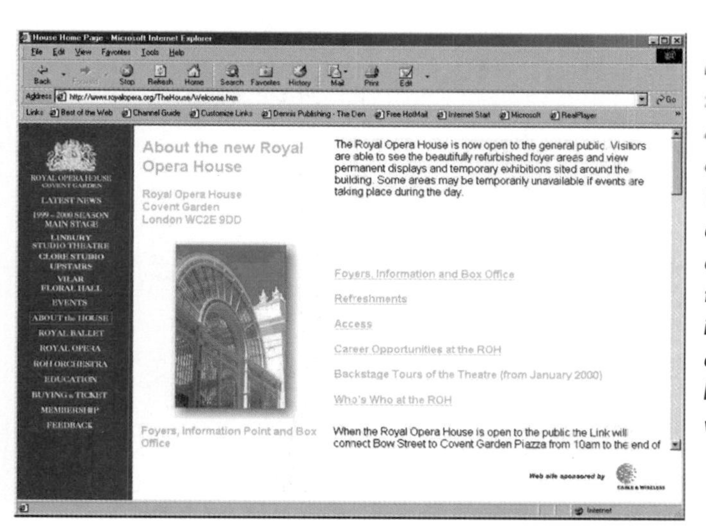

London's Royal Opera House, following its extensive – and expensive – make-over, has an attractively revamped Web site (www.royalopera.org). You'll find just about everything you need here, from details of the building itself to thorough listings of the many opera and ballet performances in its various auditoria.

SITES TO @ VISIT

The Web is alive with historical detail about classical music plus huge databases of composers' works to be accessed and listened to.

Classical Composers Database
http://utopia.knoware.nl/~jsmeets/abc.htm
If the list of composers on the reviewed CD isn't enough, try this growing site where there are details of more than 1,000 composers. It includes a biography and list of works for each, and some critical appraisals of the music.

J.S. Bach Home Page
www.jsbach.org
Here is a wealth of information about the life and work of Bach. There are ample pictures and examples of his music throughout.

CONTACT POINTS

An Introduction to Classical Music
Price: £10* approximately
Guide to the Orchestra
Price: £15* approximately
Attica, available from www.cdaccess.com

*UK prices

Exploring the world's art galleries

Don't worry if you haven't got the time to visit the art galleries that you'd like to – art gallery CD-ROMs allow you to savour the world's finest paintings from your PC.

Fashion

The first **Famous Museums of Europe CD-ROM** *takes you to London, Vienna, St Petersburg and Munich (top). It's possible to search the collections for particular topics, such as fashion (above).*

A day spent wandering around an art gallery can be a delightfully rewarding experience. Such an adventure can open your eyes to a fascinating array of paintings that you may never previously have known existed. For example, the National Gallery, in London's Trafalgar Square, houses one of the most outstanding collections of paintings in the world. A visit allows you to see some of the great masterpieces of Western art from the last 700 years, including paintings by Rembrandt, Vermeer, Turner and many other great artists. Yet, even in a whole day, you'd be hard-pressed to give more than a passing glance to the entire collection, since it contains more than 2,000 paintings.

If you want to learn more about the background to the various paintings and artists, you will have even less time to view the whole range of works. In addition, unless you live in London, getting to and from the gallery will inevitably reduce the actual time you have at your disposal to browse through the many displays.

Complete Illustrated Catalogue

THE NATIONAL GALLERY
COMPLETE ILLUSTRATED CATALOGUE
DIRECTOR'S INTRODUCTION
HISTORY OF THE NATIONAL GALLERY
HOW THE CATALOGUE IS ORGANISED
HOW TO USE THIS CD-ROM
INDEX subjects, names and related terms
ARTISTS the catalogue organised alphabetically by artist
FIND search text anywhere in the catalogue

There are many quick and easy ways of searching through The National Gallery's CD-ROM.

● Your guide to the gallery

Fortunately, help is at hand – in the shape of your computer and the art gallery CDs that are available. One such example is *The National Gallery Complete Illustrated Collection*, which includes every single picture in the gallery's collection, with a wealth of background information on the artists. You can search the

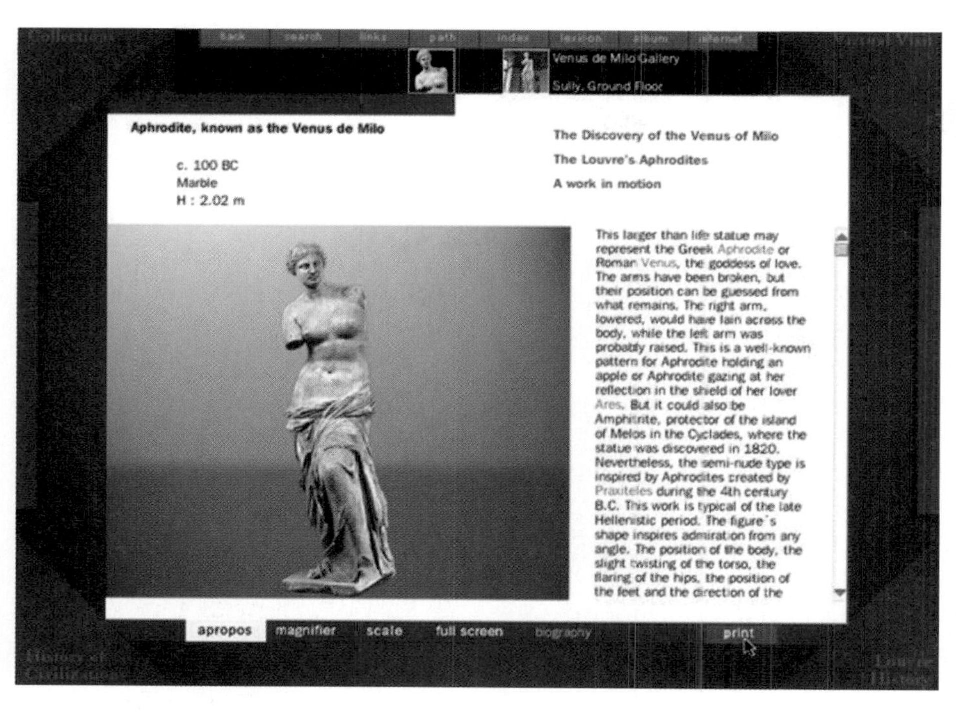

On The Louvre's virtual tour, you can view the Venus de Milo from 365 degrees, with options to zoom in, compare its scale and find out more information about the sculpture and the artist.

collection in a variety of ways, either by looking through the collection in alphabetical order or by carrying out detailed searches by artist, title, date or theme.

The real joy of the CD-ROM, however, is the quality of the images on screen. Expand the picture to maximum size and you can see each brush stroke and artistic trick in the painter's repertoire.

● Europe's finest galleries

Famous Museums of Europe – confusingly named, as it features galleries, not museums – takes a different approach. The two separate CD-ROMs do not try to be comprehensive in their coverage, but instead give a taste of the best works in some of Europe's most famous art galleries. Volume One covers the Uffizi Gallery in Florence, The Tate Gallery in London, the Hermitage in St Petersburg and the major art galleries of Munich and Vienna.

Volume Two takes in the Louvre in Paris, the Prado in Madrid, the Vatican Museum in Rome, the Galleria dell'Accademia in Florence as well as the Pushkin Museum in Moscow.

The main part of the program takes you on a 'virtual tour' of each collection. There are 3D-views of the rooms and you can examine any picture by clicking to enlarge it. In the Masterpieces option on the main menu, a selection of the paintings are examined in much more detail, with a voice-over providing lots of useful information.

Alternatively, you might want to explore the collections thematically. For example, if you select Fashion on the main menu, you'll see a selection of relevant pictures, again with a voice-over supplying information on the clothing in the painting.

The Famous Museums of Europe CD-ROMs include art galleries and look at many masterpieces, such as The Dance by Matisse in the Hermitage in St Petersburg.

● The Louvre

The Louvre DVD-ROM from Interactive Ideas goes even further – thanks to the massive amount of material that publishers Montparnasse Multimedia have been able to cram in. Over 1,000 works from the Louvre are detailed, from paintings such as the Mona Lisa to sculptures such as the Venus de Milo.

You can work your way through the Louvre in a virtual tour of the museum's 25 rooms, galleries and crypts. When you want to find out more about a work of art, you click on it to see it full screen and find out more about it. Of course, if time is tight, you can use the full index to go straight to a particular work.

DVD really makes this massive art museum come alive: there's room for a stereo soundtrack, an hour and a half of full-screen video covering the development Mediterranean civilization from 10,000 BC to 1848 AD, and a 30-minute film on the history of the Palais du Louvre itself.

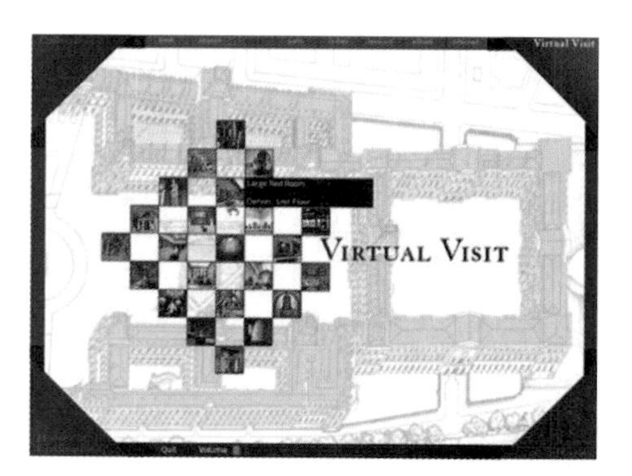

To enjoy a Virtual Visit, click on a picture icon to go straight to a particular area of the Louvre.

CONTACT POINTS

The National Gallery Complete Illustrated Collection
National Gallery Publications
Tel: 020 7747 2870
Price: £55*

Famous Museums of Europe (in two CD-ROMs)
Price: £24.99 each*

The Louvre (DVD-ROM)
Interactive Ideas
Tel: 020 8805 1000
Price: £34.99*

*UK prices

Impressionism

We've already discovered how you can visit an art gallery using your computer (see pages 122-123). Now we'll take a closer look at one of the most popular art movements.

Fine art is surprisingly well suited to Multimedia learning. Of course, there is no substitute for the real thing, but if it's an overview or an easy introduction you're after, a good CD-ROM can provide all you need.

And it isn't just general information you'll find. Many different areas of interest are catered for. To illustrate the point, we'll focus on the movement known as Impressionism, which covers such artists as Degas, Monet and Renoir (whose work is featured above the title on this page).

● The art and the artists

Of the many CD-ROMs available, *Impressionism to the Twentieth Century* from AVP PictureBase is a simple, but informative and well-constructed package. It doesn't quite have the slick presentation of a typical Multimedia program, but its prime concern is information and there's certainly plenty of it.

The CD-ROM is broken down into separate modules, starting with an introduction to Impressionism and then moving logically through Monet, Van Gogh, Gauguin, Cézanne, Toulouse-Lautrec and on into the 20th century. It also covers British painting from 1880 to 1912. There are 12 modules in all: each has a general introduction, displayed in a screen on the left-hand side, with all the works it discusses shown on the right. Each module covers some two dozen paintings and you can view the works, complete with text, by a simple double-click of the mouse.

● The full picture

The most interesting way to view the content is in AutoPlay mode. This puts each picture (plus several video clips) on screen in turn, accompanied by the spoken text. You can also click on a picture and call up printed text, which can then be highlighted with the mouse and copied onto your PC. This allows you to study each picture, accompanied by an historical description and artistic appreciation, and also to grab text and pictures whenever you want. There is a search facility as well, which allows you to look for works by title, artist or key word. Alternatively, you can display all the pictures thumbnail size and access them with a mouse click.

● Art and the National Curriculum

The CD-ROM also covers a wide variety of other subjects, including Art in the National Curriculum and English Architecture, as well as geography, history, foreign languages, music and science modules. All of these 'plug' into the same basic software and can be accessed from the same application.

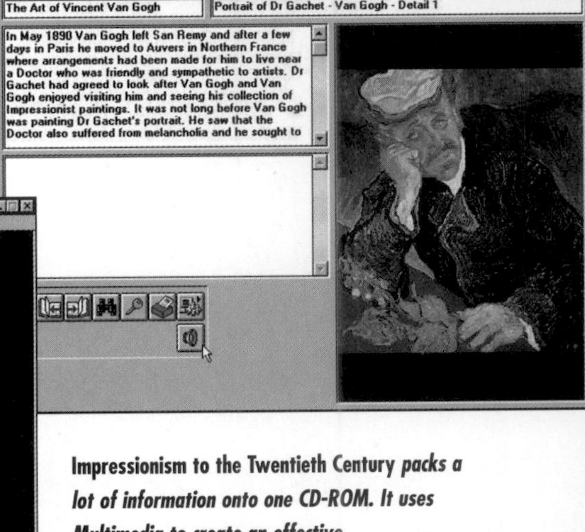

Impressionism to the Twentieth Century *packs a lot of information onto one CD-ROM. It uses Multimedia to create an effective documentary-style show, displaying textual information about each featured painting.*

The Impressionism package lets you make a virtual visit to the first-ever Impressionist exhibition in 1874. The image (left) shows the major Impressionists before they became famous. The package does, of course, allow you to examine individual works by a wide range of artists and lets you compare their styles, as shown below.

● The home of Impressionism

The beginnings of Impressionism are very French indeed (even though the style quickly spread throughout Europe), so it's fitting that an excellent examination of the movement should come from the French Multimedia company Emme. Their 2-CD *Impressionism* collection describes itself as a 'fascinating journey through a world of colour and light', which is true but gives little hint of the depth of information the package offers.

The CDs contain images of over 400 works, 200 of which are analysed in some detail. Paintings by all the big names – Monet, Manet, Renoir, Degas – are featured, but other less well-known but equally important artists, such as Caillebotte and Bazille, are also given their due. While these images and the information on them form the core of the program, and are done very well, they are not necessarily what users will find most interesting, as the package offers a much more imaginative and broader outlook on its subject matter than any simple display of pictures.

● Virtual gallery-going

For example, you can take a virtual visit to the very first Impressionist exhibition, which took place in 1874 in the Paris studio of the pioneering photographer Naclar. Rather than just showing the canvases as exhibited, the program takes you on a tour guided by the contemporary critic Louis Leroy. His voice-over tells of his delight and astonishment at this radical new way of painting, a reaction which is cleverly contrasted with that of another critic (more typical of his time) who expresses outrage and shock at what he sees as the inept daubings of the new painters. This is a very telling section, as it helps to bring alive the controversy that the Impressionists created at the time – difficult for us to grasp nowadays when Impressionism is overwhelmingly the world's favourite style of painting. In a similar vein, other modules allow you to visit the studio of the painter Bazille, to examine the places that the Impressionists loved to paint, or to hear Pissarro's words of wisdom and advice to young painters.

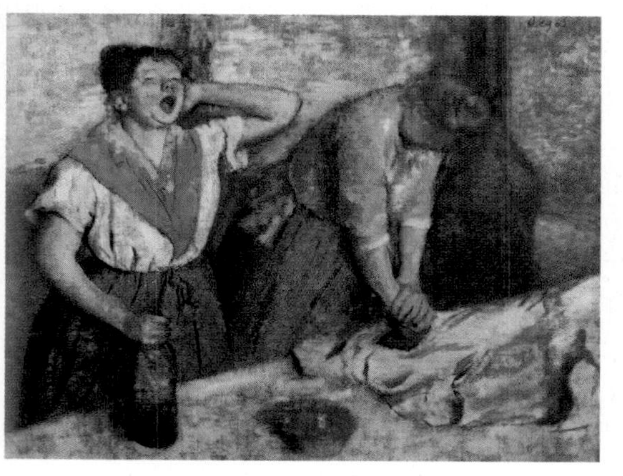

The Web Museum has special relay sites all over the world, so wherever you are you will be able to quickly download high-quality pictures, such as this work by Degas.

● Language of Impressionism

This background material actually enhances examination of the works themselves. The Language of Impressionism section gives a thorough and clear explanation of what the Impressionist painters were trying to do in their treatment of light and space, while the sections on individual painters strike just the right balance between their lives and their works. This CD package is an excellent introduction to and exploration of Impressionist art.

● Internet sites

There are plenty of sites related to Impressionism on the Internet but nearly all the links lead to the Web Museum (www.southern.net/wm) – a comprehensive site with a specialized Impressionism section, an exhibition of more than 100 Cézanne paintings and other related topics. The Web Museum uses cross-referenced *Encyclopaedia Britannica* entries, illustrated with representative works. The bigger the name, the more information there is. Monet, for example, is broken down into sections, comprising Early Works, First Impressionist Paintings, Later Impressionism and so on.

CONTACT POINTS

AVP PictureBase: Impressionism to the Twentieth Century
AVP PictureBase
Tel: 01291 625 439
Price: £69.00 (plus VAT)*

Impressionism
Interactive Ideas (Emme distributor)
Tel: 020 8805 1000
Price: £29.99*

*UK prices

How games are made

While you wait for your favourite game to load, spare a moment to think of the people who created it. Production teams sometimes labour for over a year before you get to play their latest creation.

In the early days of computer games, creating a successful game was usually a one-man operation. The same person would come up with the idea for the game, design it, program it and then place small advertisements to sell it. Now, whole teams of programmers, artists, designers and musicians work for months to create a single game, and companies invest huge amounts of money on development.

No matter what the game, they all start with a spark of inspiration. For example, in the game Populous, players can raise mountains and flood lands to help their followers. The game idea was conceived when its creator, Peter Molyneux, saw a Lego model of a mountain. Similarly, Tetris, which features shapes falling down the screen for you to scramble into place, was inspired by flat-fish swimming in an aquarium!

● From idea to icon

Even the most sophisticated idea usually starts with sketches and rough ideas jotted on paper. With the idea fleshed out, the games makers write a two-page outline that summarizes it as simply and briefly as possible.

Next comes an overview document written to sell the game to the company management, followed by a full design document. This details every part of the game, the levels and the creatures – in fact, all the information the programmers will need to create the game.

● Creating characters

Graphic artists and animators then go to work creating backgrounds and characters that feature in the game. If the game requires realistic movement, such as a footballer running or a hero jumping, then 'motion capture' is the answer. This involves attaching lights or glowing disks to volunteers and then videoing them performing actions such as hitting, kicking or catching a ball. A computer then 'captures' this video – in other words, it is imported into a computer graphics program – and the spots of light become a template for the animator to work with.

Soon, a computer stick man is performing the same actions, followed later by the finished 3D character moving realistically. Music and sound effects both help to add atmosphere

For the realistic movement of the characters in games, the games makers closely study how real people move.

Games CD-ROMs are pressed just like music CDs – many thousands at a time in a dust-free environment.

and realism and give a sense of excitement to the game: monsters scream or go 'splat' when they are killed, the crowd roars when a goal is scored and your character says 'ow!' if he or she is injured.

● Bringing it to life

Finally, the programmers become involved in order to make the computer-generated pixels come to life and to turn the animations into a fun game. Their role is still as important as in the early days – a game will succeed or fail depending on how well it plays. The efforts of the programmers should be largely invisible. Players should barely notice such things as the smoothness of scrolling and the number of animated objects on the screen at any one time.

● Testing time

Once the game itself is written, the process is far from over. Now it is sent out to play-testers who play the game again and again. Their job is to find any errors or bugs. It is a demanding task and needs an eye for detail and patience to check every aspect of the game thoroughly. Problems are reported back to the programmers, who fine-tune every detail of the game.

The finished game is then sent to the duplicator and, soon, thousands of CD-ROMs are rolling off the production line. Meanwhile the game's manual is being written and printed along with the packaging. If the game is to be exported, then translations of the rules are written and packed into the boxes. The whole product is then assembled and sent via the distributor to the shops.

● The sales pitch

While the game is in development, the marketing department sets about creating a market for it. Ideally, the makers want a demand for the game even before it appears in the shops. They engineer this with a three-pronged attack. First, samples, screenshots and information are distributed to the games magazines to give 'previews' or 'sneak peeks'. Then, full review copies are sent to magazines in the hope that they will provide pages of editorial coverage for games-hungry readers. Finally, an advertising campaign backs up the awareness already created by editorial coverage.

At the same time, the makers create tip sheets and Web sites to help and encourage players to get the most out of the game.

Meanwhile, the creative team is not idle – it is already working on the next game.

The concept for a football game, like this one from Electronic Arts, is simple enough, but making it work convincingly is an extremely sophisticated operation.

CUSTOMIZE YOUR GAMES

It is becoming increasingly common for multiplayer games, such as Quake and Total Annihilation, to have a game editor available for them. Using this editor you can customize the game to your own taste, adding new levels and graphics to give it a new lease of life.

The capabilities of these editors vary from game to game but for shoot-'em-up games, such as Quake or Half-Life (below), you are given the ability to create everything from new graphics and sound effects to completely new rooms and levels. Other games allow similar amounts of control and you will find that other enthusiasts will post their own efforts on the Internet for you to have a look at.

The only problem with customizing your games is that the editor programs themselves can be a little tricky to use. But the basics are usually pretty simple to pick up and you will find that creating your own levels can often be more fun the playing the original game!

The Internet

Browser plug-ins

Keeping up to date with advances in computer technology is often expensive, but not with plug-ins. They're usually free, and it's easy to download and install most of the plug-ins you will need.

The Web is a lively place, but only if you've got the correct hardware and software to see and hear it in all its glory. A standard Multimedia PC with sound card and speakers is the basic minimum in terms of hardware requirements. But you will also need the right software. It's often not enough just to have the most recent Web browser. To get the full Multimedia experience out of many sites, you need to supplement your Microsoft Internet Explorer or Netscape Navigator browser with the latest plug-ins.

Plug-ins are software add-ons that give extra capabilities to your browser. There are many different types, including, for example, those that let you see animations and 3D virtual worlds, play video clips and listen to music. They are usually downloadable completely free of charge from various sites on the Web.

● Netscape origins

Plug-ins originally referred exclusively to add-ons for Netscape Navigator, or, more specifically, add-ons that conformed to the Navigator standard. After a while, though, Internet Explorer became compatible with this standard, which meant that, for most plug-ins, one size fitted all. You simply download the plug-in and run the installer program, which installs itself correctly for the browser you are running. (You can install it for both browsers by running the same installer twice, specifying a different browser each time.)

● Plug-ins or ActiveX?

Internet Explorer is also designed to conform to the Microsoft ActiveX standard, which works in a rather different way. An ActiveX add-on, which Microsoft calls a control, is also designed to enhance the capabilities of your browser.

While Netscape Navigator is not directly compatible with ActiveX, there are plug-ins that allow it to run some ActiveX controls.

This might sound confusing, but it is actually quite simple. The term plug-in has become generic, and most people refer to all browser add-ons (including ActiveX) as plug-ins, whether or not they are the original Netscape Navigator-style plug-ins.

The main advantage of ActiveX controls over Netscape-style plug-ins is that you don't need to install them. As soon as you visit a page with an ActiveX control, it is automatically downloaded to your computer and starts to work immediately. If the plug-in is not an ActiveX control, detection is still automatic – your browser should tell you what it is and where to get it from.

● Download alerts

Because Netscape Navigator was the most popular browser in the early days of the Internet, its plug-ins are still the more common, so as you browse you're likely to come across plug-in download alerts quite frequently. All you need do is follow the on-screen links and instructions to track down the right file and start downloading it. Once completed, log off, close your browser and double-click on the downloaded file

It's a good idea to keep up with all the browser plug-ins, otherwise you will find you encounter several empty screens during Web browsing, where video, animation or audio should be displayed.

to run it. You'll then be presented with the usual install Wizard. Follow it through, restart your browser, log on and reload the page, and you'll see and hear what you've been missing.

Most plug-ins are effectively mini-programs in themselves, and are often basic viewers or players of files that the browser on its own has no means of handling. Without the plug-in, the files themselves are effectively useless. The authors who create these files use special programs to do so, and it's in their interests to make sure that it is easy to download and install the appropriate plug-in so everyone can view their work properly. For this reason almost all plug-ins are free.

If you visit a site that appears to be charging for a plug-in, have a look around the same site for a free version – perhaps a demonstration or trial version; there is usually one somewhere. If not, and if you don't have a compelling reason to use the plug-in's special files, then forget it; it is unlikely that you will come across the need for it often anyway.

● Complex effects from small files

Because plug-ins are effectively programs in their own right, they can appear to make a Web page look much more complex than a conventional HTML-based page. When you visit pages that contain the files that your plug-ins use, you'll often find that a surprisingly effective display can be achieved with a relatively small file. The file itself contains simple instructions, but the plug-in interprets them to display a more complex effect. Other plug-ins use compressed files which send complex video or sound files streaming to your PC, so you can watch or listen as the files arrive.

WHAT IT MEANS

STREAMING

Streaming is a technique where a video or sound clip is downloaded from an Internet site, but you don't have to wait for the download process, which could be lengthy, to finish before the clip starts playing.

● Plug-in storage

Within the Program Files folder on your hard disk will be a folder for your browser. Within this folder you'll see a Plug-ins folder.

Plug-ins are updated from time to time, so you might find yourself visiting a Web page that tells you to download a plug-in that you already have. If this happens, it's a simple matter to download and install the newer version. Delete the earlier version from the Plug-ins folder to save space on your hard disk drive.

Plug-in types

THERE ARE HUNDREDS of plug-ins out there on the Web, some of which are esoteric and many of which are doomed to obsolescence by simple lack of take-up. The holy grail of developers is for Netscape and Microsoft to embrace their plug-ins to the extent that they include them with their browsers. This has happened with Flash, one of the most popular animation and interactive plug-ins. Flash is an offshoot of Shockwave, another popular plug-in. Both were developed by Multimedia and interactive authoring developers Macromedia. Shockwave is also included with Windows and with Internet Explorer, (which comes with Windows), but not with Netscape Navigator.

With QuickTime downloaded, you can view both Web animation and videos.

To download these plug-ins visit Macromedia's site (www.macromedia.com/software). On the separate Shockwave site (www.shockwave.com) there's a selection of Multimedia content that shows off what the plug-ins can do in terms of sound and graphics. There are some excellent examples of the players in action, including interactive games (claimed to be the best on the Web, and with justification) and cartoon clips.

The leading plug-in for streaming audio and video on the Web is RealPlayer. This can be very impressive indeed. Instead of waiting some minutes for a file to download entirely before viewing it, streaming media downloads a bit at a time, compressing, buffering and uncompressing as it goes, giving you immediate sound or video. Granted, the sound is not as good, and the video has a tendency to jump occasionally, but that's a small price to pay for such instant gratification. For downloads and more audio and video clips, visit www.real.com.

With RealPlayer installed, you can watch live Web events, such as this launch of a new Boeing aircraft.

QuickTime is another useful plug-in, developed by Apple, the Macintosh people. It's another video/animation viewer, and quite common. You can see good examples of QuickTime in action on Apple's own site (www.apple.com/quicktime). Microsoft, of course, are not sitting back quietly. Their Windows Media Player performs similar functions to RealPlayer, and has extra capabilities. You can download it easily from www. microsoft.com/downloads.

Downloading a plug-in

Here we show you what happens when you access a page that uses a plug-in you don't have. Plug-ins that are downloaded and installed tend to work in the same way, so this exercise should apply for any you come across.

THE PLUG-IN we use here is Cortona, which is needed to enable us to take a 3D tour or 'fly-through' of historical reconstructions on a BBC Web site that uses VRML (virtual reality mark-up language).

1 Log on to the 3D Reconstructions section of the BBC Web site (www.bbc.co.uk/history/3d.shtml). You're told very clearly that you'll need to get the Cosmo or Cortona Player plug-in in order to view these fascinating reconstructions of long-destroyed structures in all their 3D glory. Click on the hyperlink for your version of Windows to go and get it.

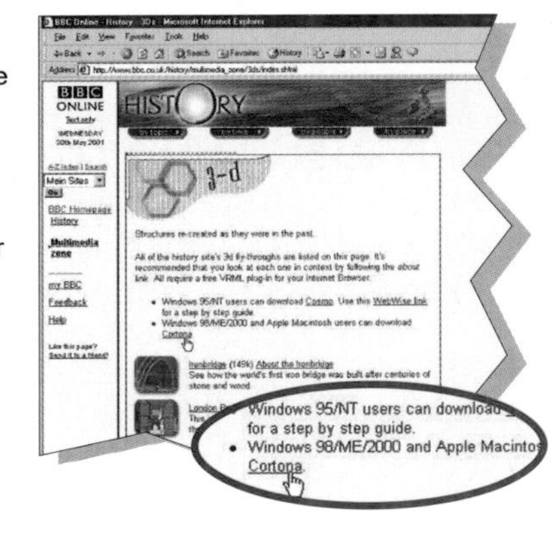

2 Windows 98 and Windows Me users are taken to the Cortona page at the Parallel Graphics' Web site. (Windows 95 users will be taken to the Cosmo site.) Click the Install Cortona link to continue with the download process.

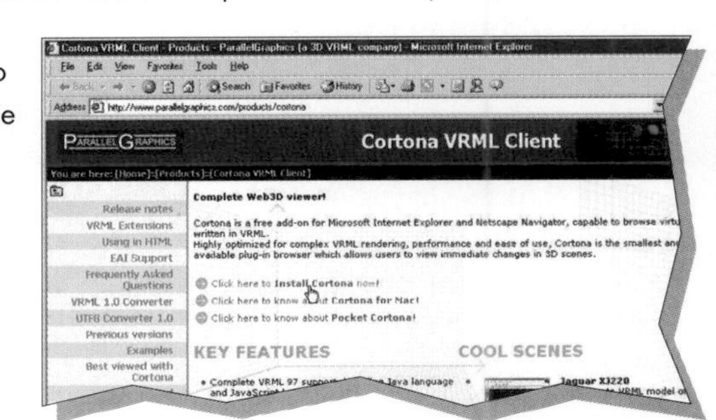

3 Modern browsers and plug-ins work together automatically. This means that you don't have to download a setup program, disconnect from the Internet and run it; instead a single button click does the whole process. On the Automatic Setup page click the large button to start the download process.

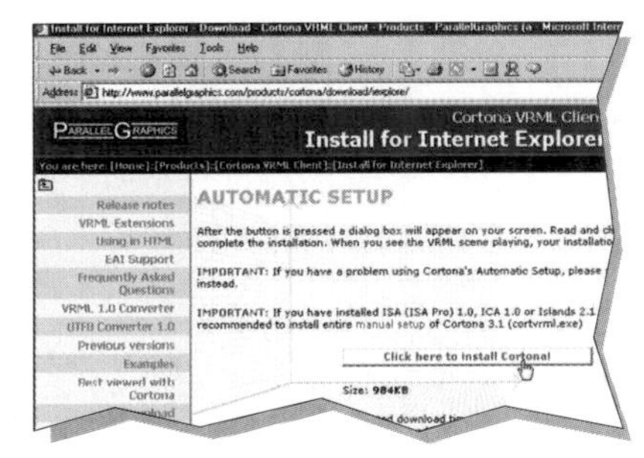

4 The Cortona file starts to download to your PC without any further intervention. A blank picture box appears to the left of the button you clicked to start the download. Wait for the download to complete.

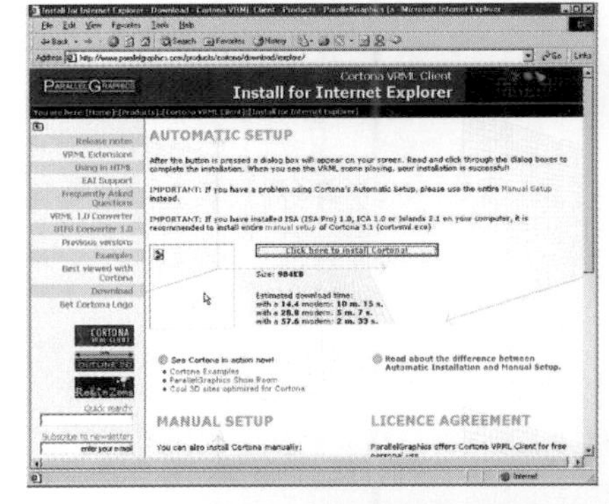

5 The Security Warning dialog box prompts you to choose whether or not to install the plug-in. Click the Yes button to continue.

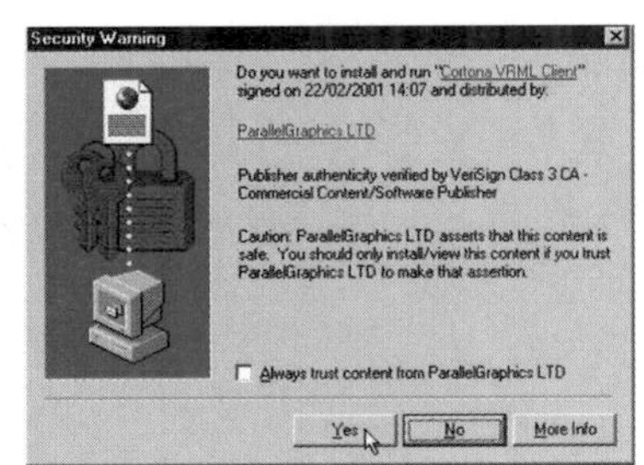

6 The plug-in can also work as your default viewer for all VRML files in Internet Explorer and Windows Explorer. Tick the options you want for the Cortona plug-in, then click the OK button. Now that Cortona is fully installed, the VRML in the Cortona Web page can be displayed: instead of the blank rectangle (see Step 4), a revolving blue cube appears.

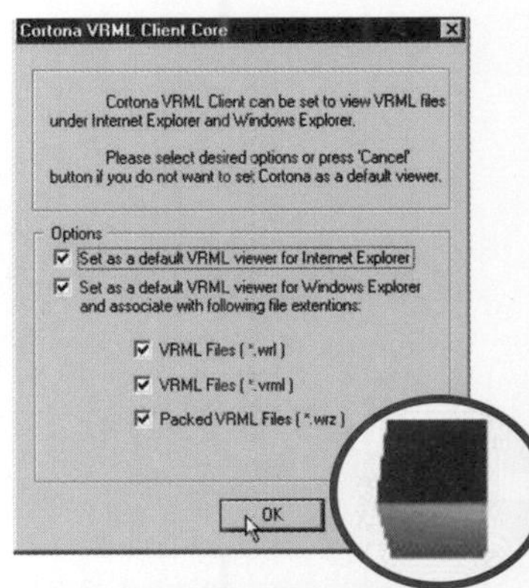

7 Now go back to the BBC 3D reconstructions site. Click on one of the links – for example, the Abbey. You can use your mouse to move around the 3D building. Use the buttons on the left of the screen to change direction.

PC TIPS

Create a Downloads folder

As you download more and more plug-ins and other files from the Internet, you'll find you start to lose track of what you have stored where. Create a Downloads folder on your Desktop and make a point of always saving downloaded files to this folder. When the download is complete, and once you have run the setup program, you can delete the file from the folder.

Downloading and using the Adobe Acrobat plug-in

In this exercise we're going to download and install the Adobe Acrobat Reader and use it to browse and print a Portable Document File (PDF), both on and offline.

1 Go to Adobe's Web site (www.adobe.com). Click on the Get Acrobat Reader button at the bottom of the page.

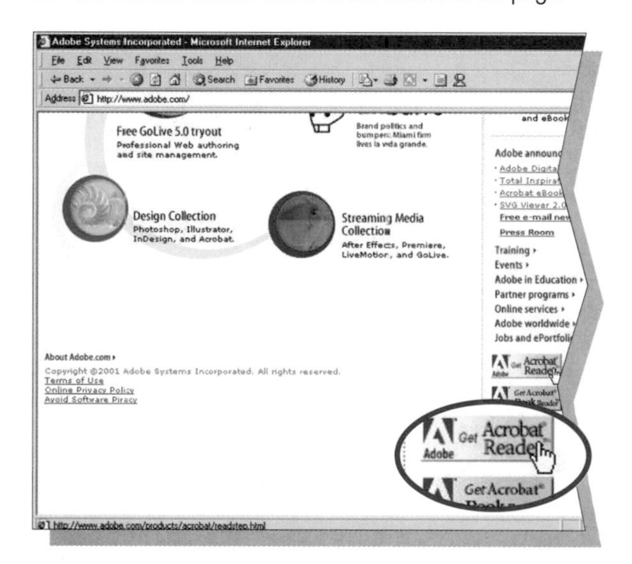

2 The next screen lets you choose between the Acrobat Reader – which is free – and the full version. Click the Acrobat Reader link and then choose your version of Windows on the next page. You also need to type in your email address before pressing the Download button.

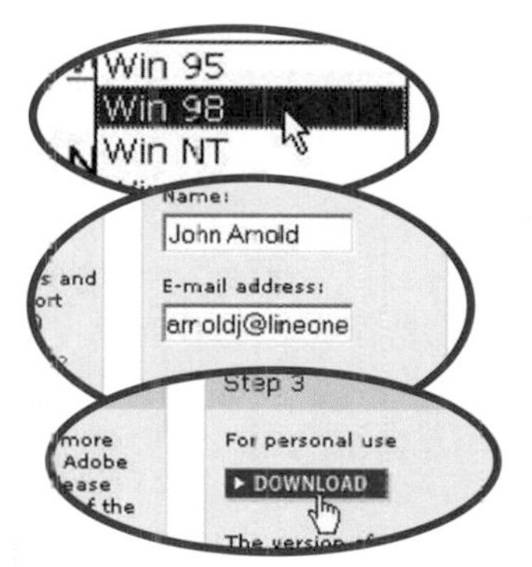

PC TIPS

Browsing a PDF file

Portable Document Files handle slightly differently to ordinary word processing documents. The arrows along the top menu bar (below) let you move through the document a page at a time, or jump straight to the end or back to the beginning.

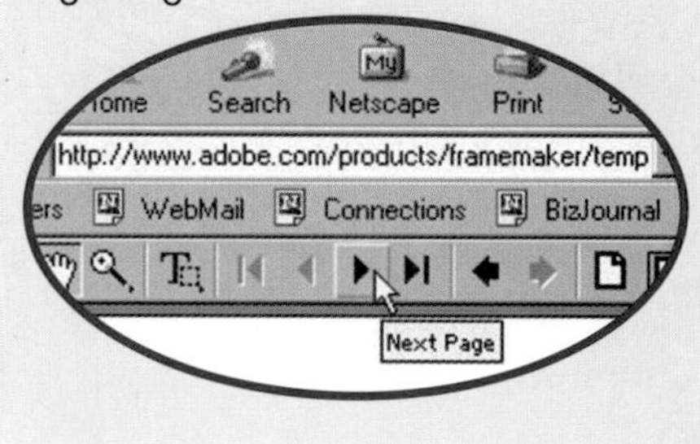

3 In the Save As window that now appears, find the location in the Save in box where you want to save the download. Click Save.

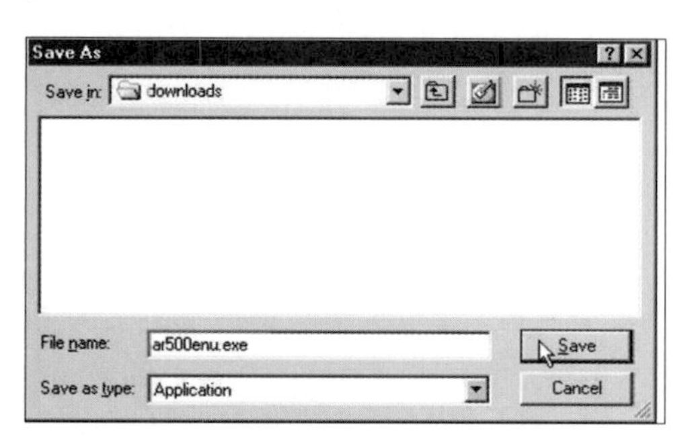

4 When the download is complete, double-click the file to install the Acrobat Reader. Go to the following location on the Adobe site: www.adobe. com/products/ framemaker/tempseries/ pdfs/primer.pdf and a PDF file for the Adobe program FrameMaker will appear in your browser window. You can save it to read and print out offline by clicking on the Save button on Acrobat's toolbar.

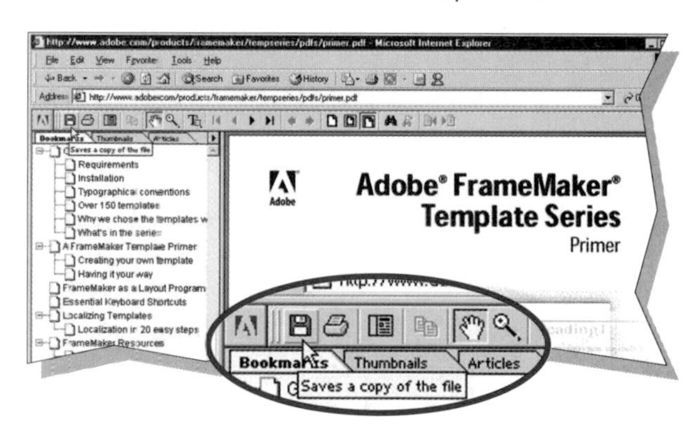

5 If you don't want to save the file you can print it out by clicking the Print button on the Acrobat toolbar.

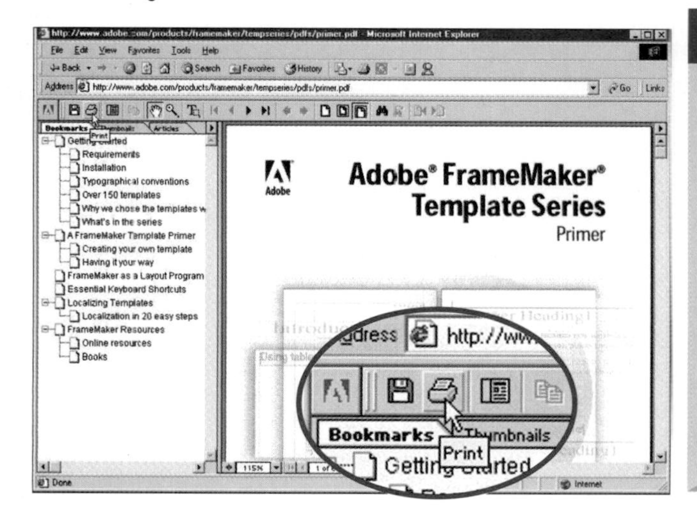

ADDING ACROBAT ADVANTAGES

There are two main reasons why Web sites use Adobe Acrobat's PDF files to distribute information. First, the PDF files are simple to produce as there's no HTML programming involved (see Stage 3, pages 154-157). This means that non-technical authors can use the same programs they use to create documents. Second, the PDF documents you see via the Acrobat plug-in look exactly the same as those seen by the authors when creating them. This solves a big problem with browsers – the layout of text and pictures on an HTML page depends too much on the shape and size of the browser window.

Adobe Acrobat is ideal for creating precise and unalterable electronic documents. Manufacturers create PDF files of equipment manuals with layouts as clear and simple as a printed manual. Achieving this through a Web page with HTML is impossible.

Using FTP programs

A Web browser, such as Navigator or Internet Explorer, is fine for viewing Web sites. But for transferring files to and from sites on the Internet, File Transfer Protocol programs are more efficient.

WHAT IT MEANS

UPLOADING

Most of the time when you use a Web browser you are downloading files (HTML text files and graphics used in Web pages) to view on your PC. You can also download files from Web sites just by clicking on links on a Web page.

The opposite of downloading is uploading, where you send a file from a PC to the Web. To create a Web site for others to view, you'll need some way of uploading your files to the Internet.

In the exercise on building your own Web site (see Stage 3, pages 154-157), we worked from our own computer's hard disk. Of course, if you want to make your Web pages viewable for other Internet users, you'll need to send the files to a site that's available 24 hours a day to users around the world. It is likely that you will have some free Web space as part of the deal with your Internet service provider (ISP). However, there's still the task of getting the files from your computer to the ISP's computer.

● Transferring files over the Internet

The process for uploading your Web pages and graphics files to an ISP will depend on your ISP. Some, for example, have their own step-by-step Wizards to simplify the process. For those ISPs that don't (or if you just want to accelerate what can be a cumbersome step-by-step process), an FTP program makes sending files to and from the Internet easy.

FTP stands for File Transfer Protocol – the most efficient technique for transferring files over the Internet. FTP programs are used to upload and download files to and from FTP sites on the Internet. Most ISPs and many Web sites have dedicated areas for FTP transfers which work alongside the Web site. An FTP site is recognizable by the letters ftp at the start of its address – for example, ftp.microsoft.com instead of www.microsoft.com.

● FTP programs

There's a wide range of different FTP programs available. Most are shareware and therefore cost very little. You can also download them over the Internet pretty quickly as they are relatively small programs. FTP software tends to look and work like Windows Explorer, so learning how to use it won't take too long. You need to find your way around the site you are transferring to so that your files upload to the right place, but actually transferring the files is simply a case of dragging and dropping them.

● Examining the protocol

An important point to note is that FTP software is handy for more than just uploading files to your own Web site; it can also be used to download files from FTP sites on the Internet to your computer. Often this is a noticeably quicker downloading process than using your Web browser to download files.

Over the next few pages, we'll take a look at some of the more popular FTP programs around and see how they are used.

FTP programs available on the Web

Here we look at some of the most popular FTP programs you can find on the Internet. These are just a few of the options – try download sites or the software's own site for a wider choice.

CuteFTP

www.cuteftp.com

This is perhaps the most widely used FTP program – largely because, as the name suggests, it is very well designed, which makes it easy to use. The interface is similar to that of Windows Explorer and includes such niceties as drag-and-drop icons and Web browser-style bookmarks.

One of the best features for the frequent FTP user is the ability to resume any interrupted download (caused by phone line problems for example). Of course, you hope your downloads won't be interrupted, but in the event that they are, this feature makes sure that you don't have to start again from scratch.

There are also features specifically created to help with uploading Web sites, such as an option to compare directory structures between folders on your hard drive and those on your Web site. At the moment the registration fee is around £25.

WHAT IT MEANS

REMOTE

It can be confusing to talk about files that are on both your own computer and the Internet. To clarify matters and to standardize terminology, the Internet computer is called the 'remote' computer and your own computer is known as the 'local' computer. If you remember to adopt these terms when using the Internet, there's less risk of accidentally transferring files the wrong way. The term 'remote' is also used to refer to any computer you are connected to.

WS_FTP Pro

www.ipswitch.com

WS_FTP Pro software can upload or download your files more quickly than any of the other FTP programs around, so far.

The interface for WS_FTP Pro looks very similar to most other FTP programs. There are no obscure toolbars and all the advanced options, such as remote file editing, can be accessed by right-clicking on the file or option in question.

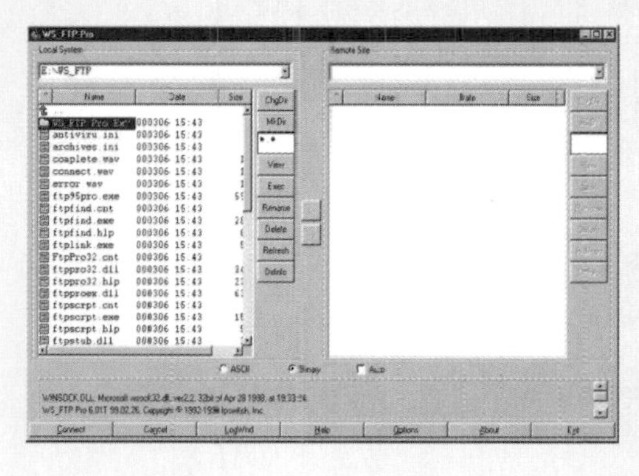

However, while the program's basic functions are easy to use, the more advanced features – of which there are many – are much trickier to access. For this reason, it's a program that is more suited to the expert programmer than the novice. WS_FTP Pro is available as shareware for a 30-day trial period, after which it costs around £25 to register.

Terrapin FTP Browser

www.nsl.co.uk/systemerk/

This works slightly differently from most FTP programs. You only need to connect once to an FTP site you want to look at and the program downloads all the details of the files and the structure of the site's folders.

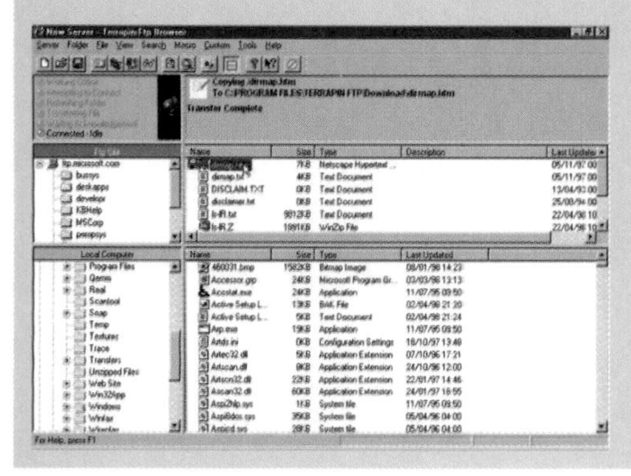

The downloading takes only a few minutes, after which you can shut down your Internet connection while you browse around the site offline. The advantage is that you don't have to pay telephone charges for the time you spend browsing. Also, you can take your time looking for the file you want. The program will reconnect to the FTP site only when you've actually selected the file or files you want to download. The only problem with Terrapin is that its interface can appear slightly complicated at first, as it is split into multiple windows and columns (left). It follows the routine of offline files on one side of the screen and online files on the other, except that this time the organization is horizontal rather than vertical. Terrapin FTP Browser is available as shareware for 30 days and then as a registered copy for about £25.

Uploading files with CuteFTP

ISPs have set up a simple procedure for CuteFTP to make it easy for you to upload files. Check the technical help area of your ISP's Web site for details and make a note of the settings you will need.

1 Download and install CuteFTP by following the instructions given on its Web site. Then start CuteFTP as you would any other program. When the program opens you will see its Site Manager screen. To begin to upload files to the Web space provided by your ISP (see Your web space box), click on the New button.

2 You must now type the FTP access data for your Web space into the Site Settings dialog box. The most important details are the FTP Host Address and the FTP site connection port: these details vary from one ISP to another, so make sure that you know them beforehand. The user name and password will be the same as your normal log on user name and password. Click the Connect button when you're ready.

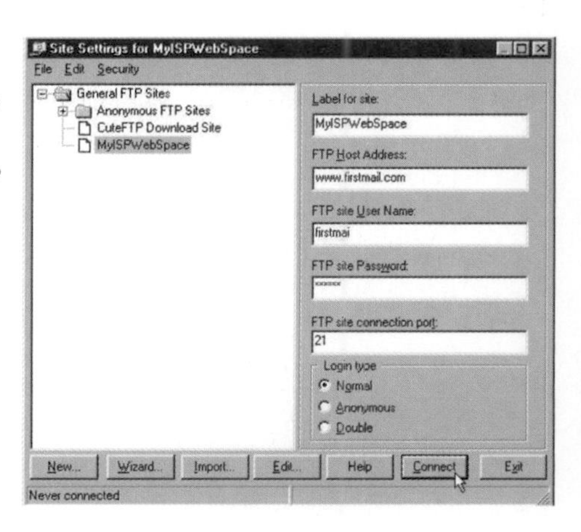

3 The top panel of the main CuteFTP window shows the progress of the connection as a series of Status messages. First of all, a message appears with the date and time and then a 'connecting' message appears while the software waits for Windows to connect to the Internet.

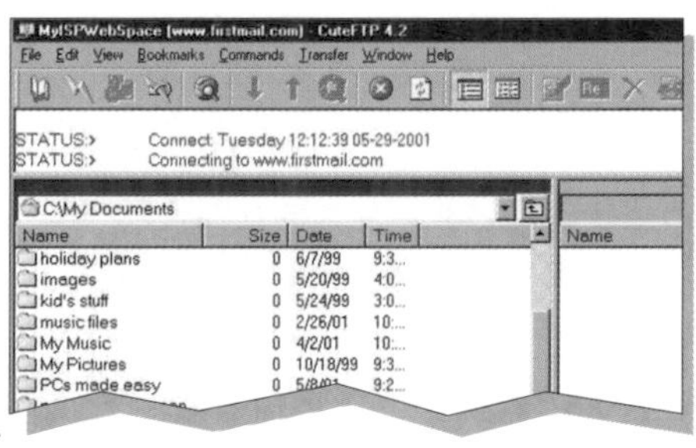

4 You will see a Login Messages window showing that you've connected successfully. Click OK.

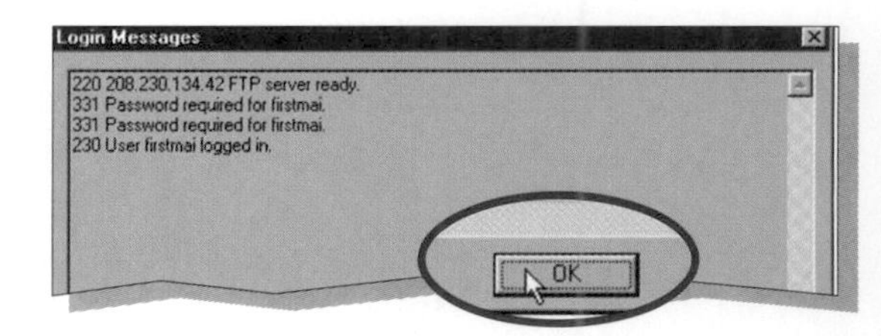

5 Within a few moments, the panel on the right of the CuteFTP window shows the files and folders on your Web server. Use the panel on the left to locate and select the files on your hard disk that you want to upload. Drag them to the panel on the right.

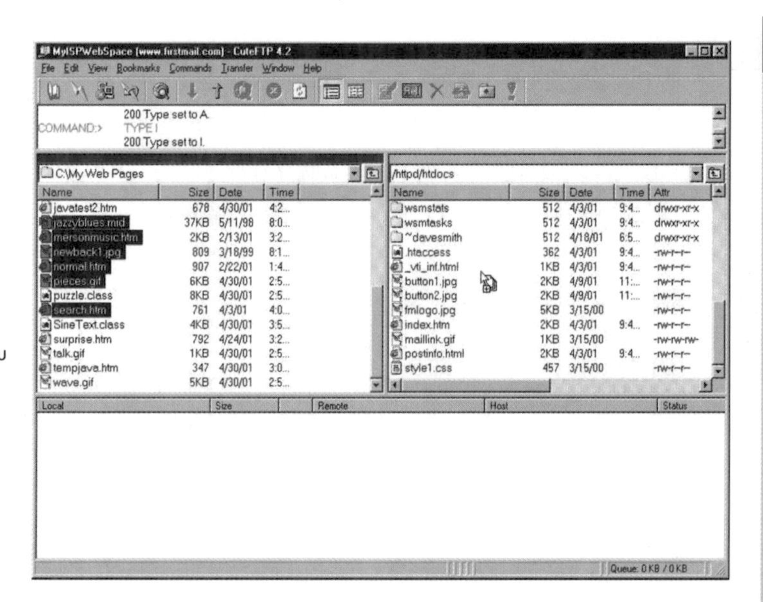

YOUR WEB SPACE

The idea of Web space on the Internet can seem a hard concept to grasp. It is simply part of a large computer – like a folder displayed by Windows on your own PC. This large computer is usually owned by your ISP. In essence, you are really renting an area of space on this computer, which is always connected to the Internet. This means that whatever files you place, they are available for viewing by millions of Internet users. In recent years, most ISPs have given away a small area of Web space, typically 5–15Mb, free to their customers. This practice is thought to have been responsible for causing the explosion of personal Web sites.

6 You will be asked to confirm that you want to upload the files. Click Yes to continue.

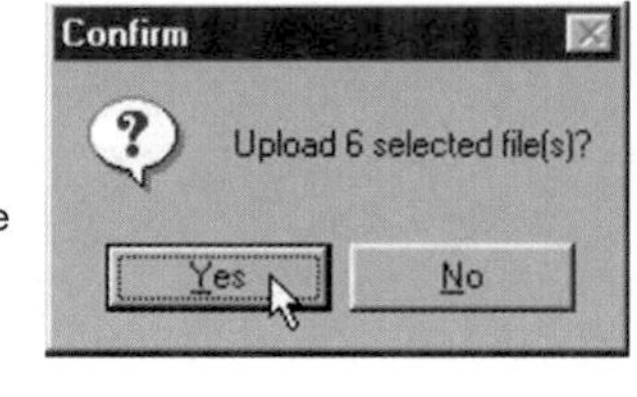

7 When the files have been successfully transferred you will see a message in the panel at the top of the screen. The files themselves will appear in the right-hand panel, showing that they are now stored in your ISP's web space.

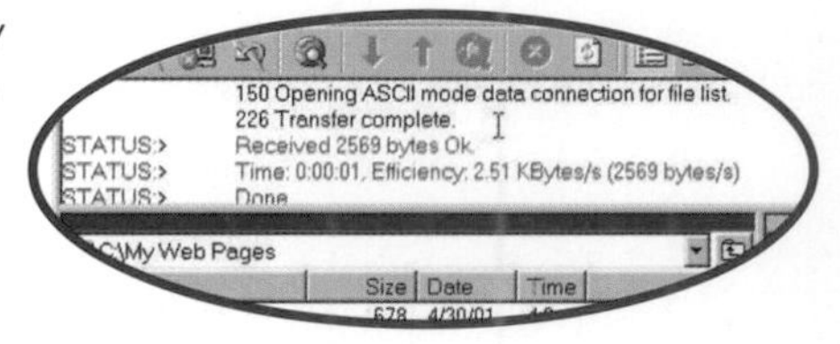

Downloading files with CuteFTP

Downloading, or transferring, files from a remote computer (the Internet) to your own PC is just as easy as uploading in CuteFTP. The program has plenty of pre-defined sites installed to make things even simpler.

1 From the Site Manager screen (see Step 1 on the opposite page), double-click on the General FTP Sites folder to show its contents.

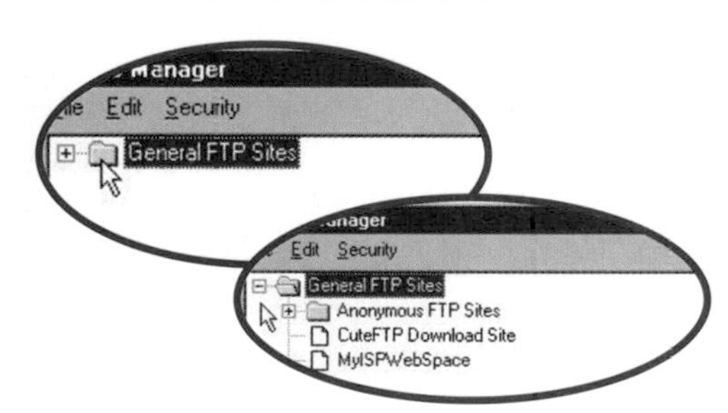

2 Double-click on the Anonymous FTP Sites folder to expand that, then on Predefined Sites, Software Sites and Archived Sites to expand each one in turn. Beneath the Archived Sites Folder you will see a list of FTP sites ready for you to connect to.

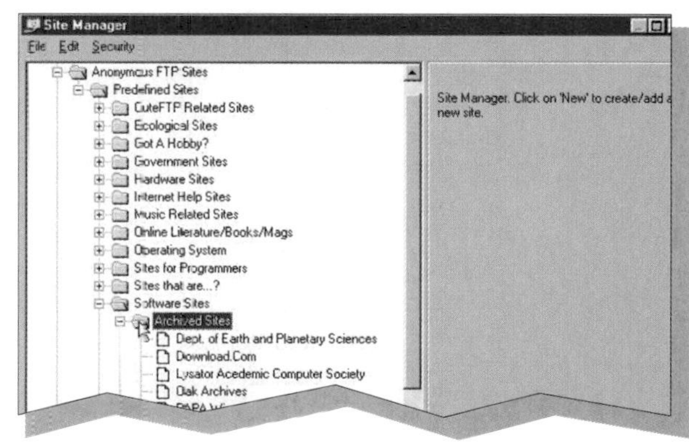

3 We'll download a file from the Various Software site. Double-click on the name and CuteFTP will connect you automatically to the site, whose address and description appear on the right of the screen.

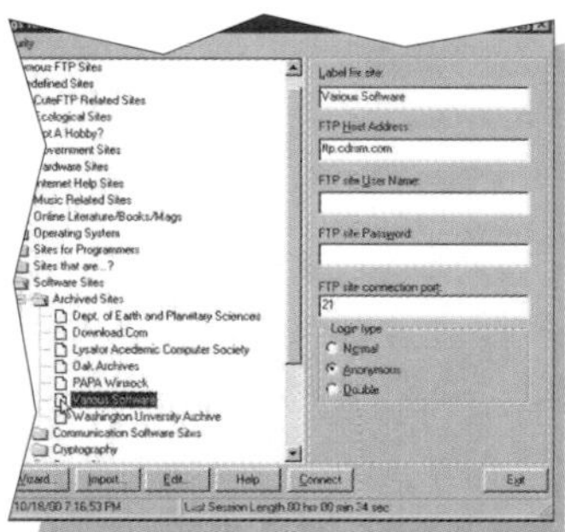

4 As you will see from the details on the Login Messages screen that now appears, CuteFTP has automatically logged you in as a guest. Click OK to proceed.

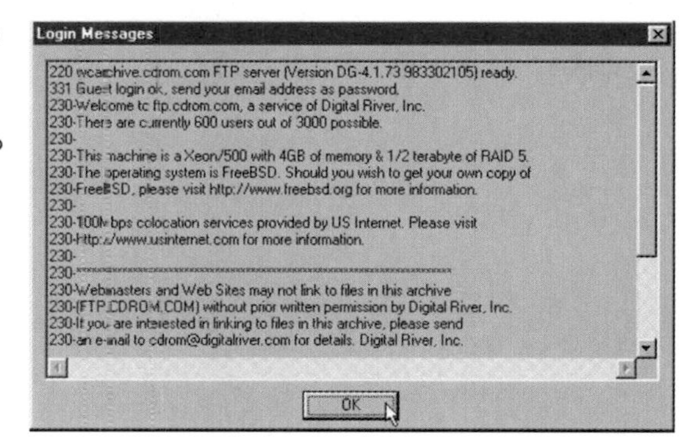

5 You'll now find the contents of the remote site's public folder shown in the right-hand panel. Depending on the site size, you might have to go down several folder levels to reach a downloadable file. We'll download an extra track for the Revolt game. Double-click on the Games folder, then Revolt and then Tracks.

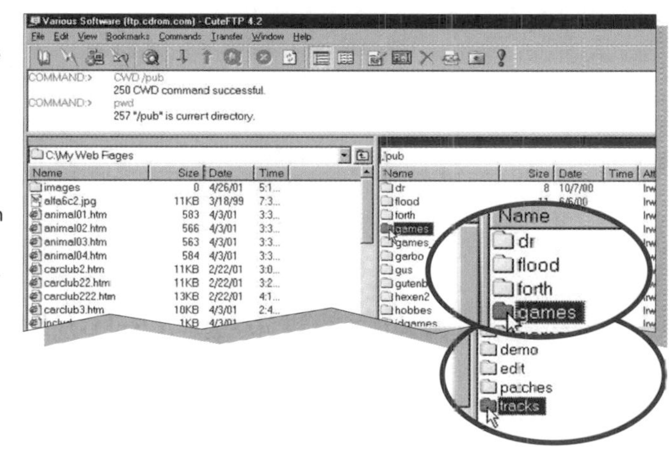

6 Now the right-hand panel displays the list of downloadable files. Drag the files you want to download to a folder on your hard disk.

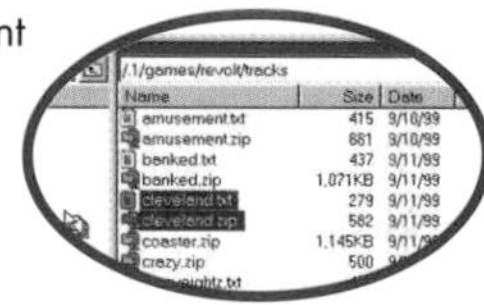

ARCHIE

Archie is short for archive and is the label given to a huge database of all the files that are known to be available by FTP. An Archie program lets you search for a file or browse for a certain type or size of file. When you've found the file, Archie lists the FTP sites from which you can download it, indicating the directory where the file is. This is a great way of finding out downloading options, especially if the file is popular and you're having trouble at the normal download sites. Try WSArchie at: dialspace.dial.pipex.com/town/square/cc83/download.shtml/

7 Click the Yes button when CuteFTP asks you to confirm the copy command. Small files like these appear on your hard disk within a few seconds. You can now disconnect and use the files you have downloaded.

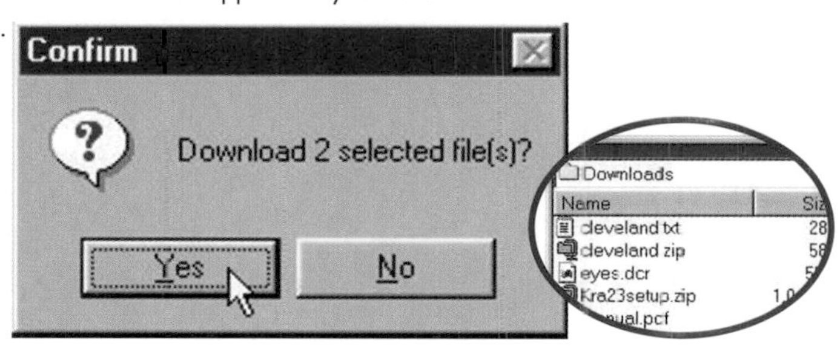

Thanks to the Internet you can listen to radio stations from all over the world. Internet radio uses the same signal that sends your email and other data through the phone line.

Internet radio

It's not possible to tune in to most radio stations on the other side of the world on your radio. But using your Internet connection, your PC can pick up the signal in the same way as it can other Internet information.

The idea of a radio station playing live over the Internet might seem a bit odd, but the activity has become very popular with stations and their listeners.

Both the number and the variety of radio stations you can listen to on your PC are astonishing. In Europe and the USA pretty much all radio stations worth their salt offer the facility for Internet radio, while even in the less Web-saturated parts of the world there is a huge choice of stations. You can listen to news and views that might otherwise be hard to come by, in languages that you rarely hear anywhere else. You can also listen to your favourite style of music at any time, night or day.

Major radio stations, such as London's Capital Radio (www.capitalfm.co.uk), are beginning to establish a presence on the Internet.

● Using a plug-in

You'll need to download special software to listen to Internet radio on your PC. There's a variety of software available, but nearly all Internet radio sites are compatible with RealPlayer, one of the most popular Internet plug-ins; it lets you play audio files as well as video files.

Broadcast quality with Internet radio is surprisingly good most of the time. By and large, the technology works well, delivering true hi-fi radio from around the world to your PC. But there are times when a station may suffer breaks in transmission if your Internet link is poor or if the station's Web site is busy. You might also experience some sound distortion if you have a slow modem. A 28.8Kbps modem is the absolute minimum: 56Kbps is much better.

WHAT IT MEANS

PLUG-IN

A plug-in is a small piece of software that works with your Web browser to give it a new capability. Usually this is something like the ability to play music, or display 3D graphics, but it can be anything. Plug-ins are often downloaded from a Web site and are compatible with most popular browsers *(see pages 130-133).*

Downloading the RealPlayer plug-in

Like most plug-ins, the basic RealPlayer software is free. The downloading process is quite simple. Here we take you step by step through exactly what you have to do.

1 In the Address panel of your Web browser, type in the address that takes you straight to the section of the RealPlayer site that deals with downloads (www.real.com/player/).

2 There's a choice of versions to download. You can try the enhanced version – RealPlayer 8 Plus – but this costs £27.99. Instead, we'll download the free version, RealPlayer 8 Basic, so click on the link for that version.

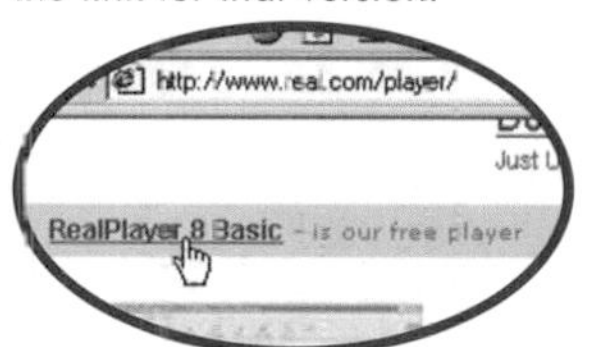

OTHER MEDIA PLAYERS

RealPlayer isn't the only option if you want to listen to Internet radio. Windows Media Player (which comes with Windows Me but can also be downloaded at www.microsoft.com/windows/mediaplayer/en/) will let you tune in and will also allow you to play video and animation delivered by Web sites. Another popular piece of software is QuickTime (download from www.apple.com/quicktime/).

3 You'll need to fill in some personal details in the boxes, such as your email address, and then answer some basic questions about your PC's configuration – you select the answers from drop-down boxes. Choose your Windows operating system in the first box and the appropriate modem speed in the final box. Then click on the Download FREE RealPlayer 8 Basic button to continue.

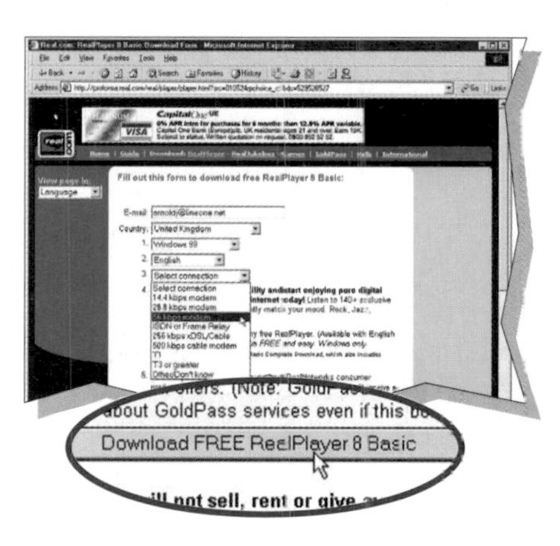

4 You can choose to download the program with all its additional elements. For a faster download you can select the Minimum setup. Click the appropriate radio button and then the Download button to continue.

5 On the next screen you are asked to select a server location for the download. If you are in the UK, select the Leeds option; otherwise, choose the nearest location from the list.

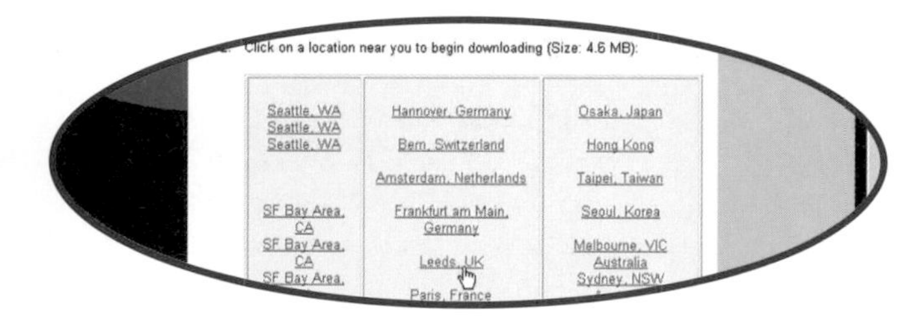

6 On the next screen select the second option to save the download to your hard disk and then click OK.

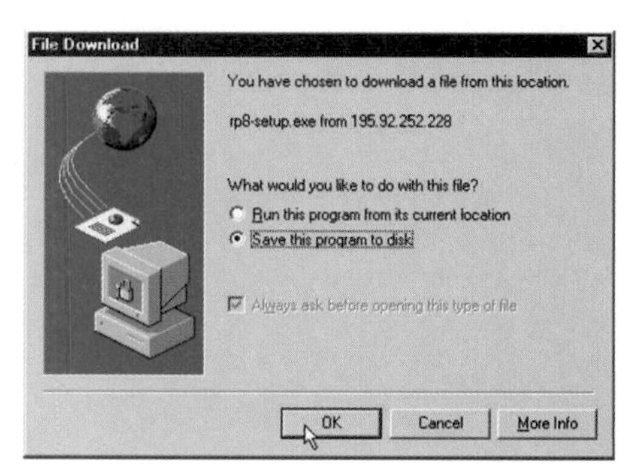

7 In the Save in panel, navigate your hard disk to find a suitable location to save the downloaded file. Click Save to continue.

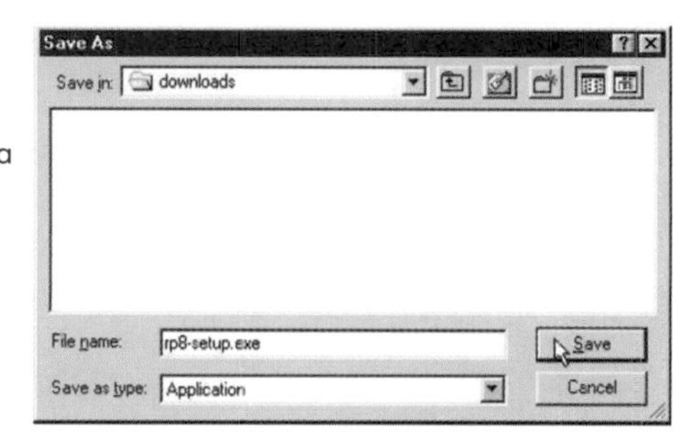

8 The program will now begin to download from the server to your hard disk. If you chose to download the program in its entirety, then the process should take 40-50 minutes with a 56Kbps modem. The minimum setup file will take about 15 minutes.

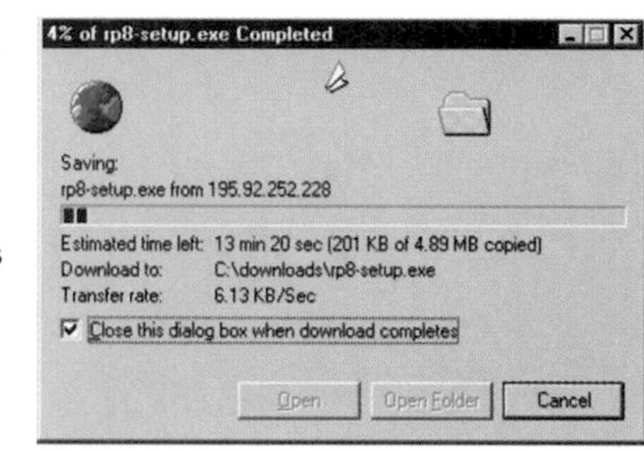

Installing and using RealPlayer

Once you have downloaded RealPlayer, just answer a few quick questions and you'll have the software installed and playing radio in no time.

1 Find the folder where you saved the downloaded RealPlayer file and then double-click on the icon to launch the installation process.

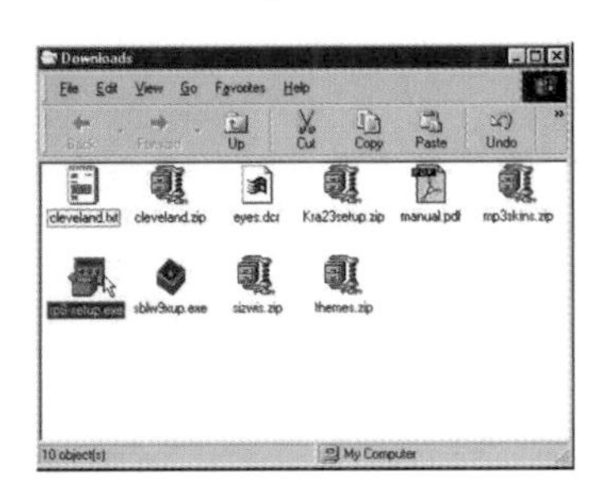

2 On the screen that follows, just click the Next button to go on to the licence agreement screen, where you simply click Accept to proceed. When the setup program asks you to confirm the installation folder, check Next.

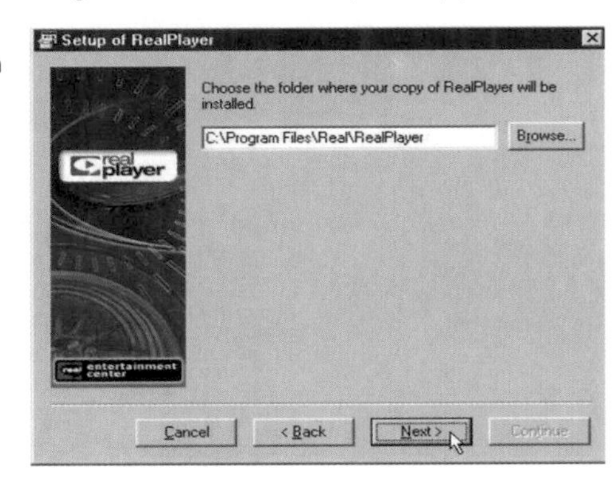

3 Now you choose where RealPlayer will place shortcuts to the program. The simplest option is to leave all boxes ticked and remove the shortcuts later if you find they are not necessary. Check Next to continue.

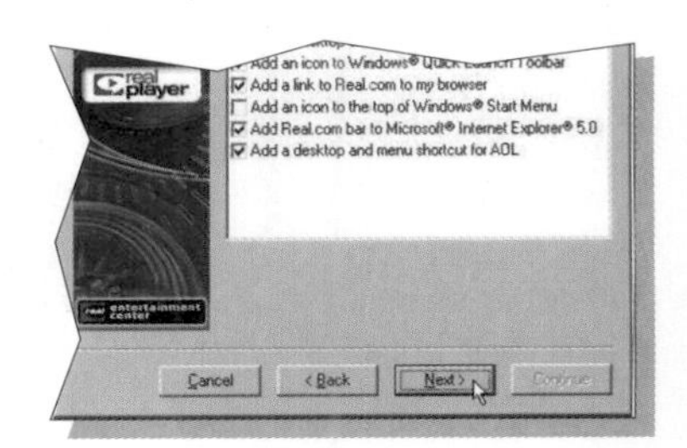

4 The configuration process begins and you then have to register the product by filling in your email address and adding your location. Check the 'E-mail me about product news…' box if you want to receive email from RealPlayer.

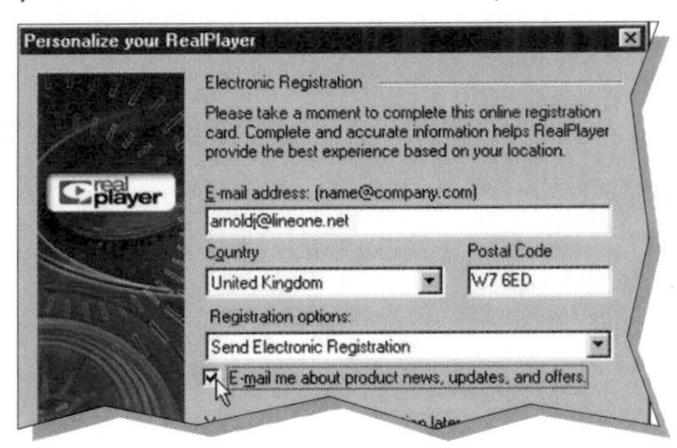

5 On the next page you need to select the type of connection you have to the Internet. The RealPlayer plug-in uses this information to ensure the best possible sound and video quality. Select your modem speed or other connection and click the Next button.

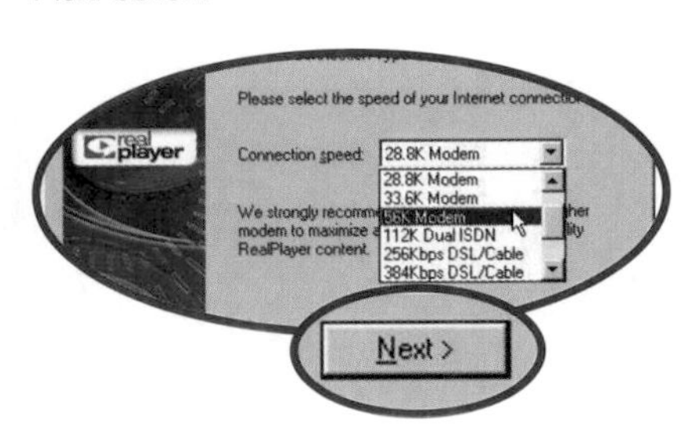

6 Now you can personalize RealPlayer by selecting which channels – related groups of media – you wish to have available. If you can't make up your mind, don't worry; you can add or delete channels later. Tick the relevant boxes or simply click on Select All.

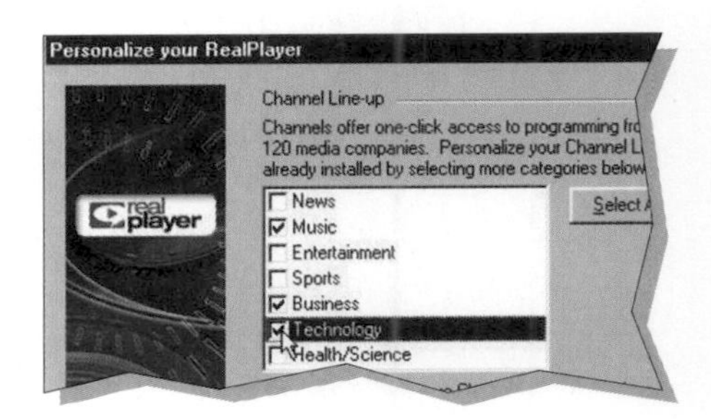

7 After selecting whether or not you want to receive product and news flashes from RealPlayer, you arrive at a screen that sets out a summary of the settings you have chosen previously. If you are happy with these, click Finish; if not, simply click the Back button to return to screens where you can modify them.

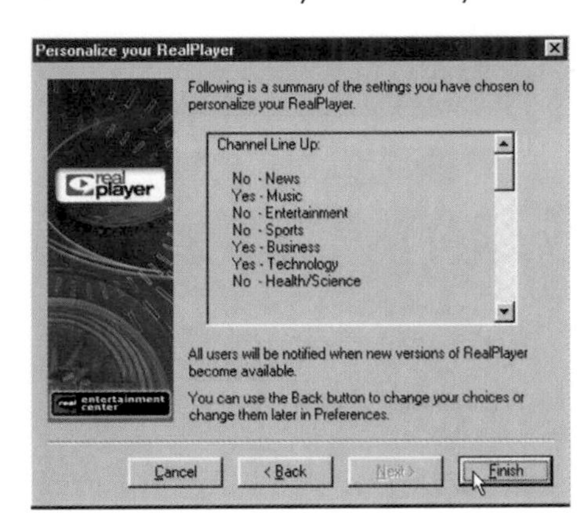

8 The RealPlayer program window now appears with a short welcome screen. Click on the Radio menu and select the Find Stations command. This connects you to the RealPlayer site.

9 Once you are connected, the RealPlayer screen opens up and shows a Radio Tuner that allows you to chose the type of music you want to listen to. Make your choices then select the Find a Station tab to get a list and click on one of the stations listed.

10 You can also listen to Internet radio by going directly to a station's Web site and tuning in from there. To access Virgin Radio, for example, just type in the Web address (http://www. virginradio.co.uk) in your browser's location bar and then click on listen now! to access the RealPlayer link to get going.

11 RealPlayer will automatically start up and play whatever is on the station at the time. You can stop or pause the transmission, then play it anytime by using the player buttons at the top of the window.

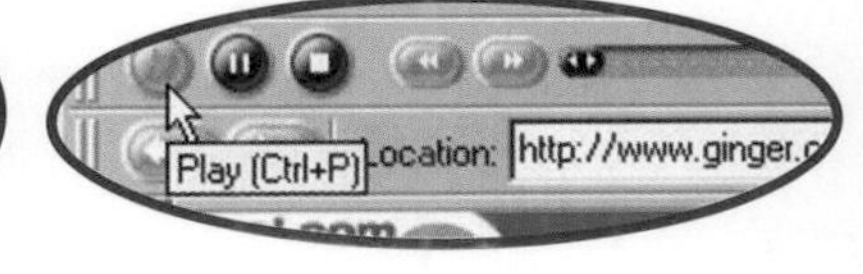

Radio sites on the Web

There's a massive range of radio stations available on the Web. You can find them via directory sites.

RealGuide

www.realguide.com

Perhaps the best place to start a search for Internet radio coverage is RealPlayer's own directory site. Just click on the RADIO TUNER link at the left of the screen to get access to hundreds of stations. There's also an excellent station search facility, allowing you to find what you want by region, language or style. Note also that RealPlayer is a 'media player'; this means that it allows you to view video as well as listen to sounds. The RealGuide site shows film trailers, special events and all sorts of other audio-visual delights, including news and sports reports, images from around the world and even some from outer space.

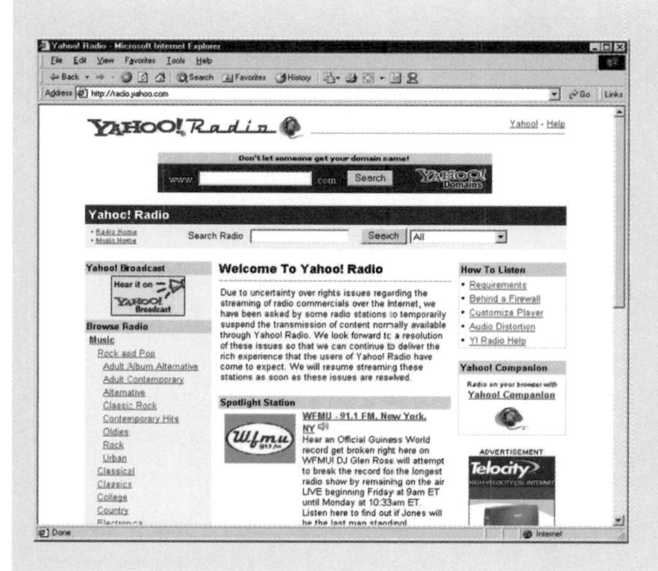

Yahoo! Radio

radio.yahoo.com

As ever, the comprehensive Yahoo! portal will almost certainly be able to supply you with just what you might need. There's a huge range of radio stations available from the site, arranged by genre from 'Adult Contemporary' to 'oldies'. There's also a lot of additional music-related information, with reviews, news and charts. The stations themselves are mostly American, but that's hardly a drawback as the variety of radio in the USA is astonishing. 'Station of the Day' introduces you to stations you might not know about, as do the Featured Stations in each category which change regularly.

Ratiostations.mu

www.radiostations.mu

This radio directory site lists more than 2000 stations, categorized by location – very handy if you want to investigate stations in only one area. The range of the stations listed here is astonishing. The California listing, for example, includes AEN Today and ranges from Christian Pirate Radio and Rave-Network down to something called Y-105. There's even a station listed under Antarctica. You can also search for stations by language or seek out those that are multi-lingual. With all these options to try out, the chances are that you'll discover a radio station that'll keep you happy, at least for a while.

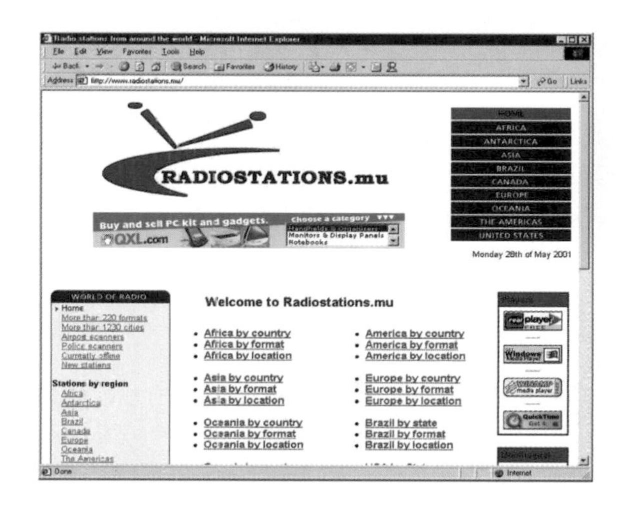

Oceanography

The environmental impact of the ocean is immense and many sites explore its mysteries.

Marine environmental issues are a popular topic on the Web, with numerous sites promoting ocean awareness.

Oceanography is the scientific study of the physical, chemical and biological processes that maintain the seas' structure and motion; it's a complex business, and one that is primarily based on reams of statistics that have been carefully compiled over time.

When surfing the Web for oceanography sites, you'll soon discover that the subject is huge. There are masses of Web sites dedicated to this subject, exploring everything from marine life and environmental issues to satellite images and maps of the oceans. Some coastal aquariums also play a vital part, providing information on certain aspects of oceanography that they may be involved in (see Aquariums box, right).

● The big picture

Jacques Cousteau, considered by many to be the father of oceanography, once said: 'The sea is so vast that when we try to study it by lowering an instrument, we are examining a macro-medium with a micro-tool. It tells us only what is happening at that moment at a single point in the ocean, but little about the sea in general'. The 'big picture' is produced from myriad sources such as countless buoys supplying data on water temperature, salinity, currents, sea levels and so on.

AQUARIUMS

Most of the sites covered here are about oceanography – the scientific study of the sea. If you enjoy watching fascinating sea creatures, take a look at the aquarium sites on the Web. One of the best is ZooWeb (www.zooweb.net), which has links to 30 or so of the world's finest. In the US, try the National Aquarium in Baltimore (www.aqua.org) which has a good collection and Web site. And don't miss the collections at the Sydney Aquarium (www.sydneyaquarium.com.au).

Clearly, many Web sites dealing with of this sort of material are of interest to researchers only, but this is not always the case. Online, for example, you'll find beautiful topographical maps of the ocean floor which would catch anyone's eye. There is also fascinating information about how oceanic changes contribute to the destructive weather phenomenon, El Niño. Oceanography also encompasses the creatures that live in the sea, as well as the sea itself. Even the most cursory search leads into ecological concerns – an appreciation of the significance of the oceans for life on Earth and the threat posed by overfishing, pollution and other harmful actions.

We touch on all of these subjects in the 10 sites on these pages. If you're starting your own investigation into oceanography, a good place to begin would be the online encyclopedia sites such as Britannica (www.britannica.com) or Encarta (encarta.msn.com). The former contains the entire text of the encyclopedia, so it provides links to articles on the subject as well as a selection of links to featured Web sites. Encarta offers less content, but has lots of good links and slick Multimedia presentation, and provides useful school or college work ideas.

Sea sites

All you want to know about the oceans of the world can be found on the Web. Although it can take a little digging about, it is worth the effort.

The Cousteau Society

www.cousteausociety.org

Founded in 1973 by the great man himself, and now boasting 150,000 members, the Cousteau Society went online in 1997. There are facts about Cousteau's teams, who have been exploring the oceans of the world for more than 40 years and making a documentary or two as well. On their nine-year *Rediscovery of the World* series, the Society's two research vessels *Calypso* and *Alcyone* circumnavigated the Earth. The *Calypso* sank following a 1996 barge-manouvering accident in Singapore but the Society has now raised it from the sea bed and renovated it for use as an educational base. There's plenty of information on all this, plus news and tasters of what you can enjoy if you join the club, such as the Dolphin Log, which offers galleries, fun facts and games for kids.

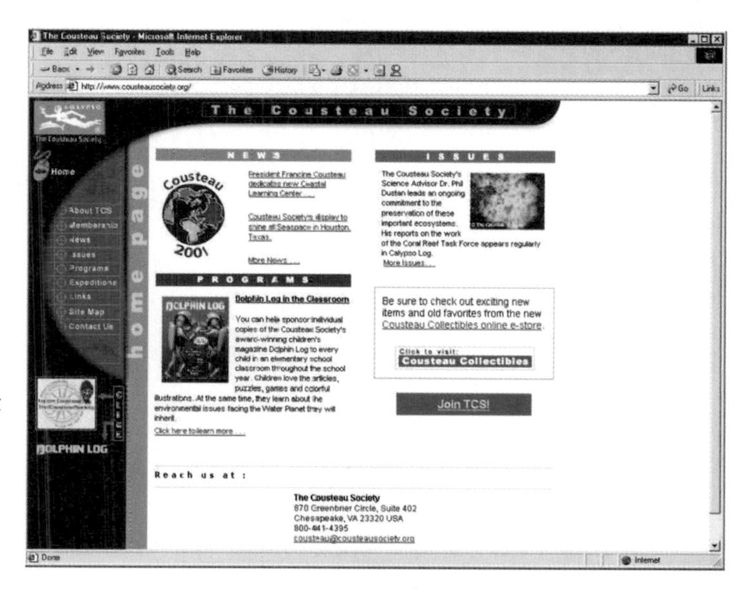

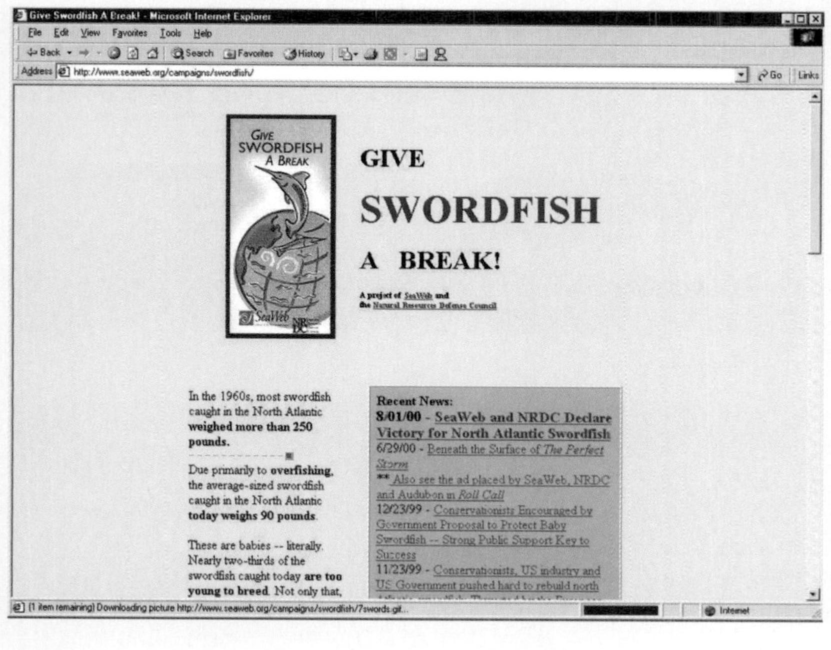

Seaweb

www.seaweb.org

A smart and comprehensive site that makes its aim 'to raise awareness of the world ocean and the life within it'. It includes the Ocean Report, comprising 90-second radio slots that are aired daily and syndicated nationally in the US. Each program, hosted by *Jaws* author Peter Benchley, features news and issues relating to the ocean. Archived and available in RealAudio format, subjects are as diverse as the danger to baby bottlenose dolphins from motorboats, the uses of seaweed as stabilizers and gelling agents in toothpaste and beer, and the extra sets of jaws owned by parrot-fish. It also offers news, ways to get involved in environmental initiatives, subscription to a monthly newsletter, facts, polls and more.

Discovery Channel

www.discovery.com/stories/nature/sharkweek2000/sharkweek2000.html
Of all the fish in the sea it's the shark that fascinates us most. And even though the Discovery Channel's Shark Week 2000 is long gone, it lives on at this Web site as a splendid all-round view of the savage predator. There's lots of action here, such as archived Webcam footage of sharks and the 3D Tank, where you can watch five different types of shark in 360° underwater splendour. In addition there are learning resources, such as a guide to shark species and populations, that are well presented and entertaining. Take a look at A Shark's Life, the story of Basker, a basking shark lurking around the coast of the Isle of Man. Overall, this is an excellent site for those interested in sharks. To get the most out of its Multimedia aspects, make sure you have both the Flash and RealPlayer plug-ins (downloadable from www.macromedia.com and www.real.com, respectively, see page 139).

Satellite Oceanography Laboratory

satftp.soest.hawaii.edu/satlab
This is quite an academic site devoted to the oceans around Hawaii. It contains satellite pictures showing, for example, the warming of the sea surface in the lee of the wind. It's an example of the type of focused sites available for specific aspects of oceanography. The images are spectacular, even if the scientific jargon is a bit dry.

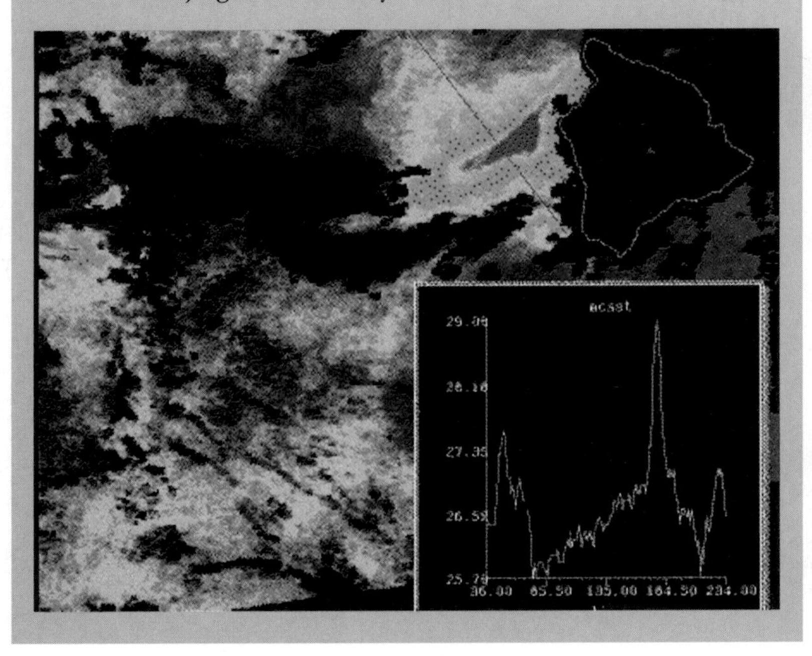

Threatened Fisheries

www.panda.org/endangeredseas/index.htm
The World Wide Fund for Nature's Endangered Seas site focuses on the dangers of overfishing, and encourages action to prevent it. It offers campaign news, press releases, video footage on pirate fishing, field reports and the WWF's map showing threatened fisheries within the world's most important marine areas.

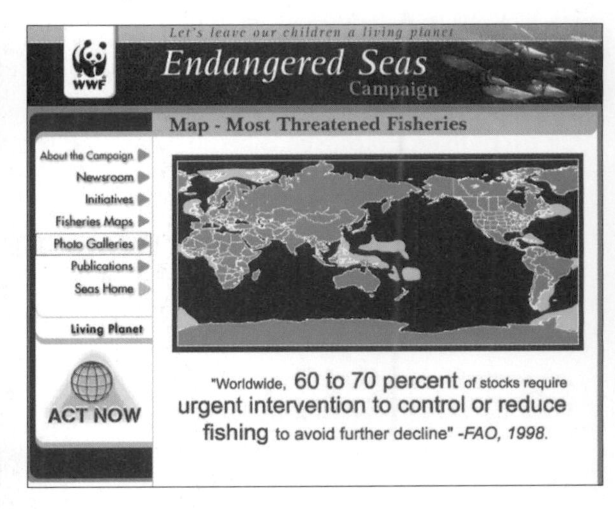

Monterey Bay Aquarium Research Institute

www.mbari.org
As you might expect from such a popular aquarium, its Web site puts a premium on accessibility. It is not academic in tone and contains, for example, satellite images of the central Californian coastline selectable via thumbnail previews. The Institute has two research vessels investigating Monterey Bay, and you can see where they are at the time of your enquiry. Naturally, there is a link to the aquarium's own site, with extensive visitor information and more. This site is like an online interactive exhibition and counterbalances the disciplined approach of some other sites.

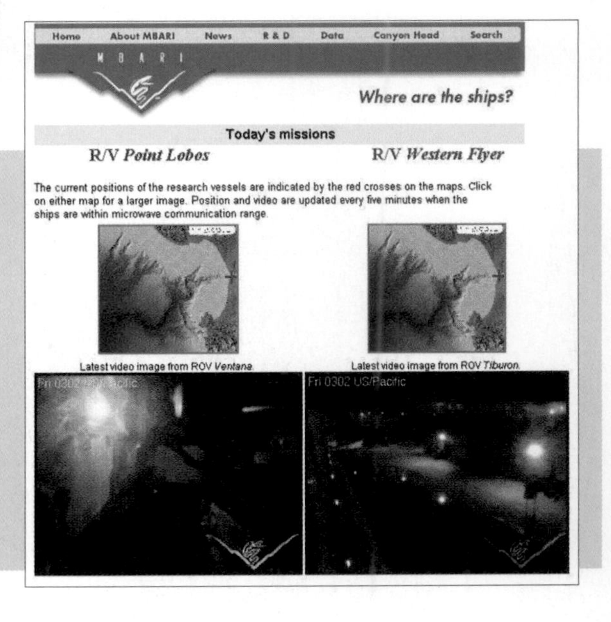

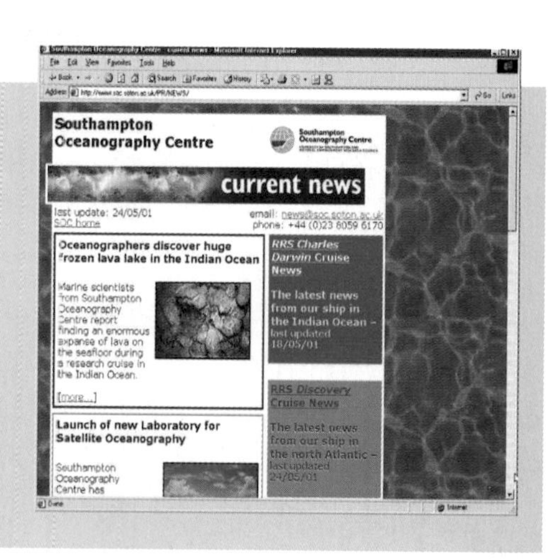

Southampton Oceanography Centre

www.soc.soton.ac.uk

Although this site showcases the Centre's research, it has been made accessible and entertaining for the non-academic visitor. Find out about the aquarium and resident and visiting experts working at the Centre who give plenty of public lectures about aspects of oceanography; you can check out past talks and see what's coming up. There's interesting information on the Centre's research ships and on the 'world's first 3D holographic camera', a £1 million gizmo designed to study plankton off the Scottish coast. And for the young person fascinated by the seas, there is some excellent advice on pursuing an oceanographic career.

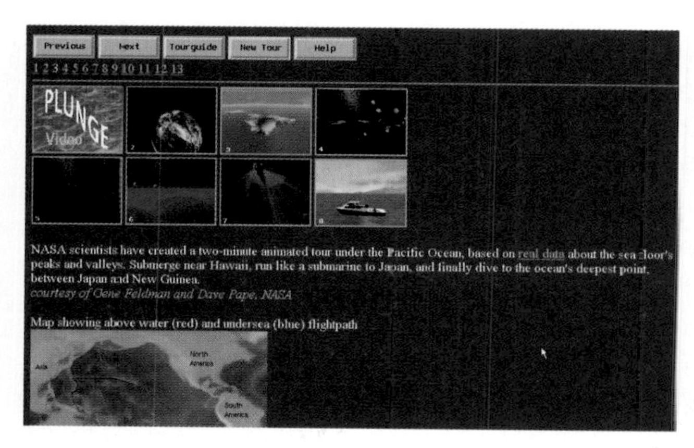

Ocean Planet

seawifs.gsfc.nasa.gov/ocean_planet.html

This is an online version of an ecologically-aware exhibition from the Smithsonian Institution. Download an animated 'fly-by' to take you from a point in space above the US, over the Pacific and then into a dive near Hawaii; 'fly' past Japan underwater, through the Mariana Trench, to resurface near New Guinea. Look at the exhibition's photo panels and read the information boards. The curator's tour offers an exhibition preview or tours about biodiversity, oceans and Africa, women and the sea, pollution and 'sea surprises'. This site is well worth a look.

Scripps Institution of Oceanography

www.sio.ucsd.edu

Part of the University of South California in San Diego, the Scripps is one of the US's top oceanographic research institutes. As a prestigious and well-funded place, it has a number of research ships at its disposal, and you can find out where they are and what they are doing. The Scripps also has Flip, the unique 'Floating Instrument Platform'. This amazing vessel for the study of underwater sound waves is shaped rather like a baseball bat, and can flip through 180° to position itself vertically in the ocean. In its Education Corner the site offers a very good explanation of Flip, together with an animation and QuickTime movies of it in action. The Scripps also has an 'interpretative center' in the form of the Birch Aquarium, which you can visit by clicking on the link on the site or going directly to www.aquarium.ucsd.edu.

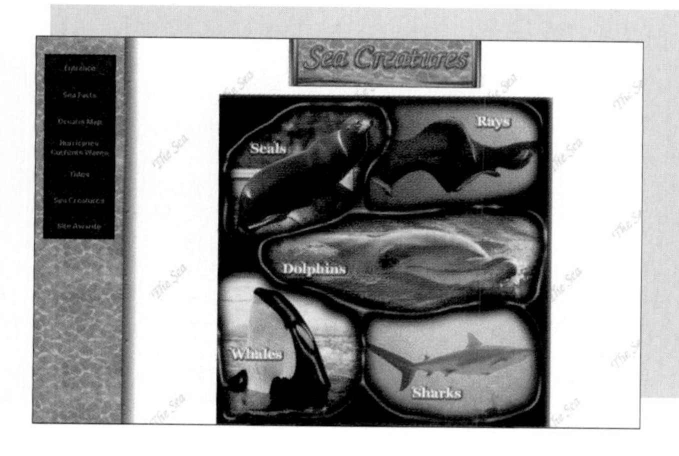

The Sea

www.the-sea.org

This is a one-man site and it gives a concise and clear introduction to many aspects of oceanography, ranging from the sea's creatures to explanations of how tides and hurricanes happen. It is illustrated with a selection of very good photographs, and although it is not a site that will satisfy a professor of oceanography, it is ideal if you want a quick introduction to the subject and lots of fascinating facts.

The Celtic world

There are numerous Web sites that provide a fascinating insight into the historic origins and specific cultural styles of the various Celtic peoples.

Some time around 3000 BC, the tribes known as the Celts were a force to be reckoned with in many parts of Europe, with a rich – if warlike – culture and civilization. As other peoples came to prominence, particularly the Romans, the Celtic tribes were driven farther west to their remaining strongholds in the western and northern parts of the British Isles and France.

Today, the Celtic heritage lives on in Scotland, Ireland, Wales, Cornwall, the Isle of Man, and even in Brittany, the most westerly part of France. It is a heritage that touches just about everyone in the Western world, be it on the superficial level of going to an Irish theme pub, or maybe in a more fundamental way for those whose genetic roots lie, however distant, in the Celtic lands.

Whether your interest lies in Celtic history and music or the equally scholarly pursuits of Gaelic languages or Celtic mythology, you'll be well served on the Web.

● Language and music

Gaelic languages are well supported on the Internet. After centuries of neglect or illegality, the native tongues of both Ireland and Scotland have undergone a revival and are now accepted academic subjects.

There are excellent Web sites to introduce you to Gaelic, from the absolute beginner stage through to much higher levels. They include plenty of useful Multimedia support, such as RealAudio files, on the Web. There are also excellent sites devoted to other languages of Celtic derivation, such as Cornish and Breton, the ancient language of Brittany. The Internet is ideal for locating both learning and reading material in these various languages.

Celtic music requires no such effort – you just listen and enjoy. Scottish and Irish music, in particular, are popular throughout the world and have given birth to many good Web sites. There are sites that list traditional music pubs all over Ireland; sites that offer CDs and videos on just about every Scottish performer you can think of; and sites that tell you all about the various instruments used in the music.

● History and mythology

Celtic mythology, especially as it survives in Irish tales, is a popular Internet topic. There's plenty of superb material on a people who ranged far and wide across Europe over two millennia, and left many fascinating monuments and artefacts. These are the inspiration for many sites on Celtic art and jewellery; you can buy various items of Celtic design, as well as discover how to make Celtic patterns yourself.

Finally, as Celtic is also the name of a famous Glasgow football club, focus your search by adding, for example, 'mythology' or 'jewellery'.

Celtic heritage

There is a wealth of data available on the Internet about the Celtic heritage – whether it be language, music, arts or crafts.

CelticLinks.com

uk.celticlinks.com

If you like the Celtic style then you will, naturally, want to buy a variety of Celt-influenced goods. This site offers a wide range of Irish items, mostly with a clear Celtic design, but some whose ethnicity may be a little more dubious. Jewellery in particular is strongly Celtic, while you might find that the attractive range of clothing and accessories is rather less so. Whatever the authenticity of the range, you're fairly sure to find something you'd like to have.

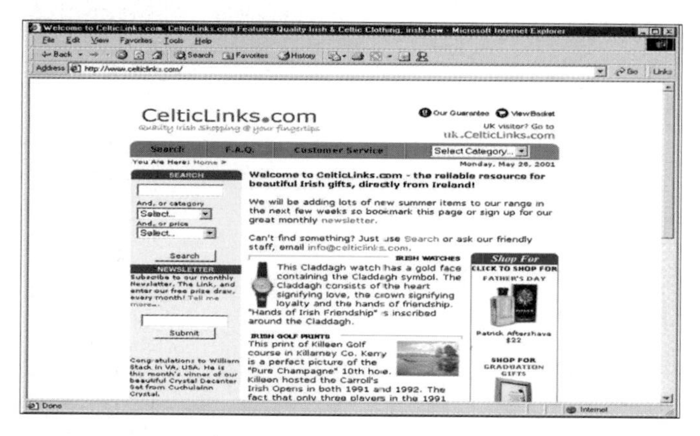

Gaelic Homepage

www.ibiblio.org/gaelic/gaelic.html

This site is 'devoted to the language and culture of the Celts' – Irish, Scottish and Manx. It is a fantastic site if you want an overview of the Celtic languages or of Celtic culture. There isn't much in the way of illustration, but the content is well written and fascinating.

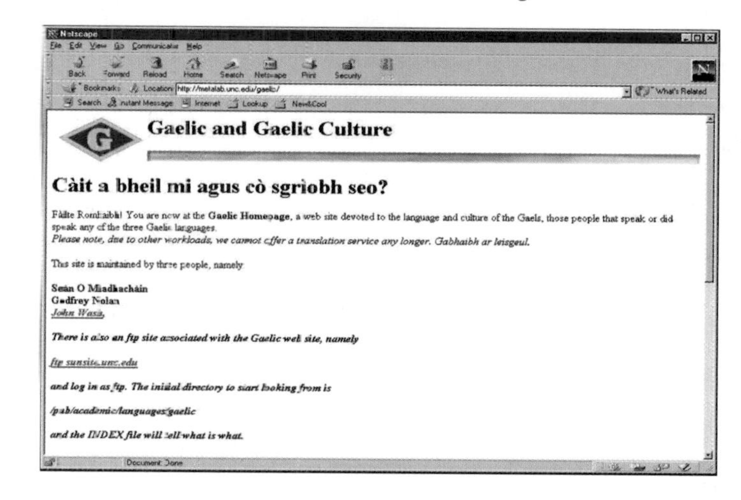

The Book of Kells

www.esotericart.com/fring/art/symbolic/BookKell/kells.htm

The Book of Kells is an illuminated manuscript of the four Gospels. Perhaps the most famous Celtic art object in the world – it has even been called the most beautiful book in the world – it is a mix of Celtic and early medieval motifs. The original, created in the ninth century, is on view in the library of Trinity College, Dublin. This site's images can be viewed in high resolution format.

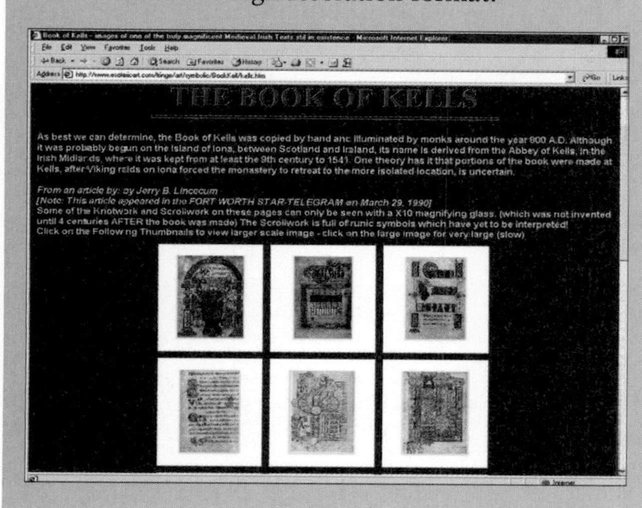

Ceolas

www.ceolas.org/ceolas.html

Ceolas describes itself as 'the home of Celtic music on the Internet'. A grand claim, perhaps, but one that is justified by the quality of the site. You get news of the Celtic music scene, record reviews, dance details, tunes in RealAudio, information on Celtic musical instruments, and profiles of Celtic musicians around the world (for example 'Duchas – quite possibly the Czech Republic's finest [and only?] Celtic band'). You also get an excellent set of links to related sites.

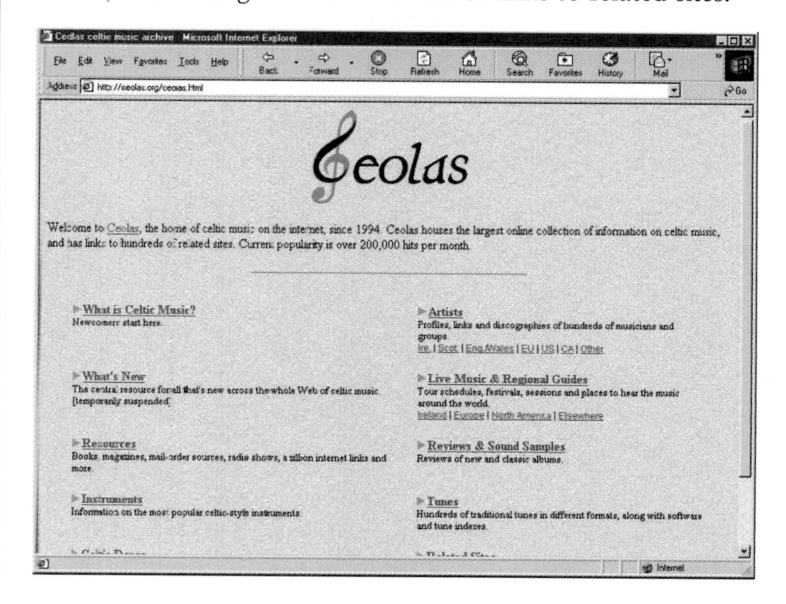

Celtic Heritage Web Ring
dandalf.com/dandalf/webring.html

Web rings – chains of thematically linked sites – can be great fun, if a little hit and miss in their quality. This Celtic heritage Web ring – whose index page is headed by the Dandalf the Dragon graphic seen below – offers a long list of sites, visible as you scroll down from the top of the page. The site expresses a great deal of enthusiasm for the Celtic cause and culture, and its content ranges from language to art, knotwork, step patterns, myth, legend and, of course, literature. A browse through this ring is sure to turn up several sites that will grab the Celtic fan's interest.

Celtic Art and Culture
www.unc.edu/courses/art111/celtic

This site is smart, attractive, packed with facts and images and presents just what it says in the title. There's an excellent timeline of the Celtic world from its origins to its spread through Europe. You can also explore other topics in detail: Irish monasteries, Celtic high crosses, burial mounds, and so on. The images are well chosen and the text is clear and informative. And there's a good lexicon of Celtic vocabulary. You can even complete a quiz to see if you've absorbed the details.

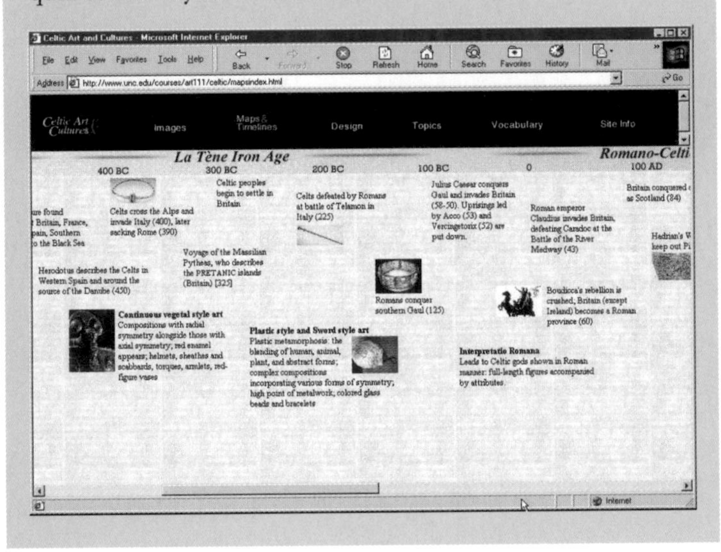

Celtica
www.celtica.wales.com/index.english.html

Wales has a rich Celtic past, highlighted here on the Web site of the Celtica exhibition in Powys, mid-Wales. Celtica is an interactive exhibition 'reflecting Wales's distinct Celtic inheritance'. The Web site gives you a good taster of the Celtic spirit and traditions, with plenty of information about the way the Celts lived – enough to make you want to visit Wales and see the sights for yourself.

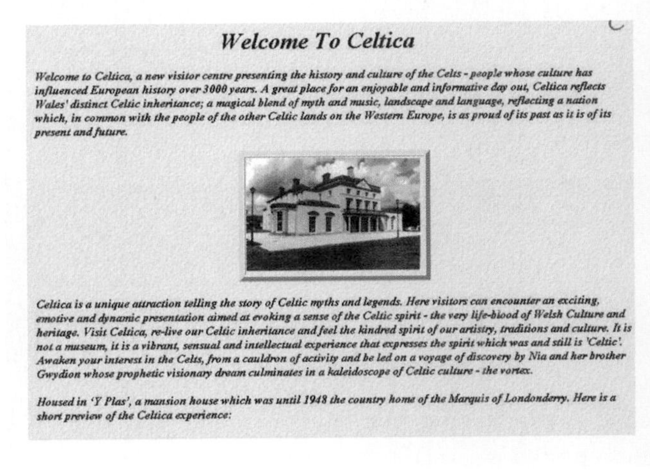

Paul's Celtic Art Web Site
village.vossnet.co.uk/p/paulkav/index.htm

This fascinating site is all the work of one Paul Kavanagh Mosson, imparting his deep knowledge of, and passion for, the basic elements used in Celtic art. There's an excellent gallery of images and, best of all, detailed instructions on how to construct characteristic designs, such as knotwork and spirals. It just goes to show that there's still scope on the Internet for the work of enthusiastic individuals. And, if you want, you can view the site in Scottish Gaelic rather than English.

Celtic Deities and Myths

www.eliki.com/ancient/myth/celts

This offers an excellent overview of Celtic mythology throughout Europe, with separate sections on Gaul, Wales and Ireland. There are very good descriptions of the gods and the role they played in Celtic life, as well as fascinating illustrations, such as the one of Cernunnos, 'the horned one', based on Celtic art.

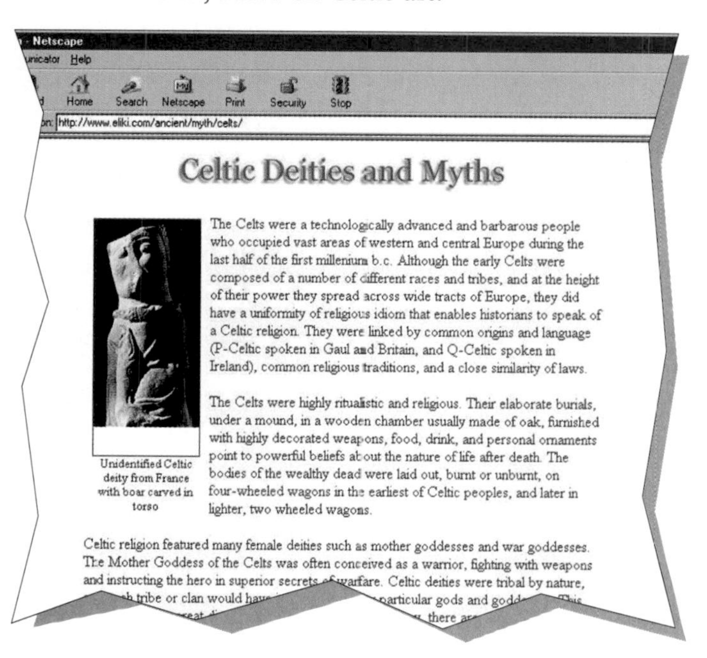

Kervarker

www.kervarker.org

Kervarker is the Celtic language of Brittany and this site is an introduction to the language, as well as to the peninsula itself. There are lessons in Kervarker, an online dictionary, a selection of short stories and a host of music themes available as downloadable files – which means you can hear them almost instantly. An interesting element of this site is its presentation of the way the Breton language has been marginalized over the centuries – a story that holds true for most Celtic languages.

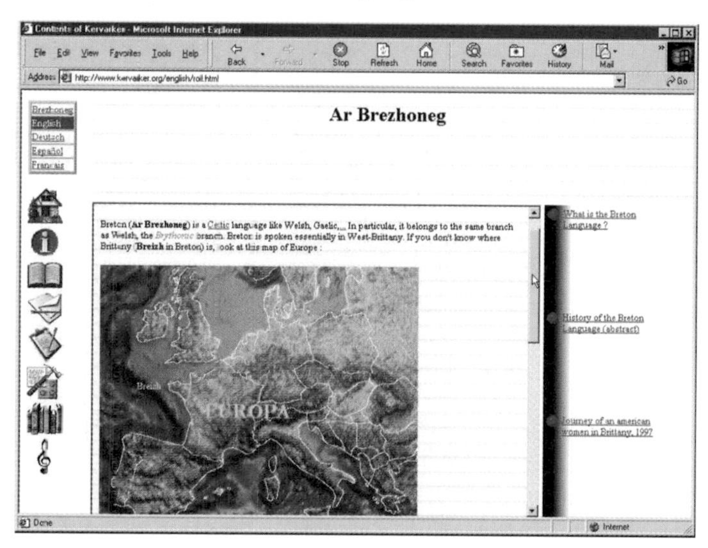

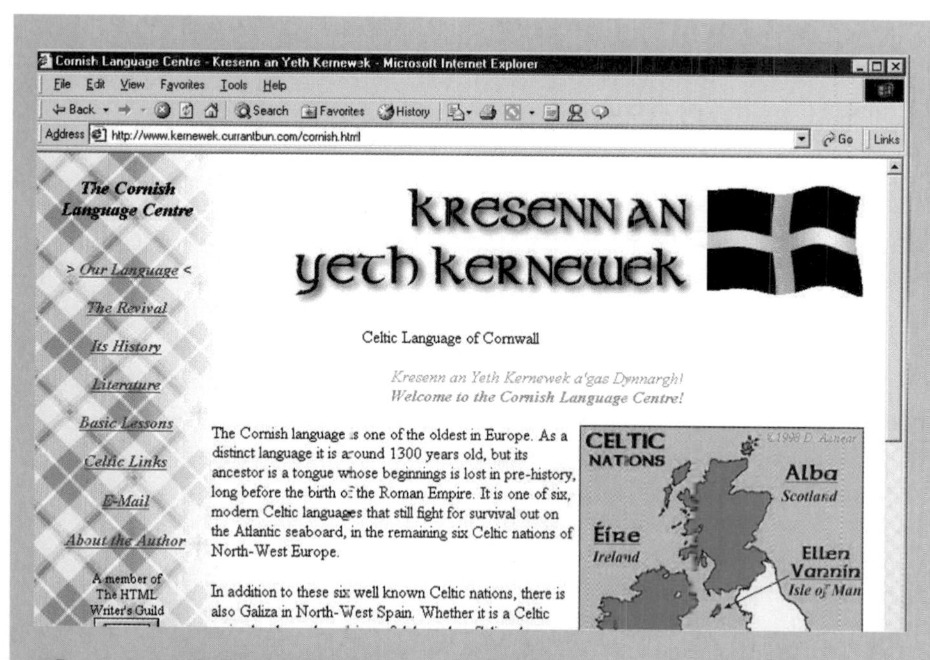

The Cornish Language Centre

www.kernewek.currantbun.com/cornish.html

Cornish (or Kernewek) was probably the first Celtic language to die out as a living, spoken language. But many people, including the producers of this site, are now making sterling efforts to revive it. You can get lessons in Cornish and hear everyday greetings. There's a history of the language, and for the more advanced student, there's plenty of literature in Cornish – and even a number of songs.

CELTIC MUSIC

Even those who do not have a single drop of Celtic blood in their veins cannot fail to be moved by the distinctive sounds of Celtic music, whether Irish, Scottish, Breton or other. The Celtic music scene thrives not just in its original strongholds, but worldwide, so there's no shortage of sites to view.

The Ireland Music List (home.wirehub.nl/~taco) is a required stop for any music fan visiting the Emerald Isle. Its aim is to list places in Ireland that have 'high quality traditional music' (mostly pubs) and it does its job with some style; the list is long and the comments are authoritative and droll.

Scotland is also well featured on the Web. Scottish videos and CDs can be obtained from Celtic Connections (www.celticconnections.com). You can also download a mail order catalogue or search online through their very extensive list of performers.

Health and medicine

Health is one of the Internet's fastest growth areas. People are increasingly interested in healthy lifestyles, diet and exercise, and in the various forms of medical care.

The founder of one health site claims that the Internet is 'the biggest thing to hit medicine since the invention of penicillin'. While this is somewhat of an exaggeration, there is no doubt that health is a boom area on the Internet – particularly in terms of US-based sites: it's been estimated that more than 18 million North Americans go online every month in search of health-related information.

● International resources

There are good reasons for this explosion of the Internet as a health resource. And it is used not only by the public but also by professionals.

There has been a huge increase in public awareness of health issues over recent years, covering everything from diet and fitness to allergies, smoking and 'mad cow disease'. But while we seem to have an insatiable appetite for medical knowledge, most of us have limited time to fit in a visit to the doctor – and many people remain reluctant to see one.

Wherever there's widespread interest in a subject, you can be sure someone will have created a Web site to satisfy it. Whether it's advice on recognising symptoms of an ailment, how to treat it or suggestions on how to avoid it, the Internet can help – and the information is available in many forms, which can be as detailed and technical as you want.

As well as a host of general interest sites, there's masses of detailed, up-to-the-minute medical research freely available on the Internet – one reason why the professionals use it as much as the public. And, fortunately for European surfers, health is one area of the Web where the US origins of many sites aren't a significant drawback: a pain is a pain wherever you live. American sites will provide a wealth of solid, practical information and tips, often presented in a very user-friendly way.

The Internet lacks the personal touch for which we still need to visit the doctor, but if it's health information you're after, it's well worth giving the Web a check-up.

● A host of alternatives

Another reason for the proliferation and popularity of health sites is that 'health' is not one single subject area. The medical profession has long been divided into a number of increasingly narrow specialities, even if the layman has only recently begun to think in a similar way.

This specialization is reflected in the way that healthcare data is arranged on the Internet. While there are many excellent sites that cover almost the entire spectrum of health and medicine, there are many more concentrating on particular areas. This is certainly an advantage for the user: instead of wading through an enormous collection of facts and features, you can go straight to a site that deals with your area of interest, whether this is children's health, skin complaints, fitness and exercise, brain structure, or the increasingly popular and widely covered subject of complementary medicine. With all this information only a click or two away, you might feel there's a danger of being swamped by obscure jargon and diagnoses. However, what you will find is that most sites are extremely user-friendly, and you can very quickly recognize when something is strictly for those who have put in several years of hard study at medical school.

● Put your mind at rest

Consulting an Internet health site is no substitute for a visit to your doctor. However, it might help to put your mind at rest as the sites often give good and clear advice on a wide range of health issues. Used wisely, the Internet might well help to make you a healthier person.

Healthcare Web sites

Here are just a few of the huge number of health sites, with links for you to pursue your queries.

InteliHealth

www.intelihealth.com

This is a very comprehensive US-based site, backed with the expertise of Harvard University's medical school. It's well presented, without too many graphics to slow downloading, and you can usually find the information you need in only a couple of clicks. The site carries plenty of breaking health-related stories, together with daily feature articles. If you know what you're after you can simply click on one of the many 'featured area' links, from Allergy to Workplace Health, to get a wide variety of information. There are excellent, clear descriptions of common ailments, together with good explanations of treatment. And the site offers some fun 'cool tools', including health quizzes and tests, risk assessments, and so on.

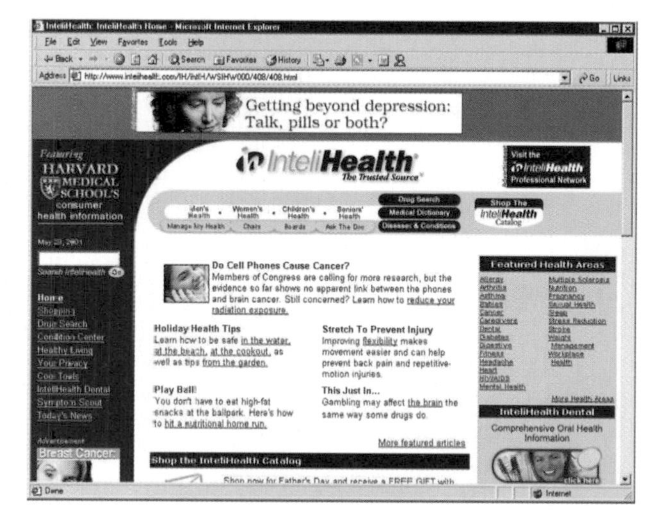

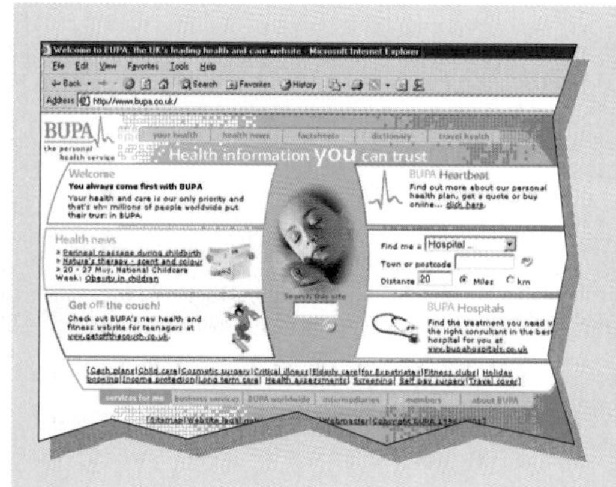

BUPA

www.bupa.co.uk

The UK's largest private healthcare insurer and provider has a colourful and well-designed site. Naturally, they would like you to take out their insurance – and you can get a quote online. But the site is more than a selling job, supplying lots of health material as well. There's news of current research; plenty of advice on health self-help (for example, coping with Alzheimer's); a Your Health section with separate areas dealing with health issues for men, women and children; and a comprehensive set of Health Fact Sheets on every conceivable complaint or disease.

Achoo

www.achoo.com

This is an impressively large and well-organized directory and index of healthcare resources. The site is organized into four main areas – Human Health and Disease Directory, the Business and Finance of Health, Organizations and Sources, and Reference Sources – each of which is subdivided with a brief summary. Aimed at both the consumer and the professional, this is a good site search engine that will help you to find exactly what you need.

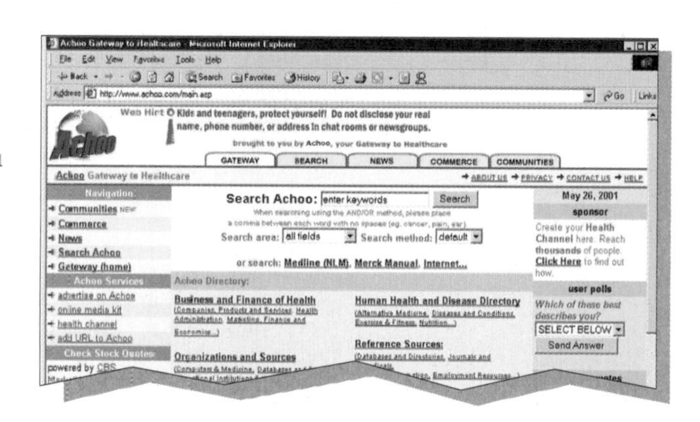

BBC Health & Fitness Online

www.bbc.co.uk/health/

The BBC's Web sites are among the best-designed, most informative sites you could hope to find on the Web. That's certainly true of this health mega-site, which you could profitably spend hours exploring. There are, of course, links and features on health-related TV programmes, both drama and documentary, but the meat of the site is in the solid information and advice it supplies. There are numerous sections devoted to health matters for particular groups or activities (women, kids, travel, etc), guides to a huge range of diseases, complaints and medical procedures, and a massive archive of health Q&As, culled from the Ask the Doctor section, where the doctor answers one featured question per day.

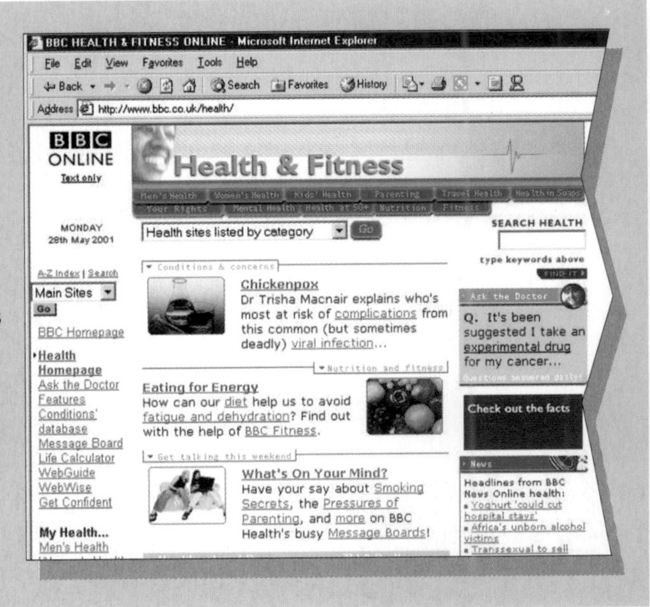

KidsHealth.org

KidsHealth.org

This site is presented by The Nemours Foundation, which funds children's medical institutions across the USA. The Foundation transcribes its work to the Internet very well indeed, with a bright and accessible site providing advice and information on all aspects of children's and teenagers' health. The site is divided into the three main areas of Parents, Kids and Teens. There are useful regular features such as Hot Topics – 'unique summaries' of what the medical professionals are up to, with an informative 'What This Means To You' section. Each of the three sections is packed with material, presented in a clear and colourful way.

Men's Health

(UK) www.menshealth.co.uk

Men's Health is a popular health and fitness magazine for men, which also has a US edition. You can access the UK site directly, or you can go to the main US site at www.menshealth.com/index.html. Both sites provide lots of useful information for anyone interested in 'working out', with a big section from the current edition of the magazine as well as a searchable archive. There are also links to various health sites where you can search, for example, a database of complaints and illnesses.

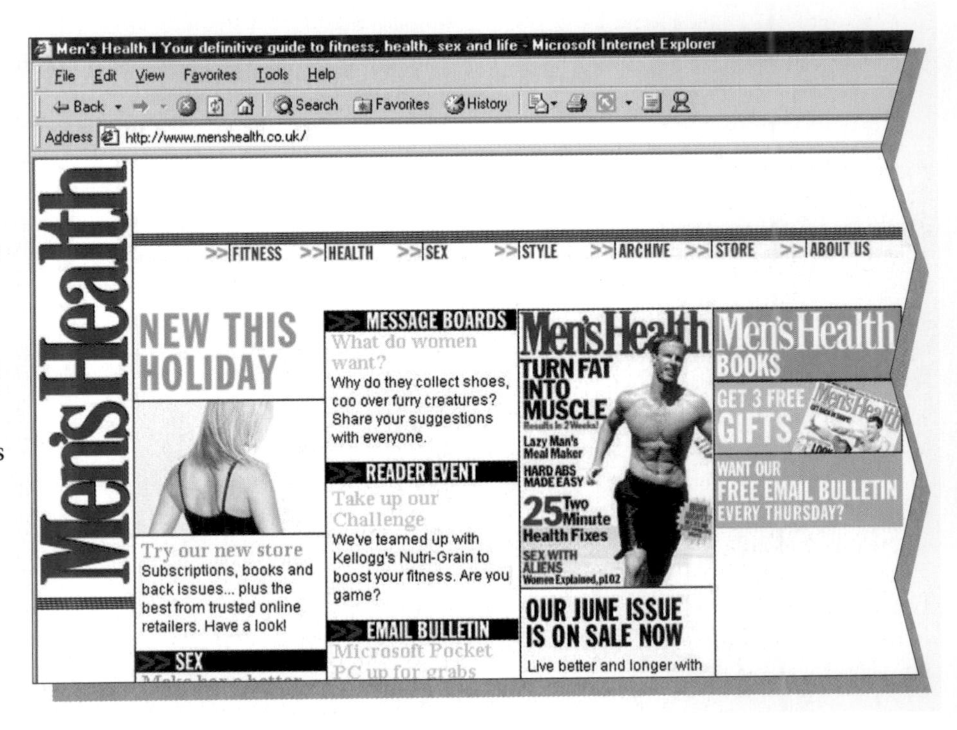

About.com Health/Fitness

home.about.com/health

This extensive area of the About network probably outstrips even the BBC in the depth and variety of information it provides. There really is something for everyone here, with sections covering every aspect of health and fitness. There are loads of features, including chat rooms dealing with all sorts of topics and even a 'symptom checker' where you can answer an online questionnaire to work out what your problem might be. One welcome feature of the site is that it's as much about fitness as disease, so there's plenty of material related to keeping well in addition to the treatment of ailments.

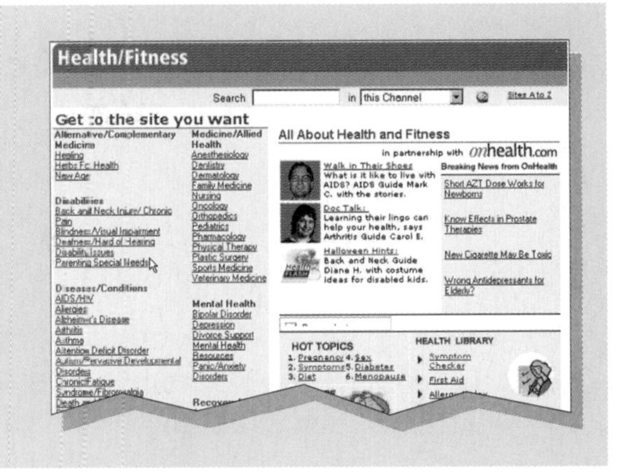

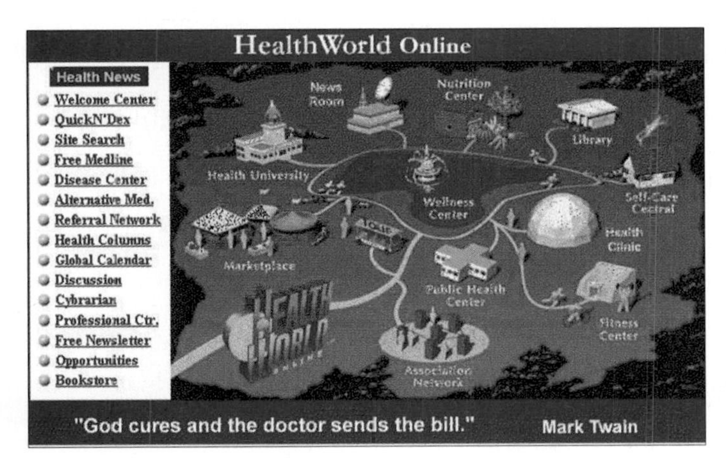

HealthWorld Online

www.healthy.net

This site is of interest mainly for its wide coverage of alternative and traditional medicine within what it calls a philosophy of 'self-managed care'. You start off with a village map in which the various buildings represent the different areas of health and fitness – with a 'Wellness Center' in the middle. Clicking on one of the subsequent links provides you with solid information, which is clearly if plainly presented. This is a well-organized and fairly comprehensive site, but it might take you a good few clicks to get down to the level of information you want.

Patient UK

www.patient.co.uk

If you can get past the garish front page of this Web site, you'll find it has some sterling virtues. Its main function is to act as a directory of all other UK healthcare sites, and it does this well, bringing up help groups as well as organizations and other information sites. If you search an ailment you get a selection of hospitals' Patient Information Leaflets, which supply trustworthy information.

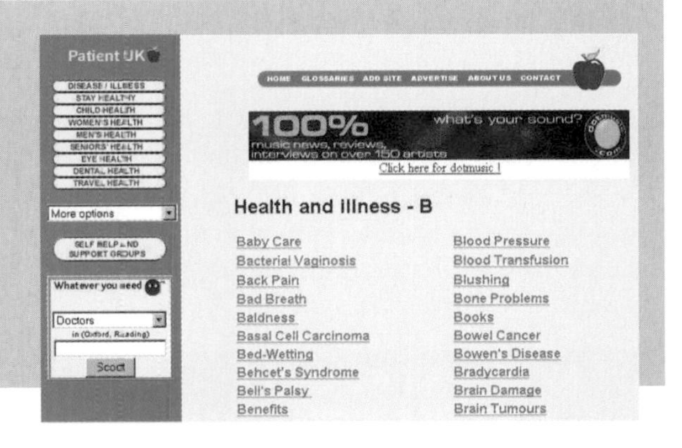

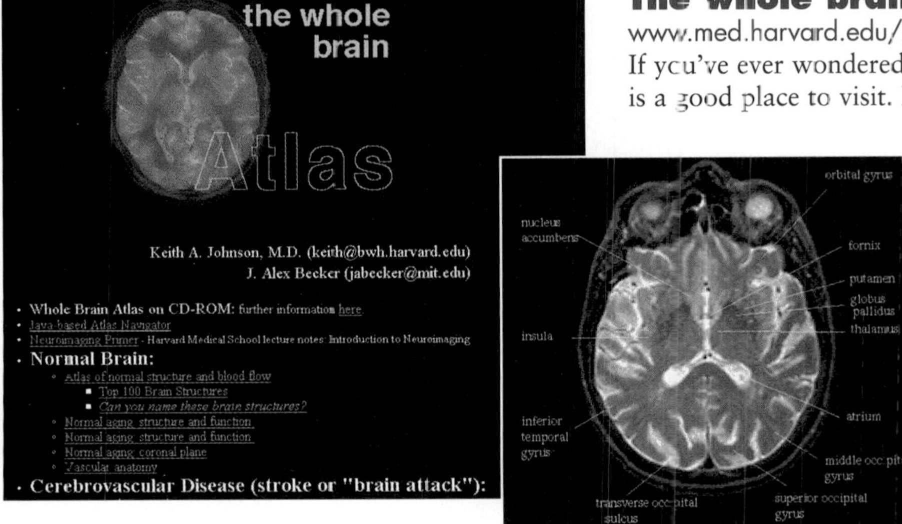

The whole brain Atlas

www.med.harvard.edu/AANLIB/home.html

If you've ever wondered what's going on inside your head, this site is a good place to visit. It presents pictures of the brain taken with the latest neuro-imaging techniques such as Magnetic Resonance Imaging (MRI). Each picture is a different 'slice' of brain, labelled and sometimes explained. Perhaps the best section is the Top 100 Brain Structures. There are lots of pictures, including many of brains that have suffered from Alzheimer's and tumours. Several of the terms might not mean a lot to the lay person (this site is aimed at medical students), but the pictures are truly fascinating.

Extreme sports sites

Although they're unlikely to make an official appearance at the Olympic Games, so-called extreme sports are some of the most popular, trendy and potentially life-threatening ways of having fun in the world today. Check out some of the sites devoted to them.

Although there is no clear definition of what an extreme sport is, the term broadly means any sport that has an element of serious physical danger. Extreme sports are not necessarily those that have been newly discovered; skydiving, surfing and rock climbing are all generally considered to be 'extreme', but have been around for a while.

The most popular new extreme sports usually involve a board of some kind, such as skateboarding and snowboarding. Both are pretty dangerous, with little chance of avoiding injury if something goes wrong. But therein lies much of the attraction. As exciting as extreme sports might be, most people would consider them to be a pursuit of the young – and generally they'd be right. Although there's nothing stopping an older athlete taking part, a significant element of the appeal of extreme sports is the underground youth culture associated with them. All these sports have their own music and fashion scenes; a number also have their own recreational drugs scene. For this reason, you should check out any extreme sports sites that your children might visit. The larger ones, such as those listed here, are fine but the more personal sites can make a lot of undesirable references. There's also the obvious warning about safety; the *raison d'être* of most of these sports is that they are inherently risky (and, therefore, thrilling), so if you or any member of your family wants to have a go, make sure you have the right tuition, the right protective gear and practise the sport somewhere with good safety facilities.

EXTREME SPORTS PC GAMES

With the current popularity of extreme sports, it should come as no surprise that computer games developers have tried to jump on the bandwagon. The only problem is that the often linear, or trick-based, nature of the sports frequently makes for unexciting games. The exceptions so far have largely been restricted to skateboarding, snowboarding and jet-ski bikes. However, most of the more successful games generally appear on the youth-orientated games consoles, such as the Sony PlayStation, although Infograme's Boarder Zone has produced a good snowboarding game for the home computer.

If you feel like risking life and limb in the pursuit of fun, settle down in front of your PC to view the mayhem before trying it yourself.

Take it to the limit

These sites reflect the diverse nature of the activities. Many offer a single sport, but a few have several to tempt you.

ESPN Extreme Sports

expn.go.com

This is part of the massive US sports network ESPN (part of the Disney empire). It is a comprehensive site, covering a wide range of sports and is snazzily presented. ESPN are sponsors of the 'X Games', a Grand Prix of extreme sports, held at various venues in the US. So it's no surprise to find plenty of coverage of X Games events, as well as athlete profiles, an event calendar and new features. If you find that exciting, then you'll want to view the video footage. There's plenty of Multimedia gimmicks here to keep the extreme fan happy; as well as videos, there are also audio chats with the stars, and in the Life & Style section there is an archived Lifestyle News section with listings by sport category.

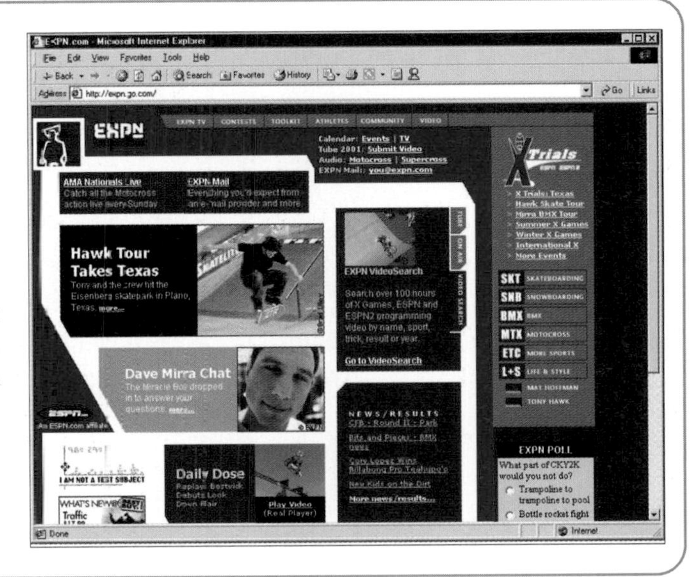

Bxtreme Net

www.bxtreme.net

If ESPN tends to stick to the bigger and more media-friendly extreme sports, this UK-based site goes for the broadest possible coverage. Just about every possible extreme activity is covered, served up in the snazzy 'youth' graphics that seem to be obligatory in the extreme world, although the site is quick to load and easy to navigate. As well as sections devoted to specific sports, there's plenty of useful, additional extreme material on Bxtreme Net. There's live chat on a wide range of topics, a WAP site to get surf reports direct on your mobile phone, and an extensive 'gear' section with direct links to online shopping services. Add the links to smaller, more specialised extreme sites, and you have a site that is definitely worth a visit.

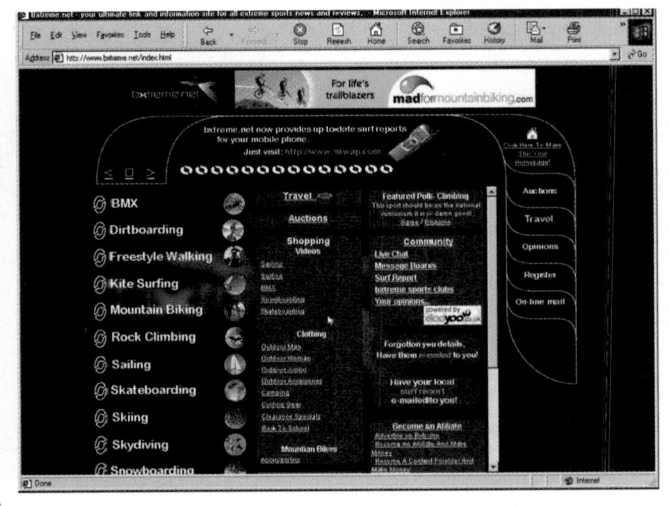

AdventureDirectory.com

www.adventuredirectory.com

This describes itself as 'the biggest single source of information on adventure sports in the world', and one would not like to dispute that claim. It contains a series of 'Handbooks' (guides written by experts) on a wide range of activities, from ballooning to white water rafting. These guides contain plenty of good advice for the beginner, as well as lots of links to equipment suppliers, holiday companies and so on. What you won't find here, however, are the more modish and youthful extreme sports; skateboarding and BMX do not feature. Instead, the site covers what one might call 'traditional' extreme sports. As such, it may well appeal to the older thrill-seeker rather than the youth market.

Surfline

www.surfline.com

Surfing is the grandaddy of extreme sports. All you need to participate is a surfboard and some large waves. This site is one of the most popular surfing sites and provides completely up-to-date surf reports from around the world. As well as meteorological data, most of the major sites also have a webcam, so you can see what a beach looks like before you visit. Catch up with what's happening on the surf scene in the magazine and find out about resorts in the Travel section.

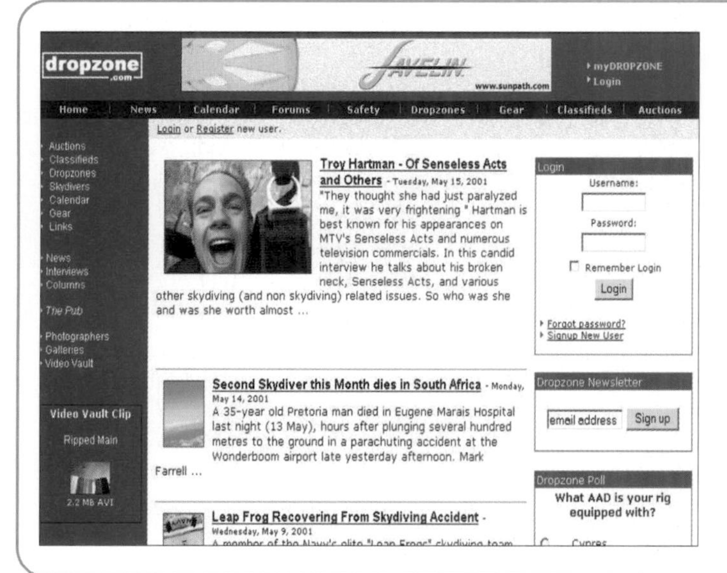

Dropzone.com

www.dropzone.com

In certain circles, skydiving is not officially considered to be a proper extreme sport. But it is still very dangerous and profoundly exhilarating. There are a number of ways to skydive, depending on the type of parachute you use. The normal canopy is considered 'old hat' because it does nothing to extend the descent time. After all, you're there for the view, not for a race. The site contains plenty of information for the best worldwide dropzones, with maps and ratings of courses and links to the operators. It also has an extensive classifieds section for buying and selling equipment and organizing trips. The photo gallery is also interesting.

Extreme mountain biking

www.extreme.nas.net

Mountain biking is never going to sound as extreme as, say, snowboarding, but it's both popular and dangerous enough to be considered a bona fide extreme sport. The rules are quite simple: using a mountain bike, you must take part in a race to the finish against a large number of competitors. The fun comes from the fact that the race usually takes place on a mountain where all manner of narrow cliff ledges, muddy pits and precipitous paths have to be negotiated. This Web site aims to aid the mountain biking enthusiast with the usual range of product reviews, tournament dates and technical tips. Judging by the amount of reader support and submissions, it's extremely popular.

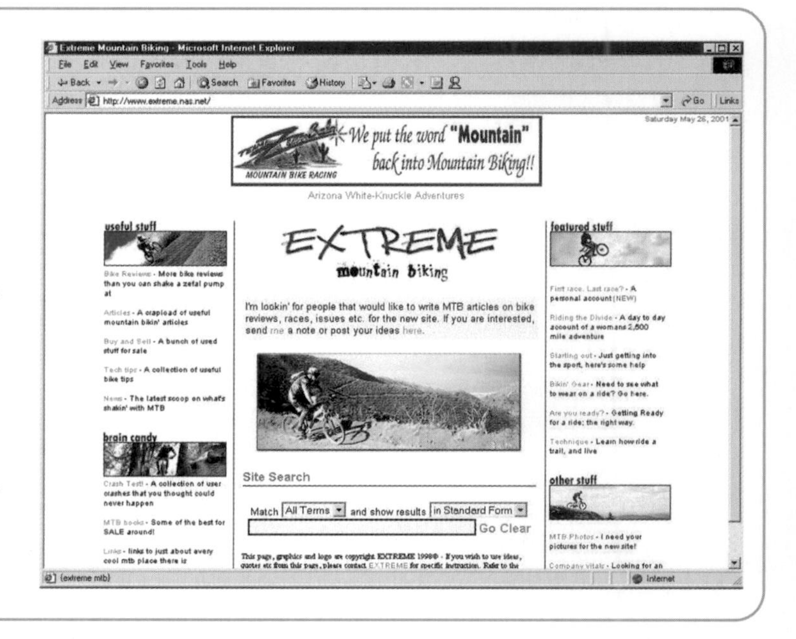

Minority extreme sports

Some pursuits are even more of a minority interest than others. Here are just a few.

OceanXtreme

www.oceanxtreme.com

This site is all about Kite Surfing, which is basically waterskiing, only powered by a kite (and a fairly powerful one at that) instead of a speedboat. As a newish sport, kite surfing needs its beginners, and this is as good a place as any to start.

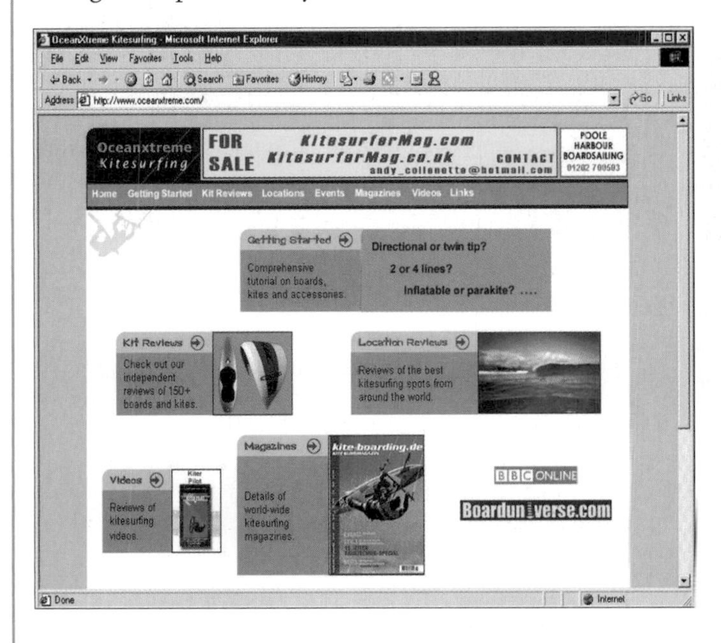

Street Luge

members.aol.com/docgofast/luge1.html

It's hard to single out one extreme sport as the most dangerous or silly, but it has to be said that street luge – where people hurtle along on what appear to be biscuit tin lids on wheels – is a leading contender.

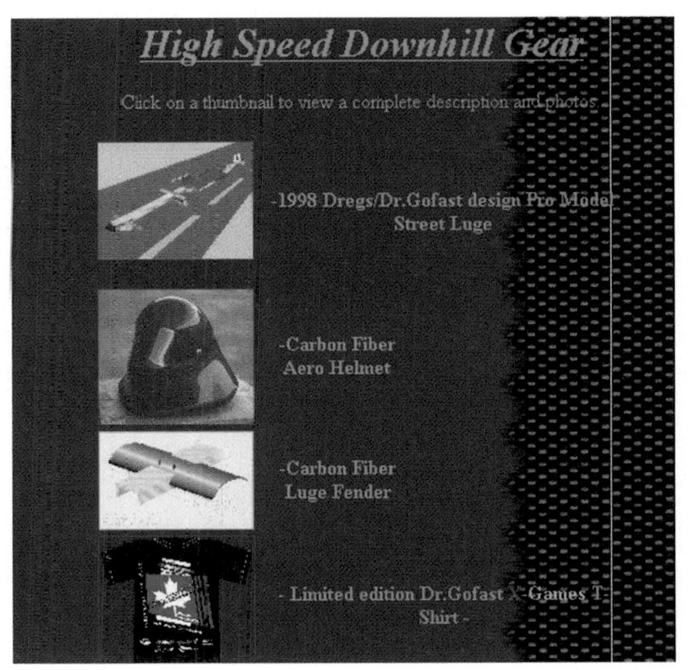

American Barefoot Club

www.barefoot.org

In many ways barefoot waterskiing is the same as ordinary waterskiing, although the boat pulling you along does have to go slower in order to avoid causing injuries to your feet as they cut a swathe through the water. If you are interested in this type of activity, there's plenty here, from a history of the sport to how to do it.

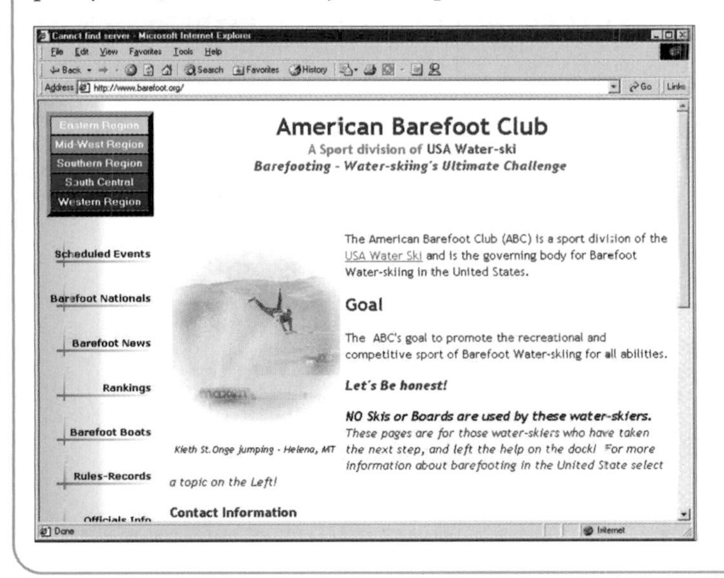

BERSA

www.bungeezone.com/orgs/bersa.shtml

The British Elastic Rope Sports Association is a grandiose name for the people who keep an eye on bungee jumping. This web site provides information on everything from the history of bungee jumping to worldwide club listings.

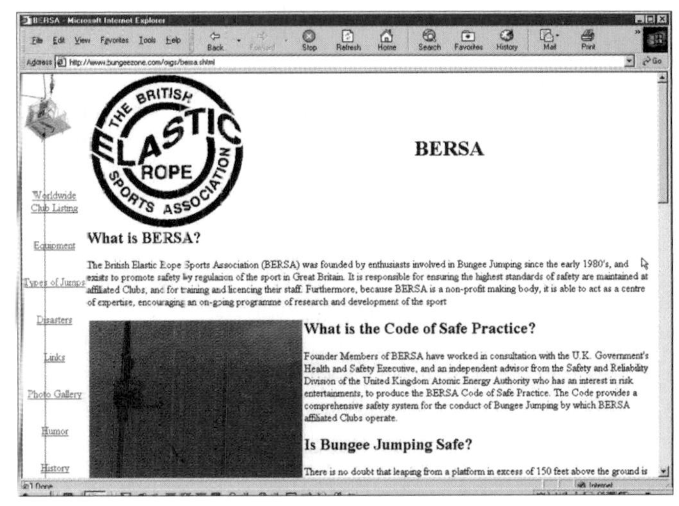

● About the index
Text in italics is used for cross-references within the index (as in *see also*...). Page numbers in bold type denote the main entries for a topic.

Acknowledgments

Abbreviations: t = top; b = bottom; r = right; l = left; c = centre; bkg = background. All cartoons are by Chris Bramley

8tr Lyndon Parker/De Agostini
11br Lyndon Parker/De Agostini
14r Lyndon Parker/De Agostini
16r Lyndon Parker/De Agostini
18r Dr L Stannard, UCT/Science Photo Library
20r Getty Images/Image Bank
22tl Lyndon Parker/De Agostini
24tr Lyndon Parker/De Agostini
26tr Lyndon Parker/De Agostini
30tr MGM (courtesy Kobal Collection)
32t MGM (courtesy Kobal Collection)
33tl MGM (courtesy Kobal Collection)
36 MGM (courtesy Kobal Collection)
38 Lyndon Parker/De Agostini
39tl Lyndon Parker/De Agostini
41tr Lyndon Parker/De Agostini
42br Lyndon Parker/De Agostini
46 S. Bartholomew/De Agostini
52 The Stock Market
54tr Adam Hart-Davis/Science Photo Library
56tr The Stock Market
58br Lyndon Parker/De Agostini
60 Getty Images/Lyndon Parker/De Agostini
62 MGM/Kobal Collection
66 Lyndon Parker/De Agostini
70 Lyndon Parker/De Agostini
71 Lyndon Parker/De Agostini
74 The Stock Market
78 The Stock Market
82 Lyndon Parker/De Agostini
84 The Stock Market/Tony Stone Images
88tr Lyndon Parker/De Agostini
90 Tony Stone Images
92t Lyndon Parker/De Agostini
96tr IKEA
96br Lyndon Parker/De Agostini
97 IKEA
98 Lyndon Parker/De Agostini
99 Lyndon Parker/De Agostini
100 The Stock Market
102 Lyndon Parker/De Agostini
103 Lyndon Parker/De Agostini
104 Lyndon Parker/De Agostini/courtesy Intel
105 Lyndon Parker/De Agostini/courtesy Intel
106 Seagate
108 Lyndon Parker/De Agostini
109 Lyndon Parker/De Agostini
110 Microsoft
111 Dvorak
114t Lyndon Parker/De Agostini
118tl,br Mary Evans Picture Library
126tl S. Bartholomew/De Agostini
126br Tony Stone Images
127tr Tony Stone Images
130 Lyndon Parker/De Agostini
132 Lyndon Parker/De Agostini
134 Claude Noridsany and Marie Perennou/Science Photo Library
138 Lyndon Parker/De Agostini
142 The Stock Market
146 Charles Walker Collection/Images
150 The Stock Market
154 The Stock Market